Librarian's Guide
to Online Searching

Librarian's Guide to Online Searching

Cultivating Database Skills for Research and Instruction

Fourth Edition

SUZANNE S. BELL

 LIBRARIES UNLIMITED

AN IMPRINT OF ABC-CLIO, LLC
Santa Barbara, California • Denver, Colorado • Oxford, England

Library of Congress Cataloging-in-Publication Data

Bell, Suzanne S.
  Librarian's guide to online searching : cultivating database skills for research and instruction / Suzanne S. Bell. — Fourth edition.
        pages cm
  Includes bibliographical references and indexes.
  ISBN 978-1-61069-998-3 (pbk : alk. paper) — ISBN 978-1-61069-999-0 (ebook)   1. Database searching.   2. Electronic information resource searching.   I. Title.
  ZA4460.B45   2015
  025.04—dc23   2014038457

ISBN: 978-1-61069-998-3
EISBN: 978-1-61069-999-0

19 18 17 16 15   1 2 3 4 5

This book is also available on the World Wide Web as an eBook.
Visit www.abc-clio.com for details.

Libraries Unlimited
An Imprint of ABC-CLIO, LLC

ABC-CLIO, LLC
130 Cremona Drive, P.O. Box 1911
Santa Barbara, California 93116-1911

This book is printed on acid-free paper ∞
Manufactured in the United States of America

To my grandfather, Augustus Hunt Shearer, librarian and teacher, and my father, Vern Coventry Bell, inventor and engineer. You may not have understood this book, but you would have appreciated it. Thank you both for the gifts that made it possible.

Contents

Preface

Welcome to the wonderful world of database searching! Roy Tennant's (2004) now famous quote that "only librarians like to search, everyone else likes to find" has perhaps been too frequently repeated—but it's hard not to, because it's *true*. There are certain kinds of minds that enjoy solving puzzles and ferreting out information, and the owners of those minds often find a good fit in library careers. Librarians do like to search, although generally we aren't born knowing it: it's a realization that emerges later, with experience or in a class. If you are a researcher or a student in the position of having to search for the information you need, you may also find that there can be some interest and pleasure in the process as well as the product.

If it is true that most people only want to "find," and are perfectly happy with the Google model of one simple search box and long lists of results, one might ask, "Why should I care about learning more sophisticated search techniques? Why should we still teach a course on database searching?" (or "Why should I buy a book on database searching?") "Will there ever be an opportunity to use this information again?"

In offering you this book, I wholeheartedly believe those questions can be answered in the affirmative. Yes, learning about more sophisticated search techniques continues to be helpful, and it will increase your effectiveness in helping others to do research, or your own productivity as a researcher. No matter how simple the initial interface becomes, it still helps to know something about database structure, that is, what is going on under the hood. This is especially helpful for understanding what is *possible* with any given database: what degree of precision in searching you can expect, and thus what you can expect in terms of results. There will continue to be advanced versions of the interface that will allow experts to do more efficient, targeted, and useful searches. Yes, people will do and are doing more searching on their own: if you are not a librarian and are looking at this book, it will introduce you to resources you might not have been aware of and help you to be more effective. For librarians and library students, searching is a part of our profession, an area in which we need to be ready to offer our users more skills than they have on their own. Indeed, as users do more searching on their own, the questions that they approach librarians with become more difficult. They have taken care of the easy questions; librarians need to be ready for the hard ones. This is still an important part of our skill set.

Most of the techniques and strategies provided in this book are not particularly complex or hard to master, but they need to be stated and learned, because they are not generally how people think. You need to *learn* to parse questions into good search strategies. You need to really internalize how Boolean logic works to understand that when a search returns only a few results, the tactic to take is to use fewer, broader search terms, not add more, and more specific, terms. One of the most essential techniques sounds like the simplest: to use your eyes and truly analyze what is on the screen. This is something that very few people really do, however, so it is also something to learn.

One of the overriding goals in this book is to remain thoroughly grounded in the real world. The examples and exercises are drawn from real life, and use commercial databases commonly available at academic and/or major public libraries. We also look at some databases that are freely available on the Web, but the free websites discussed have been carefully chosen for their expected longevity. The emphasis is not on providing every detail of every database presented, but rather how you can use a set of basic concepts ("the Searcher's Toolkit") in order to look at any interface ("use your eyes") and understand what you are seeing ("engage your brain"), so as to use effectively whatever search capabilities are provided. Once you have a basic idea of how databases are put together and have grasped the collection of concepts and techniques this book calls the Searcher's Toolkit, you should be able to plunge into any database that comes along and figure out how it works. In fact, the other main goal for this book is to help you learn to be flexible and adaptable. What more important skill can there be in our rapidly changing world?

This text will expose you to a whole range of databases: multidisciplinary, social science, medicine, science, bibliographic, humanities, and statistical/numeric. You will learn that even when you don't know anything about a subject, using some good, general principles, you should be able to use an unfamiliar database and do a reasonable search. A discussion of information-seeking behaviors and how to do an effective reference interview helps with this. Most important, you shouldn't be *afraid* of any subject area and declare it off-limits. As all of these choices begin to build up, however, the natural question is this: How do you know which database to use? Or should you use the Web? We address these issues as well. Note that although the Web does enter into the discussion from time to time, this book does not attempt to teach you to search the Web better. There are already many excellent books on the market to fulfill that purpose. The focus here is on purpose-built, sophisticated databases, both fee-based and some, incredibly, freely available. If you thought searching started and ended with Google, surprise! There's a whole other world waiting for you.

Not only will you learn to search databases, but you'll also learn something about passing your knowledge along: tips and guidance for showing others how to get what they need out of a database (and how to not have a panic attack in the process). In addition, we'll go over points to consider in evaluating a database for purposes of writing a review, or, for librarians, as part of collection development. With budgets everywhere as tight as they are, librarians are more frequently finding themselves in the position of having to evaluate and choose among current resources.

If you are a library school instructor, you'll find that the chapters after the first four are almost completely freestanding. You can pick and choose, using them in whatever order best suits your needs or teaching style. As in previous editions, exercises using the resources discussed and material that can be used as discussion-starters are included with each chapter, and "Suggested Readings" are provided for selected chapters.

There are a number of changes in this edition. There is a new first chapter to introduce the whole concept of library databases, the database vendor industry, and jumping to the far end of this topic spectrum, a discussion of Discovery Services and why these tools do not figure prominently in the rest of the text. All of the subject database chapters now include an Additional Resources section, to help students become aware of more databases or reliable websites for that subject area. In these sections I have made a very conscious effort to include free resources and databases often found in public libraries, rather than just college and university resources. Beyond the Textbook exercises using the databases discussed in these new Additional Resources sections are available on the companion website for this text, about which more below. The second half of the reference interview chapter has been given a major rewrite to reflect the much more virtual setting of reference services today. The Choosing the Right Resource for the Question chapter (previously 10, now 11) now has an extended discussion of Google Scholar; the previous list of free websites (too many of which had embarrassingly vanished) has been deleted. Subject specific sites (that are still extant and expected to remain so) have been moved to the appropriate Additional Resources sections. The final chapter, on teaching others, has been split into two chapters. Chapter 13 now provides the Teaching Principles from the previous editions, and a new section on physical preparation and in-room presentation guidance and tips. Chapter 14 goes over teaching opportunities, with a whole new section on video tutorials. Finally, you will find that the approach to illustrations in this edition is quite different: a mixture of some screenshots and some representational drawings. This again was a deliberate, although difficult, choice based on a number of factors. My hope is that the combination of illustration of key features, what you see on your screens, and visual aids provided on the companion website will be enough to provide clarity and understanding of each database.

The Student Resources site is now hosted and maintained by ABC-CLIO, at http://www.abc-clio.com/LibrariesUnlimited/product.aspx?pc=A4596P. There you will find additional detail on the history of some of the databases, Beyond the Textbook exercises to expose students to the databases presented in the new Additional Resources sections, demos of databases, updates as needed, the opportunity to leave your comments and suggestions, and more materials (such as additional Exercises) as they are developed.

About the Web, I simply wish to state the obvious: we live in the age of the Web, with its incredible capability for change; vendors and nonprofits change the appearance of their interfaces regularly, and it's crucial to be flexible. This book is intended to help you learn to adapt and change, as well as to give you the tools to understand and use what you're looking at, regardless of what the interfaces happen to look like in the future.

So what *are* these mysterious things, "library databases"? Let me welcome you to the favorite part of my world.

Acknowledgments

Grateful thanks go to the faculty who use this book in their courses and were willing to be polled about changes and to share their thoughts. I apologize to the people whose choices I couldn't accommodate, but please know your input was deeply appreciated.

Books don't happen without a publisher, and I have been truly blessed in this regard. My highly enthusiastic thanks go to Barbara Ittner, who answers emails at all hours of the day and night (which is when crazy authors write emails); and to the wonderful Emma Bailey, production manager extraordinaire and my new web mistress, for being patient, responsive, and flexible. You ladies are a total pleasure to work with.

I modified my vision of the book as text supported by (lots of) screen shots in this edition, deciding to use screen shots in some cases but conceptual drawings in others. My heartfelt thanks go to Kim Stam at EBSCO and Sara Correa at Thomson Reuters for being instant and painless in giving permission to use screen shots of their products.

Finally, where would we be without our tools and home support? Thank you, MacBook Pro and baby sister MacBook Air, for allowing me to work wherever the spirit moved. My most heartfelt thanks, however, go to my husband, a walking *Chicago Manual of Style*, who has once again put up with my being totally distracted for weeks on end, who has again patiently read page after page and provided useful editing and reactions, and altogether has been a wonderfully cheerful, supportive, and sustaining presence throughout the process. You are the very best, my dear; I couldn't do it without you.

1
Introduction to Library Databases

As they said in the *Sound of Music*, "let's start at the very beginning." In this case, a definition and some history, leading up to the current state of the database industry and its major players. Last, we'll go over the recent development known as "Discovery Services" and explain why those systems are outside the scope of this book.

Electronic access to information by means of the Web is so pervasive that we take it for granted. You have undoubtedly already used library databases somewhere in your academic life, and either heard or tossed the word "database" around yourself. But where did these "databases" come from? Why are they important? What *is* a database, anyway? Let's address that last question first, and then find out where they came from.

What *Is* a Database?

The *Oxford English Dictionary* defines "database" as: "A structured set of data held in computer storage and typically accessed or manipulated by means of specialized software." (So much for not using any part of a word in its definition.) For "data," let us substitute "information." A database is a way to structure, store, and rapidly access huge amounts of information electronically. That "information" can be numerical or textual, even visual. And as the *Encyclopedia of Computer Science* (2003) notes: "An important feature of a good database is that unnecessary redundancy of stored data is avoided." The key concepts are *structure* (an organized way to store the information, accomplished by tables, records, and fields, which are discussed later in this chapter), *efficiency* (no redundancy), and *rapid access* (the ability to search and retrieve material from the database as quickly as possible).

1

As my husband the computer scientist puts it, "a database isn't magic but it is pretty smart."

Is Google a Database?

Absolutely, in the sense that Google is a vast collection of data (the contents of web pages and material linked to web pages) that is searchable and provides rapid access to results. But Google and similar web search engines are not the focus of this textbook. These search tools build their databases automatically, from material that is freely accessible on the web, and their structure, scope, size, and many other aspects are not obvious. As far as one can tell, there is no quality control, no human intervention involved in building the database.[1]

The commercial and governmental databases considered in this text are products specifically crafted to achieve the goal of providing users access to formally published information (e.g. articles, conference papers, books, dissertations, reports), in a very organized and efficient fashion. (In the case of commercial databases, part of that crafting is a mechanism for limiting access to paid subscribers.) Let us refer to these as "library databases," since that is where you usually encounter them. Library databases tend to be targeted to specific audiences, and to offer customized features accordingly. Their structure, scope, size, date coverage, publication list and many other details are either obvious from their search interfaces, or explicitly provided. (I would like to say that library databases are more structured than Google, but I can't. Because who knows how Google is structured or how its search algorithm really works? The "black boxness" of Google is another thing that distinguishes it from the databases that are the focus of this text.) Library databases are much less well known and ubiquitous than Google, and usually not free, but there are good reasons for that. Finding out where these databases came from should help explain why (as the adage goes, "you get what you pay for").

Historical Background

Indexing and Abstracting Services

In the Beginning . . .

There was hard copy. Writers wrote, and their works were published in (physical) magazines, journals, newspapers, or conference proceedings. Months or years afterward, other writers, researchers, and other alert readers wanted to know what was written on a topic. Wouldn't it be useful if there were a way to find everything that had been published on a topic, without having to page through every likely journal, newspaper, and so forth? It certainly would, as various publishing interests demonstrated: as early as 1848, the *Poole's Index to Periodical Literature* provided "An alphabetical index to subjects, treated in the reviews, and other periodicals, to which no indexes have been published; prepared for the library of the Brothers in Unity, Yale college" (Figure 1.1).

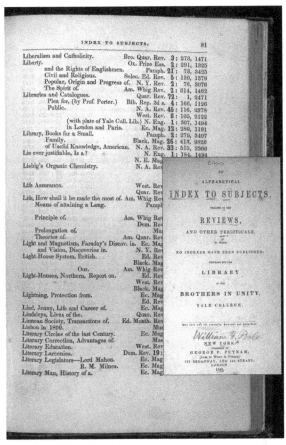

Figure 1.1. Index listing and title page (*inset*) from *Poole's Index to Periodical Literature*. Courtesy of the Department of Rare Books and Special Collections, University of Rochester Libraries, Rochester, NY.

Not to be caught napping, the *New York Times* started publishing their *Index* in 1851, and in 1896, taking a page from *Poole's*, the *Cumulative Index to a Selected List of Periodicals* appeared, which soon (1904) became the canonical *Readers' Guide to Periodical Literature*. Thus, in the mid-19th century, the hard copy Index is born: an alphabetical list of words, representing subjects, and under each word a list of articles deemed to be about that subject. The index is typeset, printed, bound, and sold, and all of this effort is done, slowly and laboriously, by humans.

Given the amount of work involved, and the costs of paper, printing, etc., how many subjects do you think an article would have been listed under? Every time the article entry is repeated under another subject, it costs the publisher just a little more. Suppose there was an article about a polar expedition, which described the role the sled dogs played, the help provided by the native Inuit, the incompetence on the part of the provisions master, and the fund-raising efforts carried on by the leader's wife back home in England. The publisher really can't afford to list this article in more than one or two places. Under which subject(s) will people interested in this topic be most likely to look? The indexer's career was a continuous series of such difficult choices.

An index, recording that an article exists and where it would be found, was a good start, but one could go a step further. The addition of a couple of sentences (e.g., to give the user an idea of what the article is about) increases the usefulness of the finding tool enormously—although the added information, of course, costs more in terms of space, paper, effort, etc. But some index publishers started adding abstracts, gambling that their customers would pay the higher price (which they did). Thus, we have the advent of *Abstracting and Indexing services* or "A & I," terminology that you may still see in the library literature.

The abstracts were all laboriously written by humans. They needed to be skilled, literate humans, and skilled humans are very expensive (even when they're underpaid, they are expensive in commercial terms). Humans are also slow, compared with technology. Paper and publishing are expensive, too. Given all this, how many times do you think an entry for an article would be duplicated (appear under multiple subjects) in this situation? The answers are obvious; the point is that the electronic situation we have today is all grounded in a physical reality. Once it was nothing but people and paper.

From Printed Volumes to Databases

Enter the Computer

The very first machines that can really be called *digital computers* were built in the period from 1939 to 1944, culminating in the construction of the ENIAC in 1946, "the first general-purpose, electronic computer" (*Encyclopædia Britannica Online* 2014). These machines were all part of a long progression of innovations to speed up the task of mathematical calculations. After that, inventions and improvements came thick and fast: the 1950s and 1960s were an incredibly innovative time in computing, although probably not in a way that the ordinary person would have noticed. The first machine to be able to store a database, RCA's Bizmac, was developed in 1952 (*Lexikon's History of Computing* 2002). The first instance of an online transaction-processing system, using telephone lines to connect remote users to central mainframe computers, was the airline reservation system known as SABRE, set up by IBM for American Airlines in 1964 (Computer History Museum 2004). Meanwhile, at Lockheed Missile and Space Company, a man named Roger Summit was engaged in projects involving search and retrieval, and management of massive data files. His group's first interactive search-and-retrieval service was demonstrated to the company in 1965; by 1972, it had developed into a new, commercially viable product: Dialog—the "first publicly available online research service" (Dialog 2005).

Thus, in the 1960s and 1970s, when articles were still being produced on typewriters, indexes and abstracts were being produced in hard copy, and very disparate industries were developing information technologies for their own specialized purposes, Summit can be credited with having incredible vision. He asked the right questions:

[handwritten in margin: Roger Summit]

1. What do people want? Information.

2. Who produces information, and in what form? The government and commercial publishers, in the form of papers, articles, newspapers, etc.

3. What if you could put information *about* all that published material into a machine-readable file: a database—something you could search?

Summit also had the vision to see how the technological elements could be used. The database needed to be made only once, at his firm's headquarters, and trained agents (librarians) could then access it over telephone lines with just some simple, basic equipment. The firm could track usage exactly and charge accordingly. Think of the advantages!

The advantages of an electronic version of an indexing/abstracting system are really revolutionary. In a system no longer bound by the confines of paper, space, and quite so many expensive skilled personnel:

- Articles could be associated with a greater number of terms describing their content, not just one or two (some skilled labor is still required).

- Although material has to be rekeyed (i.e., typed into the database), this doesn't require subject specialists, simply typists (cheap labor).

- Turnaround time is faster: most of your labor force isn't thinking and composing, just typing continuously—the process of adding to the information in the database goes on all the time, making the online product much more current.

- If you choose to provide your index "online only," thus avoiding the time delays and costs of physical publishing, why, you might be able to redirect the funds to expanding your business: offering other indexes (databases) in new subject areas.

As time goes on, this process of "from article to index" gets even faster. When articles are created electronically (e.g., word processing), no rekeying is needed to get the information into your database, just software to convert and rearrange the material to fit your database fields. So, rather than typists, you must pay programmers to write the software, and you still need some humans to analyze the content and assign the subject terms.

In the end, the electronic database is not necessarily cheaper to create; it very likely costs more! The costs have simply shifted. But customers buy it because . . . *it is so much more powerful and efficient*. It is irresistible, and printed indexes have vanished like the dodo. Online library databases are an integral part of the research process.

The Library Database Industry Today

For a line of business and a product you probably weren't very aware of until you were in high school or college, the library database business is, for the moment, surprisingly robust. The juggernaut of Google and especially Google Scholar has not put the commercial database vendors out of business (yet—I'm sure there is a constant undercurrent of fear throughout the business). Probably the largest commercial vendors, and ones you might have heard of before reading this book, are EBSCO, ProQuest, and Gale (Gale Cengage). Other major names to add to your repertoire are Thomson-Reuters (creators of the *Web of Science* and many other databases), JSTOR, LexisNexis, OCLC FirstSearch, ABC-CLIO, Alexander Street Press, Project MUSE, and OVID. Most of the databases produced by these vendors have content drawn from many sources, many publishers: they *aggregate* content, bringing it together so you can search across all of it in one database. Thus the terminology *aggregators* that is often used to describe the multidisciplinary article databases from the vendors listed above. In contrast, major publishers such as Elsevier, Oxford University Press, and Sage Publications are big enough to create databases just of the materials they publish, for example: Elsevier's ScienceDirect database, Oxford Music Online, Sage Journals and the CQ databases (an imprint of Sage).

In addition to the commercial entities mentioned above, some professional associations create and manage the subscriptions to databases of their materials. Examples include the Association for Computing Machinery (ACM), the Institute of Electrical and Electronics Engineers (IEEE), the American Society of Mechanical Engineers (ASME), the American Mathematical Society (AMS), and the American Chemical Society (ACS). Government and international agencies also produce databases. US government agencies such as the National Library of Medicine, the Department of Education, the Census Bureau, and the Bureau of Labor Statistics are the authors of key databases in their respective topical areas, which we will cover in subsequent chapters. At the international level, the World Bank,[2] the International Monetary Fund, and the Organization for Economic Cooperation and Development (OECD) all offer databases of their information.

The names of library database vendors listed above represent only the largest and/or better-known entities. As in any line of business there are, of course, many more companies, either smaller or focused on a particular audience (the number of vendors that create databases specifically for the business community, both corporate and academic, is remarkably extensive). The database vendor industry is also a *business* like any other: it is subject to consolidation and occasionally to expansion. Companies come and go through mergers and acquisitions, start-ups, and occasional deaths. Changes may not happen as rapidly as in some industries, but when they do, they can be significant. Three of the notable changes in the current decade were EBSCO's acquisition of the H.W. Wilson databases, and two major moves by ProQuest: the acquisition of the CSA databases and taking over publication of the *Statistical Abstract of the United States* from the US Census Bureau, including putting all the *Statistical Abstract* content into a new database.

At the beginning of this section, I made a reference to the database vendors' (not to mention librarians') fears about Google and Google Scholar: that these free, ubiquitous, embedded-in-daily-life resources might spell the end of the library database business. The vendors have been fighting back for many years, however, first with something called "federated search" (about which the less said the better; the title of Jody Fagan's 2011 editorial on the topic says it all: "Federated Search Is Dead—and Good Riddance!"). The latest counter-attack by the database vendors, dubbed "Discovery Services" or "Web Scale Discovery Services," is far superior. Reports on usage statistics from institutions that have adopted a discovery service indicate that these products may have a strong chance of winning ground back from the all-mighty Googleplex (Way 2010, Kemp 2012, Daniels, Robinson, and Wishnetsky 2013, Calvert 2014).

The following section will provide a brief overview of discovery services, concluding with why they will not be considered further in this text.

Discovery Services

Discovery Services are systems that harvest and pre-index a wide variety of library content from separate sources (records from library databases, the online catalog, perhaps the local institutional repository or other locally developed databases), build one giant index of all that content, and provide near-instant, relevancy ranked results through one search box (Vaughan 2011, Adams et al. 2013). Sound familiar? It is exactly the Google model, but instead of web pages it draws on all the vetted and expensive resources for which the library has already paid, making them "discoverable." These systems are frequently referred to as *Web-Scale Discovery Services*, "meaning they search library collections the way Google searches the web: by searching the entire breadth of content available in the library's collection" (Fry 2013). (The "entire breadth of content" is at least the goal if not the reality right now.) The essential key is the *pre-indexing*, getting the data from all the disparate resources ahead of time, as it were, to build that one giant index that can provide the speedy response time that users expect. Where the discovery systems start to part ways with Google is on the results page, which is loaded with options for refining and outputting results, and where library-owned full text is instantly accessible.

The vendors and products in the discovery service market at the time of this writing are EBSCO Discovery Service (EDS), Serials Solutions' Summon (note that Serials Solutions is owned by ProQuest), Ex Libris' PrimoCentral, OCLC's WorldCat Discovery Services (WDS), and, though it works differently from the others, Innovative Interface's Encore Synergy. AquaBrowser is ProQuest's discovery product aimed at the public library market.

The tricky part is that these companies are competitors both in the individual database and now in the discovery service market. Their major customers (large academic libraries) have resources from a wide variety of vendors. Achieving the goal of providing "one search" access to all that content means that each discovery service company (A) must persuade the competing discovery service companies (B), and all the *other* database vendors (C), to give A access to their databases in order to harvest and pre-index the data therein. This is a delicate dance, as you might imagine, but again, the threat of Google is actually helping, and agreements are (carefully) being negotiated. From a customer's point of view, it's obvious: "You've got to be in," says Michael Kucsak, Director of Library Systems & Technology at the University of North Florida, talking about inter-vendor discoverability. "You're in—you win. You're out—you're not long for the world" (Fry 2013).

Discovery services hold immense promise for breaking down the silos in library content, especially the one between the library catalog (OPAC) and the article databases (each one of which is in its own silo). While students may eventually understand that the catalog and the databases are separate, and that the routes for accessing each one are different, for the casual user who needs 15 good articles for tomorrow's paper—it is simply too much effort. Discovery services meet that need fairly efficiently and painlessly. And as a librarian who has made many, many purchase decisions and is painfully aware of what quality database resources cost, a "tool [that] holds the potential to significantly increase the discovery and use of such content" (Vaughan 2011) does indeed get my notice and my vote.

So how can a textbook on (individual) database searching still be justified? Why master all sorts of esoteric knowledge and get comfortable with interfaces having three search boxes (with attendant options and settings) when there is a simple, one-box option that searches the same material? The discovery services tools are a wonderful way to woo undergraduates back to library resources. But you have this textbook in hand, presumably, because you are studying to become a librarian or an information professional or technologist. For you, a higher order of knowledge and familiarity with more sophisticated tools and approaches is one of the essential *points*—otherwise anyone could set up shop and call herself an expert searcher. Google and the discovery services will take care of the lower order questions. Someone still needs to be there to deal with the harder, higher order research queries. When the discovery service search isn't providing the answer, someone needs to know how to go to next level: how to choose, access, and skillfully interact with highly crafted, subject-specific databases on an individual basis. Jody Fagan (2011) points out that "scholars working on more substantial research projects . . . have already found—or will need to find—the native interface to the subject-specific resources they need." *You* need to be the person who can point those scholars to subject-specific resources, and help them get the most out of the "native interface" (which usually provides subject-specific features) of those resources.[3] This book is designed to do precisely that. Let's get started—because searching really can be just as rewarding as finding.

Notes

1. According to the Google Guide at http://www.googleguide.com/google_works.html, the Google database is built by the GoogleBot, indexed by the Google Indexer, and searches handled by the three parts of the Query Processor. The utterly massive scale simply precludes any kind of human involvement.

2. Worth noting, the World Bank databases, formerly subscription-based, are now available to the world for free. Kudos to the World Bank for this daring and generous move!

3. Besides, it's just ever so much more interesting. What fun is plunking words in a box? Trust me, database skills make research much more efficient and satisfying.

2
Database Structure for Everyone: Records, Fields, and Indexes

Whether you are using this book in an upper-level database searching course or an entry-level intro to reference course, it's likely that you have or will have the opportunity to take a true "database" course. This means that some of you may already be familiar with the concepts in this chapter. My goal is to focus on helping you learn and develop strategies to search and interact more effectively with library databases rather than getting into the real technology of how databases are built. This chapter provides a brief and simple introduction to how databases are conceptually put together. In my experience, this is as much as you need to know to apply appropriate search techniques and use the database effectively. There's no point in piling on technical detail if it doesn't further your ultimate goal, which in this case is searching.

Database Building Blocks

Fields, Records, and Tables

In essence, databases are made up of fields and records. Fields are like one cell in an Excel spreadsheet: a bit of computer memory dedicated to holding one particular type of information, one value. For example, an age field might hold the value 28. The type of information could be text, numbers, or an image. A set of fields makes up a record, the idea being that the information in all the fields of one record relate to one thing: a person, a company, a journal, a purchase order, etc. An analogy would be a row in Excel: one row equals one record. But while you could have an Excel file with 5000 rows

Personal Data Table

ID Number	Last Name	First Name	MI	DOB	Gender
12345678	Smith	John	Q	19451121	M
23456789	Jones	Martha	A	19950401	F
98765432	Kepler	John	T	19620714	M
[etc.]					

Eye Table

ID Number	Eye color	Corrective Lenses
12345678	Blue	Y
23456789	Brown	N
98765432	Grey	Y
[etc.]		

Address Table

ID Number	Street	City	State	Zip
12345678	123 Main St	Clyde	NY	14433
23456789	60 Merriman St	Rochester	NY	14607
98765432	238 Bayview Dr	Greece	NY	14612
[etc.]				

Photo Table

ID Number	BadPic
12345678	
23456789	
98765432	
[etc.]	

Driving History Table

ID Number	Years Driving	Accidents
12345678	53	2
23456789	3	1
98765432	34	0
[etc.]		

"Show me the complete record for John T. Kepler"

ID #	Last Name	First Name	MI	DOB	Gen.	Street	City	State	Zip	Eyes	Lenses	Yrs Drv	Acc.	Pic
98765432	Kepler	John	T	19620714	M	238 Bayview Dr	Greece	NY	14612	Grey	Y	34	0	

Figure 2.1. DMV relational database example: tables, fields, and complete record.

(records), and 30 columns (all the different fields), such a file wouldn't ultimately be very efficient to search, and definitely isn't scalable (it would not, actually, be a database, but only a "flat file"). Enter the idea of *relational* databases, which are structured with tables. It's like having many Excel worksheets that can have indefinitely many rows, but only a few columns (fields). One of the fields in every table is dedicated to a unique identifier, which ties together all the material relating to the same person, company, etc. together. All of that material now represents a record. The table structure (and some additional features we will touch on presently) make possible the desired storage efficiency and speed of access even for huge amounts of information.

Think about driver's licenses. They all have an ID number, the owner's name, address, date of birth, eye color, a bad photo, etc. All of that information undoubtedly resides in a database administered by the state agency that cares about driver's licenses. It's easy to imagine the Department of Motor Vehicle's database having fields with names such as ID #, Name, Addr, DOB, Eyes, BadPic, etc. The fields are probably located in several tables: one for address information, one for driving history, one for the photo, etc. Pulled together by the ID number field, those fields make up records, each one of which represents a person (Figure 2.1).

The fields in the complete record represent every bit of information that appears on your license, and probably some that isn't actually printed on the license as well. When you send in the paperwork and the check to renew your license, they look you up in the database by your ID number, make any changes that you might have indicated in your paperwork (e.g., change the values in your fields), and hit print. Presto, you've gone from being a database entry to being a small card with an unflattering photo.

Decisions, Decisions: Designing the Database

From here on, I'm going to discuss databases only in terms of fields and records, leaving the "tables" aspect out. In the real world, yes, what is behind the interface you are looking at is almost undoubtedly a relational database, built on tables. But those tables are simply fields that make up mini-records. At essence what matters are the fields, and how many of them you need to create a complete record.

And indeed, the crucial task in developing a database is deciding what fields the records in your database are going to have, and how big they are going to be, that is, how many characters or numbers they will be able to hold. This "size" represents the computer memory allocated every time a new record is added. (Although memory is cheap now, in a huge project, how much memory will be allocated is still something to consider.) In the best of all possible worlds, a whole design team, including software engineers, subject experts, people from marketing and sales, and potential users, would wrestle with this problem. Nothing might ever get done in such a large and varied group, however, and so probably a more limited team of software engineers and content experts is the norm. The problem is that the design team had better make good choices initially, because it can be difficult, if not impossible, to make significant changes to the record structure later.[1] This is good and bad. It means there's a certain inherent stability, or at least pressure on these database products not to change too much, but when you wish that they *would* fix something, it can take a long time for change to happen. You can take a certain amount of comfort, though, in the knowledge that however much the interface to the database—the way it looks—changes, behind the scenes the same types of information (fields), are probably still there.

Figure 2.2. Database fields.

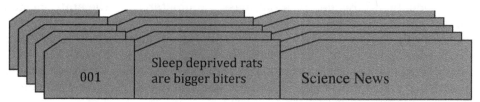

Figure 2.3. Database records.

Food for Thought

For an article database, you'd probably have a field for the article title, the name of the journal it appeared in . . . and what else? Think about the other information you would want to capture. Again, the process is something like this:

Define your fields (Figure 2.2):
. . . that make up records (Figure 2.3) . . .
. . . and form the basis of your database.

Quick Recap

In this section we have described the structure of databases in very simple terms and compared it to the structure of an Excel spreadsheet. The most basic elements of a database are fields and records. (Technically, the fields are usually structured in the form of tables, with one field in each table acting as the "unique key" to pull all the information relating to one record together.) A full set of fields makes up a record. Every record in the database has the same set of fields (even if, in some records, some fields are blank). All of the records together make up the database.

Beyond Fields and Records

Field Indexes

Fields and records are the basis, the "data" of a database. What makes a database fast, powerful, and efficient are the *indexes* of the fields. It would be very slow if every time you queried the database, it started at field1, record1, and searched sequentially through each field of each record—you might as well go back to hard copy at that rate.

An index, in the sense that we're discussing now, is a list of all the values from a particular field, with some kind of identifier indicating from which record each value came (a pointer if you will). This is much like the way the index at the end of a book indicates on which pages a word appears. In one sense, creating indexes of fields breaks one cardinal rule of databases: not to duplicate any data. But this one kind of duplication is worth the redundancy and extra storage space, because combined with sophisticated algorithms indexes make it possible to locate and retrieve the records associated with specified values in nanoseconds. The field indexes become part of the database but have a separate existence from the records. (You could think of them as really minimal table structures: just two columns, one with the values for field X, and the other containing a pointer back to the record that each field X value came from.) Again, the power of an index is that it can be sorted and in other sophisticated ways optimized for searching.

Let's return to the driver's license example. It has a field for Last Name. You'd definitely want to create an index to that field, so you'd have your computer program harvest all the values from the Last Name field, along with the associated ID Number value for each one. Given that the data is textual (a name), you'd probably want to sort the index alphabetically.[2] Then if you wanted to find the record for Smith, John, your computer program could zip to the Ss in the Last Name index list (and then to the Js in the First Name index), find a set where the ID Numbers matched, and based on that pull up the full record for Mr. Smith. And do this all in *much* less time than it takes to write about it. Using indexes to find records also means that the order of the rows in your database, that is, what order you enter your records, doesn't matter at all. You simply build an index and search *that* when you want to find something in your database. Or you can build several indexes; you can make an index of any field you want. However, as always, there are costs and reasons why you might not index every field.[3]

A Very Simple Example

Say we have three articles:

Milky Way's Last Major Merger.
Science News. v. 162 no. 24 p. 376

It's a Dog's Life.
The Economist. December 21, 2002. p. 61

Manhattan Mayhem.
Smithsonian. v. 33 no. 9 p. 44

Let's enhance these just a little by adding a one-line description to each record (so that we have a few more words to search on):

Record 1:

Milky Way's Last Major Merger.

Science News. v. 162 no. 24 p. 376.

New clues about galaxy formation indicate early collision affected Milky
  Way's shape.

Figure 2.4. A very simple database record.

Record 2:

It's a Dog's Life.

The Economist. December 21, 2002. p. 61.

From hard labour to a beauty contest, a history of the work and whims of dog breeding.

Record 3:

Manhattan Mayhem.

Smithsonian. v. 33 no. 9 p. 44

Martin Scorsese's realistic portrayal of pre–Civil War strife—*Gangs of New York*—re-creates the brutal street warfare waged between immigrant groups.

My database will have just four fields (Figure 2.4):

1. Record number (four-number places, e.g., my database will never grow to more than 9,999 articles)

2. Article title (50 characters allocated)

3. Journal name (50 characters allocated)

4. Abstract (200 characters allocated)

Now let's index the fields.
The initial list of words from the Article Title field looks like this:

Milky

Way's

Last

Major

Merger

It's

a

Dog's

Life

Manhattan

Mayhem

More Database Decisions

There are various things about this list that one might question. What will our indexing program do with those possessives and contractions? Do we want to clog it up with little words like *a*? There are many decisions for database designers to make:

- How will the indexing program handle apostrophes and other punctuation? We take it for granted now that the system will simply preserve it, and users can search for contractions or possessives, but you may still encounter systems that insert a space instead of the apostrophe (dog s), or ignore it and treat the letters as a string (ending up with "dogs" for "dog's").

- What will the indexing program do with the "little words"? That is, words such as *a, an, by, for, from, of, the, to, with*, and so forth, which are usually referred to as _stop words_. These are words that are so common that database designers usually decide they don't want to expend time and space to index them. Indexing programs are programmed with a list of such words and will "stop" indexing when they hit a word on the list. A more descriptive term would be _skip words_, because that is what really happens: the indexing program skips any stop list words and continues to the next word. Almost all databases employ a stop word list, and it can vary greatly from one vendor to the next. (Even Google has stop words, words it doesn't index.)

- Should the system be designed to preserve information about capitalization, or to ignore the case of the words? We are so used to systems that do not distinguish upper and lowercase (so that you don't have to worry how you type in your query), but there are times when you would really like the system to know the difference between, say, AIDS (the disease) and aids (the common noun or verb).

Because this is a modern system, we'll decide to preserve the apostrophes and to make *a* one of our stop words, so it won't be included in the index. We can then sort the list alphabetically:

Dog's

It's

Last

Life

Major

Manhattan

Mayhem

Merger

Milky

Way's

Can you see the problem here? We have neglected to include an identifier to show which record a word came from. Let's start over.

Better Field Indexing

Let's make sure that our index list includes the record number and which field the word came from:

0001	Milky	TI
0001	Way's	TI
0001	Last	TI
0001	Major	TI
0001	Merger	TI
0002	It's	TI
0002	Dog's	TI
0002	Life	TI
0003	Manhattan	TI
0003	Mayhem	TI

One more thing: we can include a number representing the *order* of the word within the field (why might this be useful?). We now have something like this:

0001	Milky	TI	01
0001	Way's	TI	02
0001	Last	TI	03

Now we'll sort again.

0002	Dog's	TI	03
0002	It's	TI	01
0001	Last	TI	03
0002	Life	TI	04
0001	Major	TI	04
0003	Manhattan	TI	01
0003	Mayhem	TI	02
0001	Merger	TI	05
0001	Milky	TI	01
0001	Way's	TI	02

Note how even though we deleted the stop word *a* in the title "It's a dog's life," the numerical position of "dog's" reflects that there was an intervening word there: its position is recorded as 3, not 2.

Because people might want to search on the name of the publication, it would be good to index that as well. Our index of the Journal Name field looks something like this:

0002	*Economist*	JN	02
0001	*News*	JN	02
0001	*Science*	JN	01
0001	*Science News*	JN	01, 02
0003	*Smithsonian*	JN	01

Note the multiple indexing of *Science News*. The technical term for this is *double posting*.

To make things even faster and more efficient, after indexing each field, combine the indexes so that you have only one list to search:

0002	Dog's	TI	03
0002	Economist	JN	02
0002	It's	TI	01
0001	Last	TI	03
0002	Life	TI	04
0001	Major	TI	04
0003	Manhattan	TI	01
0003	Mayhem	TI	02
0001	Merger	TI	05
0001	Milky	TI	01
0001	News	JN	02
0001	Science	JN	01
0001	Science News	JN	01, 02
0003	Smithsonian	JN	01
0001	Way's	TI	02

We undoubtedly want to index the content of the one-sentence "abstracts," as well. Here is a list of the words in raw form:

new	beauty	Pre-Civil
clues	contest	War
about	a	Strife
galaxy	history	Gangs
formation	of	Of
indicate	the	New

early	work	York
collision	and	Re-creates
affected	whims	The
Milky	of	brutal
Way's	dog	street
Shape	breeding	warfare
From	Martin	waged
hard	Scorsese's	between
labour	realistic	immigrant
to	portrayal	groups
a	of	

Decisions and cleanup are needed on this list of words:

- Stop words—what will they be?
- Hyphenated words—how will they be recorded?
- Proper names—"double post" to include the phrase too?
- Alternative spellings—do we do anything about them or not? (What might you do?)

Luckily, software does almost all of this work for us. You probably will never see any indexes in their raw state. What we've been going over here is in real life very under the hood, often proprietary material for the database vendors. You don't need to know exactly how any particular database works; you simply need to grasp some of the basic principles that govern how databases in general are put together and how they are indexed. This determines how you search them—and what you can expect to get out of them.

Quick Recap

This section discussed the idea of field indexes and the importance of good planning in the design of huge databases. Field indexes refer to the idea that the values in a database's fields can be extracted and put into their own lists that consist of just the value and a pointer back to the record it came from. These indexes exist separately from the records in the database, and make rapid, efficient searching of huge databases possible. Much thought goes into the initial database design (i.e., what fields to include, what they are called, how much space to allocate for each one), because the design cannot be easily changed later. Many decisions go into the design of indexes as well, for example, which fields will be indexed, how contractions and possessives will be handled, which words will be treated as stop words, and if and how identification of phrases will be supported.

Examples of Indexes in Common Databases

In the examples that follow, see if you can relate what we've just gone over with how the field indexes are presented to you as a user in these common databases. We'll start with two multidisciplinary databases: *Academic OneFile* from Gale, which has a single Subject list, and EBSCO's *MasterFILE Premier*, which offers separate Subjects, Places, and People indexes. Last, we'll consider the very elaborate indexing used by OCLC's WorldCat.

Gale's *Academic OneFile*: One Subject List

Academic OneFile, one of the Gale Company's "Infotrac" suite of databases, prominently offers a Subject Guide Search. If you choose the Subject Guide Search from the navigation bar, useful Search tips are displayed on that interface page (Figure 2.5). The tips text suggests using this search mode "when you want to browse a dynamic list of topics, people, products, locations, organizations and more."

Once you have searched for a term, then you can browse forward through the list, as long as there are headings containing your search term somewhere within them. But the Gale system doesn't offer unlimited, free-form browsing capability, unlike *MasterFILE*'s true browse access (i.e. *MasterFILE* presents you with the very beginning of whichever index list you choose, and you could, if you wanted, simply page through—browse—the whole thing without any searching at all). An advantage to the Gale subject list over *MasterFILE*'s is that it is all-in-one: you don't have to think about the nature of what you're looking for (Is it a subject? a person? a place?). You can look once and know for sure whether the topic you're looking for is there or not. For example, *Academic OneFile* at the time of this writing

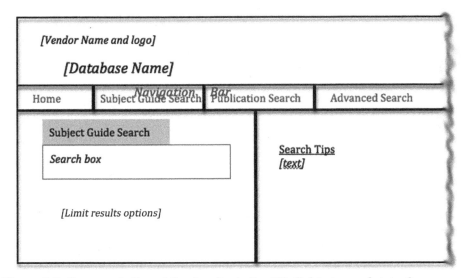

Figure 2.5. Representation of the *Academic OneFile* Subject search interface.

does not appear to have any articles on the singing group Chanticleer. The only Subject Guide entry is for *Chanticleer and the Fox*, which is helpfully glossed "(Novel)." Being an all-in-one list, these parenthetical notes are very useful. Other examples include "(Planet)," "(Medication)," "(Motion Picture)," the names of sports (to distinguish the different "World Cup" events), and various others. In the Subject Terms results list, links to Subdivisions and Related Subjects are provided if applicable, as well as "See" entries to get you to the term Gale has decided to use (e.g., "Coffee addiction See *Coffee habit*"). If one is willing to slow down enough to look through the list of Subdivisions, it is well worth it, as examining the list can make finding articles on *exactly* the aspect of [topic x] very easy and efficient. Looking at the Subdivisions for Coffee (Beverage) provides an excellent example: just looking for how much coffee is consumed? Try the Subdivision Consumption data. Environmental aspects, Market share, Prices, Research, Risk factors, Statistics—the Gale indexers have done an excellent job identifying the kinds of things people look for most often and which can be hard to find without the human intervention of applying intelligent subject headings. The Gale subject list also includes the number of results for every heading and subdivision, which is extremely helpful. Being able to see the count lets you know that *Academic OneFile* is probably a good place to find articles about the "Health aspects" of coffee (945 results in May 2014), but perhaps not for learning more about "Diseases and pests" of coffee (only 4 results in May 2014).

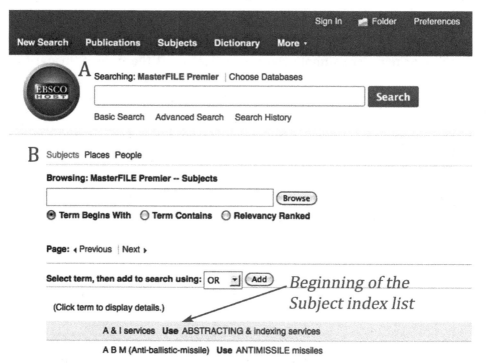

Figure 2.6. Initial Subjects Index interface in EBSCO's *MasterFILE Premier*. © 2014 EBSCO Industries, Inc. All rights reserved.

EBSCO *MasterFILE Premier*: Subjects, Places, & People Indexes

Even in a fairly simple display, there is a lot to look at and look for. In this view of the subject index interface in EBSCO's *MasterFILE Premier* (Figure 2.6), *A* is the area identifying where we are: who is providing the database, which database it is, and a search box to collect the results of our choices from the Subjects, Places, and People indexes.

The section marked *B* tells us we are accessing the Subjects lists: there are separate indexes for the Subjects, Places, and People fields. The interface to these index lists allows us to simply start at the very beginning of the list and browse forward, page by page, or to jump to any point in the index by searching on a word or phrase, with the option of having our search term at the beginning of the Subject entry ("Term begins with"), or anywhere within it ("Term contains"). The third option, "Relevancy ranked," will return all of the Subject headings containing your search term arranged by relevance rather than alphabetically (although it is hard to tell how "relevance" is being determined).

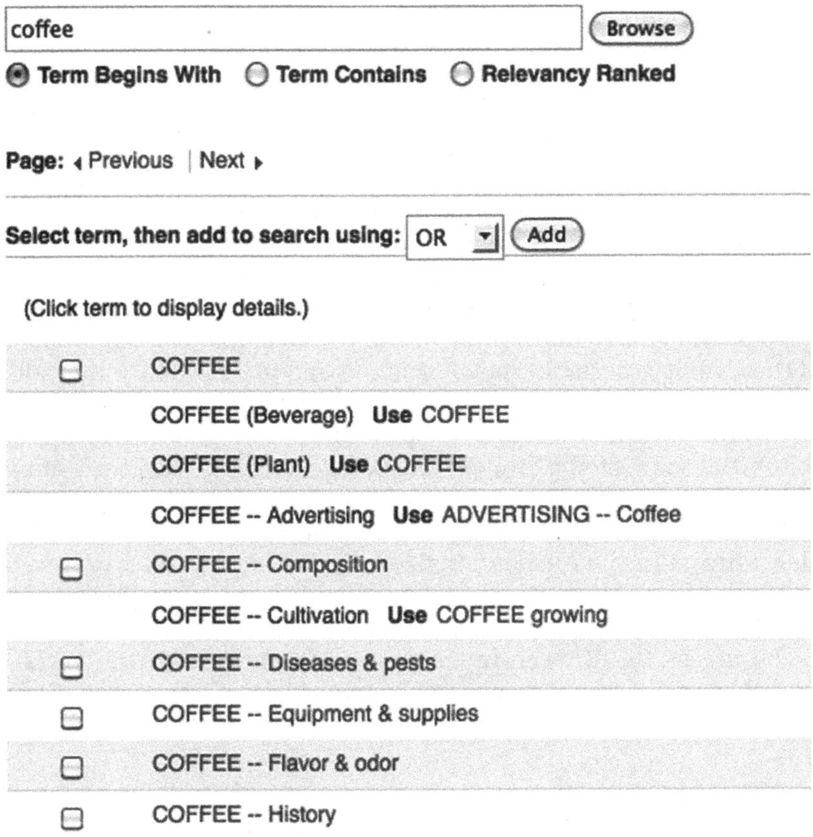

coffee	Browse

⦿ **Term Begins With**   ◯ **Term Contains**   ◯ **Relevancy Ranked**

Page: ◂ Previous | Next ▸

Select term, then add to search using: | OR ▾ | Add

(Click term to display details.)

☐ COFFEE

COFFEE (Beverage)   **Use** COFFEE

COFFEE (Plant)   **Use** COFFEE

COFFEE -- Advertising   **Use** ADVERTISING -- Coffee

☐ COFFEE -- Composition

COFFEE -- Cultivation   **Use** COFFEE growing

☐ COFFEE -- Diseases & pests

☐ COFFEE -- Equipment & supplies

☐ COFFEE -- Flavor & odor

☐ COFFEE -- History

Figure 2.7. The Subjects Index in *MasterFILE Premier*, showing the beginning of the "coffee" entries. © 2014 EBSCO Industries, Inc. All rights reserved.

In Figure 2.7 we see the results of searching the subject list for the word coffee. The entries in all caps are values from the field designated as *subjects* in this database: terms the EBSCO indexers have chosen from the predetermined list of subject headings for this database, that they feel capture the essence of the article's content. We will talk more about this idea of the "predetermined list" of subjects in chapter 3, but for now, just tuck away the idea that entries in the Subjects list are not random: the indexers have deliberately compiled this list of terms.[4] Thus every article about the history of coffee is assigned the subject: COFFEE—History. But, as indicated by the helpful "Use" note, if you are looking for articles about the cultivation of coffee, rather than "COFFEE—Cultivation" you should "**Use** COFFEE growing." The number of results for each entry is not provided, which is a bit annoying.

The "Places" list contains, obviously, names of places that have been the subject of articles in this database, helpfully glossed with the name of the country or state where they are located to disambiguate them (e.g., "abbeville (ala.)," "abbeville (france)," and "abbeville (la.)" etc.). In the "People" list you would find, obviously, names of people, but also of orchestras, musical groups, and musical events, all glossed with the parenthetical note "(performer)" (e.g., "boston early music festival (performer)"). The entire content of the Places and People lists is lowercase, which seems a little odd, but in both of these lists the number of records for each entry is provided, which is very helpful.

Field Indexes for the WorldCat Database

Moving on to our third example, OCLC's WorldCat database (a union catalog of library holdings from around the world) provides even more examples of the use of separate indexes for many fields. As in EBSCO's Subject, Places, and People lists, the WorldCat Browse Index interface provides the opportunity to roam around in the indexes, discovering what is there (and thus, what is possible), before committing to a search. Some fields (such as Author) are even indexed twice, in separate lists, creating one index for single words only, and another for phrases. Figure 2.8 provides a drawing of the initial view of the Browse Index interface (*A*), and an example of a single-word and a phrase index for the same field. In the part of the drawing marked *B*, the drop-down menu has been changed to Author, and in *C* to Author Phrase. In the Author (single-word) index, you could browse only for an author's last name, for example, Austen. In the Author Phrase, you could browse specifically for Austen, Jane.

You access the Browse Index screen via an icon in the WorldCat Advanced Search interface, discussed in greater detail in chapter 7. For now, simply observe how it works.

Using the Subject Indexes

Figure 2.9 provides a stylized representation of looking up the word *librarians* in the Subject index of the WorldCat database. (Note that the

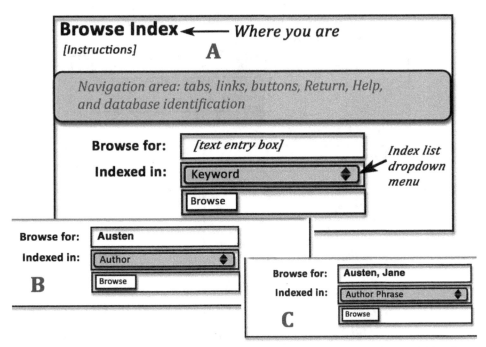

Figure 2.8. Representation of the initial Browse Index screen for the WorldCat®
database and examples of single-word and phrase indexes offered for some
fields.

dropdown for choosing which index you want to browse has been changed to
Subject, a single word index.)

The lower part of Figure 2.9 represents the results of searching this
index. In this stylized drawing, I have only written out the terms of most
interest and highest counts. The other entries represented by *"[term]"* are
almost always odd spellings or outright typos,[5] and have counts in the
single digits. The Count column indicates how many records in the database have been assigned that Subject. Since the Count numbers change
steadily, I have represented them with hash marks indicating the size of
the number. When you are actually using WorldCat, these count numbers
provide a rough indication of the content of the database, and how useful
it might prove for the topic you're working on. In this case, WorldCat appears to have a wealth of material on librarian*s* (plural) and librarianship,
but far fewer entries for "librarian" in the singular. Last, observe that the
term we searched for appears in the *middle* of the list, and is in bold. Why
do you think the database designers have chosen to display the results
this way?

In Figure 2.10, we see the results of a search for *information retrieval*
in the Subject Phrase index. This drawing uses the same conventions as in
Figure 2.9. Were you to get online and browse forward in this list, you would
find literally hundreds of entries beginning with the words: "information
retrieval."

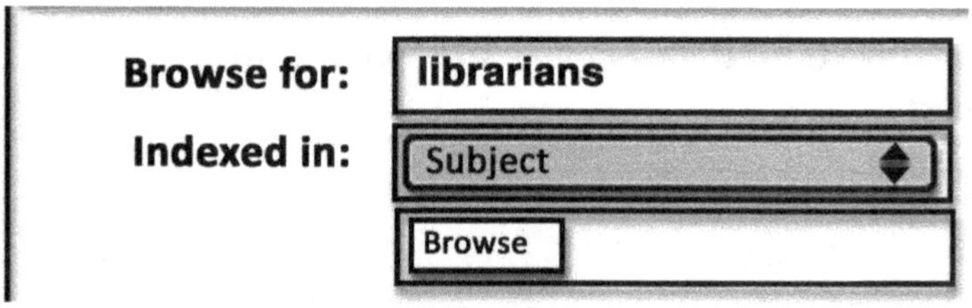

Browse for:	librarians
Indexed in:	Subject ◆
	Browse

[Back Forward navigation]

Term/Phrase	**Count**
librarian	####
[term]	#
[term]	#
[term]	#
librarians	#####
librarianship	#####
[term]	#
[term]	#
[term]	#
[term]	#

Figure 2.9. Representation of results from the single-word Subject index.

Record Structure Reflected in Fields Displayed

As a reminder, indexes are built from the fields included in a database record. The fields can be called the *record structure*, and you can get a sense of how simple, or elaborate, a database's record structure is by studying the fields displayed when viewing a record from the database.

The WorldCat database has quite an elaborate record structure; these database designers were making sure that they didn't leave anything out, and that the most complete set of bibliographic information they could assemble would be available to users. The OCLC interface designers have the task of conveying a large amount of information as clearly as possible.

Get online, and look up the record for your favorite book in WorldCat. Take time to study the full record display, noticing how the designers have used different fonts, colors, and alignments to convey meaning. Notice how the field names are lined up on the left, followed by colons, and the contents of the fields appear to the right. Find the section labeled "Subject(s)," and notice that the terms below are labeled "Descriptor." (We will encounter some odd terms for subject headings in the course of this book.) Some of the fields may seem quite mysterious, but think about the purpose of the others, and why the database designers might have decided to include them. WorldCat has been

Browse for: "information retrieval"

Indexed in: Subject Phrase

Browse

[Back Forward navigation]

Term/Phrase	Count
[term phrase]	#
[term phrase]	#
[term phrase]	#
[term phrase]	#
information retrieval	#####
[term phrase]	#
[term phrase]	#
information retrieval & textual information access	####
[term phrase]	#
[term phrase]	#

Figure 2.10. Representation of results from the multiple word Subject Phrase index.

around since 1967, and has probably struggled to adjust its record structure ever since to stay abreast of developments. If the WorldCat database had been invented today, the database designers might have made different choices.

Exercises and Points to Consider

1. What would *your* ideal database record for a journal article look like? Choose any article that interests you, and design a database record for it, keeping in mind that what you do for this one article you will do for every other article (how much do you expect your database to grow?). What fields will you use? How big will each field be? What will you call the fields? Sketch out what the overall database would be like (and why this article would be included), and justify your choices.

2. Why do you think WorldCat has separate one-word and phrase indexes for the same fields?

3. What is a useful piece of information that is provided when you browse the indexes (in *Academic OneSource* and WorldCat)? How might this affect your search strategy?

4. Using the *MasterFILE* Places index, look up: mars. What is EB-SCO's preferred term for the "place" Mars? Switch to the Subject index, and look up: self acceptance (no hyphen). Notice how EBSCO clearly and easily gets you to the right form of the term, for this and so many other "self-" entries.

5. Can you do a field search with Google?

6. People generally think of Google as indexing all the words of all the web pages that it visits.[6] With a few exceptions (it recognizes the markup codes for the page Title, for example), it offers only one huge index labeled "all the text." Why do you think the commercial database vendors go to so much trouble to provide an elaborate record structure with indexed fields?

7. In the early days of online searching in libraries, only librarians performed searches, after a detailed and careful interview with the patron requesting the search. The librarian would plan the search carefully, and then "dial up" to connect to the database, using a password and employing a very terse, arcane set of commands to perform the search. Access fees were charged by the minute, with additional charges for records viewed. Try to picture this scenario, and then compare it with the situation today. How do you think the totally open, end-user access has affected databases and their interfaces? Can you think of anything about the current situation that is not an improvement?

Notes

1. If you're wondering why it would be so hard to change the record structure, remember to think of these databases as huge things: true, adding a new field to a database of just five records would be trivial. But a database of 500,000 records? How are you possibly going to retrospectively fill in the new field for all the existing records?

2. Computer scientists can cringe here. I'm sure it would actually be something much more sophisticated than a simple alphabetic sort.

3. For one thing, the process of initially building the index can take hours. Although this does not mean that it can't be done, remember that every index has to be updated frequently to reflect any changes in your database. It just adds to the complexity of the whole operation.

4. And each vendor's list is different. EBSCO has decided rather than "Coffee (Beverage)," the subject should just be "Coffee" in the *MasterFILE* database. Meanwhile, the folks over at Gale decided that "Coffee (Beverage)" was preferable to simply "Coffee," and that's the preferred subject heading in *Academic OneFile*.

5. Go online and take a look: these are odd and sometimes amusing entries. What this shows is that the indexing process, that is, the harvesting of terms from the Subject field, is done by a computer program: it simply picks up whatever is there, typos and all. (The errors come from the humans who typed the values into the field. For fallible humans, they are impressively accurate.)

6. Does Google have stop words, words that it ignores? And does it really index every page all the way to the end? Does this matter?

3
The Searcher's Toolkit: Part 1

In my experience, there are a finite number of concepts, techniques, and strategies for searching databases that make all the difference between aimlessly groping around and efficiently and effectively retrieving useful material. If you spend your whole day searching, then you'll probably discover or develop many more, but for most researchers or reference librarians, the topics in this chapter and the next are most likely all that you will ever need. I've dubbed this set of concepts the *Searcher's Toolkit*. All of them have applications in searching commercial databases, and some can be used with Web search engines (and once you've grasped these concepts, you'll start to see what's missing in the Web search products and understand better why searching the Web is, well, the way it is: sometimes perfect, sometimes very frustrating).

The First Basic Tools

Let us plunge right in with the most fundamental concept of all.

Basic Tool No. 1: Boolean Logic

In fact, this concept is so fundamental that you've probably run into it before, possibly several times through grade school, high school, and college. But do you *really* know what Boolean logic is and how it works? Do you really understand how it will affect your searches? Bear with a discussion of it one more time—you may be surprised!

In the database context, Boolean logic (after a fellow named George Boole [1815–1864])[1] refers to the *logical* (rather than arithmetical) operations on sets. That is, rather than manipulating numbers using symbols for

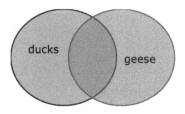

AND

Figure 3.1. Boolean AND:
Ducks AND Geese.

plus, minus, multiply, or divide, Boolean logic controls what happens to sets of things when acted on by *logical operators*. The Boolean operators used in database searching are:

AND

OR

AND NOT (frequently expressed simply as *NOT*; more on this later.)

Venn Diagrams

Arithmetical expressions (e.g., 2+2) result in some value (i.e., 4). Boolean expressions result in either a sub- or superset of the original sets; rather than producing a specific value, logical operators have an *effect* on the sets, producing a different output set. The effects of Boolean expressions are traditionally illustrated with drawings called *Venn diagrams*. Venn diagrams are always done with circles and shadings as in Figure 3.1, which keeps them nicely abstract. Feel free to start thinking of the terminology "sets," and these circle illustrations as "sets of database records," to make the concept more concrete. With just one operator in effect, Venn diagrams are quite simple to draw and to understand what the operator's effect is.

Boolean AND

In Figure 3.1, the circle on the left represents the set of all the database records that include the word *ducks*, a few of which also include the word *geese*. The circle on the right represents all records that include the word *geese*, a few of which also include the word *ducks*. A search for *ducks AND geese* retrieves only those records that mention *both* terms, represented by the smaller, overlapping section. It is easy to get confused here, because our regular use of the word *and* is additive, that is, it produces more (e.g., "two scoops, and sprinkles, and some whipped cream, please"), but a Boolean AND is very different: an AND operator will always, in practice, return a set that is *smaller* than either of the original sets. Theoretically, the largest set it could return would still be only of equal size to the smaller of the original sets. For example, at one point in time, the ProQuest Research database contained 760 records that contained *Obama, Michelle* in a field called Person, and 28,790 records containing *Obesity* in a field called Subject. A search on

Obama, Michelle in the Person field,

AND

Obesity in the Subject field

produced 50 records.

Notice how even when the initial sets are quite large, the combined, "ANDed" set is considerably smaller. When one of the initial sets is much smaller than the other, as is the case here, the resulting set is affected even more.

AND says that *all* criteria must be met for an indicated action to happen (usually retrieval of a record). What the Boolean operators are really doing is evaluating true or false. The computer's thought process goes something like this:

If (ducks) is true (e.g., present in the record)

AND (at the same time, in the same record)

If (geese) is true

Retrieve the record.

So, to reiterate: the number of records meeting multiple conditions is, in practice, always smaller than the set of records meeting just one condition, and it is usually significantly smaller. The more conditions (criteria, terms) that you set, the smaller the number of records that will be retrieved: there will be fewer documents about ducks AND geese AND loons than there are about just ducks AND geese. If one of the initial sets is very small, ANDing it with some other term is likely to reduce the results to zero. But our next operator, OR, is here to help with that potential problem.

Boolean OR

In Figure 3.2, the circle on the left represents all the database records that include the word *banana*, and the circle on the right represents all the database records that include the word *orange*. In this case, we don't care

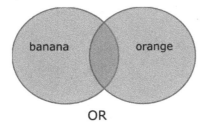

Figure 3.2. Boolean OR: Banana OR Orange.

what other words they contain, or how much they overlap. Thinking of this as a search, the OR retrieves *all* the bananas records, plus *all* the oranges records (including records mentioning both), for a total of a LOT of records! Again, our common parlance can make this confusing: usually we use the word *or* to mean "either one or the other"—"I'll have the banana *or* the orange." We wouldn't expect to be handed both fruits in response to that statement. But in Boolean logic, OR means "either the one, or the other, or both." Either of the criteria can be met for the computer to retrieve the record:

If (banana) is true (e.g., present in a record)

OR

If (orange) is true (present in a record)

Retrieve the record.

Think of it this way: in practice, Boolean OR is (practically) always more. By employing a judicious combination of Boolean AND and OR operators, you can "grow" small results sets in a controlled fashion, as we'll see later in this chapter.

Boolean NOT

Finally, Figure 3.3 represents the Boolean exclusion operator, which you'll see expressed as AND NOT and simply NOT with almost equal frequency. For our purposes, the terms are interchangeable, and this text will generally use simply NOT to make the operators as distinguishable as possible.[2] If this feels confusing, take comfort that at least the effects of this operator are more in line with our common usage of *not*: rivers NOT lakes retrieves records that include the term *rivers*, as long as they do NOT also contain the word lakes. Both criteria must be met, in the sense that the first term must be present, and the second term must *not* be present, for a record to be retrieved. The set of records retrieved can be thought of as just the lighter area of the *rivers* circle; anything from the darker *lakes* circle would not be in the results set. Note how the syntax is subtly different (which is further proof that even when a database vendor just uses NOT, what is really going on is AND NOT):

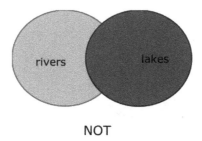

NOT

Figure 3.3. Boolean NOT: Rivers NOT Lakes.

If (rivers) is true (present in a record)

And

If (lakes) is NOT true (not present in the record)

Retrieve the record.

As you would expect, like AND, NOT almost always reduces the number of records retrieved. In general usage, you'll find that you don't often use the NOT operator in commercial databases: the possibility of missing useful records just because they happened to include the "NOTed" out term is too risky. If too many results are coming back, the better strategy is almost always to AND in another term, rather than to NOT out a term.

Order of Boolean Operations

A statement using just one Boolean operator—ducks OR geese—is straightforward. But just as you can write arithmetical expressions with several operators (2+2–3*9), you can write Boolean expressions with multiple operators. You will encounter plenty of searches that require more complexity than simply (word) AND (word). Again, just as in the arithmetical statements, the Boolean operators have very specific effects, and the order in which they are processed has a powerful effect on what ends up in the results set. When there is more than one operator in a search statement, they are generally evaluated in this order:

- NOT operations are performed first.

- Then AND operations are evaluated.

- Finally, OR operations are performed.

This is called the *order of operation*. This is the standard order for processing Boolean operators, but some systems simply evaluate statements left to right, the way you read. The results could be very different, depending on which order is used. Although it's important to be aware of the idea of order of operation, luckily you don't have to figure out what it is on each system you use. There is a simple way to take control and bend the order of operation to your will.

The Power of Parentheses

To control the order of operation, many systems allow you to group your ANDs, ORs, and NOTs with parentheses: ( ). Just as in arithmetic statements, the use of parentheses is helpful either to make the order of operation explicit, or to override it. What happens is that the expression in parentheses will be evaluated first, and then the order of operation (standard or left to right) will take over.[3] Throwing parentheses into the mix can dramatically change the way the system interprets the search.

For example, the statement

ducks NOT migration OR geese

produces the same result set as

(ducks NOT migration) OR geese

because in this case, putting the parentheses around the NOT statement (causing it to be executed first) is exactly the same as what happens in the standard order of operation (NOT first, OR last). The set of documents retrieved would be fairly large, and it would contain records for ducks (as long as those records didn't mention migration) and any records mentioning geese—even records that discuss geese and migration. OR really opens the door to let things back in, sometimes in surprising ways.

Represented as a Venn diagram, the statement (ducks NOT migration) OR geese looks like Figure 3.4.

The results of this search would include all the records except those represented by the visible dark area of the "migration" circle. Note that records about geese that mention migration *would* be included in the results; the NOT only affects the duck records. However, writing the search statement as

ducks NOT (migration OR geese)

will produce quite a different result set, much smaller and more focused. These would be records that mention ducks, and only those duck records that don't mention either migration or geese—the lightest area in Figure 3.5. The Venn diagram for this statement is shown in Figure 3.5.

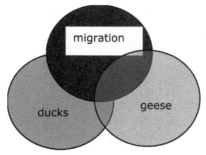

Figure 3.4. (Ducks NOT Migration) OR Geese.

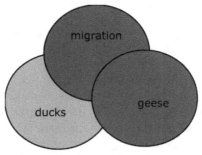

Figure 3.5. Ducks NOT (Migration OR Geese).

Quick Recap

This section introduced the first and most fundamental tool in the Searcher's Toolkit, Boolean logic. The Boolean logical operators are AND, OR, NOT (also expressed AND NOT). Adding terms to a search with AND will reduce the number of results, as will "NOTing" out a term. "ORing" more terms into a search will increase the number of results. Boolean expressions are often represented graphically with Venn diagrams. The standard order of operations for Boolean statements is to evaluate any NOT statements first, followed by AND statements, and finally by OR statements. Putting part of the statement in parentheses changes the order of operations, because the parenthesized section will be evaluated first.

Basic Tool No. 2: Controlled Vocabulary

The conundrum of online searching is that "We want to look for concepts, but we are forced to search for words" (Walker and Janes 1999). Think about it: if you wanted an *overview* of some topic, or a *discussion* of the pros and cons of some action, or especially *one good article on* . . . how do you express these squishy notions to a digital search engine? Even if you can search the full text, the item you want might not include in its text "this is an overview" or "here is a discussion" and certainly not "here is the latest best article" on topic xyz. All that you can do, in each of these cases, is to search on words that represent the topic. In the world of commercial, subscription databases, there is an additional, powerful option: the provision of *controlled vocabulary*, also known as *subject headings*, a *thesaurus*,[4] *descriptors*,[5] or *authority control*.[6] (Note that the discussion that follows will use the terms controlled vocabulary and subjects or subject headings interchangeably.) Controlled vocabulary is one of the added extras, one of the contributions of the companies that put together the databases, and one of the reasons they charge a subscription fee to access them. Remember the indexers from chapter 1? You are paying for a bit of human analysis on each entry in the database. If done well, this analysis is worth the price of admission for the efficiency that it provides.

Advantages of Controlled Vocabulary

Why is controlled vocabulary so valuable?

- Controlled vocabulary saves you from having to come up with, and then search for, every possible synonym (or alternative spelling) for a term. For example, if all of the articles discussing various kinds of clothing are assigned a subject heading of "clothing," you don't have to worry about looking for all the possible ways clothing might be expressed, for example: dress, raiment, drapery, costume, attire, habiliment, vesture, vestment, garment, garb, apparel, wardrobe, wearing apparel, clothes, outfit, trousseau, suit, trappings, togs, day wear, night wear, zoot suit . . .[7]
  - *Note*: Don't let your synonym neurons atrophy completely, though, because if you try a term in a subject or thesaurus search and get

no results, not even a "see" or "use" reference, you'll need to think of another term with which to start. And, of course, there is no controlled vocabulary on the Web.

- Theoretically, the use of controlled vocabulary should make your search more complete: if the indexers at the database company have reliably assigned a subject heading of *waterfowl* every time an article mentions geese or goose, duck or ducks, loon or loons, or any other waterbird, it should only be necessary to search on *waterfowl* as a Subject to retrieve everything.

- Subject headings lists disambiguate words that have several meanings (e.g., mercury—a planet, a car, a god, or a metal?), aiding in the precision of your search results. (*Precision*, in searching, is an important technical term, rather than just descriptive. See Searching Lexicon 3: Recall versus Precision later in this chapter.) For author names, *authority control* provides *one* way to look up an author known by more than one name (e.g., Mark Twain/Samuel Clemens).

- Controlled vocabulary provides a safe and helpful entry point into an unfamiliar subject area. Even if you know nothing about the subject, you have the assurance that the terms in the subject list are correct and appropriate. By browsing in the list and getting a sense of the terms (especially if there are "see" or "use" or "see also" references), you can often get ideas to help you develop or refine a search strategy.

Expressing these points in more formal terms (Walker and Janes 1999), controlled vocabularies

- Facilitate the *gathering of like items*
- Help with *comprehensiveness* of results
- Help with *precision* of results
- Help *broaden understanding* of a topic in an unfamiliar subject area

Basic Tool No. 3: Field Searching

This tool harks back to the discussion of database structure in chapter 2: how records in databases consist of a series of fields, each designated to hold a particular value. *Field searching* simply means the ability to restrict your search to a specific field, for example, to search just the *author* field for a particular value (a name). Most databases offer some kind of default set of fields that are searched, so if you're unsure, in a hurry, or just getting a sense of what the database might contain, you can always throw a word or phrase into the first available search box and hit search, just like you usually do on the Web. Taking a few moments to determine what fields are available for searching can be very valuable, however. Field searching focuses your search, and usually makes it more efficient. For example, say that you wanted to search a database of English literature for works by an author named—English! Just searching on the keyword "English" without limiting it to the author field would result in hundreds of irrelevant results, because a great many of the records undoubtedly mention the word in a title or abstract, or English might appear in a Language field that gets included in a Default Fields search. The database designers spent all that time deciding what fields to have—so definitely exploit this feature if it is available.

Combining Field Searching and Controlled Vocabulary

The combination of field searching with controlled vocabulary is especially effective; that is, finding an appropriate term in the list of subject terms and then searching on it, restricting your search to the Subject Terms field. Of course, you will often construct searches combining all three of these initial tools (Boolean logic, controlled vocabulary, and field searching), to produce a search such as

Hanushek → in the Author field

AND

Education → in the Subject Terms field

You can even make use of Boolean operators *within* the same text entry field. Remember the Michelle Obama example from earlier in the chapter that only produced 50 results? We could increase the number of results in a controlled, efficient way by ORing in related terms for one of the concepts, like this:

Obama, Michelle → in the Person field

AND

(Obesity OR weight control OR nutrition) → in the Subject field

This search produces 80 results. Can you explain in your own words what is happening in this search? This is a very important and useful concept; we will visit it again before leaving this chapter.

There are more tools for your Searcher's Toolkit waiting in chapter 4. Before going on, however, there are some terms in what we'll call the Searching Lexicon that, while they may not make you a better searcher, are useful to know because they give you a way to describe or better understand your search results.

Terms in the Searching Lexicon

Searching Lexicon 1: False Drops

A *false drop* is a document that is retrieved by your search terms, but the terms in the document are not used in the sense you intended, for example, a search on "employment or jobs or careers" that retrieves articles about Steve Jobs. False drops epitomize the problem of wanting to search for concepts but only being able to search for words! They are not *wrong* in a technical sense: the words in the records match the words you typed in—they just aren't being used to express the meaning you had in mind. (To make up for the inconvenience, such results are often quite humorous, if not downright bizarre.) When you get what appears to be a completely off-the-wall result, don't immediately assume that the system is defective or that something is wrong. Now you have a term for such a result; it might simply be a false drop.

Controlled vocabulary and field searching can help avoid the false-drop problem, although even those tools may not make it go away completely. Systems that search large quantities of full text are especially prone to the false-drop problem.

Searching Lexicon 2: Stop Words

Stop words were mentioned in chapter 2 but are worth revisiting here. Stop words, aka *noise words*, are those little words that most systems (commercial database or Web search) do not index. Typical choices for a stop-word list could include *an*, *by*, *for*, *from*, *of*, *the*, *to*, *with*, *be*, *where*, *how*, *it*, *he*, *my*, *his*, *when*, *there*, *is*, *are*, *so*, *she*, and *her*. There is no standard list of stop words that all databases adhere to, which is good in a way, because it allows for the possibility of a database having a relatively short list of stop words, or possibly even none at all. This means, however (if you determine that stop words might be interfering with your search results), that you'll have to dig around in the database's help files and hope that the list of stop words is documented somewhere. There will be occasions where the words that a database or search engine has chosen *not* to index are very important, and you'll need to come up with creative ways to get around the problem. (One of the most famous examples is a search on that famous line, "to be or not to be"—can it be done?)

Searching Lexicon 3: Recall versus Precision

Recall and precision have to do with the number and quality of the results retrieved by your search:

- *Recall* refers to retrieving more results—spreading your net as wide as possible, and probably picking up a number of less relevant results along with the good results. *High recall* means that you are unlikely to miss any relevant items.

- *Precision* refers to focusing your search down, retrieving fewer, but more perfectly on-target and relevant results. *High precision* means that you are unlikely to retrieve very many, if any, irrelevant results (no false drops).

What might be the pros and cons of each?

- With greater recall the chances are better that you won't miss any relevant materials, but you'll invest more time going through your results, reviewing them after the fact to filter out the irrelevant items (in other words, you might have to wade through an awful lot of junk to find the gems).

- The more precise your search is, the more likely it is that you'll miss some things. There will be items in the database that might well meet your needs but that your search didn't pick up because your choice of terminology or fields or limits was just a little *too* specific.

Google provides a great example of both ends of the recall–precision spectrum: ultimate *recall* is all the matches to a simple search. Ultimate *precision* is represented by the "I'm Feeling Lucky" search button, which takes you to just one (theoretically ideal) result.

Should I Aim for Recall or Precision?

Neither one—recall or precision—is intrinsically good or bad; they simply describe an outcome. But recall and precision also provide a useful way to think about your search, to guide how you go about it: what database or search engine you use, and what search techniques you employ. The outcome desired dictates the search style employed: someone who is testing a choice of PhD thesis topic wants to spread the net as wide as possible to make sure that no one has looked at their particular problem before. For that situation, high recall is crucial. Similarly, if you believe you're looking for an obscure topic, but you want absolutely everything and anything that can be found about it, you'll want to try for maximum recall. You might start with a Web search, or in an appropriate database, enter a very simple style of search (e.g., no controlled vocabulary, not limited to any specific field). An undergraduate writing a short paper or a community hobbyist investigating a new topic, however, may be perfectly served by a high-precision search that identifies a few recent, relevant articles, even though many more related, or equally relevant, articles remain behind in the database. In that case, choose an appropriate database, check for subject terms, perhaps combine two or more with Boolean operators, and use some field searching.

Quick Recap

This section of the chapter has introduced two more tools in the Searcher's Toolkit, as well as three terms in the Searching Lexicon. You now have these major tools in your search arsenal:

1. The concept of Boolean logic for combining terms: the operators AND, OR, and NOT, and the use of parentheses to affect the order in which the Boolean operators are processed.

2. The concept of controlled vocabulary: terms that the vendor has applied to help you get all the articles on a topic without having to keyword search every variation or synonym, and to disambiguate among various meanings.

3. The concept of field searching: restricting your search to specified fields to make it more precise and efficient.

You also now know that database indexing programs have lists of certain words they do *not* index, known as *stop words*. In addition, you have some new language to describe the results of your searches:

- False drops
- Recall
- Precision

Applying the Tools

Now we will return to EBSCO's *MasterFILE Premier*, a multidisciplinary database, and see how these tools apply there. After looking at *MasterFILE*'s advanced search interface and learning how it implements the first three Tools, go to any of the other common multidisciplinary databases that are available to you, for example: *ProQuest Research*, EBSCO's *Academic Search* (*Premier* or *Complete*), Gale's *Academic OneFile* and *General OneFile*, and LexisNexis *Academic*. Find the Advanced Search interface, and when you have, again figure out if the first three Tools are available. In most cases, you will start to see commonality: a look very similar to *MasterFILE* (obviously the other EBSCO databases will look almost exactly the same). Others may be a little different. This is an excellent exercise in training your eyes for what to look for every time you encounter a new interface.[8]

MasterFILE Premier: Notes and Search Examples

The first challenge with any database is to be able to look at and interpret what is presented in the interface. We're so used to looking at busy web pages that we look—but we don't really *see*. To turn yourself into a more efficient and effective searcher, however, it is important to be able to look over an interface and quickly translate what's there into the tools you are looking for:

- Does it use Boolean operators for combining terms?
- Is it possible to search in specific fields, and if yes, which ones?
- Is any kind of controlled vocabulary available? (Can you browse it?)

Determining Availability of Search Tools

Most databases offer two search modes: *Basic* and *Advanced*. Usually the previous questions won't be answered by looking at the Basic search interface, but there should be good information in the Advanced screen. Figure 3.6 shows the Advanced Search interface in *MasterFILE Premier*. What do you see? Are your first three tools available?

Check: Boolean operators are available here. In fact, there appears to be an alternative way to achieve a Boolean effect: note the *Search modes* area, and the "*Find all . . .*" and "*Find any . . .*" options. (You will explore the SmartText option in one of the Exercises at the end of the chapter.) The

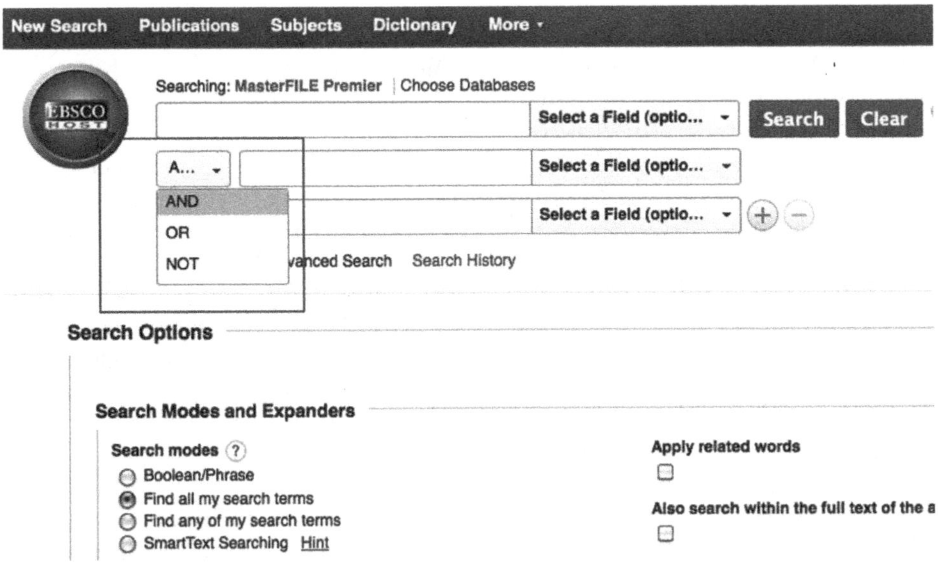

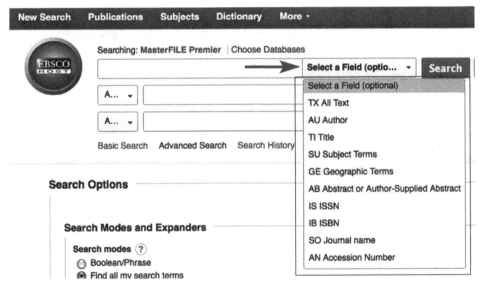

Figure 3.6. Advanced Search interface, showing Boolean operators, in *MasterFILE Premier*. © 2014 EBSCO Industries, Inc. All rights reserved.

Figure 3.7. Fields available for searching in *MasterFILE Premier*. © 2014 EBSCO Industries, Inc. All rights reserved.

whole lower area of the screen is devoted to *Limit* options, but we haven't talked about limits yet, so we won't go into those.

Now take a look at Figure 3.7: do we have the option of restricting our search to certain fields?

Check: there are fields available for searching. The list of fields gives a clue, reinforced by the top bar in the interface, that some kind of controlled vocabulary might be available, and that it can be browsed. See the entry for SU Subject Terms in the field list, and the word *Subjects* in the bar across the top?

Controlled Vocabulary: The Subjects, Places, and People Lists

In chapter 2 we saw three examples of how different database vendors handle their lists of controlled vocabulary: the all-in-one approach used by Gale, the many different index lists used by WorldCat, and *MasterFILE*'s separate lists for Subjects, Places, and People. As described in chapter 2, the EBSCO lists provide instant guidance to the term the EBSCO indexers have decided will be the one they "Use," with the preferred term handily linked. There are several ways to build a search right from this page.

If you look up 'social media' in *MasterFILE*'s Subjects index, and let your eyes drift to the right, you will see a column labeled "Explode." Good grief, what can that mean? And only some of the entries have an Explode check box. If you were to select the Explode check box for social media, then "Add" it to your search using OR, you would see something like the image in Figure 3.8. It's an explosion, all right.

Where did all those additional terms come from? The answer lies in Figure 3.9: the hint, "(Click term to display details)" has been there all along. Clicking the linked term social media reveals a whole sophisticated *thesaurus* structure, that is, a Scope Note to explain when the term is used, and then Broader, Narrower, and Related Terms. When you choose to Explode a term, the system will automatically include all the Narrower headings as well as the main heading; it is a great demonstration of "getting more with OR." (You will encounter this concept and functionality again when we look at the PsycINFO database in chapter 5.) It can also be very useful to see what terms are listed as Related Terms, especially if you are familiarizing yourself with a new topic area.

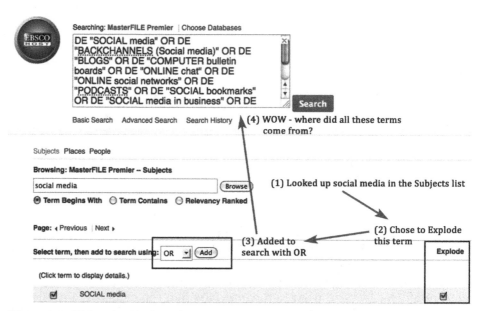

Figure 3.8. Using the Explode function in the *MasterFILE* Subjects list. © 2014 EBSCO Industries, Inc. All rights reserved.

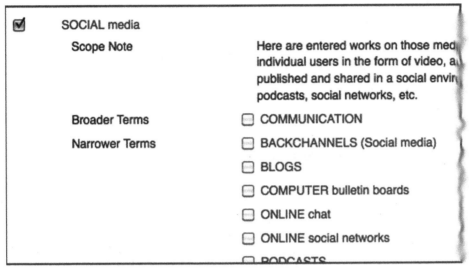

Figure 3.9. Displaying the details for a subject term with Broader, Narrower, and Related Terms in *MasterFILE*. © 2014 EBSCO Industries, Inc. All rights reserved.

You can also choose multiple terms from the same list, or from any of the three index lists to build a search. Say you were looking for articles about the laws governing organic farming or organic foods. In the *Master-FILE* Subjects list, we could search for: organic farming and then scan the results for useful headings. Aha! Two perfect subject headings: ORGANIC farming—Law & legislation and further down, ORGANIC foods industry—Law & legislation. You have only to select both, then use the "Select term, then add to search using: OR" feature. The whole search string will be pasted into the search box at the top, ready to be run, complete with all the codes that will search these two headings as subjects and the correct Boolean operator to retrieve articles about *either* the first *or* the second heading (Figure 3.10).

You can also select headings from different lists to build a search. For example, you could look up and select "mars (planet)" from the Places list, Add it to your search (it doesn't matter which Boolean operator is selected in the "add to search using" feature). Then go to the Subjects list and look up the word life, then choose the entry "LIFE (Biology)." At this point you *do* need to pay attention, and be sure to choose "add to search using AND" as your operator. Voila, another precise search full of mysterious codes ready to run:

(ZG "mars (planet)") AND (DE "LIFE (Biology)")

Go and see if you can replicate this search.

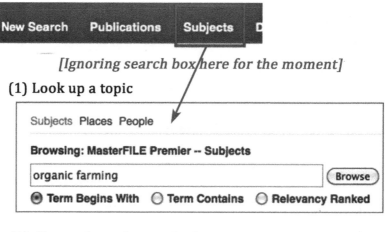

[Ignoring search box here for the moment]

(1) Look up a topic

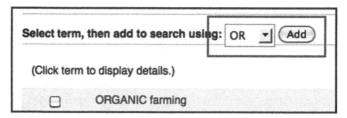

(2) Choose from the results list:

☑   ORGANIC farming -- Law & legislation

☑   ORGANIC foods industry -- Law & legislation

(3) Scroll back up, choose how to combine multiple headings:

Select term, then add to search using: OR ▾ (Add)

(Click term to display details.)

☐   ORGANIC farming

(4) Click "Add" and presto - your search is ready to be run:

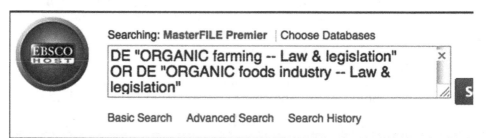

Figure 3.10. Building a multi-heading search within the Subjects index in *Master-FILE*. © 2014 EBSCO Industries, Inc. All rights reserved.

Multiple Field Searches in MasterFILE

If setting up a multi-concept search from the Subjects, Places, and People indexes proves too fiddly or confusing, however, you can definitely just use the Subjects (or Places or People) lists to determine the correct form of the terms you want to use, then click on Advanced Search and type the terms in yourself, setting the field to be searched to Subject (or Author, etc.). Note that in the field dropdowns in the Advanced Search, the field to choose for a "Place" is Geographic Terms.

Search Challenge 1

Our topic is China's involvement in space exploration, specifically, manned space flight. First try this search by constructing it within the Subjects and Places indexes:

Go to the Subjects interface, and look up: manned space flight.

ADD that term to your search.

Now select the Places list, and look up China.

ADD that term to your search. Which Boolean operator do you need to set the "add to search using" feature to achieve the right effect?

Run the search. How many results do you get?

Now go to the Advanced Search interface, and replicate this search there:

In the first text entry field enter: manned space flight—and set the field dropdown to SU Subject Terms.

In the second field, enter China and set the field to GE Geographic Terms.

Run the search. How many results do you get now?

You should get more results from your second search. Why? Look carefully at the search syntax that the system generates when you construct your search from the Subjects and Places indexes, and compare it to the syntax generated by the Advanced Search (Figure 3.11). Ignoring the codes, what does the system add to your terms when you select them from the lists?

Figure 3.11. System syntax for "Advanced" versus "Index built" searches. What is different? © 2014 EBSCO Industries, Inc. All rights reserved.

This one difference explains the different number of results. See if you can figure it out (see also endnote 8).

Boolean Logic: Advanced Search versus Basic Search

As a final note to this chapter, unfortunately we have to reveal that there are no comfortable absolutes in this business. The Advanced Search screen may not always be the best answer, as shown in the following two screenshots. In Figure 3.12, a Boolean search was set up in the Advanced Search screen, using the operators in the drop-down menus. The huge number of results and the presence of only one of our search terms (space vehicles) in the most recent result should set off alarm bells in your mind. Something has gone awry.

What the searcher *meant* was outer space exploration and (space probes or space vehicles), that is, anything about the exploration of space using mechanisms sent there. If the searcher thought to type: "outer space exploration" in the first field, and to AND that with "(Space probes OR Space vehicles)" *all in the second search field*, the search would work the way it was intended (Figure 3.13) and would produce a much smaller number of on-target results. The interface structure doesn't lead you to think of doing it this way, however, and so the results of the Figure 3.12 search are full of false drops (unless you choose the "sort by relevance" option, and then they are not as recent). Always remember that you are not bound by Boolean dropdowns in the interface: YOU are in charge, and can type in your own Boolean operators when the situation calls for it.

However, if you know your Boolean logic and remember your powerful parentheses, you can also be assured of your search doing what you intended by typing it in the Basic search box:

outer space exploration AND (space probes OR space vehicles)

Figure 3.12. Boolean logic pitfalls in the Advanced Search screen. © 2014 EBSCO Industries, Inc. All rights reserved.

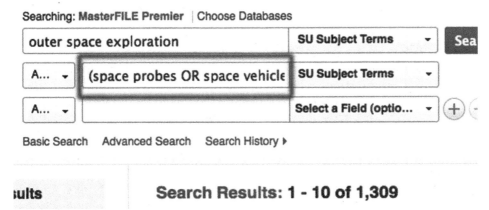

Figure 3.13. Use of Boolean operator *within* a search field to achieve the desired results. © 2014 EBSCO Industries, Inc. All rights reserved.

Yes, you give up the power of field searching (you could type in the codes if you really wanted to impress your friends), but sometimes it's more important to get started in the right direction and produce a reasonable set of results. You can always refine them by Subjects on the results page.

This is a point to keep in mind: *basic* doesn't necessarily need to mean simplistic. Because you are now a master of Boolean operators and parentheses, it can be *easier* to do some searches in the Basic mode. For quick iterations of a search, testing various terms and combinations, the Basic search box is very useful.

Exercises and Points to Consider

1. Consider these statements:

   ducks OR geese NOT migration

   (ducks OR geese) NOT migration

   (ducks AND geese) OR loons

   ducks AND (geese OR loons)

   (ducks OR geese) AND migration

   ducks OR (geese AND migration)

   (ducks OR (geese NOT migration)) AND lakes

   Try drawing Venn diagrams for the paired statements to see how (or if) they differ. Then try describing in words what the content of the documents retrieved by these statements would be. Test out the statements in the Basic search mode of any of the multidisciplinary databases mentioned at the beginning of this section: *ProQuest*

Research, Academic Search (Premier or Complete), Academic One-File or General OneFile, or LexisNexis Academic.

2. Pick three terms relating to a subject that interests you, and explore searching them in various ways in at least two of the databases you used in question 1. Try a number of Boolean combinations in Basic search mode, try setting up similar searches in Advanced mode, and see if your terms appear in the Subjects list. Even though we didn't discuss them, experiment with the various limits options, both in the search screen and in the results screen.

3. Open two browser windows so you can look at two databases at the same time. Of the databases mentioned in Question 1, open any one of the ProQuest or EBSCO databases in one window, and either one of the Gale databases in the other. Click around a bit, closely observing the interfaces, how they are different or the same, the terminology used and the functionality offered. The Gale databases are usually found in public libraries, the ProQuest or EBSCO products in academic libraries. Do you get any sense of "different audiences" being catered to? Now experiment with the search topic: history of drugstores. How precise can you make this search? Can you find appropriate subject headings in both databases that produce a small, focused set of results?

4. In the *MasterFILE* Advanced Search, try searching for something you know is incorrect, such as "mars lunar lander," but set the Search mode to SmartText Searching. For the suggested (incorrect) search, you will get results, and you might not even realize that there's no such thing as a Mars lunar lander, because the results are so appropriate. Experiment with the SmartText mode for a while. Would you want to set this as the default in your library? Why or why not?

5. In describing the benefits of controlled vocabulary, you will have noticed a consistent use of terms such as *should*, as in "use of subject headings *should* ensure that you retrieve everything on a given topic," rather than the more certain term *will*. What do you think might prevent controlled vocabulary from being a perfect retrieval panacea?

6. Say you set up a search and set the field drop-down for one of your terms to Subject. But you didn't check the Subjects index list first; you're just taking a shot in the dark. Your search results are zero. Why?

7. If you had part of a citation and were trying to find the rest of the information (a *known item search*), what type of search would you probably try first: one that had high recall or one that had high precision? Based on your answer, what type of resource (commercial database or Web search) and techniques would you use? What if your first approach didn't work?

Sidebar 3.1. Analyzing Recall versus Precision

Say that there are N relevant items "out there." You have a search engine that retrieves items based on a query. We can make a chart that describes the efficacy of the search in terms of the four possible types of results (Sidebar Table 3.1). You can think of actual numbers being substituted for all the types of results.

True positives are search results that indeed are relevant items. You can clearly count these.

False negatives are failures of the search: relevant items that are out there but are not retrieved. If you know there are N relevant items altogether, then this number is N − (true positives). This is called a *Type II* error in statistical hypothesis testing (the test wrongly reports that a true hypothesis is false).

False positives are search results that are useless and irrelevant. You can count these because you're looking at them. This is called a *Type I* error in statistical hypothesis testing (the test wrongly reports that a false hypothesis is true).

True negatives are all of those items not found that indeed you don't care about because they are irrelevant. There are presumably a great many of these unless something is really off in the system. We don't usually use this number.

Considering the *number* of these types of results, we can define the following:

Recall: the number of relevant items found divided by the number of relevant items out there (N):

Recall = (True positives)/[(True positives) + (False negatives)] = (True positives) / N.

Precision: the number of relevant items found divided by the number of items found (relevant and irrelevant):

Precision = (True positives) / [(True positives) + (False positives)].

One error measure is the number of false results divided by the number of relevant items out there (N):

Error rate = [(False positives) + (False negatives)] / [(True positives) + (False negatives)]
= [(False positives) + (False negatives)] / N.

So if you have good recall (near 1), you don't wind up with lots of missed but relevant items, but your results could be diluted by lots of false positives, or items that are wrongly retrieved as being relevant when they are not.

If you have good precision, on the other hand, you can be more sure that your results are actually relevant, but you might be missing a lot of other relevant items in your search (you could have a large number of false negatives). Error rate is just the proportion of both types of errors to the total number of relevant items you ideally would like to retrieve.

Self Test

You're looking for information on a guitar maker called David Daily.

Google finds 4,130,000 hits on "Daily Guitars," two of which (the first two, not surprisingly, as this is Google) are relevant. You have reason to know that there are actually two relevant websites out there. What are the recall, precision, and error rate for this search?

Google finds 31,500 hits on *hog farm waste runoff problems* (entered without double quotation marks), of which we will declare that 2,600 are relevant. The authoritative document you are consulting says there are "several thousand" relevant items on the Web. What are reasonable ranges for the values of recall, precision, and error rate for this search?

Sidebar Table 3.1. Retrieval versus relevancy chart.

	Retrieved Items	
Actual Items	**Relevant**	**Irrelevant**
Relevant	True positives	False negatives
Irrelevant	False positives	True negatives

Notes

1. Boole was a British mathematician and philosopher. "As the inventor of Boolean algebra, the basis of all modern computer arithmetic, Boole is regarded as one of the founders of the field of computer science." This and more details about George Boole are available from *Wikipedia*, the free online encyclopedia, http://en.wikipedia.org/wiki/George_Boole.

2. Strictly speaking, in mathematical logic the terms NOT and AND NOT are different. NOT is a unary operator, that is, it can take just one argument: NOT argyle, for example, if you were offered a world of socks and were willing to take anything but argyle. AND NOT is a binary operator, that is, it takes two arguments: pie AND NOT banana cream—you must provide a first set, and then a second set that you wish to exclude. Databases and Web search engines, even when they express the operator as NOT, mean AND NOT. This is subtly conveyed in the advanced search interfaces of databases: the "AND OR NOT" options don't start until *after* the first text input field.

3. You can have multiple levels of parenthetical expressions, a syntax known as *nesting* or *nested statements*, in which case the most deeply nested statement will be evaluated first, followed by the parenthetical expression around it, and so forth. You may very seldom, if ever, need to construct a nested statement, but it's interesting to know that you can.

4. Thesaurus, plural thesauri. A formal term for a particular variety of controlled vocabulary. When used in the context of bibliographic databases, a thesaurus may provide the list of subject headings in a hierarchical fashion, showing relationships between the terms (broader, narrower, related), and it may provide pointers to the best terms to use.

5. Certain databases use the term *descriptors* for subject headings.

6. Most often associated with library catalogs, *authority control* refers to a system of controlled vocabulary specifically for author names.

7. With thanks to the *ARTFL Project: Roget's Thesaurus, 1911*, http://machaut.uchicago.edu/?action=search&resource=Roget%27s&word=clothing&searchtype=headword.

8. If you get totally stuck, check the Student Resources website for hints.

4

The Searcher's Toolkit: Part 2

The tools covered in chapter 3, Boolean operators, controlled vocabulary, and field searching, are the most fundamental. The tools that we'll add here are further refinements: additional search functions; a simple search strategy that can be used in any situation that will enable you to execute ever more sophisticated searches; and finally a list of "mental tools." The intent is always to enable you to get the information that you're after more efficiently and effectively.

Completing the Toolkit: Basic Tools 4–7

Basic Tool No. 4: Proximity Searching

In addition to allowing you to specify that your search results must include certain terms (Boolean AND: ducks AND geese AND loons), most of the subscription database systems also allow you to set up an even more sophisticated search, in which you set a rule for the relationship between those terms. That is, you can state how close to each other, and sometimes in what order, they must appear in the text to qualify for retrieval. This is known as *proximity* searching.

Proximity searching allows you to specify that termA must appear within so many words of termB. For example, if you were trying to discover names of consulting firms that work with the food and beverage industry, it's possible that such a thing would only be mentioned as an aside—neither concept would be enough to merit a subject heading. Searching "consulting AND (food OR beverage)" would probably result in a large number of false drops, because the words could occur in the documents but have nothing to do with each other (e.g., consulting could show up in the first paragraph and food or beverage in the last paragraph, in a totally different context). The only way that you're going to have any chance of getting something meaningful is if the terms are somewhat close to each other: at least within the same paragraph, and even better, within the same sentence, within five to ten words of each other. There's also nothing to prevent you from combining the two approaches: termA within five words of (termB or termC).

When your search topic falls below the radar of subject headings (controlled vocabulary), and you have some text to work with (at least an abstract, if not full text), proximity searching is a wonderful way to get greater precision in your results. You will still get false drops, but not nearly as many as you would using only Boolean operators.

Proximity Searching Strategy

In setting up a proximity search, start by trying to envision how the writer might have expressed what you're looking for: in this case, it might be phrases such as "consultants to the consumer packaged goods, personal care, and food and beverage industries . . ." or "a leading food industry consultant . . ." or "has chosen ABC, a Boston consulting firm, for their new beverage marketing campaign . . ." This helps you to decide whether to set the proximity number lower (4 or 5), or higher (8 or 10). In this case it would be good to set it higher, because it's possible that the writer might have listed several industries, as in the first phrase example. Obviously, this presupposes that you are fairly familiar with the literature of the topic at hand. What if you aren't? In that case, simply experiment: start with a proximity of five words, and (as described in Tool No. 7, below) learn from the results, increasing or decreasing the proximity number as seems appropriate.[1] There's no rule that says you have to get it exactly right the first time!

Proximity Operators

Like a Boolean search, a proximity search is expressed with special operators. Unfortunately, unlike the universal and easily recognized AND, OR, NOT (AND NOT) used for Boolean expressions, proximity operators vary from system to system, so it's harder to produce a nice neat list to memorize. Even the syntax—the operators—can be mysterious looking, using simply N (for *near*) or W (for *within*), and a number to indicate the number of possible intervening words. Some systems, such as EBSCO, even offer two flavors of proximity operators: one for specifying just proximity, the other for dictating both proximity and word order (termA must occur within so many words, and *before* termB). Let's look at some examples.

Proximity Search Examples

ProQuest

ProQuest offers two types of proximity: NEAR and PRE, which can be shortened to N and P (capitalization is not required, I am simply using it for clarity). The NEAR command only requires that your search terms be within <number> words of each other. The PRE command specifies that the first term must appear within so many words of the second term, *in that order*. The syntax for these commands is N/<number> and P/<number> (e.g., command slash number). An example of the first type of proximity search would be:

homeless n/4 teenagers

In response to this search, the ProQuest system will return records where the word *homeless* appears within four words of *teenagers*, regardless of word order. All of the following phrases would meet the search criteria:

teenagers who have been homeless for more than . . .

Chicago district ponders residential program for homeless teens . . .

those involving teenagers, prostitutes, and the homeless . . .

even teenagers who are not homeless . . .

has been homeless ever since he was a teenager . . .

EBSCO

As noted above, EBSCO also has two proximity operators, but its syntax is slightly different: N<number> and W<number> (note there is no slash between the operator and the number). They are used as follows:

Near

teenagers N5 homeless

That is, the word *teenagers* must appear from zero to five words away from *homeless* in the text for a document to be retrieved. The terms can be in any order: teenagers first, or homeless first.

Within

homeless W3 teenagers

This means that the word *homeless* must appear within three words of *teenagers*, *in that order* (homeless first), to be retrieved. In a ProQuest database you would express this as: homeless P/3 teenagers. These subtle variations are the norm, so be prepared to be flexible and to take a quick glance at each database's Help file for guidance.

Factiva

In another variation on this theme, in *Factiva* you spell out *near* and append a number, such as near5, to set the parameters for your proximity search. If you were looking for information about gourmet or specialty pickles, you'd probably be interested in an article that mentions "the specialty market now extends to pickles, teas . . ." The search

specialty near5 pickles

would pick up this article. The pickle reference is so casual that the subject headings for the whole article give no clue that it might mention pickles. (And trust me: if you are trying to find information about the specialty pickle market without spending a fortune for a market research report, you'll take any reference, no matter how casual.)

Factiva also provides a conceptual rather than numerically bound operator called "same" to specify "in the same paragraph." For example, "Merck same research" retrieves articles in which Merck and research occur in the same paragraph, in any order.

Determining Proximity Operators

Unlike Boolean operators, proximity operators usually don't appear as drop-down menu choices in the database interface. While the use of N or near and W or within is fairly standard, the way they are interpreted and the use (or not) of additional characters such as a slash mark, make each database just a bit different. Given that there are several subtle variations that might be used, it's best not to just guess. To find out whether a database provides proximity searching and what syntax to use, you'll need to check the Help or Examples files provided by the database.

Importance of Proximity Searching in Full-Text Databases

Proximity, although requiring a bit more effort to discover, is becoming an ever more valuable function as vendors strive to provide more and more searchable full text. A database that is just an electronic version of an index simply doesn't offer that many words to search on. The text fields (i.e., author, title, journal name, and abstract) aren't that big, so the use of Boolean operators in that situation is usually fine (using proximity in such a situation might well reduce your results to zero, in fact). Matches on termA AND termB in the limited realm of index fields are likely to be relevant because the terms are, in a sense, by definition close to each other. In a full-text situation you could certainly still restrict your search to just subject headings (if they are available), or a field such as title, and use Boolean operators, but by searching the full text you have the opportunity to get at more deeply buried aspects of an article, to tweeze out nuances and secondary topics that cannot possibly be covered by a limited number of subject headings. The more searchable full text a database has, the more important the ability to do proximity searching becomes, because it is the only useful way to really mine all that text for everything it has to offer.

Really Close Proximity: Phrase Searching

Searching on exact phrases can be extremely important in some cases, and the inability of some databases to do this (easily) can really inhibit how effectively you can search. In the commercial database world, enclosing the phrase in double quotes is now almost universally the way you tell the system "this is a phrase search." EBSCO, ProQuest, LexisNexis, Gale, JSTOR, and the Web of Science databases all follow this convention of enclosing the terms to be searched as a phrase in double quotes. You can even bend Google or Bing or other web search engines to your will and force them to search for phrases by enclosing the words in double quotes.

The one prominent outlier in this arena that I am aware of is *Factiva*, which performs phrase searches without quotation marks or indicators of any kind. Their search function treats any and all multiple word entries in the search box as a phrase search, and is not forgiving about it. This can give rise to problems for the unaware. If you are used to simply plunking in a string of terms and being handed results, searching: gourmet specialty pickles markets in *Factiva* and getting no results could be quite puzzling. *Factiva* is searching that series of words as an exact phrase, so of course there are no results.[2]

Other than the automatically-assumed phrase searching in *Factiva*, the only other oddity you might encounter are databases that don't support phrase searching: they don't recognize double quotes or any other syntax for indicating "search this as a phrase." At the time of this writing, *Market-Line Advantage* is an example of a database that doesn't support phrase searching. It can be annoying, but on the other hand it saves you from doing a phrase search, getting no results, and giving up—a situation where your search was perhaps "too tight" and you simply needed to search on the words, not the bound phrase.

Uses for Phrase Searching

Phrase searching is useful any time you're searching for things such as the name of a place or an organization (especially if the name is made up of common words) or a multiword concept or topic (latch key children, gourmet pickles, missile defense shield), or—especially on the Web—if you're tracking down more complete information from incomplete fragments. Problems such as the rest of the lyrics, or indeed the real title, of a song whose only line you can remember is "is the moon out tonight?" can be quickly resolved and put in context (and possibly bar bets won) by plunking the quote-bound phrase into Google. In a more academic scenario, say you have a bad or incomplete reference to a thesis or a journal article. If it is available to you, head for a database such as *Dissertation Abstracts*, or an appropriate subject database, and try a partial phrase from the title, or the author's name and a word from the title, depending on what information you (seem) to have.[3] (If that doesn't work, try only the most distinct words as a title field search, and if that doesn't work, go to the Web. You might not find the actual item, but at least you might find a more accurate, complete reference to it from someone else's bibliography.)

Proximity and phrase searching are useful for reducing and focusing your results; they tend to increase the precision of the search. The next tool takes us back the other way, providing a way to broaden the search net (to increase recall).

Basic Tool No. 5: Truncation

"Truncation" is an efficient way of extending your search to pick up many variations on a word without having to (1) think of all the possible variants or (2) input them with endless "ORs". Truncation allows you to search on a word stem and retrieve any word beginning with those letters, for example,

harmon*

to retrieve harmony, harmonious, harmonica, etc.

In another database, the syntax and results for the truncation function might be

employ$

to retrieve employ, employs, employee, employment, employer, employed, etc.

Note that when the stem (the letters being truncated) is a word in its own right, that word will be included in the search results. Truncation generally means the word stem, and any number of characters following, from zero on up.

While it can be argued that many databases are now picking up word variants automatically, thus reducing the need to be aware of and use truncation, my position is that this is still an important concept to at least understand (so you know what the databases are doing behind your back). In addition, the word variants that are picked up automatically are generally limited to plurals or other very simple variants, and some systems (online catalogs come to mind) do *not* do any kind of "auto-variant" searching. Such systems are very literal, and if you want to search for variations in an online catalog, you will need to know what truncation symbol it uses. As professional searchers, you should know what truncation is and how to use it effectively.

Using Truncation

Truncation is a tool that is equally useful in field searching and in full-text searches in commercial databases. In a field search, for example, truncation is a wonderfully efficient way to pick up several related subject headings at once (searching poet* to pick up poet, poetics, poetry) or variations on author names (with and without a middle initial, for instance, or even with or without a first name being spelled out: Adams, J!). In a full-text search, obviously, truncation greatly increases the number of documents that are eligible for retrieval. When you are fishing around for a concept or topic that you think might be rather rare, and that isn't expressed with any set phrases or words, the combination of truncation and a proximity search can be invaluable. The earlier example of trying to identify any articles mentioning companies that act as consultants to the food and beverage industry is a prime candidate for this technique:

Consultan* near10 (food or beverage*)

to retrieve consultant, consultants, or consultancy, within a 10-word radius of food or beverage or beverages.

Common Truncation Symbols

Truncation symbols vary somewhat from database to database, but the ones most frequently used are:

- ' * '
- ' ! '
- ' ? '

Factiva uses the symbol "$," which is more unusual, but always strikes me as appropriate for this resource from the financially focused Dow Jones company.

Determining Truncation Symbols

As is the case with the other tools in this chapter, there is likely to be nothing in the initial search interface to indicate whether truncation is supported and, if so, which symbol to use. There are databases that don't offer a true truncation function, but simply search on a limited set of variants (e.g., plural forms) automatically. Some information is supplied in Table 4.1, but if the database in question is not listed, or if you want to check the most current usage (it could change), look for links to "Help" or "Examples" to determine how the database at hand handles truncation.

Table 4.1. Truncation and wildcard symbols used by various vendors.

Vendor	Truncation Symbol	Wildcard: 1 for 1 match[a] Symbol
EBSCO	*[b]	?
Endeavor (OPAC)	?	N/A[c]
Gale	*	?
Innovative Interfaces (OPAC)	*	?
LexisNexis	!	*
ProQuest	*[d]	?
Web of Science	*[d]	?

[a] Replaces characters on a one-for-one basis: wom?n to retrieve woman or women
[b] May also be used between two other words in a phrase to replace any whole word, for example, "type * diabetes" retrieves type 1 diabetes or type II diabetes
[c] Not available
[d] Can be used at either the beginning or end of a word (right- or left-hand truncation).

Wildcards

Closely related to truncation are *wildcard* symbols, in the sense that a symbol is used in place of letters. Whereas truncation symbols represent any number of characters, wildcards are used to substitute for characters on a one-to-one basis. Be prepared for confusion: the symbols used for wildcards are the same as those used for truncation, but the effect changes, depending on the vendor. That is, one vendor may use "!" for truncation and "*" for a wildcard, while another exactly reverses those two meanings. For example, LexisNexis uses "*" as its wildcard (one-to-one replacement) symbol and "!" as its truncation symbol. In EBSCO, ProQuest, and the *Web of Science*, "*" is used as the truncation symbol (for any number of characters at the end of a word) and "?" is used as the wildcard symbol, replacing characters on a one-to-one basis. These vendors also offer additional wildcard symbols that substitute for exactly zero-to-one character, for situations in which you want to pick up alternate spellings (most commonly, US/UK variants). The symbol used is different in each case; see Table 4.1 or check the database Help for the most up-to-date information.

Using Wildcards

Wildcards are probably most frequently used to replace just one letter, for example:

wom?n

retrieves woman, women, womyn. Multiple wildcards can be used to substitute for an equal number of characters, for example,

manufactur??

will retrieve manufacture, manufactured, or manufactures, but not manufacturing.

As noted earlier, a search situation in which the zero-to-one character wildcard symbol can be very helpful is for picking up US/UK alternative spellings, such as

labo$r   to get either labor or labour

globali#ation   to get either globalisation or globalization

If you were searching a database that included British publications, and you wanted to be sure you picked up relevant material from them, this use of wildcarding could be very important.

Truncation/Wildcard Symbols Reality Check

The very existence of wildcards, and the differentiation between wildcards and truncation probably strikes you as a fairly esoteric capability, and perhaps you won't need to use such functionality very often. (It doesn't even enter into your use of web search engines, which do not support any kind of truncation or wildcarding.) In real life, you're much more likely to stick a truncation symbol on the end of "manufactur" and be done with it. But knowledge is power!

Sidebar 4.1: Department of Confusing Things

In everyday speech, the term *wildcard* is often used to mean truncation. For example, you'll hear the symbol used at the end of a word to retrieve multiple endings expressed as a wildcard. I'm quite guilty of this myself: when working with a student who has never heard of truncation, the easiest course of action is to call the odd thing being demonstrated a wildcard, because almost everyone immediately grasps the sense of that notion. If you are getting serious enough about searching that you're looking at the Help files, however, you should know the technical terms used in the business and understand that different symbols can have different effects (one replaces only one character, while another is used to replace any number of characters).

Quick Recap

This part of the chapter has introduced Tools 4 and 5, proximity searching (which tends to reduce the number of results) and truncation and wildcards (which increase the result set). *Proximity searching* allows you to search for documents containing terms within a given number of words of each other. Proximity searching is particularly valuable for searching full text. *Phrase searching* is the closest form of proximity searching and can be very important for retrieving accurate results. *Truncation* refers to the use of a symbol to substitute for 0 to N characters at the *end* of a word. *Wildcards* are symbols used to substitute on a one-to-one basis for characters *within* a word. Proximity and phrase searches tend to narrow and focus results; truncation and wildcards help to increase the potential set of results. To determine the symbols or syntax to use, in all cases consult the database's Help or Examples files.

Basic Tool No. 6: Limits to Constrain Your Search

Limits or *Limiters* are preset options in the search interface that can be used to further define your search. They are described here as *preset options* to distinguish them from the words or subject terms that you have to come up with and type in. Limits make use of fields in the database record that are used to store attributes of the record rather than conceptual content: you could say limit fields are about the article, not what the article is about. Limiters usually appear as check boxes or drop-down menus. Typical Limit choices include the following:

- Scholarly (or *peer reviewed*)
- Full text (e.g., in a database that offers some records with full text and some without, this limit will constrain the search to retrieve only matching records offering full text)[4]
- Date
- Source type (scholarly journals, magazines, books, conference proceedings, etc.)

- Document type (article, review, editorial, case study, book chapter, etc.)

- Language

The Date Limit

The Date Limit is a bit of an anomaly. In the context of a known citation, you would consider it a "content" field: the date would be part of the unique information identifying that citation (Joe Blogg's 2004 article is not Joe Blogg's 2013 article). However, if you are searching for material published before or after a certain date, or in a particular date range, the date information becomes an attribute used to limit your search results. The way the date option is displayed in the search interface is frequently hybrid as well, offering both a drop-down menu of preset choices and fields for specifying a specific date (or date range).

Basic Tool No. 7: "Learning from Your Results," A Useful Search Strategy

In previous editions of this book I referred to this Tool as "Pearl Growing," a charming expression[5] for the process described below, but one that likely means nothing to students today. Thus my decision to change the name to exactly what the strategy actually *is*. Learning from your results refers to the process of doing a very simple search first, with the intent of achieving high recall, and then examining the results to find appropriate subject headings or to discover additional or alternative terms to search on from the most on-target hits. You then add one or more of these terms to your search strategy, or replace your previous terms with the new ones, to produce a more precise list of results. This is very useful when you are venturing into a new database or unfamiliar subject matter, or when you simply don't have the time or inclination to do formal preparatory work by hunting around in the subject indexes. To be honest, this is one of my favorite and most frequently used techniques.

A Search Example Demonstrating Learning from Your Results

For example, let us say that you're an engineer, and you are tired of your straight engineering job. A colleague suggests that you look into jobs in engineering sales. Whenever you're working with someone and doing this sort of career exploration—What is the work like? How is the pay? Are there openings, or is it a stagnant market?—a good first thing to check is the *Occupational Outlook Handbook* (OOH).[6] If you had come to see me, we'd start there. At the OOH, a search for "engineering sales" (with the quotes) produces no results. Hmm. Maybe this is a case where the phrase search is too constraining: trying this search again without quotes does it, and we find that such people are referred to as "sales engineers." This is useful. Let's move on to a database and try for some articles about sales engineers.

Going to a database of business articles, ProQuest's *ABI/Inform*, we can start by seeing if, by chance, "sales engineer" is a subject term. It's not (drat). So then we can try the quick-and-dirty approach: simply searching "sales engineers" (with quotes) in the "Anywhere except full text—ALL" field option, hoping to learn from the results. We can prescreen the results a bit by choosing the "Scholarly journals" limit. Among the results is an article titled "The Impact of Sales Engineers on Salesperson Effectiveness." The very first words of the abstract indicate this might be just what the patron needs: "The role of the sales engineer within the firm is defined . . ." From the subject headings—Studies, Impact analysis, Salespeople, Performance evaluation, and Sales management—we decide that the subject term Salespeople could be useful. Examining some of the other results, we notice that Sales is also a subject term. We go back to the advanced search interface and try:

Engineers in the → Abstract—AB (field)

AND

(Sales OR Salespeople) in the → Subject heading (all)—SU (field)

which nets us 42 results. (The arrow symbol is a convention you will see throughout this text, indicating that the material following represents a choice from a field dropdown menu.)

The ProQuest system also automatically provides helpful, usually insightful search suggestions in the results interface, in this case:

Engineers AND Personal profiles (both terms will be searched as subjects).

Sales AND Training (both terms will be searched as subjects, you'd want to then AND in your Engineers as a subject or a keyword).

To reiterate, the strategy in learning from your results is to start with a fairly simple, broad search, examine the most likely results, and learn how to refine or improve the search based on subject headings or other terminology used in the on-target results. This technique is really only useful in the structured, subject-headings world of commercial databases. On the Web, you may encounter links in search results saying "More like this," which are trying to do the same thing. How well they do it, and what they are basing the similarity on, are open questions.

Quick Recap

This section of the chapter completed our survey of the seven tools in the Searcher's Toolkit: number 6, Limits; and number 7, Learning from your results. *Limits* are preset options built into a search interface that enable you to search by document attributes such as full text, peer reviewed, date, source or document type, and language. *Learning from your results* is the strategy of starting with a very simple keyword search, examining the results, and discovering useful subject headings or additional terms to search on from the most on-target records.

Your Mental Toolkit

Understanding and being able to use concepts such as Boolean logic, controlled vocabulary, proximity searching, and limits will definitely go a long way toward making you a more efficient and effective searcher. In addition, there are certain mental attitudes that will help you a great deal as well. Of course, there are some aspects of mind or personality that you either have or you don't: general curiosity, interest and enjoyment in puzzles, and an ability to think out of the box, that is, to make connections or have ideas (lightbulb moments) *beyond* the research request as it is explicitly stated. But there are important mental tools that you don't have to be born with; rather, you can make a conscious effort to develop them. These are tools to employ in any search, which can be just as important in your success as a searcher as your knowledge of search functions.

The mental toolkit:

- *A healthy skepticism*: Do not trust anything someone tells you that "they remember," or even anything that is printed in a bibliography.

- *Willingness to let go*: Someone may offer a great deal of information, but if the results keep coming up zero, or wrong, *let go* and drop pieces of information, one at a time.

- *Maintain mental clarity and patience*: Be systematic about your searching; don't just thrash around rapidly trying this and that. It may seem to take longer to stop and think and try one change at a time, but in the end it will save time.

To emphasize the second point: one of the biggest pitfalls in searching is not being willing to *not* look for a part of the information provided. In general: be flexible, not fixated. Taken altogether, these three "mental tools" support and reinforce the phrase that should become your searching mantra:

The search you start with is seldom the search you end up with.

Think about what this sentence is saying. Then remember it every time you do a search, and ask yourself, "Have I tried a sufficient number of variations? Have I let go of anything, or added something I learned from my results? Am I satisfied with these results, and do they seem reasonable?" Ordinary people may do one search, not find what they (think) they want, and give up. You are pros, and aren't allowed to do that.

Summary and Advice

And that's your toolkit. You now have some concepts, some tools that you'll use over and over, in various combinations, and some attitudinal tools to use as well. My advice for how to employ this information to the best advantage is fairly simple:

1. Master the concepts.

2. Do not attempt to memorize exactly which databases offer which capabilities. Instead . . .

3. Train your eyes!

Learn to scan an interface quickly. Look for *Help* or *Search Guides*. (Actually read them, although be prepared: sometimes the *Help* is not updated as quickly as changes are made to the database.) You now know *what* to look for,[7] so simply look for it. Nothing on that screen should be "noise" or ignored. This is the most important thing you can do: LOOK with your trained eyes. Why? Because

> Things can change at any time—and they will change!

The Web fosters change, and commercial databases are not exempt: while their interfaces may be slightly more stable than most web pages, the lure and the ability to change things so easily is hard to resist. Indeed, by the time you see this book, the interfaces shown in the figures here may have already changed anywhere from a little to a lot. (Which is why in many cases I have opted to use stylized drawings instead.) You need to be flexible, and able to relearn continually as the interface designers move things around and change their terminology. Let me assure you that you will become good at it, but you need to be alert and ready for change ("oh, now all the tabs are soft grey, and they've changed the name Filter to Refine. Same thing. OK."). I cannot emphasize this enough:

USE YOUR EYES. They are the best tool that you have.[8]

Exercises and Points to Consider

1. Consider again this search: homeless N/4 teenagers, which produced this result:

   has been homeless ever since he was a teenager . . .

   Count the words between *homeless* and *teenager*. Why would the article containing this phrase be retrieved by this search?

2. What do you think would be the best way to search for a personal name, especially if you wanted any article that made any mention of the person? Would you use a phrase or proximity search? What are the pros and cons of each method?

3. Consider again this search: Consultan* near10 (food or beverage*). How might you alter this slightly to make even more documents eligible for retrieval? What might be the pros and cons of doing that?

4. Going back to ProQuest's suggestions when we did the "sales engineers" search, if you clicked the View All option to see all the suggestions, you'd find the suggestion mentioned above plus an additional one about Engineers:

Engineers AND Personal profiles (searched as Subjects)

Engineers AND Polls & surveys (searched as Subjects)

What would be an elegant way to accomplish both of these searches at once?

5. One major vendor whose proximity capabilities weren't addressed in this chapter is Gale. Go to a Gale database, and see if you can find out the following: Does it support proximity searching, and what is the syntax, if so? How about phrase searching?

6. Similar to Question 5: if you have access to any of the databases produced by Alexander Street Press, go into the Help files and see what you can find out about proximity searching, truncation, and wildcards. If you have access to more than one database from this vendor, definitely look at several of them. Their Help is always easy to find, but it is not necessarily the same from database to database. A very interesting and different set of products.

Suggested Reading

Tenopir, Carol. "Are You a Super Searcher?" *Library Journal* (March 1, 2000): 36–38. The date is old, but the discussion of characteristics of what makes a good searcher are just as relevant today as when this article first appeared.

Notes

1. When dealing with a totally unfamiliar subject area, it's also very useful to do a Google or Google Scholar search, just to get a sense of how people write about the topic.

2. In order to get results, a search such as: (gourmet OR specialty) SAME pickles AND ns=cmarkr is needed. The final mysterious bit of syntax is the code for market research as a subject.

3. Bell's Reference Desk Rule No. 1: citations almost always have a mistake in them somewhere.

4. Beware, though, that if the database is enabled with a technology for linking to full text in other databases to which the library subscribes, turning on the full-text limit could eliminate potentially useful results.

5. Why "pearl growing"? Well, you throw out a small bit (one or two words, say), a seed. Then from all the results, you add layers, the way a pearl adds layers of nacre around a grain of sand. I guess you could call it "onion growing," but it doesn't sound quite so nice!

6. Available at the U.S. Bureau of Labor's website (http://www.bls.gov/ooh/).

7. Just in case you had a momentary mental lapse, "what to look for" is Boolean operators, controlled vocabulary, fields you can search, proximity operators, truncation and wildcard symbols, and limits that you can set.

8. Well, they need to be connected to your brain, of course . . .

5
Social Science Databases

Introduction to Subject Databases

Before plunging directly into the nuts and bolts of the following databases, let's pause for a moment to think about the whole idea of subject-specific databases. The following statement might fall into the "duh" category, but sometimes it's good to start with the absolute basics: a subject-specific database is a searchable, electronic resource devoted to a particular topic. It focuses on a subject area by including only the journals, books, conferences, or other published materials in that discipline. Naturally, there are journals that are useful and interesting to more than one subject area, and you will discover that some journals are indexed in several different databases. In general, however, if you are doing research that falls into an identifiable subject area, working with the appropriate subject databases is the most efficient and effective way to pursue that research. Why is a subject database better than a Web search in this case? A Web search is just that: it will find *web pages* and various other media that are freely available on the Web, but it is not an organized, structured index of commercially published material (Google Scholar muddies the waters here; more on that in chapter 11). A Web search is by definition "all subjects"—it's anything the search engine's indexing program has picked up. A Web search may well find someone's paper, if they have put it on the Web, or a reference to a paper within another paper that someone put on her website. But it is *not* a complete, orderly scan of the appropriate journals and other published materials in a subject area. That kind of organized, thorough, ongoing effort implies an organization, staff, and money, and it is not something anyone is going to give away for free. They are each very powerful in their way, but subject databases and Web search engines are very different animals.

How do you know what databases there are for your subject? Go to the website of any major university, find the university library page, and look for links such as "databases," "electronic resources," "subject guides," or "resources by subject." Almost all institutions of higher education will have enough of these databases that they will offer a list of them by subject. Simply scanning the alphabetical list, you will probably be amazed at the number and variety of different databases that are out there.

The number and variety of databases on the market is remarkable. But who knew? Why don't at least some of these databases have the name recognition of Google? Is it simply the difference between free and fee? Access to the subject databases is almost all by subscription, but you certainly get value for money. Yet compared with Web search engines, subject databases are almost unknown among the general public, and this is a shame, because they are so good at what they do.

This chapter looks at databases that support research in the social sciences. We'll look at three that are the key resources in their respective subjects, which will give us exposure to one familiar and two new interfaces. We'll conclude with a discussion of other resources notable in this area.

Library Literature & Information Science

Background and Coverage

Since many readers of this book probably are librarians or library school students, it seems only right to start with the original database of librarianship: *Library Literature & Information Science*. Started as a print index in 1921 by the H.W. Wilson Company, *Library Literature* is now an EBSCO database. The *Library Literature* database provides indexing for materials back to the early 1980s and full text dating from 1997. Although there are two other library science–specific databases (LISA—*Library & Information Science Abstracts*, and LISTA—*Library, Information Science & Technology Abstracts*), *Library Literature* has historically stood out for "its high-quality indexing, full text, complete coverage of the journals that are indexed" (Tenopir 2003). In addition to journal and review articles, *Library Literature* has records for books, book chapters, conference proceedings, library school theses, and pamphlets. Coverage is international.

Notes and Search Examples

You have seen a bit of the EBSCO interface in chapter 2, and you will get more in chapter 8, so learning about *Library Literature* should simply be a matter of mapping this particular content onto an interface with which you are already familiar.

Advanced Search Interface

Go to *Library Literature*, and take a look at the Advanced Search interface. Figure 5.1 provides a reminder and guide to what you have available to you:

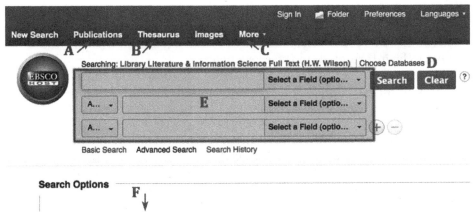

Figure 5.1. *Library Literature & Information Science* Advanced Search screen, annotated. © 2014 EBSCO Industries, Inc. All rights reserved.

A—Access to the Publications list. Used for checking to see if a database indexes a particular journal, how many years are available, whether full text is available and if there is a embargo on current material.

B—Access to the Library Literature Thesaurus. Useful for determining subject terms and broader, narrower, and related terms.

C—More provides access to the other field indexes, such as Author.

D—Reminder of which database you are in, and access to other EBSCO databases available through your institution's subscription. Tip: you will very likely find LISTA in this list (because it is free), and it is very handy to click Choose Databases, select *Library Literature* and LISTA, and thus search both of the major library resources at once.

E—The familiar three-box Advanced Search interface, with Boolean operators and the option to search in specific fields provided by drop-down menus.

F—Points down to the extensive Search Options area, which provides Search Mode options and a plethora of limits.

Which fields are available? Take a moment to open another EBSCO database in another window or tab, and compare the fields and field names in *Library Literature* to the other database: Are they the same? Different? Now examine (and compare) the options available in the "Limit your results" area: Are there any features specific to this database within the EBSCO format? Also investigate the More link (C): besides Author, mentioned above, what are the other indexes available for browsing? Try some look-ups and see what you get. Do the choices of fields to index make sense to you?

Library Literature Thesaurus

One of the great strengths of the *Library Literature* database has always been its Thesaurus, a hierarchical guide to the subject headings of this database. In a sense, this is a guide to the language of librarianship. The

Thesaurus will do its best to guide you to the correct controlled vocabulary to use (via *Use* terms), show you how terms interact hierarchically (which ones are *Broader, Narrower,* or *Related*), and explain how each term is intended to be interpreted (in the *scope note*).

When you access the Thesaurus using the link at the top of the screen, you will see an interface that looks very similar to Figure 2.7, the screenshot of access to the *MasterFILE* Subjects, Places, and People indexes back in chapter 2. The differences are that in *Library Literature*, there is only one list, and it carries the official title: Thesaurus. Again as shown in Figure 2.7, note the radio buttons below the search box: if you try looking up a term and do not even get a Use suggestion, try your search in the *Term Contains* or *Relevancy Ranked* options before deciding that there is no subject heading for your concept.

Try looking up OPAC, the acronym for Online Public Access Catalog, using the default Term Begins With search option. You should discover that you are directed instead to *Use* the term Online library catalogs. Click the correct heading to jump to that part of the list, take a moment to scan down and see some of the subheadings for Online library catalogs, but then click the Online library catalogs heading itself to access the full Thesaurus record for it. Here you will find out what it means (the scope note), what terms are Broader, what terms are Related, and what terms the indexers have decided *not* to use, that is, the *Used for* terms. These *Used for* terms represent all the ways that the *Library Literature* indexers have anticipated that people might look for this idea, as we just did. How many *Used for* terms have been assigned to Online library catalogs? (Count them.) This means we have that many opportunities to be guided to the correct term in the Thesaurus, and to access relevant results in the main database even if we don't search on the preferred term. As noted before in discussing controlled vocabulary, otherwise we might have to think of all these variations and search them all. A good set of subject headings, consistently applied, makes searching so efficient.

Online library catalogs is the term that the Thesaurus designers have decided will be the subject heading assigned to all articles on this topic, no matter how the concept is referred to in the article itself. Thus, theoretically, if you searched for Online library catalogs as a subject, your results should include every relevant record in the database. ("Theoretically" because even indexers have bad days: there might be articles that are mis-indexed.)

Search Example 1: Identifying Terms Using the Thesaurus

We'd like to find articles on how library school curriculum is changing in response to advances in information technology (IT).

Since we know that this database is already focused on libraries and librarians, do we need to include the "library school" part? See what you get if you only type in curriculum, using the default Term Begins With search. See any likely headings? Try it again using the Relevancy Ranked option. Aha! Now we're talking: "Library schools—Curricula." Perfect. Click the heading to look at the full record display for that term. Where does it fall in the Thesaurus hierarchy, that is, are there any Broader terms? How about Narrower, Related, or Used for terms? The terms have check boxes so that you can select more than one, and then you can add them to your search with a choice of Boolean operators, just as we did in the *MasterFILE* database. Select the two headings that look most pertinent to you, and add them to your search using OR. This operation will be reflected in the search box at the top of the same page. Add parentheses around those two OR'd terms, and add the following to that search statement: AND "information technology" (with the quotes). The search statement should look like this:

> (DE "Library schools—Curricula" OR DE "Information science—Study & teaching") AND "information technology"

Run that search.

The Results screen should look familiar: as in other EBSCO databases, the search interface is available above the results list, and the usual (very useful) "Refine Results" tools are all there on the left side. How are the results sorted? Can you change that? How do the results look to you—anything interesting or pertinent to our topic?

Search Example 2: A Lesson in Problem-Solving

You want to find some information on chat services as part of reference. You start by looking up "reference chat" in the Thesaurus (hint: use the Relevancy Ranked option). See if you get the following subject headings (you should):

Online chat

Electronic reference services (Libraries)

These subject headings look exactly right. Select both and add them to your search with AND (because you want articles that have been assigned *both* headings). The search statement should appear in the search box as:

DE "Online chat" AND DE "Electronic reference services (Libraries)"

How many results does this search return? If you feel the number of results is underwhelming, what can you do? Here is a tidied-up version of what goes through my head during my debugging process for this search:

- The search that was just run specified that both terms had to be Subjects. Must be too constraining. I'll change one of those terms to search just a keyword. [Mental toolkit: letting go]

- Remove 'DE "Online chat" AND' from the first text input box on the results screen. Instead, type 'chat' in the second text box, leaving the Boolean set to AND; don't select a search field. Search now looks like:

  ○ DE "Electronic reference services (Libraries)" → *[no need to specify the Subject field, because the code DE does that already]*

    AND

    Chat → *[leave as default: Select a Field (optional)]*

- Gets a few more. Hmm. Can I come up with any other terminology from what's in my results? There's "instant messaging"—that could count as a synonym for chat. I'll OR that with chat, still not specifying any field. [Get more with OR]

- Nuts. ORing in "instant messaging" didn't help a lot. What else? I'm seeing the subject "Library reference services" in a lot of records (right along with Electronic reference services). Worth a try . . .

- I want to OR the Library reference services with the Electronic reference services, and have them both searched as subjects. I think I'll strip out the DE code and control this myself. My search now looks like this:

  ○ "Electronic reference services (Libraries)" OR "Library reference services" → SU Subject

  AND

  Chat OR "instant messaging" → *[no field selected]*

- WOW. Ok, that made a difference, and they look relevant, too. Great, I'm done, for now. [The search you start out with is seldom the search you end up with.]

Your turn: go to the Advanced Search in *Library Literature* and see if you can set up and run the final version of my search. What do *you* think of the results? Now try approaching this search as if you knew nothing about the Thesaurus or subject headings. What words would you type in? (Hints: this activity is also variously referred to as virtual reference, reference chat, chat services, and AskALibrarian.) Try your search, maybe do some learning from your results or make some adjustments, but in the end—how do your results look? It's okay to say they look just as good to you as the results produced by a lot of fiddling with subject headings. Which set of results do you feel would work better for you if you were writing a paper on this topic? (There is no right or wrong answer to that question!)

Working with Results

No matter how good your search skills are, there are bound to be items in your results that are not as useful as the others. The database vendors understand this, and therefore generally offer a way to collect selected records. EBSCO databases use a folder analogy: for any records you want to output, click the associated Add to Folder link. (Another common implementation you will see in other databases is for each record to have a check box for marking or collecting it.) Typical output options are to print, save, email (send records and/or full text to yourself or someone else), and export to a citation manager program, all of which are offered by EBSCO databases. The folder and output options will be discussed in more detail in chapter 8 when we look at *America: History and Life*, another EBSCO database.

Quick Recap

In this section we looked at *Library Literature & Information Science*, the oldest and longest-running index devoted to the library field. *Library Literature* indexes journal articles, books, book chapters, conference proceedings, and library school theses. Materials are mainly in English, but coverage is international, and a number of other languages are represented. The *Library Literature* Thesaurus is custom built for this database, and it is an important tool for discovering subject headings and relationships between headings. LISTA, another database of library literature, is also available from EBSCO. This allows you to choose both databases and search all of their content simultaneously.

ERIC on the Web

Background and Coverage

ERIC, the *E*ducation *R*esources *I*nformation *C*enter, is another database with a long history of excellence that has gone through some significant changes in its lifetime. ERIC was established in 1964 by the Department of Education, to "gather, index, and input bibliographic information" (Tenopir 2004) for documents known as *grey literature*[1] and for journal articles. At more than 1 million records, the ERIC database is now the largest and foremost subject resource for education. (For more details on the history of ERIC, go to the Student Resources tab at http://www.abc-clio.com/LibrariesUnlimited/product.aspx?pc=A4596P.)

ERIC also has a long history of different database vendors licensing its content and then offering the database through their own search interface.[2] In addition to these choices, the Department of Education itself provides free access to ERIC, and it is this version we will work with here. While you will find it a far cry from the commercial vendors' implementations, this version *is* available to everyone, all the time. Access is not dependent on an institutional affiliation (e.g. being a college student) or going through a special portal (e.g. for remote access to a public library database). Let us see what the ERIC interface designers think the world wants.

Notes and Search Examples

ERIC Homepage

The ERIC database is available at http://eric.ed.gov. Go and take a look; as of this writing the landing page had the smooth, streamlined look, as shown in Figure 5.2. In fact, it looks lot like—guess who? (Google.) This search interface allows us to switch from searching the "Collection" to searching the Thesaurus, and to invoke the two most common

Figure 5.2. Home page for the free version of ERIC from the U.S. Department of Education, as of June 2014.

Limits: Peer reviewed and Full text. There is a link in very small print to access "Advanced Search Tips" but . . . where is the Advanced Search interface?

Oh brave new world that has almighty Google in it—there isn't an Advanced Search interface. No typical three input boxes with Boolean and field drop-downs. Instead, if you want to do something "advanced," you need to know what you're doing. Mastering the material in the initial chapters of this book suddenly seems like less of an academic exercise.

Advanced Search Tips

Indeed, the Advanced Search Tips page (http://eric.ed.gov/?advanced) should read like a refresher of chapters 3 and 4: searching phrases by enclosing them in double quotes, Boolean operators, parentheses to control the order of execution, and field searching, in this case by specifying the field name. (The "DE" code we just saw in the *Library Literature* search is the same idea, and we'll get another example of searching by field names when we look at PubMed.)

The list of fields available for searching is quite brief (see below), consisting of the fields you'd expect (Author, Descriptor, Source, Title) and a couple that are subject-specific to this education database (Audience, Education Level).

- abstract
- audience
- author
- descriptor
- educationlevel
- pubyear
- source
- title

As you can see by looking at the interface, there are no other limits or options available at the point of creating your search.

Search Example 1: Using the ERIC Thesaurus

The first search example that we'll use for our tour of the ERIC database is to find material on training teachers of deaf students. We will approach this search as sophisticated searchers, in contrast to the second search example, and then offer some thoughts about which techniques are best suited to this resource.

Let's start by using the Thesaurus to find the right Descriptors (or subject terms) we might use for this search. Clicking the Thesaurus tab above the search box, the interface changes slightly. We can leap into searching the Thesaurus, with the options to Include Synonyms or Include Dead Terms (e.g. former Thesaurus terms that are no longer being used)—A in Figure 5.3. But we can also start by *browsing* the Thesaurus (B in Figure 5.3), where we find we can browse alphabetically or by category.

Going to the Alphabetical list for "D," we get to entries starting with "Deaf (1966–1980)" and continuing through the term "Deafness." (Tip: the Find in Page search, Control-f in Windows or Command-f on a Mac, can be useful for finding what you want faster in these long lists.) Notice how many of the entries in the list are in italics: this indicates that the term is a *synonym*. It is not dead, but it isn't a valid subject heading either. Clicking an italicized term will show you which term to use instead. In the case of Deaf (1966–1980) it directs us to use: Deafness.

In contrast, searching the Thesaurus for the word deaf returns the three active Thesaurus entries: Deaf Blind, Deaf Interpreting, and Deafness. (Do this same search for 'deaf' in the Thesaurus yourself, but choose both of the "Include" options below the search box. See how the results

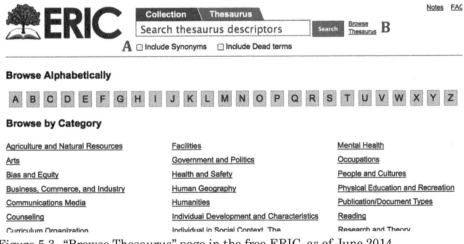

Figure 5.3. "Browse Thesaurus" page in the free ERIC, as of June 2014.

change, and remember that terms in italics are synonyms, not valid subject headings.)

ERIC Thesaurus

We now know the correct subject heading is Deafness. Clicking that, we get a full Thesaurus record (Figure 5.4).

This is informative: it tells us what this term means to the indexers (the Scope Note), the Category it falls into (Disabilities), Broader, Narrower and Related Terms, if any, and all the terms *not* to use. We could start a search just on the subject heading Deafness right from here (*A* in Figure 5.4), but we haven't finished discovering the rest of our search terms. I also like the heading "Partial Hearing" listed under Related Terms, but there is no built-in facility for choosing two terms from the same display and searching on them (unlike, say, the EBSCO subject index).

No matter what you do in this version of the ERIC database, the search box remains displayed at the top of screen, which is handy. Make sure it is still set to Thesaurus, and search for: teacher (do not use either of the Include options). How many Thesaurus Descriptors does this term retrieve?[3] (It is the education database after all.) Let's do a more specific search. How many Thesaurus terms are retrieved when you search for teacher education? Yes, quite a few, but two of them look particularly useful. Keeping in mind the guidance from the Advanced Search Tips page, let's use some syntax to construct an expert search:

descriptor: "Deafness" OR descriptor: "Partial Hearing" AND descriptor: "Teacher Education" OR descriptor: "Teacher Education Programs"

Back to Search Results

Deafness

Scope Note: Deprivation of the functional use of the sense of hearing -- usually a loss of more than 75 decibels
Category: Disabilities

🔍 Search collection using this descriptor **A**

Broader Terms
  Hearing Impairments

Narrower Terms
  N/A

Use this term instead of
  Deaf (1966 1980)
  Deaf Children (1966 1980)
  Deaf Community
  Deaf Culture
  Deaf Education (1968 1980)
  Deaf Research (1968 1980)
  Profoundly Hearing Impaired

Related Terms
  Deaf Blind
  Deaf Interpreting
  Hearing (Physiology)
  Manual Communication
  Oral Communication Method
  Partial Hearing
  Total Communication

Figure 5.4. Full ERIC Thesaurus record for Deafness, as of June 2014.

It only seems to work if we rather pedantically repeat the field name before each subject, and it also seems better *not* to use parentheses, which is not what I'd expect. How frustrating—that was a lot of work to try to do something smart and precise. Unfortunately, the system doesn't echo back to you how it interpreted your search (as most of the commercial vendors do), so we'll never know what it is doing behind the scenes. How many results does this search produce? Even more important: how are the results arranged? Can you change it?

Results

The Results display is laid out in what has become a very common format, with many options for focusing the results in the panel on the left side, and the results list occupying the rest of the screen. Result entries include citation information, the beginning of the abstract, and the first several Descriptors. Having a partial abstract and some Descriptors is helpful for evaluating the usefulness of each result without having to click into the record. An indicator of the item's "Peer reviewed" status and full text access is provided for each record. Although it is not explicitly stated anywhere, the results are sorted in order by relevance. And unfortunately, there is no option to change the order and sort them by date.

The number and nature of the options provided on the left side of the results display is the most powerful and sophisticated feature in this implementation of the database. It echoes and in one case goes beyond the list of fields on the Advanced Search Tips page. These options provide an easy point-and-click way to focus a large set of results (a way to invoke expertise without any learning curve). You can refine the results by:

- Publication Date
- Descriptor (subject headings)
- Source (journal or other publication name)
- Author
- Publication Type (articles, reports, legal materials, speeches, etc.)
- Education Level (elementary, middle school, higher education, etc.)
- Audience (practitioners, teachers, policymakers, administrators, parents, etc.)

The entries in each left side panel are listed in order by *frequency*: the number of records they are associated with in the current results list. The Descriptors tend to be our first go-to refinement, but you can enhance your overall knowledge about the topic simply by scanning the other lists. For example, from the Source titles, Author names, or Education Level lists, you can learn who are the experts in this area (or at least write on the topic most often), what the major journals (or other sources) are, and what level in the education system is most concerned with the topic. Figure 5.5 shows three examples of these left side panels.

SOURCE		
American Annals of the Deaf	176	
Language, Speech, and Hearing...	110	
Volta Review	96	
Perspectives for Teachers of...	26	
Perspectives in Education and...	23	
Journal of Speech, Language,...	20	
Journal of Deaf Studies and...	16	
ProQuest LLC	16	
Communication Disorders...	11	
Exceptional Children	11	
More ▼		

AUTHOR	
Luckner, John L.	18
Martin, David S.	16
Kluwin, Thomas N.	12
Stewart, David A.	9
Phay, Robert E.	7
Woodward, James	7
Easterbrooks, Susan R.	6
Frels, Kelly	6
Justice, Laura M.	6
Mertens, Donna M.	6
More ▼	

EDUCATION LEVEL	
Elementary Secondary Education	93
Higher Education	75
Elementary Education	47
Early Childhood Education	36
Secondary Education	25
Postsecondary Education	24
Preschool Education	22
High Schools	21
Middle Schools	16
Adult Education	11
More ▼	

Figure 5.5. Three of the panels for refining results in the free ERIC, as of June 2014.

Search Example 2: Refining on the Results Page

The thing is, most people do not know or do not care about taking the time for a very structured approach. The world of users on the web is not going to carefully check the thesaurus entries before deciding on search terms and setting up the strategy. Sally the busy graduate student looking for resources on corrective feedback in second language acquisition is much more likely to go to ERIC and simply type in:

corrective feedback second language acquisition

and assume the results will be ordered to provide the most relevant ones at the beginning. She may not even be conscious of this expectation.

Her strategy appears to have worked: there are certainly a *lot* of results, and at first glance they look on target, thanks to the relevancy ranked order. Indeed, the first two results are "perfect" because the real motivation for Sally's research is that she's an instructor for a freshman composition class of international students. What she really wants is research about the use of corrective feedback in writing classes where the students are not native English speakers. Her most likely response to the situation is not to examine the options on the left side, but to simply add the word writing to her search, which does seem to help get the results in line with what she wants. Now we can only hold our collective breath and hope she notices the Descriptors panel on the left, where the entry Writing (Composition) is now visible. Choosing that will focus her results nicely; having seen how that works, she might look again at the Descriptors panel and notice the entry English (Second Language), choose that as well, and focus her results even more. The system is attuned to the non-expert searcher.

What might have happened if Sally had gone to Dan, the librarian in the social sciences division of her city's public library? With what she initially told him (including that second language acquisition is frequently referred to by its acronym, SLA), and sensing her "I'm in a hurry" vibrations, he might have gone to ERIC and typed in:

corrective feedback AND (second language acquisition OR SLA)

This produces a hefty list of results, but still only about half of what Sally's initial search produced. In this case, Dan would encourage her to scan them, and see if any appear to be particularly "on target." She does, and the article titled "Second Language Writing Research and Written Corrective Feedback in SLA: Intersections and Practical Applications," gets her attention because she notices one of the Descriptors for this article is "Writing (Composition)." Now it comes out that she's an instructor for a freshman composition class of international students, and that's the real reason for her research. On the same record, Dan notices that "Feedback (Response)" seems to be the official Descriptor for the concept of corrective feedback, and he immediately turns his attention to the list of Descriptors on the left. Feedback (Response) leads the list, which bodes well: to Dan's "searcher mind" knowing the first filter he applies has lots of records associated with it means there will still be plenty of records for further refining. Clicking the Descriptor applies it, and the list of results goes down to the number associated with that term. Eyes back to the Descriptors panel: aha, English (Second Language) is there now, and Dan applies that. Now what about the composition class aspect? Writing Instruction is visible in the Descriptors list, but not Writing (Composition)—until Dan clicks to see More, and then it appears with 50+ records associated with it: perfect. What a difference a search professional makes!

The series of steps described in the preceding paragraph paints a picture of an inevitable march to success. Life, as we know, is usually messier than that; therefore a third scenario for how this search might have gone is depicted in Figure 5.6.

What is the ultimate lesson from all these results screen scenarios? My suggestion is that this free version of ERIC is optimized for very simple, non-expert *searching* but sophisticated (although still very easy to use) *refining* of results. If that is how it is meant to work, you might as well go with the flow: you are allowed to use only your minimal 'searcher brain' in this version of ERIC (but, as always, make sure you are using your eyes to see what is in the left hand panels).

At this point we would normally go over how to collect and output records. In the "streamlined" version of ERIC released in August 2013 that we have been looking at, the system designers evidently decided to do away with all of that functionality. There isn't any way to mark records and then perform any kind of collective action on them; no printing, emailing, exporting, etc. It's rather shocking, because these capabilities were available in the previous version: it was on par with any commercial vendor's database functionality. Perhaps adding some of this functionality back in will be part of the "Further enhancements to increase usefulness" planned for the remainder of 2014 (US Department of Education 2014).

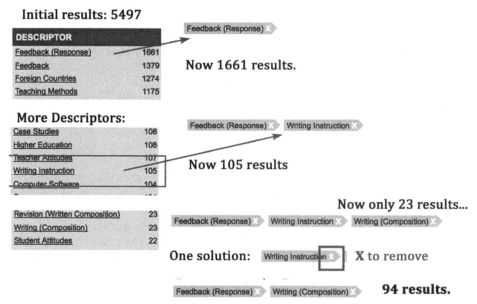

Figure 5.6. Iterative refining by Descriptors process in the free ERIC, as of June 2014.

Quick Recap

We have just looked at the free Web version of ERIC, the Education Resources Information Center, the premier database for education. ERIC is produced under the aegis of the US Department of Education and dates back to 1964. ERIC indexes journal articles and *grey literature*—scholarly works that have not been commercially published. The Department of Education provides the ERIC database freely to the world at http://eric.ed.gov; ERIC is available from many different commercial database vendors as well. The free version is highly simplified compared to any of the commercial vendors' implementations, almost certainly an attempt to appeal to and be easy to use by the widest possible audience. Some advanced searching is possible using field codes and Boolean operators, but this implementation seems to be optimized for searching by keywords and then refining on the Results screen. There are currently no output options in the free version.

PsycINFO from Ovid

Background and Coverage

PsycINFO is the online version of the American Psychological Association's venerable *Psychological Abstracts*, started as a print abstracting and indexing service in 1927. *PsycINFO* is the largest, and most well known, index of the literature of psychology and the behavioral sciences. The American Psychological Association (APA) draws on US and international sources, including US dissertations, journals in more than 29 languages (99% of which are peer reviewed), and English-language books and book chapters from all over the world. The Thesaurus terms (subject headings) used to index entries in the *PsycINFO* database are developed and applied by APA indexers.

Two other notable features of PsycINFO are the range of time it covers, and the extensive set of search fields in the database structure. PsycINFO has summaries of materials dating to 1597 and abstracts of books and journal articles dating from 1806, but most of the journal coverage is from the 1880s to the present, and most of the books are from 1987 to the present. The database is updated weekly, and the latest updated week is reflected in the search interface. Database records include over 40 fields, as detailed in the online Field Guide at the APA website.[4] The Guide indicates whether a field is searchable or display-only (indicated with an asterisk), and provides helpful information about what the field is used for: content or possible values. Note especially the presence of a Cited References field (containing the article's bibliography; very important in tracing the development of research), and the Methodology field (indicating what kind of study, e.g., clinical, field, qualitative, quantitative, is discussed). Capturing this information and being able to search it is very valuable to psychological researchers.

Like ERIC, the *PsycINFO* online database is available from several different vendors. We're going to take a look at *PsycINFO* as offered by the database vendor Ovid.

Why Look at Ovid's *PsycINFO*

The Ovid platform interface is quite different from the ones that we have seen so far in two interesting and, to me, quite useful ways:

- It has a built-in map-to-subject-heading feature that tries to offer you the best subject heading choices based on the terms you type in.

- It encourages you to build your search one concept at a time, which turns out to be very handy because when you have all the conceptual pieces, it is then very easy to experiment with putting them together in different combinations.

Notes and Search Examples

It's time to jump in and see what the Ovid interface is like. As you should be beginning to expect, we will go directly to the Advanced Search interface—after all, we are not Basic searchers.

Advanced Search Interface

What do you notice about the interface as represented by the drawing in Figure 5.7? The first thing that registers for me is the emphasis on the Search

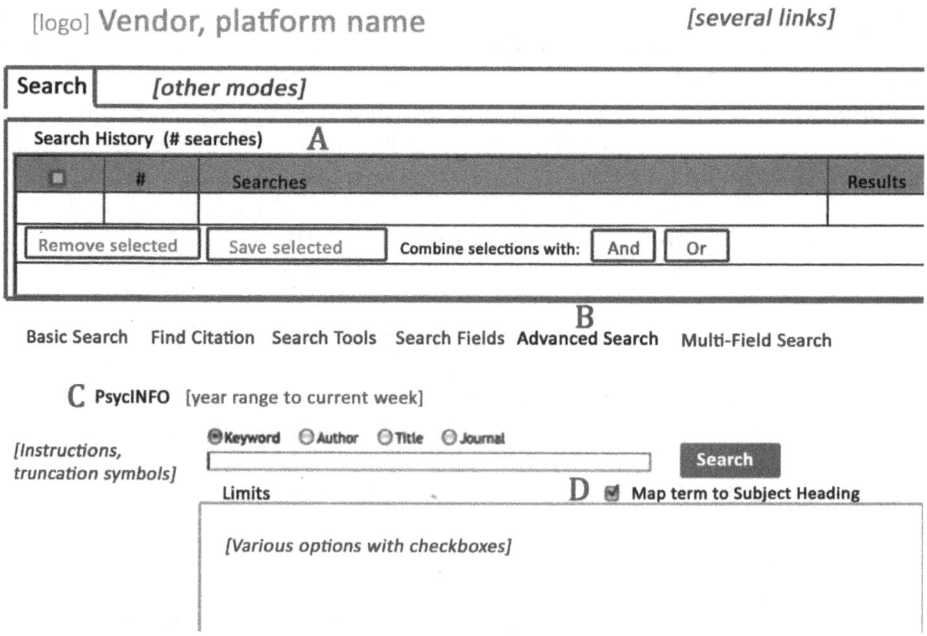

[logo] Vendor, platform name   *[several links]*

Search | *[other modes]*

Search History (# searches)   **A**

☐	#	Searches		Results

| Remove selected | Save selected | Combine selections with: | And | Or |

B

Basic Search   Find Citation   Search Tools   Search Fields   **Advanced Search**   Multi-Field Search

C PsycINFO   [year range to current week]

[Instructions,   ⦿ Keyword   ○ Author   ○ Title   ○ Journal
truncation symbols]
                        [   ]   **Search**
                        Limits   **D** ☑ Map term to Subject Heading

                        [Various options with checkboxes]

Figure 5.7. Representation of the PsycINFO Advanced Search screen on the Ovid platform.

History area: my eyes see that first (*A* in Figure 5.7). Then note: we are in Advanced Search mode (*B*), but there is only one text-entry box. There are links for several other search options (Find Citation, Search Tools, etc.), which are obvious enough but not intrusive. You are reminded of which resource you are now in—*PsycINFO*—with the date coverage available in this institution's subscription (*C*). The four radio buttons above the single search box tell you the four types of searches possible in the current Advanced Search mode. When the text-entry field is set to "Keywords," the "Map Term to Subject Heading" option (*D*) is turned on by default, which is important: this is one of the special powers of the Ovid interface, that it gets you from Keywords to Subject Headings as an integral part of the search process. Directly below the search box is the Limits area; it provides access to the most frequently used limits and the option to see more. (The drawing only indicates their location; more detail will be provided when we make use of some Limits.)

Here are some additional notes about this interface.

As mentioned previously, the most effective way to use this database is to build your search one step at a time, with the results of each step recorded in the Search History. Thus, putting the Search History table first and foremost in the display makes sense, because it becomes very important as you work in this database. The individual searches can then be quickly and flexibly combined and reused, as we shall see.

To quickly describe the other search-mode links:

- Find Citation provides a set of fields in which you can enter whatever parts of a citation you have in order to complete the citation and see if there is a record for that work in the database.

- The Search Tools link allows you to search supporting materials, such as the Map Terms list, Thesaurus, Permuted Index, or Scope Notes (definitions of subject headings), which govern the content of *PsycINFO*.

- The Search Fields link takes you to a screen where you enter your term in a search box, then restrict your search to a particular field or fields by clicking its check box. (This is quite different from the drop-down menu approach.)

- The Multi-Field Search provides what should now be a familiar-looking interface: three text entry fields with drop-downs to restrict that part of the search to a particular field, connected by Boolean drop-downs.

As mentioned earlier, the most frequently used limits are available directly below the search box area. Once a search has been performed, an "Additional Limits" button becomes visible and offers other, more detailed limits. Note that a standard limit in this subject area is "Human" (to rule out articles about tests or studies on animals).

Here is what the Ovid interface is like to use.

Search Example 1: Building Your Search Concept by Concept

We'd like to search the psychological literature for material on the "effect of peer pressure on self esteem." We'll start by typing the following into the search box:

peer pressure

and running the search. This brings up the "Mapping Display" screen, depicted in the drawing in Figure 5.8.

The Mapping Display

Because the "Map Term to Subject Heading" feature was turned on, the system automatically tries to match, or "map," what you type in against its Thesaurus, the hierarchical list of subject headings for *PsycINFO*. The results can be quite fascinating, because even in the case of an exact match (as we have here: Peer Pressure is a subject heading), if you click the term

[indicates if term is a thesaurus term]

Combine selections with: [OR ⬍]   [Continue >>]

Select	Subject Heading		Auto Explode	Focus
✔	Peer Pressure		✔	☐
☐	peer pressure *search as Keyword*			

Figure 5.8. Representation of the Mapping Display for the term Peer Pressure.

you are taken into the Thesaurus, where you can see all the terms that have a relationship to this heading, that is, they are broader, narrower, or "related." The immense amount of thought that the Thesaurus designers put into their product can make your searching life so much easier, by suggesting relationships and lines of thought that might not have occurred to you.

Each subject heading has two options: *Auto-Explode* and *Focus*. Remember the "Explode" feature in the *MasterFILE* Subjects index in chapter 3? This is the same: Auto-explode will pick up the heading and any narrower headings, i.e., ones indented below it in the hierarchy. *Focus* means that the indexers decided that the heading was a main aspect, or focus, of the article. Only a few of the subject headings assigned to an article will be designated as a Focus, so you may want to use this option sparingly in the initial phases of your search.

For the current search, we'll leave Auto-Explode on, but we won't check Focus—we'll leave it a little more open. Clicking the Continue button returns us to the main search page, which now displays our search history with the number of results from the Peer Pressure search, the interface to start another search, and the beginning of our results list.

Building the Search

Now to add the second concept of our search, by typing

self esteem

into the search box. Again, this maps exactly to a subject heading.

This time on the Mapping Display screen we'll click the Focus box, because we really want the main theme of these articles to be about self-esteem. There should be more than 16,000 results for this search.

Combining Search History Sets

Now we will combine the results of these two searches. In the Search History box, we could check box both searches and use the "Combine Selections with" AND button. Note, however, that each search in your history is numbered: an insider's shortcut is that you can simply type

1 and 2

into the search box, as shown in Figure 5.9 (or whatever numbers correspond to the searches in your search history that you wish to combine.)

You can use any of the Boolean operators, and parentheses for making nested statements, to combine Search History set numbers in this way. Each variation will, of course, produce a set of results that differs to a greater or lesser extent. If you have built up a series of searches, this is a very fast and easy way to experiment with them to arrive at an optimal set of results.

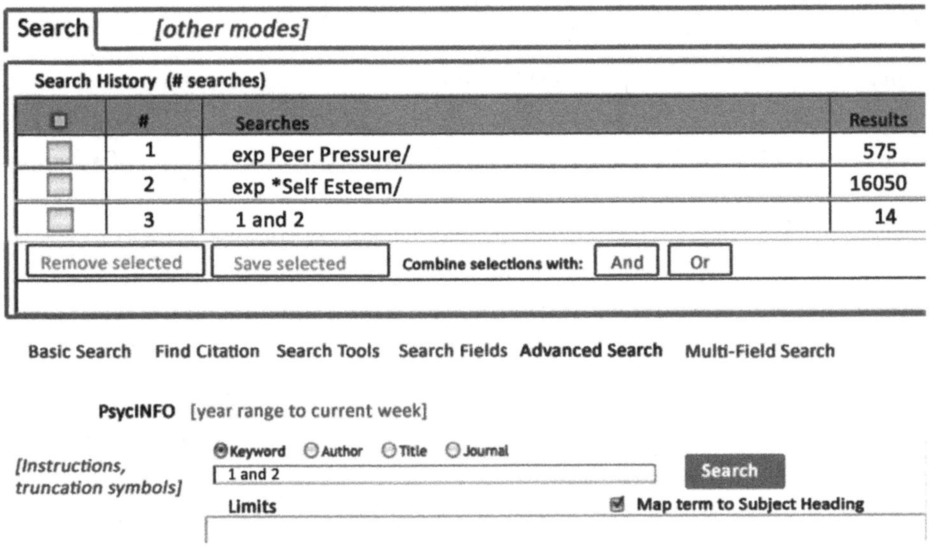

Search	*[other modes]*

Search History (# searches)

☐	#	Searches	Results
☐	1	exp Peer Pressure/	575
☐	2	exp *Self Esteem/	16050
☐	3	1 and 2	14

Remove selected	Save selected	**Combine selections with:**	And	Or

Basic Search   Find Citation   Search Tools   Search Fields   **Advanced Search**   Multi-Field Search

PsycINFO   [year range to current week]

[Instructions, truncation symbols]   ⦿ Keyword   ○ Author   ○ Title   ○ Journal

| 1 and 2 | | **Search** |

Limits   ☑ **Map term to Subject Heading**

Figure 5.9. Representation of short cut for combining searches in the Ovid platform.

Results

Presto: our combined sets result in 14 articles, as indicated both in the Search History display and at the beginning of the results list. A useful feature of the Ovid interface is that it allows us to see the search history, search interface, and results all on the same (long) page. These results seem on target, but 14 isn't a lot. How might we get more?

Search Example 1 Redone: Getting More with OR

Let's do this search again. This time, to *avoid* mapping directly to a term, type "pressure from peers" into the search box. This causes the Mapping Display to show us a whole list of possible subject headings, from which we can select several terms in addition to Peer Pressure. Think about your choices, selecting headings that are the most similar, that are getting at essentially the same concept (which is what I tried to do in Table 5.1– Mapping Display Table). In this case, headings about Tobacco, Alcohol, or Drugs would represent the *effects* of peer pressure, so I won't choose those. Note the "Combine selections with" drop-down above the list of subject headings (Figure 5.8). By default, it is set to OR, which is what we want. After picking several headings and ORing them together, yes, the number of results is enormous: more than 33,000.

Don't panic.

Combining from the Search History

There were LOTS of hits for self esteem when we searched it before, so let's reuse that search, and combine it with our new set of "peer" topics (here is the beauty of being able to quickly and easily reuse previous sets). Simply

Table 5.1. Beginning of all the suggested Subject Headings in the Mapping Display generated in response to a search for 'pressure from peers,' with several selected.

Select	Subject Heading	Auto Explode
☑	Peer Pressure	☑
☑	Peer Relations	☑
☐	Peers	☐
☑	Interpersonal Influences	☑
☐	Human Sex Differences	☐
☐	"Conformity (Personality)"	☐
☐	Coping Behavior	☐
☐	Tobacco Smoking	☐
☐	Age Differences	☐
☐	Alcohol Drinking Patterns	☐
☑	Adolescent Attitudes	☑

type the numbers of the sets that you want to combine into the search box, in this case: 2 and 4.

Applying Limits

OK, it's still a fairly big set of records, but still, don't panic. Let's make use of some of those limits that are provided by default in the search interface, which include: Ovid Full Text Available, Latest Update, Abstracts, Human, All Journals, English Language and Publication Year. We will limit by English Language, All Journals, and Publication Year 2008—Current. Simply select the Limits that you want to use, and click the Search button. It feels odd, because there is nothing in the input field next to the Search button, but the system understands that you are applying limits. This set of limits whittles the results down to 107, a good set of results for a serious research project.

There are also options to "Filter" (e.g., narrow) your results in the panel to the left of the results list, as shown in the drawing in Figure 5.10. The lists for each Filter (Subject, Author, Journal, Publication Type) represent the most frequently occurring entries from the total results list; thus, you might decide to look only at the articles from the journal that had the most articles on this topic, or articles by an author who publishes on the topic frequently.

More Search History Advantages

The Ovid piece-by-piece approach to searching is also helpful if you decide to change direction as you're working. If you get a new idea, you simply

Filter By
Add to search history
+ Selected only (0)
- Years
[Various Year Options]
+ Subject
+ Author
- Journal
All Journals
Journal of Adolescence
Personality and
Individual Differences
Psychology of Sport and
Exercise
Social Behavior and
Personality
Body Image
More . . .
+ Publication Type

Figure 5.10. Representation of some of the Filter By options on the PsycINFO results screen.

start that new thread, and then experiment with combining it with previous searches. You can delete searches if you're really sure they aren't useful (using the Remove Selected button in the Search History box), but you can also just keep adding new ones. Although the interface will default to showing you only the four most recent searches, the small Expand tab on the upper right of the Search History table will reveal them all.

Table 5.2 shows an example of the results you get when you add two new searches (for material about body image and about advertising) and combine them with previous searches. We find that the new search set 8 produces only one result when ANDed with search set 6, so we might simply try combining set 8 with the large set on self esteem, set 2. This combination results in 26 citations (not pictured in the screenshot), perhaps not enough, so we OR set 7, about Body Image, with set 2, and then AND that with the advertising set to get a substantial set of 98 records—all with a few flicks of the keys.

Working with Results

The first 10 results of the latest search are always listed on the main search page, starting below the Search interface. As with many databases, you select citations of interest by clicking their check boxes. Just above the results are the usual options for handling your results: selected items can be printed, emailed, or exported to a bibliographic software application. You

Table 5.2. Search history list showing quick experiments with different combinations of search sets.

Select	#	Subject Heading	Results
☐	1	exp Peer Pressure/	575
☐	2	exp *Self Esteem/	16050
☐	3	1 and 2	14
☐	4	exp Peer Relations/ or exp Peer Pressure/ or exp Interpersonal Influences/ or exp Adolescent Attitudes/	33241
☐	5	2 and 4	645
☐	6	limit 5 to (all journals and english language and yr="2008-Current")	107
☐	7	exp Body Image/	9482
☐	8	exp Advertising/ or exp Television Advertising/	9213
☐	9	2 or 7	24808
☐	10	1 or 8	9784
☐	11	9 and 10	142

can choose exactly which fields to include, which citation style you want them formatted in, and whether or not to include your search history. There is also an Order feature that ties in with the subscribing institution's Interlibrary Loan system, allowing quick and easy ordering of documents not locally available. The My Projects option allows you to create your own personal account in the system to store results over time, useful if you are engaged in a long-term research project. There are also various customization features provided in this area: you can choose how much detail you want displayed in the results list (Titles, Citations, or Abstracts), and how many results to display per page. All of these options are represented in the drawing in Figure 5.11.

Additional Feature: The *PsycINFO* Thesaurus

You can directly access the *PsycINFO* Thesaurus by going to the Search Tools link, selecting Thesaurus from the drop-down menu, and entering a term, as shown in Figure 5.12. You can also access the Thesaurus from the Mapping Display screen in the course of a search by clicking on any of the linked subject headings.

In either case, you'll get taken to the Thesaurus display for that term. This allows you to see how the term fits into the hierarchy, all the narrower

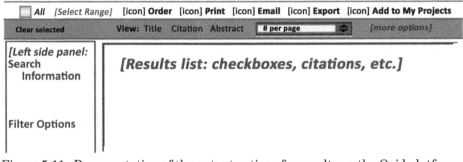

	All *[Select Range]* [icon] **Order** [icon] **Print** [icon] **Email** [icon] **Export** [icon] **Add to My Projects**

Clear selected   **View:** Title   Citation   Abstract   **# per page**   ⇕   *[more options]*

[Left side panel:
Search
   Information

[Results list: checkboxes, citations, etc.]

Filter Options

Figure 5.11. Representation of the output options for results on the Ovid platform.

;ic Search   Find Citation   **Search Tools**   Search Fields   Advanced Search   Multi-Field Search

PsycINFO   [year range to current week]

| Thesaurus ⇕ | motivation | **Search** |

Figure 5.12. Representation of how to access the PsycINFO Thesaurus via the Search

terms that will be included if you leave the Auto-Explode box checked, what terms are broader, and what terms are related. For example, my Thesaurus search for motivation tells me it is "Used For" Drive, meaning that instead of drive, the indexers voted to use the term Motivation. It also reveals that there are 17 "Narrower Terms." In addition to the terms you might expect (e.g., Intrinsic and Extrinsic Motivation, Employee Motivation, Monetary Incentives, Hunger, Sex Drive), there are always some surprises, such as:

Animal Motivation

Drug Seeking

Educational Incentives

Fear of Success

Procrastination

Temptation

There are also *23* Related Terms, from Activity Level to Wishful Thinking. It can be quite interesting to wander around in the PsycINFO Thesaurus for a bit—it is a fascinating insight into how a discipline has codified and classi-fied the idiosyncrasies of the human psyche.

Quick Recap

PsycINFO is the preeminent index to psychology literature, and is pro-duced by the American Psychological Association. The complete version of the online database provides journal indexing back to 1806, and covers journals, books, book chapters, technical reports, dissertations, published conference papers, bibliographies, and more. Sources are international. Using *PsycINFO* through the Ovid interface takes advantage of the Ovid "Map to Subject Heading" functionality, which automatically provides a list of suggested terms from the *PsycINFO* Thesaurus for any word or phrase typed into the search field. Specialized functions in the Subject Heading Mapping Display are Auto-Explode, that is, automatically search the indicated term and all narrower subject headings, and Focus, that is, restrict the search to records in which the indicated term is a major aspect (or focus) of the article. The optimal search style to use in the Ovid interface is to build a search one concept at a time, and then combine sets from the search history. This is very different from the other databases considered so far. The most commonly used Limits appear in the Advanced Search interface, and many more are accessible by means of the Additional Limits button. In addition, options for filtering a search by Subject, Author, Journal, or Publication Type are available in the results interface. The Ovid interface offers a number of customization and personalization features.

Additional Resources for Social Science

This chapter has considered in detail three databases that are the most important for their respective disciplines, but these are only a representative sample. Almost every discipline has one or more subject databases devoted to it; a sampling of academic disciplines, databases and vendors is provided in Table 5.3 to give you a sense of what is available. Notice how often the vendor names EBSCO and ProQuest appear: they are definitely vying for dominance in the library database industry. In addition to the subject specific databases listed in this table, the multidisciplinary databases JSTOR and Social Sciences Full Text (from EBSCO) are usually recommended for all of these subject areas.

There are also two significant, long-standing *free* resources that need to be mentioned here, one for economics and one for our own library science. *Ideas* (ideas.repec.org), hosted by the Federal Reserve Bank of St. Louis, is the largest collection of economics materials on the Web. (RePEc stands for Research Papers in Economics.) It includes both citations and full text for working papers, articles, chapters, and books in every area of economics. If you don't have EconLit, this is the place to go. For librarians, *Library, Information Science & Technology Abstracts* (LISTA; available via www.libraryresearch.com), is a full-featured EBSCO database that the company provides for free to "anyone interested in libraries and information management." Indexing goes back to the mid-1960s for close to 600 periodicals and other materials, making its depth and breadth of coverage somewhat greater than that of *Library Literature*. If you had no access to *Library Literature*, a wealth of scholarly information and EBSCO's powerful search platform would still be at your fingertips with this resource.

You'll notice that one big area is not represented in Table 5.3: business. There is such a wealth of databases for business, from so many vendors, I

Table 5.3. Table of Social Science Disciplines, Databases, and Vendors

Discipline	Database (Vendor)
Anthropology	AnthroSource (American Anthropological Assoc.) Anthropological Literature (EBSCO) eHRAF World Cultures (Human Relations Area Files, Inc.) Early Encounters in North America (Alexander Street Press)
Economics	EconLit (EBSCO) NBER Working Papers (National Bureau of Economic Research) World Development Indicators (World Bank)
Law	Criminal Justice Abstracts (EBSCO) HeinOnline (William S. Hein & Co., Inc.) Index to Legal Periodicals & Books (EBSCO) LexisNexis Academic (LexisNexis) ProQuest Congressional (ProQuest) Westlaw (Westlaw)
Political Science	CIAO—Columbia International Affairs Online (Columbia University Press) CQ Researcher (CQ Press, an imprint of Sage) PAIS International (ProQuest) Political Science Complete (EBSCO) Polling the Nations (ORS Publishing) Public Affairs Index (EBSCO) Worldwide Political Science Abstracts (ProQuest)
Sociology	SocIndex (EBSCO) Sociological Abstracts (ProQuest)

was afraid if I started, I'd get carried away! I am going to attempt to restrain myself, and give you just the following four databases, three from the "Big Three" vendors: EBSCO, ProQuest, and Gale, and one from a vendor we haven't encountered before: Infogroup.

ABI/Inform (ProQuest)

Business Source Premier, Business Source Complete (EBSCO),

Business Insights: Essentials (Gale)

ReferenceUSA (Infogroup, Inc.)

ABI/Inform and *Business Source* (*Premier* or *Complete*, EBSCO offers different subscription levels) are two of the most well known business *article* databases in academia. In addition to articles, both levels of the EBSCO database also offer industry reports, company profiles, and country economic reports. If you need articles from business publications, these are the names to know.

Business Insights: Essentials used to be known as *Business & Company Resource Center*, which was a more descriptive (but less exciting) title. It is

---

Sidebar 5.1 – Expert Tip

An efficient and effective way to tap into the collective, expert knowledge of the library community is to search the LibGuides Community site. Literally thousands of institutions of all kinds use LibGuides, a product of Springshare, to create online "library guides." Librarians create guides for topics, specific courses, anything and everything they think might be of interest to their community. Because all the guides created live on Springshare's servers, it is possible to search across all of them (unless the guide has been designated "private" by its creator), and instantly tap into this huge and ever-growing body of expertise. Simply entering:

libguides.com

will pull up the LibGuides Community site. (The complete URL when it does so is: http://libguides.com/community.php?m=i&ref=libguides.com.)

You can limit your search to guides from institutions like your own (e.g., Academics, Publics, K-12), then search by topic, database name, anything! For example, are there any guides to business resources at K-12 institutions? Find out instantly, and see what they recommend. The LibGuides Community site is an excellent way to learn about the resources for a subject, or to learn how to use a particular resource. The expertise of librarians all over the world is at your fingertips! Take advantage of it.

---

a very useful all-in-one resource for industry and company research that brings together content from many Gale products: their article databases, *International Directory of Company Histories* series, encyclopedias of *Global Industries* and *American Industries, Directory of Associations, Market Share Reporter*, and other sources either produced by Gale or licensed by the company. Gale's *Business Insights: Essentials* is a useful one to remember because it is one of the few business databases found in public libraries.

ReferenceUSA has the very unusual distinction of being equally at home in public and academic libraries. It is actually a suite of databases, not just one, but is usually primarily known for its company directory database. The company database has entries and information for companies down to the very smallest enterprises, and a sophisticated Custom Search for creating lists of companies based on a wide variety of criteria. The other databases-within-the-database offer more than we can go into here, but it is likely that either your school or your public library system subscribes to *ReferenceUSA*. Go and take a look for yourself.

Business research is an area that deserves a whole book unto itself, and indeed, there are a number of such books available. My particular favorite is Celia Ross' *Making Sense of Business Reference* (American Library Association Editions, 2012), an excellent, down-to-earth resource for beginners through professionals.

Exercises and Points to Consider

1. I'm looking for articles or anything about movies that had librarians in them—surely *Library Literature* would be the place to find out? Try going to the Thesaurus and searching for "librarians in film." Can you spot the right heading? (What happens if you try searching for "librarians in movies" in the Thesaurus?) See what happens if you had started by doing a keyword search on "librarians in movies" (don't use quotes). How many results do you get? When you don't get many results from a keyword search, always remember to look at the subjects associated with the results. You should see the heading you spotted earlier in the Thesaurus. Click into the record that has just "Librarians in Motion Pictures" as a Subject, then click the linked Subject. You should get the same results you did when you did your search from the Thesaurus.

2. Search example 2 in *Library Literature* was about chat services as part of the Reference function. Go to the database, reproduce the suggested searches, then compare the results with what you get by simply typing in Reference chat as a keyword search and, if you want, applying one or more Subjects that you discover in the Refine panel. To take a devil's advocate role here: aren't these results just as good as those that we retrieved with a much more elaborate search? Carefully compare the results—are there any records not found in the last set (the keyword search here) that really would have been bad to miss? Not to undermine the more sophisticated techniques that this text has been encouraging you to learn, but the reality is that most people simply do a keyword search, and in some—perhaps many—cases, that approach does the job. When it doesn't work, you need to be ready with better techniques. Message: Don't get rigid, either about what you're seeing, or what you're doing.

3. Say that you want to catch up on what's being written about information literacy classes in college or school libraries (whichever you are more interested in). Rather than using the Thesaurus, you simply do an Advanced search on "information literacy" (with the quotes) in Keyword, AND "college" [or "school"] in Subject, and let *Library Literature* do the work of informing you about appropriate subject headings by observing what comes up under Subject in the left panel of the Results screen. What is the Thesaurus term for this kind of teaching? Pick a subject heading under the Subject suggestions and see how it affects the number of results. Try adding a keyword, such as "evaluation," to your last search. Finally, go into the Thesaurus and look up "information literacy." What can you learn about this term?

4. One last quick search in *Library Literature*: as discussed in chapter 1, a hot trend in database searching is to search many databases (and other resources) at once using a Discovery Service search.

What is the latest news in *Library Literature* on "discovery services"? What is the subject heading that seems to be used most often for this topic? (Note: it is an unfortunate choice. Federated search systems were totally different from Discovery Services: they queried each database at the time of the search, and thus could only deal with a limited set of databases, and they were *agonizingly* slow. Discovery Services are a vast improvement.)

5. In the first Search example for ERIC, we used a very structured approach, carefully checking the Thesaurus before deciding on our search terms and setting up the strategy. Compare that with the following much less structured approach. Try simply searching either or both of these variations:

   Teaching the deaf

   (deafness or "partial hearing") AND ("teacher education")

   How do the number of results compare? What do you think about the *precision* (relevance) of these results? If you had started with one of these searches, what would you immediately start doing to increase the precision of the results? (Note: "recent" doesn't necessarily mean more relevant.)

6. It is likely that your school has access to ERIC via a commercial vendor. Repeat all the example searches in that version, observing the differences between the free and the fee versions. Leaving aside any familiarity and comfort-level issues you may have with the commercial version's interface, how do the search experiences compare? Do you get the same results sets? How easy is it to get to full text? (And of course, the commercial versions allow you to output your results in various ways, which the free ERIC doesn't.)

7. (Questions 7 and 8 are structured for *PsycINFO* via Ovid. If this interface is not available to you, see Question 9.) Your sister recently had a baby, and is upset because the baby's sleep patterns aren't settling down at all. She wonders if the baby has some kind of sleep disorder, and if it's going to affect her (the baby's, not the mother's!) development.

   You start by going to *PsycINFO* and typing in "sleep disorders" (without quotes).

   That maps directly to a subject heading, but you're curious about what might be included "under" it, or near it in the Thesaurus list. Click the subject heading to find out.

   Now look down through the list. Hmm—"Sleep Onset"—that's kind of the problem. What lies beyond that in the list? Oh look! "Sleep Wake Cycle"! That sounds good. Select that, and click its Explode box. Click the Continue button.

   Next term: type "infants" in the search box, and see what comes up on the Mapping Display.

   "Infant Development"—that looks good. Select that and Continue.

Now combine those two searches by ANDing their search set numbers together.

Do you like the results?

8. A friend has a child with Asperger syndrome (a form of autism) and is worried about how this could affect his verbal and writing skills, that is, his language development. In *PsycINFO*, what happens if you search and then combine Aspergers Syndrome (this is how the term appears in *PsycINFO)* and Language Development? (You don't get very many.) Maybe we could "widen our net" on the "Language" aspect of the search. Type in the broad term Language, and see if the Mapping Display offers more subject headings that we could use. Choose several.

Now combine this new (very large!) set with the Aspergers Syndrome set. It should result in more results than before.

9. I choose to demonstrate *PsycINFO* on the Ovid platform to expose you to a very different interface and approach to the search process. If your institution subscribes to *PsycINFO* from another vendor, go to your version and experiment with the same searches we created here. Can you recreate them? How is the experience different? Do you get different results? How do you access the *PsycINFO* Thesaurus, and is anything about the display (order of material, labels) different from the Ovid display? (See the web companion for screenshots of the Ovid display, and for a hint on how to achieve a similar search in the EBSCO version.)

10. As you compare what is discussed about these databases with what you see on your screen, you will undoubtedly spot additional features or functionality not mentioned here. Figure out what these other features or functions do, and ask yourself why they were included. Think about which users would most benefit from [feature X], and how you might market it to them (i.e., get them to use it). Discussing this as a class or in small groups will help to generate more ideas as you bounce ideas off one another.

Consider doing this Exercise for every chapter that discusses specific databases in this book.

Beyond the Textbook Exercises

Exercises using databases from the Additional Resources section are available on the Student Resources tab at http://www.abc-clio.com/Libraries Unlimited/product.aspx?pc=A4596P.

Notes

1. Grey literature is material that has not been commercially published, but that has scholarly value: papers presented at conferences, progress reports, working papers, technical reports, lab notebooks, student papers, curriculum guides, etc.

2. As of March of 2014, the ERIC database and thesaurus are freely available for download, which may encourage even more vendors (or anyone with database expertise) to offer this database.

3. Hint: there's no need to count.

4. http://www.apa.org/pubs/databases/training/field-guide.aspx.

6
Databases for Science and Medicine

The databases in this chapter, besides being intrinsically interesting and well-crafted systems, provide a view into their respective disciplines that goes beyond their content. Obviously, medical databases index medical material, and science databases index scientific publications. But the two subject databases considered here are functionally quite different, and I believe the difference reflects a basic tenet of each discipline.

Every discipline or profession has its own language: a specialized vocabulary is one of the things that unites and defines a profession (think of all the jargon we use in libraries). In almost no area is this truer than in medicine: a major part of the study of medicine is mastery of its language. The language is crucial, and *the* medical database, PubMed, reflects this. One of the key components of PubMed are MEDLINE records, which are distinguished by their detailed system of subject headings and subheadings for *terms*, painstakingly applied by trained professionals. We will see in PubMed that the system will do its best to translate whatever terminology you enter into subject terms, as well as search your terms simply as words. Consider this as you experiment with PubMed, and see if you agree: the basic tenet here is a focus on *"what."* Medical terms represent *"what"*: what organ, what condition, what symptoms, what drugs, and what outcome.

In contrast, the approach taken by the scientist who developed the *Science Citation Index* (and later similar indexes for the other disciplines) was that the *citations* were of paramount importance: the references associated with scientific papers. To me, this represents *who*. *Who* was cited? *Who* was citing? Although it is used in other organizations, the *Science Citation Index* is a very *academic* product, and in academia, a great deal rides on who you are (which you establish by publishing your work) and who has recognized your work (by citing it). You will find that the *Web of Science* citation indexes do not use subject headings (in the sense that we've seen so far) at all.

93

Another way this difference in emphasis (what versus who) is reflected in the functionality of each database is the way they arrive at "Related records." In PubMed, an algorithm based on words (what) identifies related records. In the citation indexes, shared citations (who) identify related records.

As you work through this chapter and become familiar with these databases, keep this idea in the back of your mind: that medicine is focused on what (terms) and the citation indexes are focused on who. See if you can spot additional aspects of the databases' functionality to support it.

PubMed and MEDLINE

It's easy to know where to start a consideration of medical databases: it has to be PubMed, the über medical database freely available to the world on the Internet at http://pubmed.gov. PubMed is developed and maintained by the National Center for Biotechnology Information (NCBI), at the U.S. National Library of Medicine (NLM), which is part of the National Institutes of Health (NIH). The difficulty is knowing where to stop: the major component of PubMed is MEDLINE, a huge, immensely detailed, highly specific, and sophisticated resource for an elite professional field, and PubMed extends this resource to be even larger and richer in its content. Let me declare right here: this text is not going to attempt to teach you to be a medical researcher. If you get a job in a medical library, you will receive thorough training from professionals in the field. Instead, in the spirit that you can achieve *something* reasonable, no matter what the subject area, by employing the same basic strategy (i.e., engaging in a reference interview, using your searching techniques, and keeping your eyes open), what follows will be a demystifying look at doing medical literature searching through PubMed. Like ERIC, many commercial database vendors offer this content, but the government also provides it freely to everyone who can get online (and PubMed still offers sophisticated searching capabilities). The idea that the most respected resource in the area of medical research is freely available to everyone is really quite staggering.

As noted above, a major component of PubMed is MEDLINE (Medical Literature Analysis and Retrieval System Online), the detailed journal citation database focused on the life sciences that is produced by the NLM. Everything about MEDLINE is vast: the number of journals covered, the number of source countries, the total number of records (which grows daily), and especially the detailed indexing applied to every MEDLINE record. This indexing is a key distinguishing feature of this database: the *Medical Subject Headings*, or MeSH, thesaurus system is probably as famous as MEDLINE itself. A whole branch of the NLM is devoted to continuous maintenance, revision, and updating of the MeSH vocabulary.[1] The impression one gets is that this is a dynamic system, continually growing and changing in response to developments in scientific and medical research and practice. For more details about MEDLINE, see the Student Resources tab at http://www.abc-clio.com/LibrariesUnlimited/product.aspx?pc=A4596P.

An important thing to remember about the MeSH terms applied to MEDLINE records is that indexers are instructed always to choose the most specific terms available. Although there are broad terms such as "Digestive System Diseases" at top of the MeSH hierarchy, if an article is discussing a specific malady, such as Crohn Disease, *only the more specific term* will be applied as a heading. All the layers of headings between Digestive System Diseases and Crohn Disease (e.g., Gastrointestinal Diseases, Gastroenteritis, and Inflammatory Bowel Diseases) would *not* appear as additional subject headings. So you have full permission to enter very specific terms here.

PubMed: More than MEDLINE

As a database of medical citations, think of PubMed as what you'd get if databases were like hamburgers: "Give me MEDLINE—and super size it!"[2] PubMed goes beyond MEDLINE in many ways:

- Newer material: PubMed includes "ahead of print" citations: records for articles that have not yet been published (tagged "Epub ahead of print"); and "in-process" citations: records for articles that have been published, but have not yet been indexed with MeSH. (All that detailed indexing takes time.)

- Older material: Date coverage for the MEDLINE database as offered through commercial vendors is generally from 1966 to the present, but PubMed includes material back to 1945 and even older: as early as 1809.

- Additional material beyond the subject or document types in MEDLINE:

  o Citations for articles in journals otherwise indexed by MEDLINE, that were not selected for the MEDLINE database because of their non–life sciences content.

  o Citations to additional life science journals that submit full text to PubMedCentral®.

  o Citations to author manuscripts of articles published by NIH-funded researchers.

  o Citations for both the entire work and each chapter of "the majority" of ebooks available on the NCBI Bookshelf.

  (U.S. National Library of Medicine 2014).

Overall, be aware that PubMed is going in both directions, backward and forward.

PubMed is much more than a super-sized database of medical citations, however. It is also a portal to databases from the NCBI—of gene sequences, molecular structures, etc. ("Resources"), to "Tools" such as citation matchers and a special interface for clinical queries, and to "More Resources" such as the MeSH database and the government's Clinical Trials website. It's huge, first-class, professional information, and it is freely available on the Web. I'm afraid we won't do more than touch the surface of the possibilities here, but

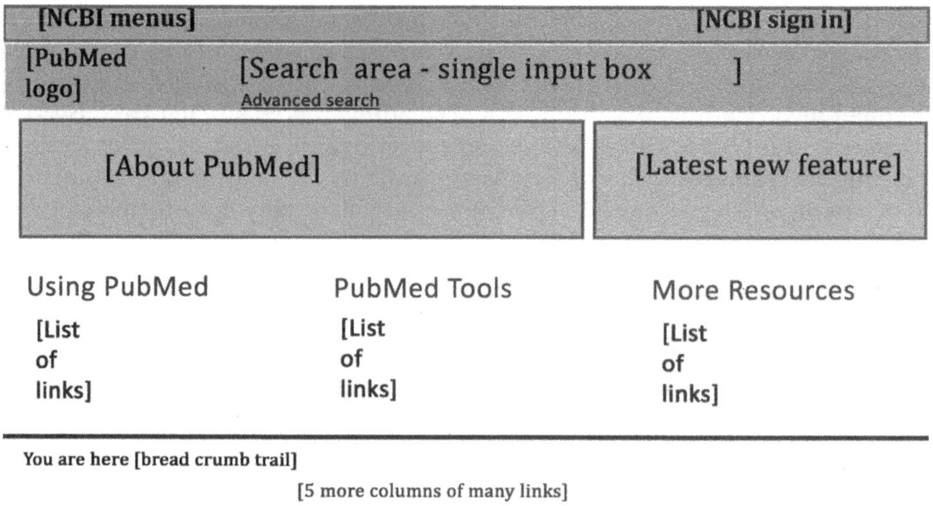

[NCBI menus]		[NCBI sign in]
[PubMed logo]	[Search area - single input box] Advanced search	

[About PubMed]	[Latest new feature]

Using PubMed	PubMed Tools	More Resources
[List of links]	[List of links]	[List of links]

You are here [bread crumb trail]

[5 more columns of many links]

Figure 6.1. Schematic of PubMed home interface, as of June 2014.

at least you'll now know that it exists, and you can explore further when and if the need should arise.

Introduction to the PubMed Interface

Let's take a look. Get online and go to: http://pubmed.gov. What a clean, neatly laid out page! The topmost blue bar is devoted to the wider world of NCBI: Resources, how to use them, and "Sign in to NCBI"—again, you are being offered a personalized experience and a way to carry results over from one search session to another. Then the search area: one Google-box search field with an "Advanced" option link just below it. (Note: this text will work only with the basic search.) A bold banner area provides descriptive information about what PubMed is and the latest new feature, followed by three categories of links below. The guide and tutorial links under Using PubMed in the first list are excellent; one of our search examples will make use of the citation matcher function in the second list, and if you are interested in searching the MeSH database, it's first in the More Resources list. If you keep scrolling there are many more links in small print below the blue bar (which obviously represents "below the fold" for this page). Figure 6.1 presents a schematic view of the PubMed homepage.

Notes and Search Examples

This section will take you through four types of searches: a topic search, a simple field codes search, a known item search, and an author-subject search.

Search Example 1: A Topic Search

Our first search in PubMed is looking for material on heart failure in young adult women: a "topic" search. (Note: this condition, also known as

---

Sidebar 6.1

Beware the trap of expectation that because PubMed is a free Web resource and is apparently easy to use that somehow the content will be "easier." Not in the slightest. As noted in the opening discussion of this section, PubMed contains the highly sophisticated MEDLINE database content, plus additional material not indexed by MEDLINE, and links to advanced scientific resources such as the NCBI genome databases. In other words, despite the fact that this is a free Web resource that is open to the world, this may not be the place for the average mortal to try and find an answer to a medical question. If you are working with a health professional, researcher, or student in the health sciences, yes, this is the place. If you want to help your mom or your neighbor find some health information, go to MedlinePlus.gov.

---

congestive heart failure, is common in older women but unusual in young adult women.) Starting from a very simple keyword search, we will learn some ways to focus our results using the Search details information and Limits.

As we start typing the word: heart in the search box, the system starts offering us "suggestions," a la Google and many others. Note that although I use the term "suggestions," these are really just things other people have searched for: they are not recommendations or in any sense better. They can be handy, and they might give you ideas, but don't feel as if you have to choose any of them over your own terminology. If you find the suggestions distracting, you can turn them off. The suggestions include "congenital heart disease" and "congestive heart failure" among others. We will just type our concepts, however: heart failure women.

This produces a daunting set of results, but fear not. We will learn why there are so many, and how to bring the number down to something more manageable (and on target). Look down the results screen and find the Search Details "portlet" shown in Figure 6.2. The system is telling you how it interpreted your search. Clicking the "See more . . ." link produces a full interface to this information, also shown in Figure 6.2.

The Search Details screen provides a full Query Translation, the total number of results, the Translations for each phrase or single word, which database was searched (because there are a number of other biomedical databases available here besides PubMed), and your original "User query." Both "translation" areas show us immediately why there are so many results: heart failure and women were searched as subject headings (since they happen to be MeSH terms), plus they have been searched simply as words in "All Fields," with a lot of ORing going on. We can start learning from this information and focusing our results right here. We could search the appropriate terms only as MeSH Terms—but then we are losing out on all the extras, all the newer material available in PubMed.[3] So let's not do that. We'll just create a new search query that is slightly smarter than our first one. Note that Boolean operators are always entered in caps:

"heart failure" AND women

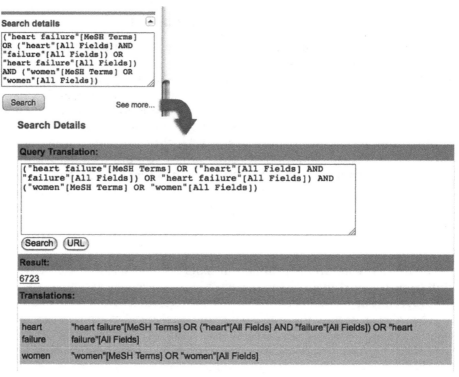

Figure 6.2. Search details "portlet" and full Query Translation screen in PubMed, as of June 2014.

We click the Search button and our results are reduced somewhat. Now to apply some Filters.

Hopefully you already noticed that something was going on at the left side of the results screen. Just like the EBSCO interface, ERIC, and in the Web of Science later in this chapter, there is an emphasis on refining or "filtering" your results on the results screen (rather than upfront in the search), and like the other interfaces, the PubMed filter options are listed on the left side of the interface.

As of this writing, the default filter options displayed were:

- Article types

- Text availability

- PubMed Commons (Reader comments)

- Publication dates

- Species

For this particular search, none of the default filters look very useful: what we really need is a way to get at the *age* of the women being studied or reported on. Time to see what's available behind the "Show additional filters" link. And indeed, there is a filter for Ages, and since it's frustrating to discover a result in a language one can't read, I'm going to also choose to

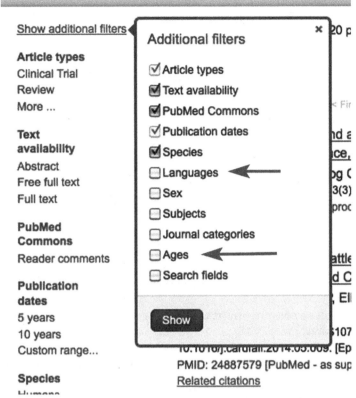

Figure 6.3. Choosing additional filters to display in PubMed, as of June 2014.

display the Languages filter so I can limit the results to English (Figure 6.3). Adding the filters for Language and Ages to the left side display, I can now choose English and the Adult: 19-44 filters. (If I decide those aren't the best filters, I simply click them again to turn them off.)

This reduces our results to 1,600, which of course is a still a great many. The next step would be to determine what *about* heart failure in young adult women—the effects of exercise? diet? simply the incidence? and add that additional concept to the search.

The newly applied filters and initial results are shown in Figure 6.4. Several aspects of the display have been highlighted. You can change the Display Settings (arrow), something you might well want to do because the default sort order for displaying the results is by "recently added," which is *the date the citation was added to the database*, **not** the publication date. In this case, I have left it at the default (*A*), but don't hesitate to open the Display Settings and change the order to Pub Date. It can make a difference in the initial results. We will come back to (*B*) Send to: when we discuss output, and just note that any filters you have applied are echoed back to you, along with the option to clear them all (*C*).

PubMed provides a number of useful features on the right side of the screen in addition to the Search Details box. What is offered changes

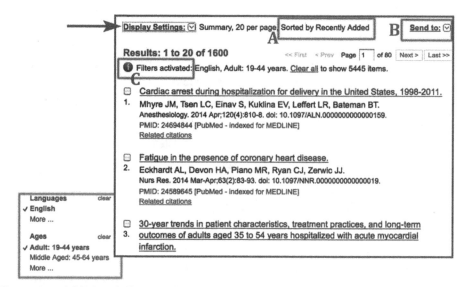

Figure 6.4. Additional filters applied and results in PubMed, as of June 2014.

depending on the search, but at the time of this writing could include any or all of the following:

- New feature (highlighting any recently added functionality)
- Results by year (bar chart of publication activity, downloadable in CSV format. Useful if you were analyzing research activity on a topic.)
- Find related data (in another NCBI database)
- Related searches (search suggestions)
- PMC images search (images from PubMed Central)
- Titles with your search terms (One of the best ways to get a quick list of articles on your topic that you can mine for additional search terms, no matter what their publication date.)
- [Number] free full-text articles in PubMed Central (open access articles)
- Recent activity (your search history; allows you to jump back to the results from a previous search)

Experiment with some different searches and see what interesting and informative options come up on the right side of the screen.

Search Example 2: Searching with Field Codes (and More)

Search 1 was all very well, but what if you wanted just a quick and dirty way to get a few on-target results? Rather than figuring out ways to focus a huge set of results, you could then take the approach of "Learning from your results" from the best items in a small set to learn headings or other terms so you can create a new strategy that retrieves more, but still on-target, items. Our second search example will demonstrate the use of the title field code in a PubMed search string to specify that terms be searched only in the title field. Using field codes is like setting a drop-down menu to a particular field.

Field codes are always encased in square brackets, and the field code for the title field is pretty obvious: [title]. You can spell it out, or use the two-letter version (and look extra-cool to your friends): [ti]. You can use truncation and other search operators (parentheses, Boolean, phrase quotes) with field codes. To look for articles on burnout in the nursing profession, we might enter this search:

nurs*[ti] AND burnout[ti]

in the PubMed search box. Wow—at the time of writing, this search produced close to 550 results, and a quick scan shows it to be a worldwide issue (Malaysia, Iran, Brazil, Japan, Korea, China, Cuba and Cypress appear just in the first two pages of results). That scan of the first two pages (sorted by Pub Date) also shows that there aren't any articles that have been "indexed for MEDLINE" until the bottom of the second page. (That would be our way of learning some subject headings.) The best tactic at this point might be to add another term as a keyword: we're really interested in the *prevention* of burnout in nurses, so let's amend the search to:

nurs*[ti] AND burnout[ti] AND prevent*

The number of results is less daunting now, and seems on target. There are several ways this search could go from here:

1. We could look for a record that is marked "PubMed—indexed for MEDLINE" and see what MeSH terms have been applied to it. We could then use those terms to build a new, highly structured, very precise search, but it would consist only of MEDLINE records. We would lose all the additional records PubMed gives us.

2. We could find a record with MeSH terms, but rather than searching the appropriate terms exclusively as MeSH headings, we could type in significant words from the headings, connecting them with AND.

3. Rather than either of the above, we could add "AND United States" to our current search (since that is the geography we are interested in) and simply start reviewing the results.

To experiment with these different approaches, enter the following (author) search in PubMed in order to retrieve a record with good MeSH headings to work with:

Fearon[au] AND Nicol[au]

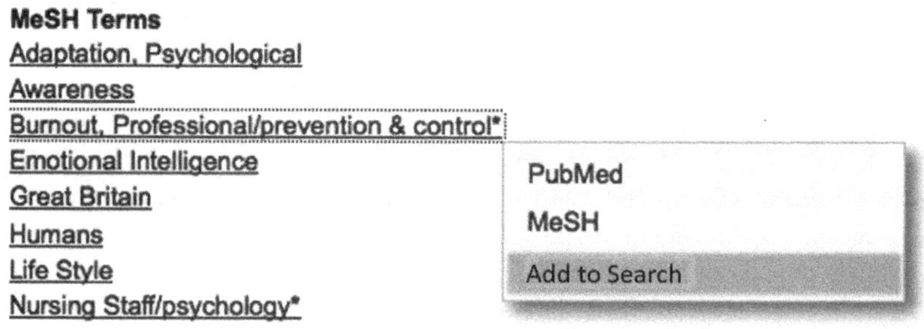

MeSH Terms
Adaptation, Psychological
Awareness
Burnout, Professional/prevention & control*
Emotional Intelligence
Great Britain
Humans
Life Style
Nursing Staff/psychology*

> PubMed
>
> MeSH
>
> Add to Search

Figure 6.5. Using the MeSH terms mini-menu in PubMed, as of June 2014.

In the record this search brings up, click on the area labeled MeSH Terms to see the headings assigned to this record. You'll discover that burnout (and its prevention) is such a common phenomenon that it has its own subject heading. Nurses are "Nursing Staff," and the country where this study was done is also listed as a MeSH term. If you click a MeSH term in a record, it brings up a tiny menu with the options to [start a new search in] PubMed, [look this term up in the] MeSH [database], or Add [the term] to Search (Figure 6.5). Use the "Add to Search" option for the Burnout and Nursing Staff headings. This represents option 1 above. How many results do you get? Focus your results on whatever country you want to by simply adding: AND "[country name]" to your search (e.g., AND "United States").

Now open a new window or tab, go to PubMed, and this time try searching the terms you learned about, but not restricting them to the MeSH field:

burnout AND prevention AND "nursing staff"

Again, how many results? Compare them to the other set of results—how do they compare in terms of precision? Which has the most recent results? Try ANDing in a country name to this search; again, how does it seem to affect the results? There really is no one right way to do these searches; it's a matter of trying various approaches until the results look appropriate for the information needed at the time.

Our next example is a common type of search: a citation search for a known (or half known) item that might turn into a topic search.

Search Example 3: A Known Item Search

Clicking the PubMed.gov logo always returns us to the home screen (Figure 6.1). In this search example we will use the Single Citation Matcher link (listed under PubMed Tools) to look up a known item. In this case, we are working with a person who has partial "known" information: she remembers that the title of the article mentioned tamoxifen and singing, and that it appeared in one of the PLoS (Public Library of Science) journals. Figure 6.6 shows this search ready to run (and the result); carefully note how the journal title has been entered: PLoS[space]* (wildcard), indicating any of the PLoS [Word] journal titles. Entering this as PLoS* (no space between PLoS and the asterisk) will not work.

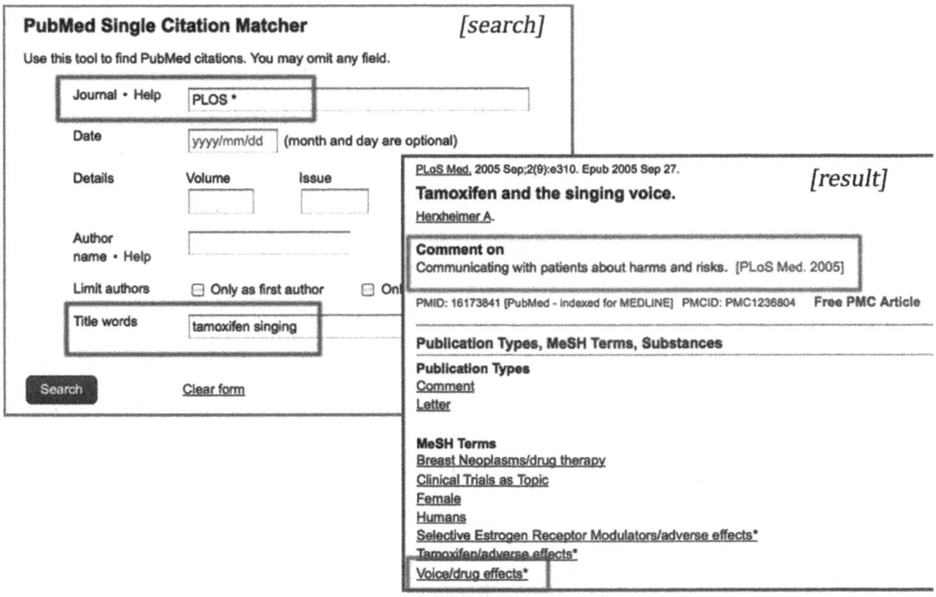

Figure 6.6. Using the Single Citation Matcher to find a known item and the result in PubMed, as of June 2014.

The result is what the person remembered (also Figure 6.6), and because it is a PLoS journal the full text is freely available. However, she didn't realize it was only a comment on another article (first rectangle in the "result" screenshot). Luckily, that article also appeared in *PLoS Medicine*, so the full text would again be available, or this might be the time to look at the MeSH Terms for this article and start a new search. And there is just the right MeSH term: Voice/drug effects. The patron could then add the name of a drug or a substance to the search box to focus the results. For example:

"Voice/drug effects"[MAJR] AND (estrogen OR "oral contraceptives").

Search Example 4: An Author-Topic Search

Our final search example is a type of search frequently done in medical research: an author-topic search. With the knowledge that author names are entered lastname[space]firstinitial (or two initials), and that the field code for author is [au], you can execute this type of search very easily and efficiently. For example, to find a set of articles that Mary Story, PhD, RD, authored (alone or with others) on the topic of obesity, we simply enter

Story M[au] AND obesity

This produces a set of 164 articles at the time I ran it—prolific author, Mary Story!

Now you have several strategies for searching in PubMed. We will leave discussion of the Advanced search screen to classes specializing in health sciences librarianship. It's time we took a good look at a complete record from PubMed, which will lead us into our last topics: outputting citations and getting to the full text.

A PubMed Record

Figure 6.7 illustrates the major components of a PubMed record. To see everything (I had to abbreviate parts for space reasons), get online and look up this record yourself: simply search "chocolate intake and incidence of heart failure" as a phrase in PubMed. The original article appeared in Circulation: Heart Failure (abbreviated Circ Heart Fail) in September 2010. (There is now a letter commenting on this article, complaining that the study is flawed. Give and take at work in scholarly discourse!)

In the upper portion of the record notice first that your search interface stays with you, even at the record level. To me, this is part of a trend to reduce clicks, to help you keep searching (and thus finding), to keep moving ahead rather than having to go back. Below that, looking across from left to right, you can control how the record is displayed (Display Settings), choose output options (Send to), and (perhaps) access the full text via the publisher's button. (More on this under Output.) Just below that are listed "Related citations in PubMed," which are related based on terminology. (Examine these, and store your impressions away, to compare with the "related results" you get from the *Web of Science* later in this chapter, where relatedness is based on shared citations in the papers' bibliographies.) Below that, you find that this article has been cited by "4 PubMed Central articles"—again, something to tuck away: the citation indexes in the *Web of Science* used to be the only game in town in terms of tracking who is citing whom. Back on the left, the bulk of the record consists of familiar things: the full citation and a detailed abstract. (The complete citation for the letter commenting on this article appears again just below the abstract under the heading "Comment in." This part of the record is not shown in Figure 6.7.)

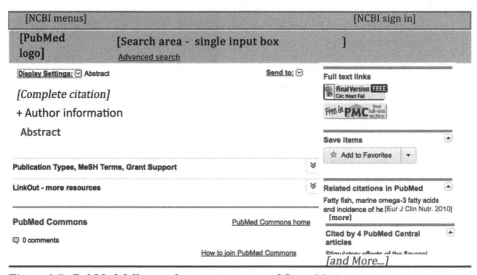

Figure 6.7. PubMed full record components, as of June 2014.

In the lower portion of the record are the two expandable sections "Publication Types, MeSH Terms, Grant Support," and "LinkOut - more resources." Click on the sections to open them. You'll see the incredibly detailed work of the NLM indexers in the full list of MeSH Terms applied to this record, and note the list of grants that supported this research. The LinkOut section provides links to known sources of full text, and note especially the link under the word Medical that goes to MedlinePlus Health Information. This is the stepping stone from the professional world of medicine (where the air may be a bit thin for us mere mortals) to information that is authoritative yet accessible. It's a very nice touch, I think. Finally, a section called PubMed Commons invites users to leave comments. (PubMed meets social media?)

Output in PubMed

The *Send to* link at the top of the record display offers a brief, telegraphic menu of choices (Table 6.1).

Table 6.1. Send To options in PubMed

Choose Destination	
File	Clipboard
Collections	Email
Order	My Bibliography
Citation manager	

File is analogous to "save" in many other databases: it will simply download and save the current record as a text file. *Collections* (and *My Bibliography* at the end of the list) are options available to those who create their own account in PubMed (known as "My NCBI" after the parent organization): again, the emphasis on personalized access, and long-term research projects. *Order* will be addressed in the next section, Getting to the Full Text. *Citation manager* will generate a generically formatted file that can then be imported into your citation management software of choice (RefWorks, EndNote, etc.). *Clipboard* is like the Folder in an EBSCO database: the place to store records during the course of a session, to be emailed or otherwise output en masse. The email option is self-evident. Now on to the murky world of accessing full text, often subscription-based, from a website that is not part of your institution.

Getting to the Full Text

Accessing full text in PubMed can present issues in certain situations. PubMed provides as many links as it can to full text, some of which are free (titles in the collection called PubMed Central and other open access journals), and others that are subscription based. If subscription based, PubMed will link directly to the publisher's website and to any other sources, as described earlier. If the local library has a subscription to one of those sources, and the user is onsite, access from the library or organization is thus "recognized" by the external subscription site, and the user will get the article he or she needs. If the user is offsite, but using something like virtual private networking (VPN) that makes them appear to be within the IP range of the organization, again, the user will connect seamlessly to the desired full-text article. The organization can also set up a customized access link to PubMed, which will then display the institution's link resolver service (for getting to full text) in every PubMed record . . . but the user has to go to the library site and use that link. When a user is offsite, has not used the institution's special link to PubMed, and is *not* running VPN—then things get complicated. In that case, the subscription site will not recognize the user, and he or she will be presented with a screen asking him or her to pay for access. The user would have to know to go back to the library's website, and either start the session again using the customized access link, or look up the journal name to see if the library has paid for electronic access, follow links from there into the journal, the right volume, issue, etc. It's much more complicated than most users are willing to master, remember, or put up with. Librarians are naturally bothered by the idea that their users are not getting to material that is actually available to them under the right circumstances. It is very hard to train people to use a special link—after all, it's so easy to simply type "pubmed.gov."

Of course, libraries can't afford to subscribe to every journal, so there will be plenty of cases where the subscription sites would ask a user to pay no matter what the circumstances were. This is what Interlibrary Loan (ILL) is for. But in PubMed ILL also becomes complicated.

Order

As mentioned earlier, there is an option called *Order* in the Send to menu. The Order function in this case will take the user to an NLM function known as Loansome Doc (cute or what?), which has nothing to do with the local library and will charge the user for document delivery. *Only* if an offsite user has accessed PubMed by way of the local, customized access link, and he clicks the icon for the link resolver service, will he get link(s) to the local ILL system. It makes life—tricky.

However, in both cases (full text that actually *is* available or redirection to the local ILL service) human nature works in our favor. Most people will balk at having to pay, and instead shoot an email to the library: "How can I get this?" It's a perfect opportunity for the librarian to either direct them to the local ILL service, or to make their day by informing them "we have this, and here it is."

Quick Recap

This part of the chapter has provided an introduction to the pre-eminent database of medical literature citations, PubMed. PubMed is part of a portal to scientific databases provided by the National Center for Biotechnology Information (NCBI), all of which are freely accessible online. The primary component of PubMed is MEDLINE, but PubMed also includes additional material: items older, newer, and beyond the scope of MEDLINE. MEDLINE is the product of the U.S. National Library of Medicine (NLM), and is an index to medical journals from around the world. A defining feature of MEDLINE is its thesaurus, known as "MeSH" (*Medical Subject Headings*). The search examples in this section demonstrated four ways to search PubMed. First, you can simply enter terms in the search box and then refine the results by applying filters (on the left side of the screen), looking at the options and suggestions on the right side of the screen, learning from those records, etc. Second, you can specifically search for words in article titles using the field code for title: [ti]. Third, the Single Citation Matcher interface is useful for looking up known, or partially remembered, items. Last, author-subject searches can be constructed using the author's name (in the form: lastname initial[s]) and the author field code: Smith JL[au] with a word or phrase indicating the subject. Overall, keep in mind that the PubMed search box accepts Boolean operators, parentheses for nesting statements, double quotes for phrases, and truncation. Remember to put Boolean operators in all caps (AND, OR, NOT).

PubMed provides links to full text whenever possible, to either free or fee-based resources. Users can encounter difficulties accessing full text from subscription services when they are using PubMed from outside their institution. It is possible to customize PubMed so that it provides linking services to local resources, but users must then access PubMed using a special, institutional link, which can be hard to train users to do.

Additional Resources for Medicine

Two additional resources for health professionals include BioMedCentral (www.biomedcentral.com) and CINAHL. Despite the .com web address, BioMedCentral is an open access publisher, and provides free full text access to over 250 peer-reviewed journals in biology and medicine. PubMed indexes all of the journals published by BioMedCentral.

CINAHL (*Cumulative Index to Nursing and Allied Health Literature*) is always (and appropriately) described as the "premier indexing and abstracting database for nursing and allied health literature" (Marcin 2006, Bardyn 2009). A database with a venerable history, it started life as a print index in 1956, went online in 1984, and has survived and thrived ever since. Originally a grass roots effort at the Glendale Adventist Medical Center, Cinahl Information Systems (CIS) was acquired by EBSCO in 2003, which has enabled CINAHL "to expand and implement" new ideas (Bardyn 2009). In addition to new features and content, EBSCO has added four additional subscription options for this database since 2003: *CINAHL with Full Text*, *CINAHL Plus, CINAHL Plus with Full Text*, and *CINAHL Complete* (released 2013).

CINAHL is unusual in many ways, from the breadth and variety of document types included (everything from journal articles to government publications, audiovisuals, and materials created by the CIS: quick lessons, evidence-based care sheets, etc.) to the degree that EBSCO has customized their interface for this database.

Both the Basic and Advanced Search screens offer access to three additional searches, of Publications, CINAHL Headings, and Cited References.

In addition, there are several special purpose Limits unique to this database, such as Clinical Queries (e.g., Therapy—High Sensitivity, Prognosis—Best Balance).

The Advanced Search interface has a "Suggest Subject Terms" option that functions quite like the Map to Subject Headings feature in Ovid's PsycINFO. Typing in a word or phrase with this option checked will bring up a screen of suggested subject terms and the options to Explode or have the term searched as a Major Concept (Focus in PsycINFO). The subject mapping in CINAHL goes further, however, by bringing up a list of subheadings for any subject term selected, providing the option to choose only certain aspects (e.g., Drug Therapy, Prevention and Control) of the subject term to search on. Quite different from any other EBSCO search I've ever encountered. (Relevant results are also completely possible with keyword searches, however.)

The provision of Cited References, and *citing* reference links, demonstrates again the importance of this approach to finding related literature. We will see this again in another EBSCO database, *America: History & Life* in chapter 8.

Health resources for consumers include Gale's *Health Reference Center Academic*, a database equally at home in academic and public library settings. Although generally marketed as a health information resource for the lay public, it definitely includes material for professionals as well.

First reviewed as a CD-ROM product in 1993, HRC has been receiving positive reviews since 1999. Described by the company as: "full text of nursing and allied health journals, plus the wide variety of personal health information sources," it actually goes much further, providing a range of reading levels with academic journals, magazines, books, and news, as well as images, audio, and videos. The single search box has four search mode options: Keyword, Subject, Publication Title, and Entire Document, and provides suggestions as you type. The type-ahead suggestions can be particularly valuable in the Keyword search mode, since choosing a system-supplied suggestion beginning with a capital letter turns your keyword search into a subject heading search.

The results pages offer typical refine options and limits, plus the fascinating (if somewhat mysterious), visual "Analyze term clusters" feature. One caveat about the results page: the results are grouped by publication type, that is, Academic Journals, Magazines, Books, and News. Only one publication type's results are shown at a time, and the Academic Journals results appear first by default. It can be disconcerting to do a simple search for "tmj" and be faced with results such as "A lectin from the green seaweed Caulerpa cupressoides reduces mechanical hyper-nociception and inflammation in the rat temporomandibular joint during zymosan-induced arthritis." A combination of publication type News and limiting by the Related Subject "Temporomandibular joint disorders" produces much more accessible, yet still authoritative, results.

There are actually a number of reputable free websites for consumer health now[4], but the one that was probably the first still leads the list: Medlineplus.gov, created by the National Library of Medicine at the National Institutes of Health, the organizations that also bring us PubMed. Medlineplus.

gov, is completely consumer-oriented, and offers a trove of accessible health information of all kinds. Included are essays on common health topics, which can be accessed as a complete list or by categories (Seniors, Men, Women, Children), medical dictionaries and encyclopedias, information about drugs, links to directories of doctors and hospitals, and an A-Z list of links to health-related organizations. Finally, what self-respecting website would be without a whole section of "Videos and Cool Tools"? Included here are Interactive Tutorials, Anatomy and Surgery Videos, Calculators and Quizzes, Games, and guides such as "Evaluating Health Information." (The material here really is pretty cool; I am very impressed at the ability of the creators of MEDLINE to meet the consumer on his own terms.)

The *Web of Science* and the Citation Indexes

Citations and the Academic Researcher

Now we're going to take off the stethoscope and get into the mind-set of the scholarly academic researcher. Think of yourself as Joe(sephine) Bloggs, PhD. When you write a scholarly paper, it almost always involves a literature review, or at least a process of consulting previous articles that you can quote to support various points throughout your paper. You are drawing on past knowledge in this way, building on the ideas of previous researchers and taking them further, or moving tangentially. If we look at your list of references, we can trace the lineage of your ideas back in time. For J. Bloggs, undergraduate, this is still a common and accepted way to get started writing a paper: to find a recent work that is related to what you want to write about and trace its references. This is fairly easily done, because the references provide the information about the other articles (accurately, you hope). However . . . there are works in every field that achieve the status of classic papers, which are cited by subsequent authors over and over again. As Carol Tenopir (2001) put it: "The power of citation searching lies in the capacity to take a seminal article and uncover who the author was influenced by (who was cited) and go forward in time to discover how that seminal research affected newer works (who is citing it)." What if you wanted to trace that evolution, that is, all the people who had *cited* a particular paper or book? A professor could hand you a classic work from 1985 and tell you: "that's the authoritative work in this area." What do you do with that? A place to start would be to see who has cited that work recently, and in what context. You want to trace the evolution of those ideas *forward* in time. How in the world do you do that?

An Index Focused on Citations

Brief History of the Citation Indexes

The concept of tracking and indexing not just articles, but the references associated with those articles, was the brainchild of Dr. Eugene Garfield, founder of the Institute for Scientific Information (ISI). From a concept first outlined in a 1955 article in the journal *Science*, the oversize, print, multivolume sets known as the *Science Citation Index* (1964–), the *Social Science Citation Index* (1973–), and the *Arts & Humanities Citation Index* (1978–) have been providing researchers with a unique and powerful way to trace the evolution and impact of ideas over time for 50 years. From print to CD-ROM to the Web, the *Citation Indexes* have gone from strength to strength. Acquired in 1992 by the Thomson Corporation, these three indexes are now all part of the *Web of Science*, an ever-growing suite of research tools offered by Thomson Reuters.

What it Means to Index Citations

The unique feature that the citation indexes introduced was simply that they retained and *used* the list of cited references for each journal article record added to the database. That had never been done before because of the size and complexity of the task (i.e. the one-to-many relationship between each article and its references). So rather than bibliographic records having only the usual fields of author, article title, journal name, volume, issue, year, the citation indexes also include a field to hold the article's bibliography. In addition, each of those references is also recorded in another part of the database as an independent, "cited reference" record, which can be searched separately. Thus the *Web of Science* databases have a dual nature: think of them as having one database containing journal article records *only*, and another database containing records for every item cited by those articles. The latter, the cited reference records, can be articles but also books, reports, unpublished papers, or whatever an author has cited in his article. (If your brain is starting to hurt, don't despair: it's actually surprisingly clear and easy once you get into the database.) What can you do with all this information?

Topic Searches and Tracing *Back* by Means of Citations

You can use the *Web of Science* databases just like any other indexing and abstracting product: to perform a keyword or field search to find articles on a particular topic, to find articles by a particular author, or to track down a specific article when you have only partial information. Having identified one or more articles, you can then see the list of references for each article. If that reference list cites other journal articles for which there are records in the database, you can immediately start tracking the ideas in a current article *back* in time.

Tracing Forward and Tracking Citations for Tenure

On the other hand, because the cited references are stored as their own searchable database, you can look up a particular work (of any publication type) and see which subsequent articles have cited it. Researchers look at this as tracking the development and influence of an idea from when it was first published to now—a way to bring research forward, from old to new. In addition to helping students and scholars in the process of writing papers, citation indexes also provide important—even crucial—functionality. Researchers use this database to find out who is citing their work, and in what context. In the "publish-or-perish" scramble for academic tenure in the United States, faculty who are up for tenure use these databases to show how many times their papers have been cited by others, which can be a key factor in proving their eligibility for tenure.

Relating Records by Citations

The *Web of Science* databases determine that records are "related" by their having at least one cited reference in common. Articles that both cite the same four, five, or more references are likely to be discussing the same topics. The *Web of Science* Related Records system is a completely different way to locate relevant papers on a topic that might not have been found with a traditional author or subject search. Think of it this way: this is about as close to "searching by concept" as opposed to "searching by words" as you can get. True, you start with a word search (to produce the initial results), but then, based on shared references—shared *concepts*—you can move into related intellectual territory. This is a powerful concept and tool.

Additional Differences in Fields Available

Present: The Address Field

The article records in the *Web of Science* databases also include an Address field, used to record where each author works. This is useful in several ways. From a librarian's perspective, it provides a quick way to get a sense of the total output of a particular department or person (if they publish in journals covered by the *Web of Science*) and what sorts of things they write about. Used in conjunction with the Analyze function (discussed as an advanced feature at the end of this chapter), it can be used to determine where your institution's faculty publish most frequently, and thus, which journals to lobby hardest for during a serials review. It allows an academic or corporate researcher to track what a colleague (or a competitor!) at a specific institution is publishing. The researcher could search on just an author name, or an author name combined with address (to disambiguate common names), to track known people. Using a keyword(s) and address search, the researcher could track the output of a department or unit at another institution, without knowing any specific names at all.

Absent: Subject Headings Fields

Finally, there is one thing that hasn't been mentioned about these remarkable databases. Did you notice? Having just discussed MEDLINE, where subject headings are crucial and heavily emphasized, here at the *Web of Science* we haven't mentioned them at all, because . . . the citation indexes don't use subject headings! Yes, it's true. All the databases we've discussed so far have used some kind of subject indexing, and I've made a big point of emphasizing it. Now we come to a set of databases that don't use subject terms at all, but that are every bit as powerful and compelling (if not more so) than the previous databases. The determination not to employ subject headings was another part of Dr. Garfield's vision. The labor- and thought-intensive process of having humans analyze each article and apply subject terms slowed down the production of the indexes too much for the needs of the burgeoning scientific research community. Such indexing also tends to be very subject specific, trapping work within one discipline and its terminology. Scientists were "recognizing that they had to be aware of, if not completely familiar with, work in a number of different subject disciplines" (Thomson Reuters 2014). Automating the process of creating a database of citations and using them as retrieval terms sped up the process of research and discovery, and allowed researchers to search across disciplines seamlessly. (There is also an advantage that in the sciences, paper titles tend to be more descriptive and express the true content of the work, thus providing a richer source of keywords for searching.) So, you will not find indexer-applied subject headings here. But I can almost guarantee you won't miss them.

Web of Science Coverage

In all, the *Web of Science* citation databases cover more than "12,000 high impact research journals worldwide" (Thomson Reuters 2014), and index the complete content of those journals. Depending on the subscription package, coverage can go back as early as 1900 for the Science Citation Index and 1956 for the Social Sciences. The "deep date" subscription is, as you can imagine, very expensive, so most institutions opt for access only back to a particular year, for example, 1987. A "1987 subscription option" means users can access *journal articles* back to 1987. They can look up a *cited reference* from any time period, but will only be allowed to see records for articles citing that reference that were published from 1987 to the present. Keep reminding yourself that these databases have two parts: the *cited references records*, which can be from any date, and the *journal article records*, which may be restricted depending on the subscription.

As you might imagine (if you haven't, you should), an undertaking of this size and complexity involves thousands of workers, incredible feats of programming, etc. It is big, and frankly, it's expensive. You are likely to find it only at major research libraries, but it's worth being aware of as part of your overall understanding of how research works, and how our current knowledge builds on past work. If you work in an academic environment, this is part of understanding the scholarly animal. Let's take a look.

Searching the *Web of Science*: Main Search Interface

Figure 6.8 shows the initial search screen for the *Web of Science* databases (the details will depend on your subscription, but this should be close). Compared to the interface shown in previous editions of this book, we again see a trend towards a spare and minimalist search screen.

Just one search box, with no immediate, visible clues that Boolean searching is available (Basic Tool #1), but at least they let you know you can "Add Another Field." There is a dropdown associated with that one input

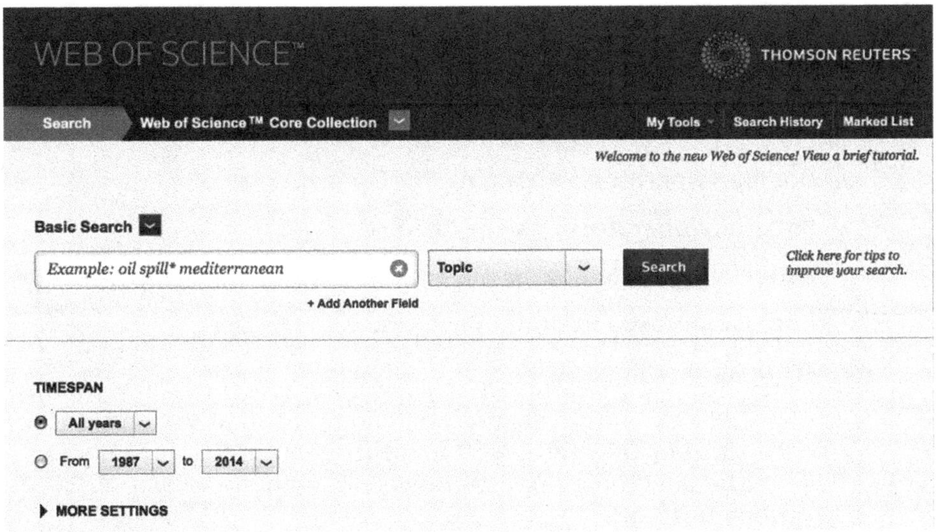

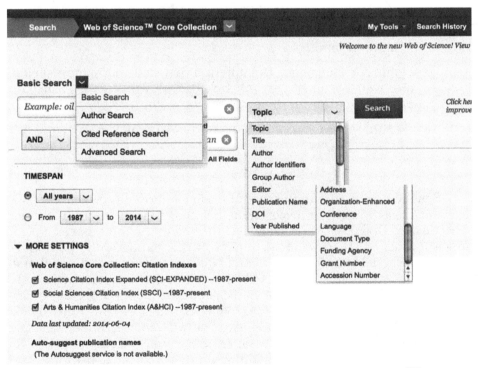

Figure 6.8. The *Web of Science* initial search screen. Web of Science™. © 2014 Thomson Reuters. All rights reserved.

Figure 6.9. View of all menus in the Basic search screen. Web of Science™. © 2014 Thomson Reuters. All rights reserved.

box, implying that we have fields to search (Basic Tool #3). The only other visible option is Timespan, so we do have at least one limit (Basic Tool #6). Oh dear—it really seems very limited. Is this going to be another ERIC-on-the-web experience? Thankfully, no: when you start opening menus, the hidden power starts to emerge as shown in Figure 6.9.

Sidebar 6.2

Here's an inventory of your Searcher's Toolkit for the Citation databases:

- Boolean operators: AND, OR, NOT
- Proximity operators: SAME, NEAR/#
- Order of precedence: NEAR/#, SAME, NOT, AND, OR
- Enclose phrases in double quotes.
- Truncation/wildcards:
  - *—zero to "many" characters, can be used at the end *or the beginning* of a term (left-hand truncation). Note: This cannot be used on a publication year search, for example, 200* does not work.
  - ?—substitutes for characters on a one-to-one basis, for example, ? = one character, ?? = two characters, etc. Can be used within a word or at the end of a word.
  - $—zero or one character only, for example, labo$r to get labor or labour
- Limits for Language, Document Type, and many more fields are available in the search box drop-down menus. *(You can even search by funding agency or grant number.)*
- No stop words: you can search for phrases such as "Vitamin A."

Sensibly, right next to the search mode you are in is the access point to change to a different form of search, including the essential Cited Reference Search. Opening the dropdown at the end of the input box you begin to get a sense of the meticulous quality of this database by the number and nature of fields available to search, demonstrating that Basic Tool #3 is definitely available. Clicking Add Another Field gives you another text input box, and the familiar Boolean dropdown menu also appears—phew! Basic Tool #1 accounted for. Clicking "More Settings" reveals that you can choose which of the Citation Databases you wish to search (i.e., one, two, or all three). That is it for the basic search screen. When you get to the Results pages, you'll find many additional limits you can apply to "Refine" your results.

I've noted some of the Searcher's Toolkit items in the discussion of the search interface earlier; see the Sidebar for additional details. Remember, though, there will be no Basic Tool #2 in this database: no controlled vocabulary.

We're going to start with a search on a scientific topic, so we'll leave only the *Science Citation Index Expanded* checked under More Settings.

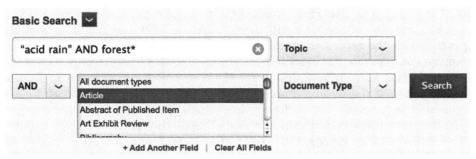

Figure 6.10. Setting up a topic search. Web of Science™. © 2014 Thomson Reuters. All rights reserved.

Search Example 1: A Topic Search

We'll get our feet wet with a simple search (Figure 6.10):

"acid rain" AND forest*—as Topic.

Add Another Field

Set drop-down menu on this second search box to Document Type, and then choose Article from the list that appears where the text box was.

Search Results

The power of the *Web of Science* really becomes apparent on its results screen, with options to Create [an] Alert, *12* ways to sort the results, various ways to output results including saving them to a citation manager (indicated by the menu beginning with EndNote, another Thomson product), Analyze Results, or Create [a] Citation Report. (If you can't get online, peek ahead to Figure 6.12 to see some of these features.) But the most prominent feature is the Refine Results panel on the left, with many options for refining your results, from Web of Science Categories[5] to Open Access (e.g., status: yes or no). Not only does it provide a chance to immediately refine your results by applying any of the limits listed, but by providing the hit counts for each one, you also get a sense of who writes on this topic most frequently, which journals are most important, and which institutions are most interested in this area. You don't need to know which limits you might want to use up front; you can decide afterward and then easily choose the ones that seem most promising. With this database's emphasis on citations, it's no surprise that the whole right side of the display is devoted to the Times Cited count, providing an immediate sense of the impact the papers are having on their field. (There hasn't been time for the newest articles to get cited, obviously.)

That initial search produced a lot of results, however, and really what we had in mind was material about acid rain and forests in the United States. Nothing could be easier: examining the Refine Results panel, we find we can limit by Countries/Territories, as shown in Figure 6.11. (Another approach that might not have immediately occurred to you would be to limit by the "Organizations" the authors are associated with: in this case, one might try the top two institutions listed, the U.S. Department of Agriculture and the U.S. Forest Service.) We will check USA and click the Refine button. As promised by the record count associated with "USA," we are now looking at a more manageable 211 results.

Selected parts of the first page of these results are shown in Figure 6.12: the top of the results display and part of the first result, which hasn't had time to be cited yet, and record 6, which *has* been cited. In only nine months since its publication in September 2013, this article has been cited— by articles in other journals indexed by the *Web of Science*—four times. This paper is making an impact.

You can look at the abstract of any record without leaving the results list by simply clicking the View Abstract button (*A* in Figure 6.12). After reading the abstract for record 6, we decide this is a good one, and we go into the full record display.

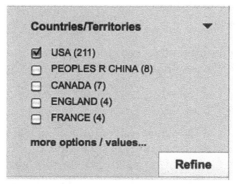

Figure 6.11. Refining the results by country. Web of Science™. © 2014 Thomson Reuters. All rights reserved.

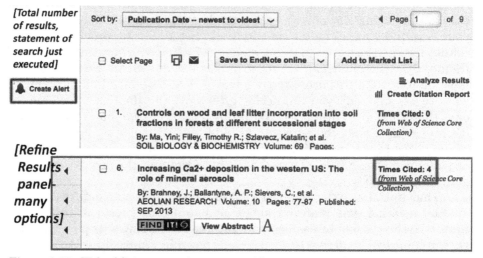

Figure 6.12. *Web of Science* results screen with annotations, highlights. Web of Science™. © 2014 Thomson Reuters. All rights reserved.

A lot of information is being presented here, but let us focus on the citation information. This is all gathered for us in the "Citation Network" panel on the right side of the screen, shown in the 3 clips in Figure 6.13. Included are:

- [##] Times Cited (link): in larger font and leading the list, obviously the most important data point

- [##] Cited References (link) for this article: the information next most often of interest to researchers

- View Related Records (link): remember these are related based on the number of citations they have in common. Take a look and see what you think about the efficacy of this way of "relating" results.

- View Citation Map: a visual representation of the cited references and citing articles surrounding this article.

- Create Citation Alert: be notified whenever the *Web of Science* adds a new article that cites this article.

- All Times Cited Counts: which *Web of Science* databases the citing articles came from. Note all the new *Web of Science* database products: the *Chinese Science Citation Index, the Data Citation Index, the SciELO Citation Index.*

- Most Recent Citation: shows the bibliographic information for the most recent citing article, with the option to View All (of the citing articles; this is really the same as the first link to "4 Times Cited." Are you getting the sense of how important being cited is?).

In the spirit of "you can learn a lot from the results page," let's return there and see who writes on this topic most often. Checking the names in the Author refine panel, someone named Likens GE leads the list with 16 out of the current set of 211 results (as of this writing). Does most prolific have any correlation with most cited? It's a snap to find out; we simply change the Sort by menu to Times Cited—highest to lowest. And indeed, an article by Likens GE leads the list, co-authored with Driscoll CT and Buso

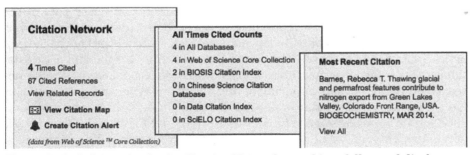

Figure 6.13. Information in the Citation Network panel in a full record display. Web of Science™. © 2014 Thomson Reuters. All rights reserved.

DC. "Long-term effects of acid rain: Response and recovery of a forest ecosystem." *Science* 272 (5259): 244–246, April 12 1996. At the time of writing, it had been cited 539 times! Obviously a very influential piece of research.

Search Example 2: An Author Search

Here's another example: say that you are familiar with Stephen Hawking's books but want a list of journal articles by him. We'll set the search field to Author, and, as prompted by the example that then appears right in the search box, enter the name as Hawking S* (no comma, and do not spell out the first name).[6] How many S Hawkings can there be? But we can add a second search box, set the search field to Address and enter: Cambridge to be sure that it's the person that we want. Your search should look like this:

Hawking S* → Author
AND Cambridge → Address

The results for this search indicate that Stephen Hawking is a prolific author, and that almost all of his articles are frequently cited, as well. If you can access this database, note too that there is great variation in how his name is listed: Hawking S. W., Hawking Stephen, Hawking S, and Hawking SW. By entering just his first initial with the wildcard symbol we easily retrieved all the variations.

Cited Reference Searching

Let's move on to the special functionality of this database: searching a *Cited Reference*. Navigate to the main search screen and click the menu icon next to the label Basic Search (Figure 6.9) to access the Cited Reference Search interface.

Cited Reference Search Example 1: Finding Articles that Cite a Book

Now let us say that you are interested in the classic book by James Watson, *The Double Helix*, in which he described the discovery of DNA. How many times has it been cited? Is it still being cited by current authors? In what contexts? This search is a perfect example of the dual nature of the *Web of Science* databases. By searching in the cited references part of the database, we can *search* for a publication that is both outside the year coverage (1987–current) and outside the material type (e.g., a book) of the journal article part of the database—but our *results* come from the journal article database, that is, articles that have cited that work. You can do a cited reference search on really ancient material, of any document type, and get results, as long as someone has cited it in a journal article since 1987 (or whatever year your subscription coverage begins). Ponder that, and Figure 6.14, for a couple of minutes: this can be difficult to get straight in your mind. We're not used to working with material that is outside of the stated year span of the database.

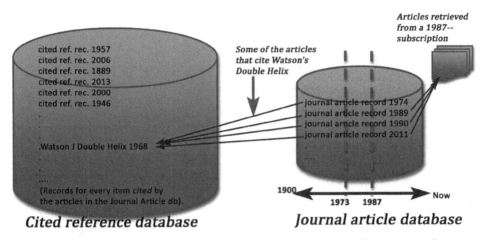

Figure 6.14. Conceptual drawing of what happens in a cited reference search.

Cited Reference Search Input

In this case, we will make use of all the fields provided in the Cited Reference Search screen and boldly type in the information as given. Later on, we'll work on an example that isn't as tidy or straightforward. (You might note that there is link to a Cited Reference Search tutorial handily placed in the interface; this link will follow you through the process.)

Type in:

Cited Author: Watson J* → Cited Author

Cited Work: double helix → Cited Work

Cited Year(s): 1968 → Cited Year(s)

Under More Settings, select all the databases: *Science, Social Science*, and *Arts and Humanities*.

This produces something called the Cited Reference Index, as shown in Figure 6.15.

Cited Reference Index Results

Yikes! A million variations! Is this all the same thing? Unfortunately, yes. This represents all the ways that people have cited this work in their bibliographies. 610 people cited it with both of Watson's initials and without any kind of page number or chapter reference, but the others ... did it differently. And every time somebody writes a reference a little differently (or even incorrectly!), that reference gets its own entry (in the actual interface, note the "Hint" in the instructions just above the results). Although Thomson does a lot of cleanup and normalization of references, it would be impossible to check and fix every reference for every article and still maintain the rate at which new material is added to the databases to keep them current.

CITED REFERENCE INDEX
References: 1 - 20 of 20

| Select Page | Select All* | Clear All | Finish Search |

Select	Cited Author	Cited Work [SHOW EXPANDED TITLES]	Year	Volume	Issue	Page	Identifier	Citing Articles **	View Record
☐	WATSON J	DOUBLE HELIX	1968			5		1	
☐	WATSON J	DOUBLE HELIX	1968			35		1	
☐	WATSON J	DOUBLE HELIX	1968			77		3	
☐	WATSON J	DOUBLE HELIX	1968			183		1	
☐	WATSON J	DOUBLE HELIX	1968			222		2	
☐	WATSON J	DOUBLE HELIX	1968			CH22		2	
☐	Watson, J. D.	DOUBLE HELIX	1968			256		1	
☐	Watson, James	DOUBLE HELIX	1968			197		1	
☐	Watson, JD	DOUBLE HELIX	1968					610	
☐	WATSON JD	DOUBLE HELIX	1968			13		2	
☐	WATSON JD	DOUBLE HELIX	1968			20		1	
☐	WATSON JD	DOUBLE HELIX	1968			68		1	
☐	WATSON JD	DOUBLE HELIX	1968			107		1	
☐	WATSON JD	DOUBLE HELIX	1968			116		2	

Figure 6.15. The Cited Reference Index display for Watson's *Double Helix*. Web of Science™. © 2014 Thomson Reuters. All rights reserved.

As a result, materials that are frequently cited produce results lists like this one. Don't panic; now you know why.

Getting to the Articles Doing the Citing

Luckily, 30 variations is no problem: we can simply click the Select All* button to grab them all, and then click the Finish Search button. Now we are presented with the articles that have cited this classic work, with the most recent ones listed first.

Amazing! What an array: subject areas from Art to Zoology (literally: click the "more options/values . . ." link for Web of Science Categories in the Refine Results panel, and then sort the list alphabetically). Here are six articles selected from the first two pages of results that demonstrate the range of disciplines referring to this work, and the international scope of the journal list.

- One hundred years of inorganic crystal chemistry - a personal view
  Baur, Werner H.
  CRYSTALLOGRAPHY REVIEWS 20(2): 64–116 APR 3 2014

- Local context, academic entrepreneurship and open science: Publication secrecy and commercial activity among Japanese and US scientists
  Walsh, John P.; Huang, Hsini
  RESEARCH POLICY 43(2): 245–260 MAR 2014

- SCIENCE AND ART IN TRIBUTE TO FRANCOIS JACOB
  Dosne Pasqualini, Christiane
  MEDICINA-BUENOS AIRES 73(6): 547-551 2013

- On beauty and truth in art and science
  Carafoli, Ernesto
  RENDICONTI LINCEI-SCIENZE FISICHE E NATURALI 24(1):
  67-88 MAR 2013

- Life Forms: Elizabeth Bishop in "Sestina" and DNA Structure
  Rogers, Janine
  MOSAIC - A JOURNAL FOR THE INTERDISCIPLINARY STUDY
  OF LITERATURE, 43(1): 93–109 MAR 2010

- Research education shaped by musical sensibilities
  Bresler, Liora
  BRITISH JOURNAL OF MUSIC EDUCATION, 26(1): 7–25 MAR
  2009

On to one more cited reference challenge . . .

Cited Reference Search Example 2: Using the Cited Work Index

Getting back to Stephen Hawking, say that you'd like to see who has been citing his book *A Brief History of Time* recently. (The book was published in 1988.) This is basically like the previous cited reference search. We would start at the Cited Reference search screen and enter the author's name, in the correct way, and the year the work was published, as shown in Figure 6.16.

Title Abbreviations and the Cited Work Index

Why was the Cited Work field left blank? In the previous example we put it in (*Double Helix*). Why not here? The book is called *A Brief History*

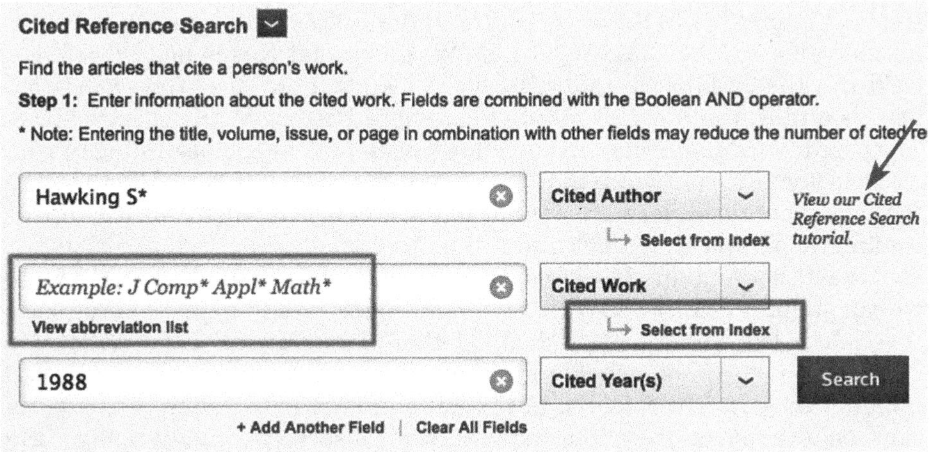

Cited Reference Search ▾

Find the articles that cite a person's work.

Step 1: Enter information about the cited work. Fields are combined with the Boolean AND operator.

* Note: Entering the title, volume, issue, or page in combination with other fields may reduce the number of cited re

| Hawking S* | ✕ | **Cited Author** ▾ | *View our Cited Reference Search tutorial.* |

↳ Select from Index

| Example: J Comp* Appl* Math* | ✕ | **Cited Work** ▾ |
View abbreviation list

↳ Select from Index

| 1988 | ✕ | **Cited Year(s)** ▾ | Search |

+ Add Another Field | Clear All Fields

Figure 6.16. Setting up the Cited Reference search for Hawking's *Brief History of Time*. Web of Science™. © 2014 Thomson Reuters. All rights reserved.

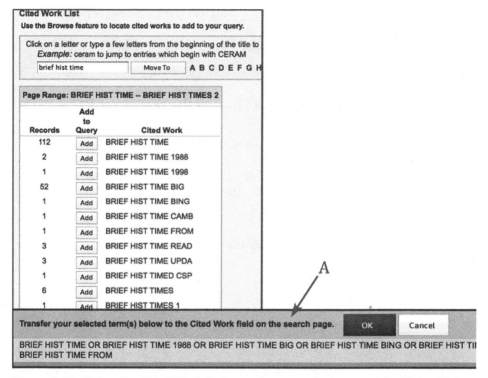

Figure 6.17. Using the Cited Work Index to choose variants on a title. Web of Science™. © 2014 Thomson Reuters. All rights reserved.

of Time, right? Well, yes, and it also has a subtitle: *From the Big Bang to Black Holes*. The issue here is that we have a Work title that is potentially many words longer, and this database is very big on abbreviations. *Very* big. Almost every cited reference title will be abbreviated in some way,[7] and it's a very, very bad idea to try to *guess* the abbreviation. (Although you might use truncation successfully.) Note the Example hint in the Cited Work search box and helpful links to the journal abbreviation list and to "Select from Index," highlighted in Figure 6.16. The Index allows you to search or browse all the values in the Cited Work List. We know that this is not a journal, so we'll use the cited work index. Because I know how this story comes out, here is a hint: the favorite way to abbreviate History in this case is "Hist." The Cited Work Index very nicely allows us to type in the beginning of what we're looking for and jump to it in the list. If we jump to "brief hist time" in the index (because there are a great many other "brief hists," as it happens) we find the list partially pictured in Figure 6.17.

We'll choose a number of variations,[8] and what a handy system this is: we can simply click the ADD button for each one, and it appears in the selection field below, intelligently ORed together (*A* in Figure 6.17). A click of the OK button inserts this whole string into the appropriate field in the search screen. Performing the search now results in another amazing list of variations on a theme on the Cited Index screen. Observe the many, many variations on how authors have entered Hawking's name and the name of his work in their bibliographies (the rest of the different entries were generated by authors who put a specific page or chapter number in their citation to this work).

As mentioned before, basically what appears at the end of an author's article is what goes into the cited reference part of the database. Remember Reference Desk Rule No. 1: citations are *never* quite accurate. If you don't believe that yet, try this: look up Hawking S* as a cited author (without any other fields filled in). Browse forward through the screens, noticing that some people referred to the book by versions of its subtitle (Big Bang, Black Holes), to the entries beginning *Breve Hist Temps* (aha—this book was translated into French—and *Brevisima*—Italian!) and beyond. Note the many variations in titles and year (probably different editions), and this is only the Hawking S section of the list! Imagine what might be waiting when you get to the two-initial part of the list.

Pause and Think

Again, take a moment to ponder this: all of these entries represent articles that *cited* this book. There is no general record for this book in this database, because it doesn't index books. There is no record for the thing itself, but endless records that refer to it. Isn't that rather interesting? Exploring the world of scholarship is lovely, but ultimately, of course, you want to identify some records and do something with them. On to output options.

Email, Print, Save, or Export Results

Marking and Outputting

The process for outputting records from the *Web of Science* is fairly straightforward, with one slight twist. Like PubMed, if you can determine which records you want to print, email, or export to a citation manager from the information given in the results list, you simply check-box those records, and then choose what to do with them using the icons or menu just above the results (shown in Figure 6.12) as you do with the Sent to menu in PubMed.

However, should you move off a page on which you've selected some records before doing something with them, the system quietly makes sure you don't lose them by adding those records to the Marked List. These records then appear with a new icon (an orange check mark) in the results list, and they are no longer "recognized" by the immediate output options on the results screen, that is, the Print or Email icons won't instantly recognize that you want to send just records 5 and 8 if those records have been added to the Marked List. If you've been marking things and moving from screen to screen of your results, you must go into the Marked List to output them.

Output From the Marked List Screen

The link to the Marked List appears in the upper right part of the screen following the links to My Tools and Search History.

The Marked List screen shown in Figure 6.18 is rather busy because it is offering you as many options as possible for handling your output,

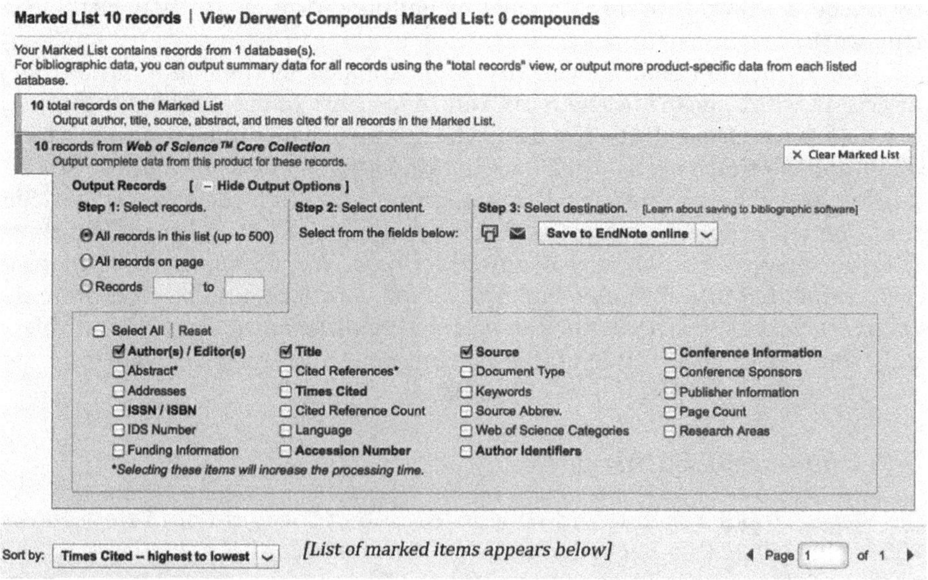

Figure 6.18. The Marked List interface. Web of Science™. © 2014 Thomson Reuters. All rights reserved.

especially which fields to include in the output. The list of marked articles begins at the bottom of the screen; by default it is sorted by Times Cited—highest to lowest. (Noted only because it again demonstrates the emphasis on and importance of *being cited*.)

The email function is good: it lets you put in your address for return address and add a note to explain why you're sending the information. If you are sending results to someone else, being able to have your email address appear as the sender rather than a strange system-generated email address from the vendor makes the message look less like spam.

Advanced Features: Advanced Search and Analyze

Advanced Search

The Advanced Search screen offers options for you real search hackers out there: searching with field codes and detailed syntax, or manipulating sets from your search history—somewhat like the experience we had in Ovid's version of PsycINFO. (You can also access your Search History in the upper right of any screen, next to the Marked List link.) Highlights of these features are shown in Figure 6.19.

Analyze Results

In everyday usage of the *Web of Science* (searching for articles or tracing citations), you probably won't find yourself using the Analyze Results feature that frequently. However, for tracking publication patterns or doing

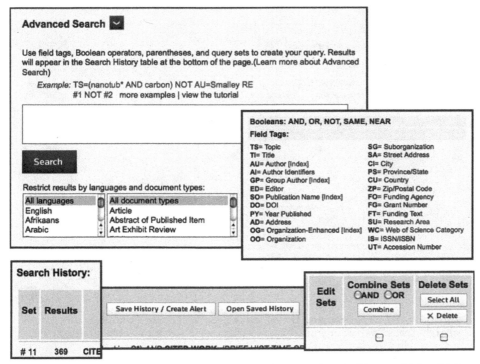

Figure 6.19. The Advanced search interface, including Search History. Web of Science™. © 2014 Thomson Reuters. All rights reserved.

general research on scholarship (e.g., Who is doing it? Where—in what countries, by which organizations? What journals are they publishing in? What subject categories does this department publish in?), the Analyze function provides a fascinating tool.

For example, searching for:

informat* studies SAME Milwaukee

in the address field retrieves articles published by members of the School of Information Studies at the University of Wisconsin-Milwaukee. If we Analyze these results by Research Areas, the majority are, as we might expect, classed as Information Science/Library Science. But other subjects are represented too, particularly Computer Science, which is quite interesting (Figure 6.20).

Quick Recap

In the second half of this chapter, we looked at the *Web of Science* databases: three citation indexes representing science, social science, and arts and humanities. The driving idea behind these databases is that *citations*, both citing articles and cited materials, are an efficient and effective way of doing research and seeing how various lines of research relate to and build

Results Analysis

<<Back to previous page

174 records. ADDRESS: (informat* studies SAME Milwaukee)

Rank the records by this field:	Set display options:	Sort by:
Languages Organizations Organizations-Enhanced Publication Years **Research Areas**	Show the top `10` Results. Minimum record count (threshold): `2`	⦿ Record count ○ Selected field

Analyze

Use the checkboxes below to view the records. You can choose to view those selected records, or you can exclude them (and view the others).

➔ View Records ✕ Exclude Records	Field: Research Areas	Record Count	% of 174	Bar Chart	Save Analysis Data to File ⦿ Data rows displayed in table ○ All data rows (up to 200,000)
☐	INFORMATION SCIENCE LIBRARY SCIENCE	145	83.333 %	▬▬▬▬▬	
☐	COMPUTER SCIENCE	95	54.598 %	▬▬▬	
☐	HISTORY PHILOSOPHY OF SCIENCE	10	5.747 %	▪	
☐	SOCIAL SCIENCES OTHER TOPICS	8	4.598 %	▪	
☐	BUSINESS ECONOMICS	4	2.299 %	▎	
☐	EDUCATION EDUCATIONAL RESEARCH	4	2.299 %	▎	
☐	MEDICAL INFORMATICS	2	1.149 %	▏	
☐	SOCIAL ISSUES	2	1.149 %	▏	
➔ View Records ✕ Exclude Records	Field: Research Areas	Record Count	% of 174	Bar Chart	Save Analysis Data to File ○ Data rows displayed in table ○ All data rows (up to 200,000)

Figure 6.20. Example of using the Analyze Results feature to rank results by Research Areas. Web of Science™. © 2014 Thomson Reuters. All rights reserved.

on each other. Unlike every other database considered in this textbook, the three citation indexes making up the *Web of Science* have no human-applied controlled vocabulary.

The *Web of Science* databases have a dual nature. One aspect is an article database, which you access through the main search page. This database of journal articles can be searched by topic (keyword searches), or by author, journal title, the author's address, or several other field choices. Records produced by such searches include both the list of all works cited by the article (its bibliography, in highly abbreviated form), and links to more recent articles that have cited that article. Each article record also has a link to related records, which are identified based on the number of cited references they share.

The other side of the dual nature is a database of records of every item cited by the articles in the journal article database (their *cited references*). This set of records is accessed using the Cited Reference search, which allows you to search for current articles that have *cited* a particular work from the past. The original cited work can be any material type, not just journal articles, and it can be from any date. Since the titles of the works in these citations are stored in a highly abbreviated format, it is important to either use the lookup indexes to pull up citations (and variations) correctly, or to make heavy use of truncation.

Altogether, the *Web of Science* databases are a quintessentially academic product, reflecting the importance of citing the work of others, publishing in the "highest impact" journals, and most importantly, getting cited. Tenure decisions—and thus an assistant professor's whole future—often depend on the latter two items; this is serious business.

Additional Resources for Science

While the *Web of Science* is a towering product, it is actually not alone in its "space" of tracking research by citations, although the competition arrived on the scene much later. "About two years" before 2004, Elsevier, a major publisher based in the Netherlands, realized they had an opportunity (Manafy 2004). They could leverage their existing A&I databases, notably EMBASE, the ScienceDirect archive of Elsevier journals and their "partner publishers' archives" (Jacsó 2004), MEDLINE, and the web sites from their Scirus product, enabling researchers to "browse, search, and navigate all science literature and all of the related information on the Web" through one interface (Manafy 2004). "All" they needed to do was enhance their A&I databases with cited references and they'd have a product to go head to head with the *Web of Science*. As Péter Jacsó said in his pre-release review, adding the cited references "must have been a massive project" (Jacsó 2004) but still, the overall product was built on existing materials.

The result was *Scopus*, which Elsevier launched in November 2004. From the perspective of 2007, François Libmann said that with this product, Elsevier "clearly had Thomson's *Web of Science* in its sights" (Libmann 2007). Trying to compare these two giants in the space of a few paragraphs is unrealistic, but we can at least list some basic facts and make some observations.

Features that are similar in both resources:

Table 6.2. Similar features in *Web of Science* and *Scopus*

	Citation tracking/ Searching	Author identification	Journal "impact" tool(s)	Analysis tools	Visualization
Web of Science	Cited Reference Search	Researcher ID, users can link their ORCID[a] identifier	Journal Citation Reports (JCR)	Analyze (15 options), *h*-index, InCites	Citation Report, Citation Mapping
Scopus	Citation Overview/ Tracker	Author ID, users can link their ORCID identifier	Journal Analyzer, SNIP, SJR[b]	Author Evaluator, *h*-index	Can view results as line charts or tables

[a] Open Researcher and Contributor ID; non-profit organization that aims to solve the author/contributor name ambiguity problem in scholarly communication by creating a central registry of unique identifiers.
[b] *Scopus*' journal impact metric alternatives to WoS' JCR. SJR = SCImago Journal Rank, SNIP = Source Normalized Impact per Paper.

The *Web of Science* has a definite advantage with their journal impact system, the *Journal Citation Reports* (JCR), because it has been on the scene for much longer and is considered the gold standard in the measurement of a journal's "impact" on its subject field. WoS is also frequently referred to as a better tool for institutions to analyze their research activity/impact (HL-WIKI Canada 2014, Schnall and Jankowski 2014). *Scopus*' option to create on-the-fly line graphs of selected aspects of your results does help you visualize at a glance output, impact, etc., putting it perhaps a notch up on the "snazzy feature" dial.

Differences between the two products:

Table 6.3   Differences between *Web of Science* and *Scopus*

	Web of Science	*Scopus*
Size and document types	Not as big, not as broad, but deeper and more consistent. Materials indexed are journals, conference proceedings, and highly cited book series.	Bigger: more journals, conference papers, plus books, patents, scientific websites; a wider variety of document types. "Scopus is 5–15% smaller prior to 1996, and 20–45% larger than WoS after 1996. For publications before 1996, the coverage offered by Scopus for the various subjects is uneven." (HLWIKI Canada 2014)
Cited reference coverage	Includes cited references for all records and has from the beginning (Core Collection has over 100 years of cited reference records)	Originally provided cited references only for materials from 1996 on; now engaged in project to add cited references to records from 1970 to 1995.
C-to-C?	For journals covered, coverage is cover-to-cover	Coverage not necessarily cover-to-cover
"Internationality"	WoS' latest offerings are regionally focused: South America (SciELO) and China (Chinese Science Citation Index)	More international journals (47% Western Europe, 32% North America [Vucovich 2014])
Home base	ThomsonReuters is based in NYC; offices all over the world	Elsevier is based in the Netherlands; offices all over the world
Topic weighting	All three major topic areas are strong, consistent, and deep.	Much more emphasis on the life and health sciences; social sciences fairly strong; arts and humanities are a much more recent addition.
Controlled vocabulary	Does not use a human-applied controlled vocabulary system	Uses (several) controlled vocabulary systems for the life, health, and physical sciences; but not for the social sciences or arts and humanities.
Age	50 years old in 2014	10 years old in 2014

My sense from the reviews, comparisons, and observations recorded by the library community (LaGuardia 2005, Libmann 2007, Salisbury 2009, Schnall and Jankowski 2014) is that WoS, while definitely covering fewer journals than *Scopus*, is deeper, more thorough, and has more clearly defined boundaries in terms of coverage. Because of the longstanding commitment to the three citation indexes, WoS is equally strong in all three areas: science and technology, social science, and arts and humanities. It has simply been in existence (and survived) for much longer. Scopus has overall a much bigger footprint with its higher numbers of journals indexed, and its inclusion of more document types including websites, but its coverage is definitely weighted in certain areas. This is especially true in the life and health sciences, since it builds on the advantage of other, existing Elsevier products (e.g. EMBASE, ScienceDirect). Following the lead of most reviewers, I would not dare recommend one over the other; if financially possible (for two products that both run in the five-to-six figure category), it would be great to have both.

ScienceDirect is also an Elsevier product; a full text database of all the extremely high quality, scholarly journals published under the Elsevier and North Holland imprints. For an additional fee, access to some or all of the Elsevier ebooks (handbook series, reference works, etc.) can also be part of an institution's subscription package.

Elsevier publishes over 2,500 journals, giving them plenty of material to make a "single publisher" database. Although weighted towards the physical, life, and health sciences (hence the database name), Elsevier does also publish in the social sciences and humanities; titles in those areas make up about 20 percent of the ScienceDirect database. Many of the Elsevier titles in business and economics are the premier publications in their field.

Since this is all Elsevier's own material, one of the interesting benefits is that they provide access to articles in advance of their being published in print (e.g., articles from a September issue being available in June), and articles still in the pre-publication stage, indicated by notes such as "In Press. Corrected Proof" or "In Press, Accepted Manuscript." This in addition to all-full-text-everything, your choice of three search modes, and decent refinement options on the results page make this a database that is very attractive to undergraduates and seasoned researchers alike. The one anomaly is that the ScienceDirect interface, despite being a commercial (and very expensive) product, includes advertisements, which strikes me as very odd.

AccessScience from McGraw-Hill is a full text online encyclopedia of science and engineering from one of the stalwarts of the reference and textbook publishing world. Building on the content of their print reference books, the 14 volume *McGraw-Hill Encyclopedia of Science and Technology*, the annual *McGraw-Hill Yearbook of Science and Technology*, and the single volume *McGraw-Hill Dictionary of Scientific and Technical Terms*, the publisher has added biographies of well-known scientific figures, suggestions for further study, links to primary source literature, articles from *Science News*, and resources for faculty such as curriculum maps. Embracing the possibilities of a digital resource, *AccessScience* also offers downloadable images, animations, and videos.

All of the encyclopedia entries in *AccessScience* are signed, and written by practicing scientists, including a number of Nobel Prize winners. The entries are not dated, however, and a 2008 review expressed concern that the entries were not as current as they should be (Turner 2008). There are now "Research Review" entries that are clearly dated, however, and are also authored by authorities in the field. The 2008 reviewer also found her search results to not be as relevant as they should be; this has evidently been addressed. Performing the same searches now produces excellent, on target results. This kind of responsive, dynamic change seems to be typical; going by the content of reviews over the years, since the database was first introduced in 2000 features have come and gone or been re-labeled, new material and functionality have been added, etc. As a non-scientist myself, I find this resource very easy to use yet very authoritative, it never feels "dumbed down."

After all these fee-based resources, let us end with one free commercial database, and two free web resources with long histories, that look likely to continue to thrive. Each of the websites is central to the researchers in its discipline.

- GreenFILE, from EBSCO. Like LISTA, GreenFILE is one of EBSCO's open access databases: freely available at http://www.green infoonline.com/. As the promo page says, this database "Cover[s] all aspects of human impact to the environment" (EBSCO 2014).

- arXiv[9] (www.arXiv.org), hosted by Cornell University. Provides e-prints in all areas of physics, plus some mathematics, computer science, quantitative biology, quantitative finance, and statistics. Physicists generally do not need (or know of) any other database.

- CiteSeer (citeseerx.ist.psu.edu), hosted by Pennsylvania State University. CiteSeer is to computer scientists as arXiv is to physicists. If you didn't have subscriptions to IEEE Xplore and the ACM Digital Library, between this website and Google Scholar (discussed in chapter 11) you could get along fairly well. Computer scientists are as familiar with CiteSeer, if not more, as they are with the commercial products from the IEEE and ACM.

Exercises and Points to Consider

1. In PubMed, start typing in male pattern baldness. Something that other people have searched seems to be male pattern baldness treatment. Choose that suggestion. Your result set should be more than 10,000 records. Come up with some strategies for focusing and refining this search.

2. In PubMed, try searching for: trigger finger guitar*. How many results do you get? How might you adjust this search to find some more on this topic?

3. Still in PubMed, find the record for an article from *Movement Disorders* that has "right hand of a guitarist" in the title, and take a look at the 'Related citations in PubMed' links. If you have access to the *Web of Science*, find the same record there (again just by searching

that phrase in the Title field), and take a look at the Related Records there. Going solely by the titles produced in each case, what is your impression of how well the different databases' "relatedness" function works? PubMed relates articles by a word algorithm, and *Web of Science* does it by number of shared citations. Does either approach seem to produce more related results than the other? (Gut impression only; no research required.)

4. For fun and amazement: at PubMed, change the search drop-down from PubMed to All Databases. Put in any term you want (diseases are good, as are substances: chocolate, coffee, wine, beer). You'll see the number of hits in each database for your term. Even if you have no idea what most of these resources represent, this is fascinating! (You can always click the "?" to get a fairly understandable description of the database content.)

5. A search scenario: You are applying for the position of librarian for physics and astronomy at the (name of university here). You want to make points when you meet the astronomy faculty, and a good way to do that is to find out what they've been writing about. In the *Web of Science* you search for:

Topic: galax*

Address: (part of school name) SAME astron* (SAME state abbreviation, if needed to distinguish). How many results do you get? Which people are publishing most frequently? Try changing the Topic word (e.g., planet* OR "deep space") and searching again. Can you put together a picture of these faculty members and their research from your efforts?

6. In the *Web of Science*, look up Hawking S* as cited author again. Note the remarkable number of variations—lots of different years, in French, etc. Select only those entries where the citation seems to be odd or incorrect in some way, then "Finish" the search and look at the articles produced—interesting titles!

7. In WoS, start in the Basic search and search for Brown C* [a fairly common name/initial] as an Author. Then use the Refine options in the results screen to differentiate the results by subject area, by organization, etc. Experiment and familiarize yourself with all the possible options. See if you can get a list of results just for Carol V. Brown, who works in the computer science area (Hints: use only the Science and Social Science Citation Indexes, then look at the "more options / values" for Categories on the results page. Don't search for her full name or you'll miss a lot of records.) Now compare this to using the Author Search, which is specifically designed for this purpose (we did not go over this in the text, but you can figure it out). For the purposes of the Author Search, she's now at the Stevens Institute of Technology in Hoboken, NJ . . . but she was at Indiana University before that, and University of Oklahoma before that. (Hints: you can pick multiple organizations in that stage of the Author Search

process, and it will help to look at the "## Record Sets" on the results page to find all the materials from the right person.) How do your results (and the whole experience) compare between these two ways of identifying materials from a particular author?

8. Now that you've seen how difficult it can be to identify "the right" person with a fairly common US/UK name, try doing a search for: Liu H* as an author. When you see the number of results, it should show you why both WoS and Scopus spend so much energy on "author identification." The first name of the particular Liu I have in mind is Huan, he works at Arizona State University, and his area is also computer science, in particular topics around social media. Again, try this as a Basic, then as an Author search. If you didn't have this additional information, do you see how difficult it could be to "find all the papers by [PersonX]"? And even with the information, how it is still not a perfect process?

9. Now that you've finished this chapter, what do you think about the opening premise: that the medical database is about *what*, and the science database is about *who*. Do you find this valid? Did you see further evidence to support this theory?

Beyond the Textbook Exercises

Exercises using databases from the Additional Resources section are available on the Student Resources tab at http://www.abc-clio.com/Libraries Unlimited/product.aspx?pc=A4596P.

Notes

1. MeSH has its own website, at http://www.nlm.nih.gov/mesh/meshhome.html. Access to the thesaurus, really a database unto itself, and everything you could possibly want to know about MeSH is there, up to and including a photo of the members of the MeSH staff and a link to their biographies, an invitation to submit vocabulary suggestions, and a link to download your own electronic copy of the whole MeSH database.

2. For the latest numbers, see the NLM's Fact Sheet MEDLINE, PubMed, and PMC (PubMed Central): How are they different? At http://www.nlm.nih.gov/pubs/fact sheets/dif_med_pub.html.

3. Among other reasons for not limiting yourself to just MEDLINE citations, this can make a big difference depending on where you are in the calendar year. The NLM stops adding records to MEDLINE during November and December, while maintenance is done on the database. During that time, and at the beginning of the new year while they race to catch up, you'd miss out on a potentially significant body of literature.

4. The Ocean City Free Public Library guide to Health & Medicine Resources has an excellent list of "World Wide Web Resources." See: http://reference.oceancitylibrary .org/health.

5. Alert readers who examine the topics listed under Web of Science Categories may find those listings looking suspiciously like subject headings. But you've been told there are no indexer-applied subject headings in this database. What's going on? Web

of Science Category is the subject category of the *journal* that the article appeared in, a value decided once and then applied automatically every time a record is added from that journal. Also, in a full record display you may notice "Author Keywords" and "Keywords Plus." Author Keywords are exactly that: author-supplied terms, a useful addition, but the addition of these terms did not slow down the process of getting the record into the database, and there is no controlled schema for them—they are simply whatever the author provided. Keywords Plus terms are automatically generated terms, representing words or phrases that show up most frequently in the titles of an article's *references*.

6. You don't *have* to use the wildcard; you can also use initials for both first and middle names, if you're sure that the author always uses the middle initial. While *Web of Science* is beginning to add spelled out first names, you are still better off using the FirstInitial* form, to ensure that you retrieve older and newer records. Not sure what Hawking's middle name is? Google for "Stephen * Hawking"—you'll be able to verify his name (and anything else about him) in no time.

7. In recent years they have loosened up and started writing out names and titles rather than the strict "first initials only" and publication name abbreviations, but still—your results will be much more complete if you adopt an "abbreviation mindset."

8. My favorite is "Brief Hist Time Bing" . . .

9. It's pronounced "archive"—the X is the Greek letter chi, pronounced "ki" (long "i").

7
Bibliographic Databases

From the beginning of this book, we have been focusing on "article" databases that serve an abstracting and indexing (A&I) function: databases that provide a means to identify (and often to supply) articles from periodical publications. In this chapter, our focus shifts to "bibliographic" databases, which we define as resources that provide information (mainly) about books. While A&I databases provide information about the contents of journals, and may include book chapters, conference papers, or other materials, bibliographic databases provide information about the contents of a particular library, or many libraries, or any collection of book titles (e.g., *Books in Print*, Amazon.com). Put another way, an A&I database is like being *inside* a collection of journals or books, seeing all the contents, while a bibliographic database is like being on the *outside*, running your eyes down the spine titles of everything (book, bound journal, video, etc.) sitting on the physical—and increasingly, virtual—shelves of a library or other collection.

You have undoubtedly used a bibliographic database many times already as a student or as a regular library user: every library's online catalog is a bibliographic database. Officially known as an Online Public Access Catalog (OPAC), the online catalog is how you find out about the contents of a particular library. If you think about it for any time at all, it's easy in today's networked, everything-is-on-the-Web world to see that it would be even more interesting if you could find out about the contents of other libraries without having to go to each of their catalogs and search. It would be incredibly useful to gather the records from many libraries and provide them as one massive "union" catalog. It would provide all the contents of all the libraries, searchable through one interface. This sounds like a totally natural idea now—but can you imagine having this vision in 1967? That is when Frederick G. Kilgour and university presidents in Ohio founded the *Ohio College Library Center* (Jordan 2003) in order to "share library resources and reduce costs by using computers and technology" (Helfer 2002). The original idea was to establish an online shared cataloging system, which

OCLC introduced in 1971, and an Interlibrary Loan system, which was introduced in 1979 (Helfer 2002). OCLC introduced the FirstSearch interface and access to several databases, including the union catalog, dubbed World-Cat, for use as a reference tool in 1991 (Hogan 1991). OCLC (the abbreviation now stands for *Online Computer* Library Center) was a brilliant idea, way ahead of its time.

Most of this chapter is devoted to an exploration of WorldCat and to its free Web version, WorldCat.org. We'll conclude with some suggestions and reminders about what to look for in your own local catalog.

WorldCat: The "OPAC of OPACs"

The OCLC website pulls no punches in describing WorldCat as "the world's largest and most comprehensive catalog" with over 72,000 libraries contributing to the database, representing 170 countries (OCLC 2014a). How was it, and is it, possible to put together and maintain such an enormous resource?

Background and Coverage

Note: in the following discussion, although it is always the same body of information being referred to, *how* it is referred to differs depending on the library context. To Cataloging and Interlibrary Loan (ILL) departments, this database is usually known simply as OCLC. To librarians and library users, the database information is presented via WorldCat. (The cataloging and ILL interfaces and programs for interacting with the database are very different from those in WorldCat.) When the discussion concerns Cataloging or ILL, the text refers to this resource as "the OCLC database." In the context of a database used by reference librarians and patrons, it is referred to as WorldCat. Again, it is all the same body of information.

Part of the brilliance of OCLC's vision for creating this far-reaching union catalog was to make it a distributed, cooperative effort, and one that had immediate benefit for those supplying the effort. The business model here is that libraries pay annual fees to be members of OCLC, as well as activity fees to search the database and download records for use in the library's local catalog. However, whenever a cataloger at a member library contributes a new record or improves an existing record, the library receives *credits*. The more the library contributes, the more credits it receives.[1] While an actively contributing library is usually also an actively "using" library (thus incurring more service fees), receiving the credits does help to keep the financial relationship from being entirely one sided. OCLC manages the contributed data and provides many services and benefits based on the database information. Thus, the OCLC database is built by catalogers at member libraries, already experts in their field, who would need to create records for their library's holdings anyway. By contributing their work, these member library catalogers offset the costs of searching and downloading records supplied by *other* member libraries. Everyone benefits in terms of time, effort, and efficiency. One of the great benefits is that this huge bibliographic collection is made available as a sophisticated database to reference librarians and patrons in the form of WorldCat, and it is freely available to the world in the form of the simpler WorldCat.org.

The scope of WorldCat is dazzling: as of this writing, the number of records in WorldCat has passed the 321 million mark, representing over two billion items in member libraries. There are works dating from before 1000 BC to the present, in nearly 500 languages. The records in WorldCat represent the whole gamut of material types, everything that the contributing libraries have cataloged: books, serials, manuscripts, musical scores, audiovisual materials (i.e., videos, DVDs, audiotapes, and other "sound recordings"), maps, and electronic resources (i.e., websites, electronic journals, e-books, etc.), and these are just the common formats. There is, literally, everything from stone tablets to electronic books, and more. As a collaborative, contributed effort, the database is updated constantly: according to the OCLC website, on average a new record is added to WorldCat every 10 seconds (OCLC 2014).[2]

A Tool for Many Parts of the Library

The OCLC database is both a creation and a tool of the *cataloging* department. Original catalogers create new records that get added to the local OPAC and to the OCLC database, while copy catalogers download preexisting records for the local OPAC and add the local library's holdings to existing OCLC records (a process known as *tagging*). As you might imagine, the OCLC database is also integral to the Interlibrary Loan (ILL) function. OCLC supplies several services that help to speed and streamline resource sharing by ILL departments (which certainly seem to work: the WorldCat facts and statistics also mention that a request is filled *every four seconds* via WorldCat Resource Sharing—OCLC 2014).

As a *reference* and *collection development* tool, librarians can use World-Cat to

- Explore new or unfamiliar topics presented in reference questions to get a sense of what is available in a subject area.

- Find resources in an area that their library is limited in.

- Find resources in a particular format.

- Find everything written by a particular author.

- Test the waters before encouraging a patron to request an ILL by seeing how many libraries own the item, and where those libraries are located.

- Identify government documents.

- Verify citations (for titles of books, journals, etc.), check publication dates, serial start dates, etc.

- Provide an interim solution if the local catalog is down (but the holdings are in WorldCat).

- Develop a collection by seeing what's out there on a topic, what other libraries own, and what they might want to buy.

Note that records for serial publications in WorldCat can include holdings records, that is, the dates of the journal run owned by the library. It has always been possible to use WorldCat to see if another library owned a particular journal, but until holdings records were added to the WorldCat records, there was no way to tell if that subscription was current or had stopped, say, in 1964. This is very useful for ILL staff, as well as reference librarians.

Notes and Search Examples

Let's get into the database, start looking for our Searcher's Toolkit items, and get a sense of how this database differs from the article databases. We have several lighthearted searches to try here in WorldCat. We'll go straight to the Advanced Search screen to begin (Figure 7.1). OCLC's database interface, known as FirstSearch, is quite dense with options and features. It is best if you access your school's subscription, and then use the schematic drawing here to interpret what you are seeing.

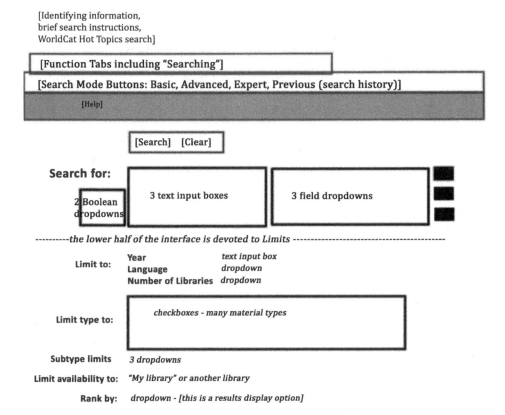

Figure 7.1. Representation of the WorldCat® Advanced Search screen, with major areas labelled.

Advanced Search Screen

The WorldCat interface includes several features that are different from what you typically encounter in an article database, which reflect its role as an access point to the contents of libraries. The immediately visible differences have to do with Limits and Ranking possibilities in the lower half of the interface. We can limit by the fairly typical Year and Language, but here is a brand new limit: Number of Libraries, that is, how many libraries own the item. The choices are 5 or more, 50 or more, or 500 or more. (Think about this one for a moment: What is the implication here? Why might you want to use this limit?) Rather than a drop-down menu of document types common in article databases, we have a whole section of the screen devoted to choosing *material* types (Books, Serials, Archival Materials, etc.). We can choose to limit our search only to the holdings of a particular library (i.e., the library that you are in, or another library that you indicate by an alpha code) using the options in the "Limit availability to:" area.

We also have new *Subtype limits* to define our audience, content, and format. Under audience, we can specify Juvenile or not Juvenile. Under content, we have options for Fiction, not Fiction, Biography, Thesis/dissertation, Musical recording, or Non-musical recording. The format options are Large print, Braille, Manuscript, Microform, not Microform, CD audio, Cassette recording, LP recording, VHS tape/Videocassette, and DVD Video/Videodisc. The options in these subtype menus say a lot about WorldCat as both a reflection of the content and as a tool for *public* libraries, which also distinguishes this database from the article databases in this book. Not that academia doesn't use WorldCat constantly; it does. But WorldCat is equally useful in any other kind of library, too: it's a database of all the libraries, for all the people. Quite an achievement!

Last in the display is a "Rank by" setting, which will control the order in which your results are displayed. The "Rank by" options are Number of Libraries (the default), Relevance, Date, or Accession Number. That the default for displaying results is Number of Libraries is another reminder that this database is all about the holdings of many libraries.

Moving back to the top of the screen, more differences become apparent when we compare the fields available for searching (the drop-down menus associated with the three text-input fields in the "Search for" section). The searchable fields in WorldCat are all about identifying books and other complete items that you would find on library shelves or, increasingly, digital items owned by libraries. There are many variations on Author (nicely gathered together and indented under *Author*), along with Publisher and Publisher Location, and specific Standard Number choices: ISBN and ISSN. WorldCat certainly has subject-related search fields, but subjects here are rather different: in addition to Subject, Subject Phrase, and Descriptor, we have Genre/Form, Geographic Coverage, Named Corporation and Conference, and Named Person. Subject is an excellent way to start exploring WorldCat, in conjunction with some limits.

Search Example 1: Finding Materials in Other Languages

You'd like to find some cookbooks for your friend's Korean mother, who doesn't speak English. Take a quick browse of the Subject index (available by clicking the black and white "up/down" button following the drop-down menus) to see the number of times each of the following has been applied as a subject: cooking, cookbooks, and cookery. You'll find that "cooking" has been applied in the overwhelming majority of cases. To be comprehensive, let's search for either cooking or cookbooks in the Subject field. We can then use our Language limit to limit to materials about Cooking in Korean.

Search for: cooking OR cookbooks → Subject

Limit to: Language drop-down: Korean

On the results page, notice the tabs above the results list, indicating the number of hits for each material type (e.g. Books, Visual, Internet, etc.). Note too that there are almost 3,000 records for cookbooks in *Korean*—isn't that incredible? Remember that the results are sorted, or ranked, by the number of libraries that own the item.

Search Example 2: Finding Materials for a Specific Audience

Your kids are beginning to show an interest in cooking, and you'd like to see if there are some cookbooks written for children.

Returning to the Search screen (the Searching tab is a good way to do this), we already have our Subjects in place. Any limits that you set previously will also still be in effect, so remember to change the language back to English. This is the perfect occasion to use that first Subtype limit, audience, to specify that we want materials for a "Juvenile" audience. The criteria for this search are:

Search for: cooking OR cookbooks → Subject

Limit to: Language drop-down: English

Subtype limits: Juvenile [first drop-down, change from default Any Audience]

There are plenty of options to explore, as indicated by the number and variety of formats shown in the Results screen—everything from Books to Internet[3] to (musical) Scores!

Speaking of the Scores tab—having that material type appear for this search seems peculiar. Whenever you see an odd result, don't immediately assume that it's a mistake. Take a good look at the record and see if you can figure out what triggered the retrieval. In a carefully crafted database like this one, where your search has been set up only in terms of subjects and field search values (rather than as a keyword search), it is highly unlikely that an odd result will be a false drop. By looking and figuring out why it's there, you'll add to your understanding of database lore in general, and you'll discover interesting and bizarre things that may bring a smile to your face (and remind you why this profession is so much fun).

The Descriptors and Notes fields are a good first place to check for clues. In this record (*Wee Sing for Halloween*) we immediately see that "Holiday cooking" is one of the subjects, and the Notes field tells us about the contents: "Songs, poems, finger plays, and recipes for Halloween." Now our Score result makes perfect sense!

Search Example 3: Finding Materials by Genre

Switching to a slightly darker vein, now we'd like to find some mystery novels with a science fiction theme.

We'll change the first field where we searched "cooking" as a Subject to the phrase science fiction and search that as a Subject Phrase. Then we'll add another field search to find materials with "mystery" in the Genre/ Form field. (Genre/Form is part of the indented list under Subject in the drop-down menu. Tip: tabbing to the menu and typing g will change the field to Genre; no mousing necessary.) Any limits that you set previously will also still be in effect, so remember to change the Subtype back to Any Audience.

Click into any of your results to experience a full WorldCat record (probably one of the longest and most detailed you will see in any database). Figure 7.2 provides a conceptual look at what is happening in a full record; compare it to what you see on your screen. Note the Amazon.com-like feature of providing the book cover and a brief blurb. In fact, the one record is really being offered two ways: the upper, generally eye-catching, easy-to-grasp-quickly section, and then the lower, nitty-gritty, all-the-details section: all the fields and their contents. Even when an image of the cover art is not provided, the basic citation information is set off in this upper section.

Search Example 4: Finding Materials on a Current Topic

Now for something a bit more serious: let's look for nonfiction materials on global warming that have been published recently. Checking the Subject Phrase index, we find that global warming is indeed a subject. For the Year limit, we'll look for the years 2012–2015. Finally, we'll set the Subtype limit to "not Fiction" to rule out science fiction horror stories. The complete strategy is:

Search for: global warming → drop-down: Subject Phrase

Limit to: Year: 2012–2015

Subtype limits: not Fiction [second drop-down, change from default Any Content]

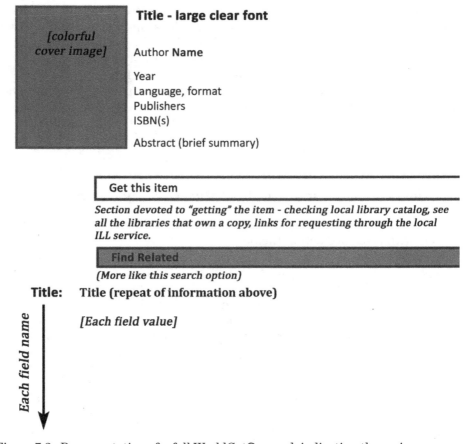

Figure 7.2. Representation of a full WorldCat® record, indicating the major areas.

The results are a dazzling array, as indicated by the tabs above the results. Books still lead the list, closely followed by Internet, but we have also retrieved Visual materials, Articles, Sound files, Archival materials, Serials, "Computer" files, a Score, a Map, and an "Updated Resource." Take a moment to explore and see what the records under some of the more unusual material types actually represent.

Using WorldCat for Citation Verification

WorldCat is also invaluable for resolving citation problems, such as determining what the *real* title of a work is, or its publication year, author, etc. You can use it to fill in information on books and other formats, or to determine what material type a title really is (i.e., a monographic series? A conference report? A serial publication?). WorldCat can be particularly useful for resolving questions about serial publications, especially esoteric titles or titles that have ceased publication (and that don't appear in a periodicals directory). If we know that something existed at some time, then it is likely that *some* library, somewhere, owns it, and chances are good that that library also contributes records to WorldCat.

Search Example 5: Finding Materials in Other Libraries

A student comes to the library service desk and says: "My professor said I should look at some journal—it's the British journal of clinical something or other, I can't remember . . . but she said she knows the library at SUNY Buffalo gets it . . ."

In doing any kind of citation verification or completion in WorldCat (or in an article database), the Searcher's Toolkit tools that you'll want to make good use of are the field indexes and truncation symbols. If at all possible, especially in tracking down journals, try to come up with the ISSN for the publication (or ISBN for books). Words are fuzzy and easily mistaken, but numbers don't lie. There is only one identifying number for every publication (exceptions exist, of course, but as a general principle you can depend on this). It's much more efficient and accurate to search by number than by name.

However, because we are unsure of the journal name, we can't determine an ISSN and look it up that way. Checking the Title Phrase field index for "British journal of clinical" we find there are quite a few *British Journal of Clinical* . . . titles, and since the student isn't sure, rather than trying to choose anything from the index list, we'll simply return to the Advanced Search screen and get ready to search: British journal of clinical* as a Title Phrase.

The patron has also told us that this journal is available at the "library at SUNY Buffalo." (SUNY stands for State University of New York, the large system of colleges and universities in New York State.) We could refine our search by finding the "Library Code" for the library at Buffalo and entering it in the "Limit availability to" section (see Figure 7.1). Clicking the "Find codes . . ." link opens the "Directory of OCLC Libraries" search in a new window. Initially, we're given only two search boxes, Institution Name and OCLC Symbol (for when you are trying to decipher a mysterious OCLC library code). We could open the "More search options" link but it looks like it's trying to be foolproof, so let's see what we get if we simply type: SUNY Buffalo into the Institution Name search box. And voila! One result, SUNY at Buffalo, symbol BUF.

Back on the search screen, our mystery journal search is now ready to run using just the first text input field and the Library Code field:

British journal of clinical* → drop-down: Title Phrase

Library Code: BUF

Upon seeing the results the student decides the professor must have been referring to the *British Journal of Clinical Psychology*, because it's for a psych class.

The student might also want to know, "Is SUNY Buffalo's subscription current?" And it would be even more convenient if the journal were here, at the University of Rochester, so she wouldn't need to drive to Buffalo—or best of all, if she could simply access it online. There is an immediate tip-off here in the results screen: the *British Journal of Clinical Psychology* entry includes the notation "Univ of Rochester," indicating that the title *is*

Table 7.1. Representation of the "Libraries that Own Item" screen: the list of libraries owning the *British Journal of Clinical Psychology* and their holdings

Location	Library	Local Holdings	Code
US/NY	Univ of Rochester	20- (1981-)	RRR
US/NY	Albert Einstein Col, Med Col		YYE
US/NY	Baruch Col		VVB
US/NY	Brooklyn Col Libr	20-35 (1981-1996)	VDB
US/NY	City Col, CUNY	20 (1981)	ZXC
US/NY	College of St Rose Libr	v.20 (1981)-	VJN
US/NY	Columbia Univ	v.20 (1981)-v.48 (2009)	ZCU
US/NY	Cornell Univ	Local holdings availa . . .	COO
(etc.)			

held locally. But are the local holdings up to date? The "Libraries worldwide" link (also in the initial results screen) will display a list of institutions that own the item, and in the case of a serial publication, the years and volumes owned are also displayed. The local holding library is helpfully listed first (Table 7.1).

This is all very nice, but what really catches the student's eye is the little globe icon and the notation "Internet Resource." There are electronic access links in the record for the print version, but to be sure you get a link that works, you look the journal title up in the local ejournals system. (Which is what you probably should have done to begin with, but you got sidetracked by the student's saying the journal was available at SUNY Buffalo. It happens to us all.) This journal *is* available online locally, which makes the student very happy.

Quick Recap

The first half of this chapter has looked at the subscription version of WorldCat, a bibliographic database that is different from all the other databases in this book. Rather than being an index to journal articles or statistical publications, it is a database of the contents of all kinds of libraries: public, academic, and corporate. The range of materials included and the audiences that might be served by the information contained here are thus incredibly broad.

WorldCat is the largest union catalog in the world, comprising records for books and many other material types from thousands of member libraries. The database is a distributed effort, built by catalogers at contributing libraries. As a reference tool, WorldCat can be used in many ways, such as for exploring topics or doing collection development, finding resources in a particular format, verifying citations for books or other materials, or discovering where materials that your library does not own are available (e.g., which other libraries own them). The WorldCat Advanced Search interface has many Limits (for material types) and Subtype limits (for audience, content, and formats) not found in other databases. The Results screen is tabbed to allow users to see all the results, or to view records by material type (serials, Internet resources, maps, etc.). Every record includes a "Libraries worldwide" link to view the list of libraries that own the item. One can also restrict a search to a particular library.

WorldCat.org

When the National Library of Medicine provides the entire contents of MEDLINE (and more) for free on the Internet in the form of PubMed or, similarly, when the Department of Education gives us ERIC, it's wonderful; it's amazing. But after all, these are government-produced resources: in the United States, these are our tax dollars at work. So while these are very important additions in terms of information sharing, they aren't *completely* unexpected. In contrast, when OCLC, a private, for-profit organization, decides to provide the WorldCat database for free on the Internet as WorldCat.org, it is, to me at least, a breathtaking move. WorldCat had only ever been offered through OCLC's FirstSearch platform; it was the result of thousands of contributing member libraries' efforts, and building it had involved a great deal of money sloshing back and forth over the years. To decide to "give it away" must have involved meetings and discussions and struggles beyond the powers of my imagination.

Brief Background

WorldCat.org appeared in August 2006, a "destination website" that was greeted very positively by librarians (Flagg 2006; Hane 2006). At last, anyone who could get online could search the entire WorldCat database, using a simple, friendly interface. Since its launch, WorldCat.org has been enthusiastically adding both technical and social media features to appeal to all sorts of audiences. Some of the notable features are personalization features that allow users to create personal accounts and private and public recommendation lists, as well as write reviews (and people actually do all of these things). There is a mobile version of WorldCat.org, or simply download an app to use WorldCat.org on your mobile phone. You can tag WorldCat records, follow it on Twitter, or watch tutorials or "why I love WorldCat" videos on its YouTube channel. Along with established features, the WorldCat.org homepage usually has one or more "Experimental" offerings for you to try, too. Where the trends go, WorldCat.org is right there with them. For more detail on the history of WorldCat.org, see the Student Resources tab at http://www.abc-clio.com/LibrariesUnlimited/product .aspx?pc=A4596P.

Notes and Search Examples

The WorldCat.org home screen offers one search box with five search option tabs, various announcements and many invitations to log in; Figure 7.3 provides a conceptual drawing. If you want to search "everything," you

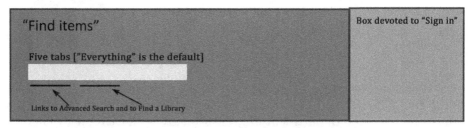

Figure 7.3. Representation of the WorldCat.org home page, indicating major areas and functions.

can, and then refine your results afterward. Or, if you know you're looking for a DVD to while away the evening, this search screen lets you specify that, or one of the other most common formats people tend to search for.

This screen is "home" for WorldCat.org. The Search menu just above the logo offers the options to Search for Library Items, Search for Lists, Search for Contacts, or Search for a Library. You might expect that the Search for Library Items interface would be the same as on the home screen, but it turns out to be even more minimalistic. Let's think of it as the basic search. No matter what screen you are on, the WorldCat.org text input boxes offer suggestions as you type, just as PubMed does (we will see this again, in a more sophisticated implementation, in *Statistical Insight* in chapter 9). Google started it, and produced another trend.

Both the home and the basic search screens also link to an Advanced search, which provides just enough additional sophistication to make it efficient but not overwhelming. The interface offers a very clean and easy to use set of useful options: a familiar pattern of three drop-down menus with text input fields (the default settings for the drop-downs are probably the types of information most commonly searched for, e.g. Keyword, Title, and Author). The area below that is labeled "Narrow your search (optional)," and the order of the limits is Year, Audience, Content, Format, and Language. But nowhere is there any whisper of "Boolean"—the WorldCat.org designers (or their usability team) have rightly divined that people will assume if they enter information in more than one box that it all relates to the same item. That is, users will assume an AND search even if they have no idea that's what they are doing.

As you work through the examples, note that every results page and record display page includes a search box, along with a link to the Advanced search, at the top of the page. This is very useful for adding terms to an existing search or changing direction on the fly: there's no need to return to a search interface page unless you need the extra functionality.

Search Examples

Here are just a few ideas for getting into WorldCat.org and exploring its features. Since it is freely available and will look slightly different in the standard versus the mobile versions, I have elected not to include screen-shots, but features to look for are described.

Search Example 1: Using the Refine Panel to Focus a Broad Search

Say that you are a student taking a course on medieval history, and you have to write a paper on some aspect of the period that interests you. A pretty broad mandate, and frankly, you're not sure if you're that interested in *any* aspect of medieval times, at least not enough to write a paper on it! Maybe if you could see a lot of results, however, something will get your attention. At the Home screen of WorldCat.org, you simply type in:

Medieval life

with the tab set to the default, Everything. Wow! Plenty of results—and observe, a feature that has become ubiquitous: the panel on the left offering a host of ways to limit or Refine your search. First and foremost for WorldCat.org are the Format options; this placement is unusual and, thus, interesting. Table 7.2 lays out the options in a tabular format to help identify what we are looking at.

On the screen, note the marvelous detail in the Format listing: there are eBooks, which we would expect, but there are also more unusual formats: Continually updated resource, Downloadable archival material—and if that's not enough, there are more, indicated by the "Show more . . ." link. If one of the titles in the results list doesn't catch your eye immediately, the most helpful way to "Refine" your search in this case might be the last option, by Topic. Clicking "Show more . . ." in this case reveals a fascinating list of topical areas for "medieval life," and surely one of them will be interesting enough for a whole paper's worth of writing (there's even a Library Science topic area for medieval life).

Search Example 2: Using WorldCat.org to Find Musical Scores

A student working on a Master's in vocal performance is home on break and preparing for a midyear vocal recital. She wants to do an all-Purcell program, but knows that her school's library isn't strong on that period. Going to WorldCat.org, she simply types in

Purcell music

and is stunned at the number of results; what a jumble of material types and authors! Sadly, she misses the "Refine Your Search" area on the left, but does

Table 7.2. WorldCat.org refine options on the results page

Section	Initial categories displayed	*Examples* of subcategories
Format	Article	Chapter Downloadable article
	Book	eBook Braille Book Continually updated resource
	Encyclopedia article	
	Archival material	Downloadable archival material
	Image	
	Computer file	
Refine Your Search	Author	[Listed in order by frequency of appearance in results list]
	Year	[Listed in order by frequency of appearance in results list [a]]
	Language	English French Latin . . .
	Content	Biography Fiction Non-Fiction
	Audience	Juvenile Non-Juvenile
	Topic	History Language, Linguistics Philosophy & Religion . . .

[a] To explain the initial year display in the Refine panel a bit more fully: the years initially listed are those with the highest publication counts in this set of results. It can be easy to misinterpret it as a "date descending" list, because the years are often in chronological order, with perhaps one year skipped, simply because the publication pattern turned out that way. Once you click Show more, the list is presented in straight chronological order, with hit counts for each year.

notice the Advanced Search link at the top, just below the search box that is echoing back her initial search. In the Advanced Search screen, she knows that her Author is Henry Purcell, and after looking at the Format drop-down for a moment, she recognizes just what she wants: "Musical score." At the last minute, she adds "vocal" as a Keyword, having noticed material on "keyboard" compositions in the earlier results. Ah! These results are more manageable. In fact, now that she's not so overwhelmed by the results, she notices the panel on the left side, spotting the Format option: Download-able musical score. Talk about score! She mines that list, and then returns to the list of all Musical scores simply by clicking that box again in the left panel. Going through those results, the material only available in print from various libraries, she creates an account and starts putting together a list to follow up on later.

Search Example 3: Finding Materials Based on Partial Information

The year is 2008, and a friend mentions to you that she was reading a great mystery novel, set in Victorian times, that really conveyed what daily life was like then (and made her awfully glad not to have had to live through the Victorian era). Of course, she told you the title, but a couple of weeks pass, and this is all you can remember about it. You could email her and admit that you have no short-term memory, or you could see if WorldCat.org could provide any ideas. In the Advanced screen, you set up a search as follows:

drop-down: Keyword → Victorian

drop-down: Subject → mystery

Narrow search by:

Year → 2006 to 2008

Content → drop-down: Fiction

Specifying "Subject—mystery" and "Content—fiction" seems rather redundant, but because this is all you have to focus your search, you do it anyway. Amazingly, you spot two likely possibilities right away in the results list: *Kept, a Victorian Mystery* and *The Worcester Whisperers: A Victorian Crime Story. Trumpets Sound No More* might be possible, too. (The results with cover images that are goofy or cheerfully colorful can be ruled out immediately. Perhaps we shouldn't judge a book by its cover, but we invariably do.) Going into the full records for each of the likely ones, the abstracts in every record, and comments from other WorldCat users, help to narrow the field quickly. *Kept* appears to be the most in-depth and Dickensian of the possibilities. That could well be it!

To find a copy, simply scroll down in the full record display, to the area labeled "Find a copy in the library." Enter your zip code and the system instantly generates a list of libraries, starting with the geographically closest, that own a copy of the item. Click the name of the library and you will be taken directly to the record for the item in that library's catalog, so you can check availability (e.g. is it checked out or not?). Really a very smooth system.

Working with Results

Results in WorldCat.org each have a check box, our clue that we can mark results of interest and do something with them. (And very intelligently the system "remembers" your selections: if you check box a couple of results, then visit a full record or the next page of results, your marked items remain marked.) At this point, the emphasis on "create an account" and "sign in" comes to the fore: you cannot do anything further with multiple marked results unless you sign in. On an individual record page, however, you can

Cite/Export, Print, Email, Share (a mixture of social media and repeats of the print and email functions), or even generate a Permalink to the record.

To aid students and other writers in their quest for easier bibliography creation, WorldCat.org can format citations in any of five common styles (APA, Chicago, Harvard, MLA, Turabian), which can then be exported to RefWorks, EndNote, or other bibliographic management software. Again, this can be done at the individual record without signing in; for a group of records, you'll need to create an account (it's free, needless to say).

WorldCat.org: A Bold Stroke in the Case for Libraries

Librarians are increasingly anxious that their profession and their institutions will be made redundant by products such as Google, but with WorldCat.org, OCLC is making a resounding counterattack. Their stated goal in providing WorldCat.org at the beginning was to "make library resources more visible to Web users and to increase awareness of libraries as a primary source of reliable information" (Flagg 2006). Almost a decade later, the public mission statement is simple and smart: "WorldCat is the world's largest network of library content and services. WorldCat libraries are dedicated to providing access to their resources on the Web, where most people start their search for information" (OCLC 2014b). The methodology is brilliant: put the content of the WorldCat database directly into the hands of everyone online, at a brief, easy-to-remember Web address, and let the site grow and participate in whatever new Web developments come along.

Quick Recap

WorldCat.org provides free access on the Web to the entire contents of the WorldCat database, with the aim of helping users discover and use library content. It is designed for easy use by any Web user, in both the "one search box" versions on the home page and the easy-to-use Advanced search page. The extensive options that appear in the left-side panel on the results page provide many ways to focus a search, and they are particularly valuable for broad keyword searches. When a record for an item is displayed, WorldCat.org displays a list of libraries that own the item, geographically arranged from nearest to farthest. While the system has automatic geographic detection based on IP address (interpreted as a zip code), that may not be the same as the user's home zip code. For most accurate results, it is best to enter your zip code in the box provided in the "Find a copy in the library" section of a full record. WorldCat.org offers features for personalization (e.g., personal accounts to create a public profile, lists, and bibliographies, or to add notes, tags, or reviews to a record), alerting (email updates), and citation management (e.g., create bibliographies or export records to RefWorks and EndNote).

Revisiting Your Local OPAC

Even though WorldCat is a (huge) union *catalog*, I always think of it as a *database*. On the other hand, I always think of my institution's online catalog as—a catalog, not a database. Now, why is that? Is it because World-Cat comes to us through the FirstSearch interface (which is an article database model) or, in the case of WorldCat.org, in a Web search-engine model, and our library catalogs come from other vendors, vendors who specialize in online public access *catalogs* that have a different kind of look and feel? Whether you have the same reaction or not, go now and revisit whatever library catalog you use most often. Try to look at it as if it were a new database, examining it with the Searcher's Toolkit in mind (going to the Advanced Search screen may make it easier to identify the presence or absence of various features). What fields does it offer? What limits? Does it offer a basic and an advanced search mode? Other search modes? Does it support Boolean searching, wildcards, or truncation? Are there stop words? What are the default search settings? Are there any special features that have been customized for *your* library?

Not to do your work for you, but in the spirit of confirming what you are likely seeing: your local catalog undoubtedly offers field searching (Basic Tool #3), and some limits, such as year, location, (material) type, or language (Basic Tool #6). It doesn't exactly leap out and announce itself, but having a field called "Subject" and the presence of "Subjects" in the records strongly indicates that Basic Tool #2, Controlled Vocabulary, is available. What about the most fundamental tool of all, Boolean operators? The Basic screen *may* include a "Boolean (and/or/not)" option in the drop-down to choose what kind of search you want to do, but it's more likely there will be Boolean drop-downs in the Advanced Search screen. So Basic Tool #1 is there; it just isn't terribly obvious. If you go nosing into the Help, you'll probably find that there is a truncation symbol (Basic Tool #5), and that you can search for phrases by putting them in double quotes. You probably *won't* find any evidence of Basic Tool #4, Proximity Searching, but you likely do not need it: you are only searching bibliographic records here, not full text. Thus most of the Searcher's Toolkit is present, but for some reason just seems harder to recognize and use. (At least, it does to me—what do you think?) And with the influx of Discovery Services, including OCLC's own offering, all these issues may become moot.

Now compare searching your OPAC with searching WorldCat and WorldCat.org. Does one seem more transparent (in terms of how it works) than the other? Look up an item owned by your library, and then find the record for it in WorldCat,[4] and in WorldCat.org. How do the record displays compare? Think about what factors might be driving the needs of a remote, *union* catalog as opposed to the local catalog for one library (or library system). WorldCat.org figures somewhere in the middle of the two: it is the huge WorldCat catalog, but it is also trying very hard to be local. How well does it succeed?

Finally, if your institution has implemented a Discovery Service that includes the content of your local catalog, do some more comparison searching between the Discovery Service and the catalog on its own. Compare searching for a known item (the specific title of a book, journal, or any kind of media recording) in both, doing a topic search (any keyword or keywords), and doing a specific subject search. Are there any cases where the OPAC does a better job, that is, it provides a more efficient way to find material?

With what you've learned so far about searching, are you able to use the local catalog in more sophisticated ways in order to get better results? ("No" is a perfectly good answer.) Discovery Services, with their "one box search," tend to focus on refining on the results page. Do you find that to be just as efficient, or perhaps more so, than setting up a number of parameters at the beginning, say, in the catalog's Advanced Search interface? You may be happy to have the Discovery Service and never have to deal with the catalog interface again, but give it one last chance—just in case it is still better at some things. It's always good to be able to use all the resources at your disposal, and to know which are best for what purpose(s).

Exercises and Points to Consider

1. In the section called "A Tool for Many Parts of the Library," we mentioned a couple of ways you might use WorldCat in a reference transaction. What other uses can you think of?

2. Find some books on fast food (what's the best way—that is, what's a good subject heading—to get books that are really on "fast food," and not about food you can prepare fast?)

3. Half-remembered reference problem: a patron comes in trying to describe some books she has enjoyed. She remembers the author's name was "something-something Smith," and the books are mysteries, about a female detective in Africa somewhere. Try just searching the author field for Smith, and the Genre/Form field for mystery, and see if you can identify this series of books.

4. If you have a favorite author or genre, see if you can use WorldCat to find all the records for those works in your local public library branch. (Tip: use the code look-up screen in WorldCat via FirstSearch.)

5. You're at the reference desk on the weekend, and some junior high school kids come in looking for information about corsets and bloomers for a project. A social history type of encyclopedia might really be best; otherwise, books would be a better way to go than articles for this age group. Try searching your local catalog and see what you can find; then try the subscription WorldCat database (unless your local catalog has a "Juvenile audience" limiter, which would be unusual) and see if you can find more materials or get some additional ideas that way.

6. WorldCat claims to have records for everything from clay tablets to electronic books. See if you can find examples of both ends of this spectrum. Hints: in each case, use a combination of keywords and Limits. For the clay tablets, note that such things would normally be housed in an Archive, thus making them—what kind of materials? Learn from your results what a more formal term for clay tablets is, that you might add as an alternate term to your search. For electronic books, try your favorite author and the "Internet Resources"

Limit. Hint: Look up your author in the Author Phrase index, last name first, to find how his or her name is most commonly entered.

7. WorldCat results are sorted, or ranked, by the number of libraries that own the item. There are three other options, but ranking is often set as the default. Why do you think that is? What would be the advantages and disadvantages of other results display options?

8. Now try the searches in exercises 2 to 5 in WorldCat.org. Do you get the same numbers of results? Which do you find easier? What are the advantages and disadvantages of searching using the First-Search interface versus the WorldCat.org interface?

Beyond the Textbook Exercises

Additional exercises are available on the Student Resources tab at http://www.abc-clio.com/LibrariesUnlimited/product.aspx?pc=A4596P.

Notes

1. Not all member libraries can or do contribute records, of course. Many small libraries simply pay to be able to search and download records for their local catalog, as it is still more efficient and economical than employing cataloging staff.

2. Visit the "Watch WorldCat grow" page at http://www.oclc.org/en-US/worldcat/watch-worldcat-grow.html. It is absolutely fascinating.

3. I find it interesting that the second most frequent material type in the results is "Internet," i.e., ebooks, in this case, e-cookbooks. For kids. Fascinating!

4. Check the "Items in my library" box to make sure that you get the version of the record with which your library is associated. Although the ideal might be one record per title in WorldCat, the reality is that there are often several records for the same title, because participating libraries have cataloged the item slightly differently.

8
Humanities Databases

Although people come to librarianship with all kinds of different backgrounds and with many different undergraduate degrees, from purely an-
ecdotal evidence it seems to me that there is still a preponderance of people
with undergraduate degrees in the humanities who enter the library field
(or am I imagining that large sigh of relief among you readers, now that
we've arrived at the humanities chapter?). In any event, it's likely you'll find
the two databases considered here, *America: History and Life*,[1] and the *MLA
International Bibliography*, to be interesting, easy to use, and a window into
their respective disciplines.

In *America: History and Life*, we have an excellent example of a familiar interface (EBSCO) that has been customized just enough to take advantage of the unique content and fields available in this particular database.
As with PubMed and the *Web of Science* in chapter 6, in *MLA* we have an
excellent example of a database structured specifically for its subject matter.
What is uniquely important to *MLA* and its users are attributes of written
(and other forms of) communication: genres, themes, influences, etc., all of
which are supported in *MLA* records, and very clearly reflected in the version of the *MLA* database described here.

We will observe some disciplinary differences between the two resources
in their approach to languages and dates. In the history database, it is sufficient to have the usual single field for language of publication. In the literature database, however, language of publication and language as the
subject of the publication are equally important and are supported by two
distinct fields. For historians, this kind of distinction arises around dates:
when something happened is part of a publication's content and needs to
be distinguished from when the item was published. Thus, two fields: one, a
special-purpose field to specify the historical period discussed in the publication, and the other, a typical date-of-publication limit field. The *MLA International Bibliography* also has the usual publication date limit field and a
separate field for the period being discussed, but their set of "Period" values

(a browsable index list) reveals a rather different mind-set about dates. As in chapter 6, while we work through these two resources, in addition to absorbing information about functionality and content, try to be alert to aspects of each database that seem specially designed to support its subject discipline.

America: History and Life

Background and Coverage

America: History and Life (AHL), and its complement, *Historical Abstracts* for world history, were the flagship products of ABC-CLIO. Acquired by EBSCO in 2007, since 2008 they have been available solely through that interface. Gail Golderman, writing for *Library Journal* in November 2008, described AHL as "the definitive bibliographic reference covering the history, culture, area studies, and current affairs literature of the United States and Canada, from prehistory to the present," whose content and functionality "has only gotten better since being acquired by EBSCO" (Golderman 2008). The introduction of *America: History and Life with Full Text* in 2010 provides continuing evidence that this is so.

In terms of scope and coverage, the journal list for AHL included over 1900 titles as of this writing. Analysis of the list shows that coverage for a few journals extends back into the 1800 and early 1900s, with the majority of the coverage starting in the 1950s and beyond. Articles, book and media reviews, relevant dissertations, and ebooks discussing any period of American and Canadian history from prehistory to the present are eligible for inclusion. The database is updated monthly, and approximately 16,000 entries are added per year.

Notes and Search Examples

If you subscribe to both *America: History and Life* and *Historical Abstracts,* you can configure your EBSCO links to search both databases at once, or each one separately. The following scenarios are based on searching AHL by itself.

Advanced Search Interface

The Advanced Search screen should look familiar, because it is almost identical to the interface for *MasterFILE Premier* introduced in chapter 3. Running through our usual mental checklist of the Searcher's Toolkit, it's easy to see we have field searching, Boolean operators, and limits—including several special-purpose limits we didn't see in the *MasterFILE* interface. Table 8.1 provides a comparison of limits offered in *MasterFILE* and AHL; the differences in features like this say a lot about the content and intended audience for the database.

Looking back up at the very top of the screen, there is a link to "Indexes" (as opposed to "Subjects" in *MasterFILE*). We can infer that we will be able to browse the values for several distinct fields (the index lists), as in

Table 8.1. Differences in the Limits interface options between *America: History & Life* and *MasterFILE*.

Limits common to both databases	Limits unique to *America: History & Life*	Limits unique to *MasterFILE*
Peer Reviewed	Linked Full Text	Full Text
Published Date	Historical Period	Number of Pages
Publication	Language	Image Quick View Types
Publication Type[1]	References Available	Cover Story
Document Type[1]		Image Quick View
		PDF Full Text

[1]Note: while the limit name is the same, the choices listed for Publication Type and Document Type differ between the two databases.

WorldCat. In the same area as Indexes are two new links: Cited References and CLIO Notes, which we will discuss a little later in this section.

Search Example 1: Finding Book Reviews

In this search example, we'd like to find reviews of two of Stanley Engerman's books, *Naval Blockades in Peace and War* and *Slavery, Emancipation, and Freedom*. The title part of the search is fairly easy: we can pick a distinct word from each title, OR them, and search that information against the Title field. We want book reviews, which should immediately make us think of limiting by document type, and indeed Book Review is a choice for this limit. Professor Engerman's role in this search is harder to define: he is the author of the *books*, but not the author of the reviews, so we can't search for him in the Author field. He is also not the Subject of the reviews, his books are. What to do? Luckily, there is a field simply called People; we will enter his name directory style (last name, first name) in that field. Our search criteria are thus:

Engerman, Stanley → PE People

AND

Naval OR emancipation → TI Title

Limits:

Document type: Book Review

Our results appear to be right on target, judging by the titles and subjects in the results. Here is a sampling showing just the article titles and their subject headings:

1. Slavery, Emancipation, and Freedom: Comparative Perspectives.

   Subjects: BOOKS—Reviews; SLAVERY; NONFICTION; SLAVERY, Emancipation & Freedom: Comparative Perspectives (Book); ENGERMAN, Stanley L.

2. Slavery, Emancipation, & Freedom: Comparative Perspectives.

Subjects: BOOKS—Reviews; SLAVERY—United States—History; NONFICTION; SLAVERY, Emancipation & Freedom: Comparative Perspectives (Book); ENGERMAN, Stanley L.

3. Naval Blockades in Peace and War: An Economic History since 1750.

Subjects: BOOKS—Reviews; UNITED States—Economic conditions—To 1865; NONFICTION; NAVAL Blockades in Peace & War: An Economic History Since 1750 (Book); DAVIS, Lance Edwin; ENGERMAN, Stanley L.

4. The Comparative Histories of Slavery in Brazil, Cuba, and the United States/Slavery, Emancipation, and Freedom: Comparative Perspectives.

Subjects: CUBA; BRAZIL; BOOKS—Reviews; SLAVERY—History; NONFICTION; SLAVERY; COMPARATIVE Histories of Slavery in Brazil, Cuba & the United States, The (Book); SLAVERY, Emancipation & Freedom: Comparative Perspectives (Book); ENGERMAN, Stanley L.; BERGAD, Laird W.

If you look at all closely at the information listed as Subjects in the examples above, there are two traps you might fall into. One is that the title of the book being reviewed seems to be listed as a Subject; the other is that the book's author (in this case, Prof. Engerman) also seems to be listed as a Subject. Are they both subjects? Why don't we search them against the SU Subject Terms field, then? (Try it: it doesn't work.) Taking a good look at a full record reveals that the book under review appears in a field called "Reviews & Products," and Prof. Engerman's name does indeed appear in the People field. I can understand the EBSCO interface designers not wanting to clutter up the results display with additional field names yet wanting to provide as much useful information as possible, and thus making the choice to list information from these other fields as "Subjects." Still, it could make for confusion. Beware, and be *aware*, that just because something is listed with the Subjects in the brief results display, doesn't mean it actually came from the "SU Subject Terms" field.

Search Example 2: Finding Material about a Topic in a Particular Period

In this search, we want to produce a list of references to works about organized crime during Prohibition, that is, the period from 1920 to 1933 when the Volstead Act was in effect. Now we get to use the Historical Period limit field, with its "Era" drop-down menu for specifying "b.c.e. (BC)" or "c.e. (AD)."[2] Figure 8.1 shows relevant parts of the search screen set up for this search.

In the results screen for this search we have many options for further adjusting our results. The search interface stays with us, which is always

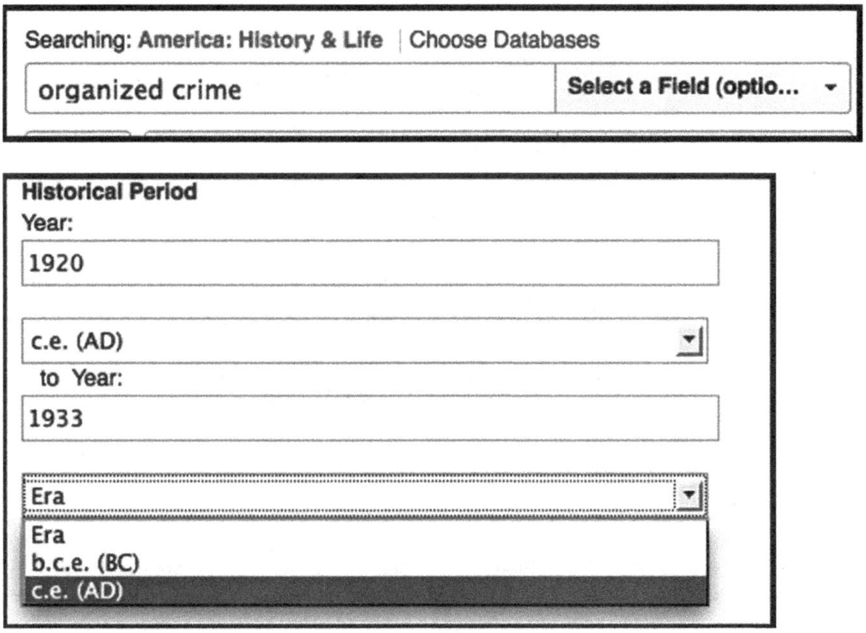

Searching: America: History & Life | Choose Databases

| organized crime | Select a Field (optio... ▾ |

Historical Period
Year:

1920

c.e. (AD)   ▾

to Year:

1933

Era   ▾

Era
b.c.e. (BC)
c.e. (AD)

Figure 8.1. Selected areas of the Advanced Search screen, set to run a topic search limited by Historical Period. © 2014 EBSCO Industries, Inc. All rights reserved.

useful for adding more terms or changing a search without having to go back to a search screen. On the left side, we have the (by now) familiar "Refine Results"[3] panel full of handy options and information. We could immediately limit these results to just those with full text, those that have a list of references available, or those that are peer reviewed. Using the input fields or the slider bar, we could limit just to records with a more recent Publication Date. Just below that, the "Show more>>" link would superimpose the full limit interface over the current screen (a functionality known as an Ajax window), so we never need to fully leave the current screen.

Scrolling down to see the rest of the Refine panel, we find options to limit by Source Type, such as Academic Journals, and/or by adding a Subject heading to the original search (it turns out that "Organized crime" is actually a subject heading. Good!). Clicking any of the options in the Refine panel instantly puts it into effect and causes the results list to refresh.

In all cases, if you don't like the new results, it's very easy to get back to your original list. All the limits you've chosen are listed at the top of the Refine panel. They can be removed from the search criteria by just clicking the X icon associated with them (Figure 8.2).

Just above the results list on the right are three low key menus providing options for your results list display and manipulation. You can set the sort order of your results (Date Newest being the default), how you'd like the results page laid out and how many results to show per page (Page Options), and the third menu provides many ways to "Share" the results:

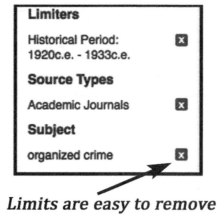

Limits are easy to remove

Figure 8.2. How to remove limits chosen in the results screen. © 2014 EBSCO Industries, Inc. All rights reserved.

Subjects: UNITED States; GANGSTERS; **ORGANIZED crime**; CLOTHING & dress -- Social aspects; AMERICAN Dream; IDEALISM, American; SUCCESS -- United States; CLOTHING & dress -- United States; PROHIBITION -- United States; PROGRESSIVISM (United States politics); UNITED States -- Social life & customs -- 1918-1945; CAPONE, Al, 1899-1947

Figure 8.3. Link to Cited References in the initial results list. © 2014 EBSCO Industries, Inc. All rights reserved.

Add them to a folder (EBSCO's metaphor for a 'marked list')

Create an alert, either email or RSS Feed

Permalink: a link you can copy and paste into another application, enabling you or others to return directly to this set of results

Series of icons: bewildering array of social media options for "sharing," as well as more pedestrian email and print output options.

Most of the records provide an abstract, and all provide their Subjects as we saw in the first search example. This causes the display to be longer but reduces the number of clicks needed to decide whether a result is relevant or not (as well as providing many more opportunities to learn new terms you might employ in your search). Records with Cited References will also include that information in the form of a link to "Cited References: (##)" as shown in Figure 8.3. (Note that not every record will have a Cited References link.) Clicking the link displays the list of references (shades of the *Web of Science!*).

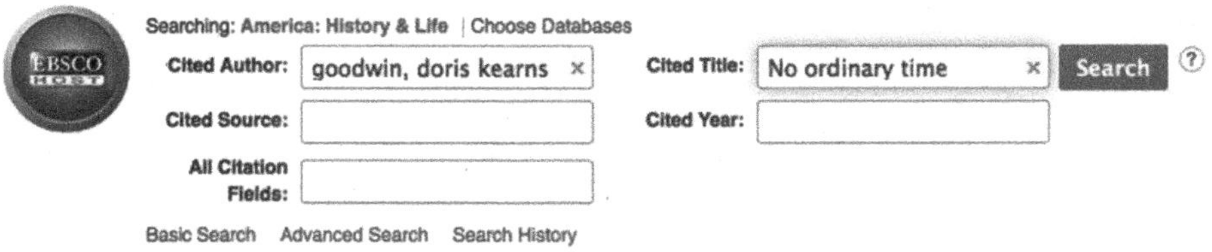

Figure 8.4. Cited reference search interface, set to run search example 3. © 2014 EBSCO Industries, Inc. All rights reserved.

Search Example 3: Searching Cited References

Citations are as important to historians as to the scientists in Thomson Reuter's *Web of Science*, and it's exciting to see another database vendor tackling this labor-intensive issue.

Here's our example for this search: We'd like to see publications that have cited Doris Kearns Goodwin's *No Ordinary Time: Franklin and Eleanor Roosevelt: The Home Front in World War II*, published in 1994. Clicking Cited References in the top bar, we get the search interface shown in Figure 8.4. The interface is set up to run our cited reference search with Goodwin, Doris Kearns in the Cited Author field, and the beginning of her book's title in the Cited Title field. (Why no year? Well, the hardcover appeared in 1994, the paperback edition appeared in 1995, followed by audio and Kindle editions—we don't really care which edition, so we'll leave it open.)

This search already feels very different from the Cited Reference searching in the *Web of Science*—no constraints on how the name is entered, no agonizing about how a title (referring to a book or an article title) or a Source (which could again be a book title or the name of a journal) are abbreviated or entered: simply enter the initial words, or even a keyword. Now look at what is displayed on your results screen. These "Citation Records" have some mysterious elements, but we can search on full words because the citation records contain full words.[4] Amazing!

You'll notice that not every result has a check box—only the references that are associated with a "citing article" *in this database* have a check box. Selecting all the available check boxes, we click the Find Citing Articles button and arrive at a screen of seven results. We are reminded of how the whole process started by the presence of the search interface at the top of the screen, and the bold reminder just above the records: "These records cite: WA goodwin, doris kearns and WB no ordinary time." (WA and WB are field codes.) We can toggle between the Cited References screen and the Citing Articles screen using the links in the bar between the search interface and the results list. (Figure 8.5)

I cannot resist giving you a sense of the fascinating, scholarly material available in this database. Here are the titles in this set of results, with the cited reference and times cited information for each:

1. "The Guiding Spirit": Philip Loeb, The Battle for Television Jurisdiction, and the Broadcasting Industry Blacklist. Cited References: (91)

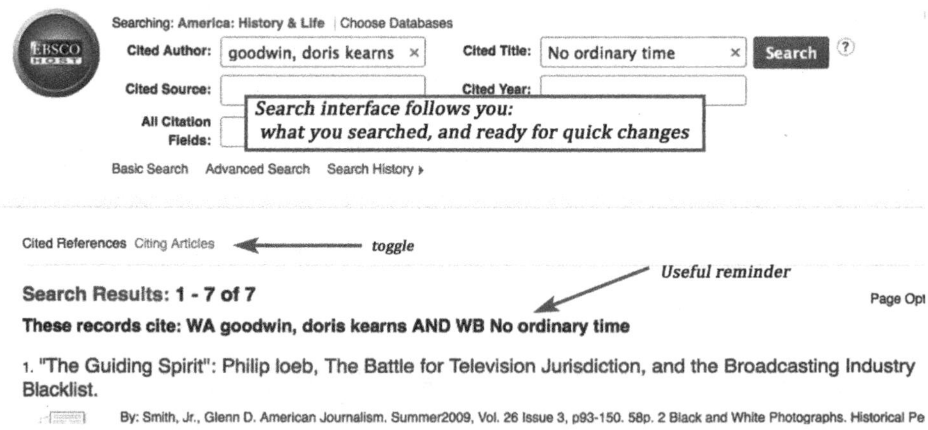

Searching: America: History & Life   Choose Databases

Cited Author: goodwin, doris kearns   ×   Cited Title: No ordinary time   ×   **Search**   ⑦

Cited Source: Cited Year:

All Citation
Fields: *Search interface follows you:*
              what you searched, and ready for quick changes

Basic Search   Advanced Search   Search History ▸

Cited References Citing Articles   ◄——————— *toggle*

                                                Useful reminder
Search Results: 1 - 7 of 7   Page Opt
These records cite: WA goodwin, doris kearns AND WB No ordinary time

1. "The Guiding Spirit": Philip loeb, The Battle for Television Jurisdiction, and the Broadcasting Industry
Blacklist.
        By: Smith, Jr., Glenn D. American Journalism. Summer2009, Vol. 26 Issue 3, p93-150. 58p. 2 Black and White Photographs. Historical Pe

Figure 8.5. Cited References search results display. © 2014 EBSCO Industries, Inc.
All rights reserved.

2. Westbrook Pegler, Eleanor Roosevelt, and the FBI. Cited References: (49)

3. Broken Circle: The Isolation of Franklin D. Roosevelt in World War
   II. Cited References: (59)

4. Preparing for a National Emergency: The Committee on Conserva-
   tion of Cultural Resources, 1939–1944. Cited References: (43)

5. Queer Hoover: Sex, Lies, and Political History. Cited References:
   (103) Times cited in this Database: (2)

6. Race, Roosevelt, and Wartime Production: Fair Employment in
   World War II Labor Markets. Cited References: (29) Times cited in
   this Database: (5)

7. Oral history and the story of America and World War II. Cited References: (29) Times cited in this Database: (2)

Using just two bits of information about a work, we have found seven newer
articles in this database that are related (and yet going in interesting new
research directions), all of very high scholarship judging by the number of
cited references (one of which is, of course, to Goodwin's book). To me, there
is nothing quite like cited reference searching for producing intriguing and
unexpected results.

The Full Record Display

Let's pause and take a look at a full record display (Figure 8.6). In addition to the detailed record itself, you can see that the left- and right-side
panels offer a wealth of options. On the left, in this case we get links both to
HTML and PDF versions of the full text, a link to the Cited References, and
the option to "Find Similar Results" using SmartText searching.[5]

In the right panel you have a plethora of Tools for actions to take on this
individual record. You can Add to folder (discussed in detail below), Print,

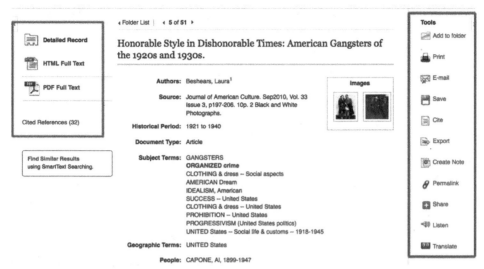

Figure 8.6. Full record display for an article. © 2014 EBSCO Industries, Inc. All rights reserved.

Email, Save, see how to Cite (in seven popular formats), or Export the record to a citation manager program. The Export function now offers seven different formats, including XML, BibTex, and MARC21, as well as the more familiar RefWorks and EndNote. For extended research projects, you again have the ability to create a personal account with the database and add your own notes on records (Create Note), obtain a permanent link (Permalink) to the record, or share it via various social networking sites (Share). All of these options use a technology that superimposes a new screen over the current one. This technique saves a great deal of screen loading/refreshing time, and it leaves you right where you were when the superimposed screen is closed. At the end of the list of Tools, you can even have the article read to you (Listen) or Translated for you (the list of language options is impressive).

It's great to have the output options at the individual record level, but usually you will want to work with a whole group of records. That is done using the Folder.

The Folder: Outputting Results

Collecting Items in the "Folder"

You may have noticed that in the results list, rather than a check box for each record, there is an icon of a folder associated with each one. The Folder is EBSCO's mechanism for collecting records on which you want to take some collective action; you can add a whole page of records using that option under the Share menu, or individual ones using the folder icon associated with each one, or you can add a record from the full record display.

Once you have added the desired records to the Folder, you then work with them in the Folder view (Figure 8.7). The Folder is accessed by the link in the topmost bar of the interface (indicated by the arrow in Figure 8.7).

Figure 8.7. Significant parts of the Folder interface: access link and display. © 2014 EBSCO Industries, Inc. All rights reserved.

The options to Print, Email, Save as File, or Export (to a citation management program) are available here, for all or selected records in the Folder. The email function has all the best features: it lets you put your own email in the "from" field, send to multiple recipients, put in your own Subject line, and add comments. In addition, you can choose a standard format, a specific citation format, or create your own format by choosing exactly which fields you wish to send.

The Folder also includes detailed information about the types of materials that you've put in it (on the right), and you can retain your Folder items from session to session by creating a "My EBSCOhost" account; again, there is an emphasis on personalization and ongoing research.

Special Feature: CLIO Notes

You may have been wondering what in the world "CLIO Notes" is: if you click this option in the topmost bar, you'll be presented with a list of historical periods. Diving into any of these reveals a list of defining aspects of the era (such as Economic Developments, Politics and Foreign Policy, Social Conflicts, etc. for "[1920–1929] The Roaring 20's") and further topics associated with each of those aspects, as shown in the left panel of Figure 8.8. Clicking on any topic provides a useful, fairly brief essay, suggested research questions, and appropriate Subject headings for researching the topics; parts of such a screen are shown on the right side of Figure 8.8. It's an "I don't know what to write about" student's dream!

Quick Recap

America: History and Life (AHL), and its complement, *Historical Abstracts*, are the leading indexes to the literature of history. AHL provides indexing, abstracts, and some full text for articles as well as indexing for

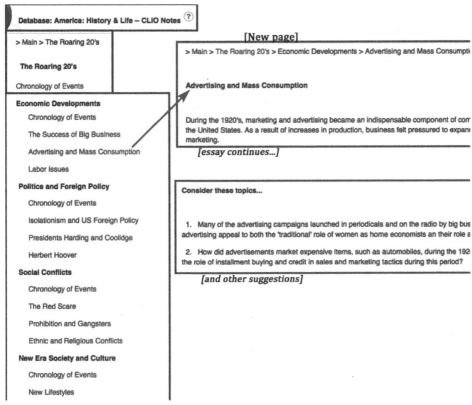

Figure 8.8. Selected views of the CLIO Notes feature. © 2014 EBSCO Industries, Inc. All rights reserved.

book and media reviews and dissertations. The scope of AHL is any period of American and Canadian history from prehistory to the present; *Historical Abstracts* covers the rest of the world. The Advanced Search interface offers field searching and limits, including the special purpose "Historical Period" limit. AHL offers a Cited References search that is friendlier to use but smaller in scale than that of the *Web of Science*. There are many options for changing the search on the Results screen, all easily reversible. Output of multiple records is done by adding them to the Folder and processing them from there. The output options are well developed, including good email features and output to citation management programs. Unique to the *America: History & Life* and *Historical Abstracts* databases is the CLIO Notes feature, which provides historically and thematically structured access to a wealth of research paper suggestions.

MLA International Bibliography

Background and Coverage

The *MLA International Bibliography* is produced by the Modern Language Association of America (MLA), and is one of the longest-running indexes still in existence. The Association itself was founded in 1883 and published a printed index from 1921 to 2009. The online database includes the index records back to 1926; the addition of records for JSTOR journals has extended coverage for certain titles back to the 1880s,[6] providing another example of an electronic product that has expanded beyond its print counterpart.

In addition to the date range mentioned above, the *MLA International Bibliography* (MLA IB) is also vast in terms of the scope of topics included, sources, document types, and number of records. Topical coverage runs the gamut of human communication, including literature, folklore (including music and art), the study of linguistics and languages, literary theory and criticism, the dramatic arts, the history of printing and publishing, and material about teaching language, literature, and rhetoric and composition. As indicated in the title (the *International* Bibliography), sources from all over the world are reviewed for entry into the database. The "Language of Publication" thesaurus list is probably the longest and most esoteric you will ever encounter. Document types covered include types that you would expect, such as books, book chapters, and journal articles, but also indexed are reference works, published working papers, conference papers and proceedings, citations for dissertations listed in *Dissertations Abstracts International*, electronic publications, and works related to teaching—handbooks, textbooks, anthologies, etc. Reviews of books or other scholarly works have to meet certain criteria to be included; reviews that simply describe or summarize a work are not included. Full details are given on the MLA *Scope of the Bibliography* web page (MLA 2014a).

The numbers for the MLA IB are equally impressive: there are "over 2.5 million citations" in the database, with "new records for 65,000 books and articles" added per year (ProQuest 2014a). Subject terms used to describe records come from the *MLA Thesaurus*, which includes "over 45,000 terms and 327,000 names" (MLA 2014b). A database about literature is, obviously, very concerned with names: the names of writers and of characters.

The MLA IB is the first database that we've encountered in this book that is purely an index. Full records are quite long owing to the number of fields included, but there are no abstracts.[7] On the other hand, opportunities for getting directly to full text are increasing. If your institution also subscribes to JSTOR and Project MUSE, your MLA IB subscription can be configured to include links to full text in those two databases. The MLA IB supports linking technologies for getting to full text in other sources as well. It is also possible to run the MLA IB as a module in a full-text database called *Literature Online* (LION), as described briefly in the section that follows.

Relationship to Other Literature Resources

Any discussion of the MLA IB should also mention two other major literature resources: the *Annual Bibliography of English Language and Literature* (ABELL) and the previously mentioned *Literature Online* (LION). ABELL has a somewhat smaller scope than MLA IB in that it focuses on just English language materials and literature in English. LION, the only full-text database of the three, also focuses on English literature, and provides the texts of over 357,000 literary works, along with criticism, reference resources, and video and audio materials (ProQuest 2014b). At this time, Chadwyck-Healey, the specialist humanities imprint of ProQuest, is the sole publisher for LION and is also a supplier of ABELL. MLA IB is also available from Chadwyck-Healey, making it possible for subscribers to all three databases from this vendor to opt to use LION as the single point of access—a very powerful combination. Although we will be looking at the Chadwyck-Healey version of MLA in this chapter, we will look at the MLA IB as a stand-alone database.

Notes and Search Examples

Any consideration of humanities databases needs to look at the MLA IB, but the question then is: from which vendor? At the time of this writing, three database vendors are offering the MLA's database. (The MLA provides a very informative and helpful chart about the distributors of their database at http://www.mla.org/bib_dist_comparison.) I have chosen to look at ProQuest's Chadwyck-Healey version, because their interface seems to be nicely tuned to the subject matter[8] and is quite different from any we have seen so far. The only downside is that one keeps hearing murmurs that ProQuest is going to bring the Chadwyck-Healey databases into the standard ProQuest interface, so becoming very familiar with this interface may be a short term investment. Because of that, I have opted to include only minimal graphics, all of which are conceptual illustrations rather than screenshots.

Standard Search Interface

The MLA IB as offered by Chadwyck-Healey provides three search interfaces: Standard, Advanced, and Directory of Periodicals. We'll work with the Standard search and briefly describe the Advanced options; notes about the Directory of Periodicals appear under "Additional Feature" later in this chapter.

The Standard Search (Figure 8.9) offers support for the kinds of searches users need to do most often: a straight topical search (using Keyword[s], Title Keyword[s], or Subject—All), a search for literary criticism or interpretation (Author as Subject, Author's Work), and the need to fill out a citation from incomplete information (using a combination of Keyword, Article Author, Journal, and Publication Year). What I find compelling about this interface is that there are no drop-down menus: every field available in this search mode is in plain view, clearly labeled. How to search for articles *discussing* other works (literary criticism) is a search that students are frequently required to do but which most don't know how to do (searching on an author's name or the title of a book as a *subject* is not instantly intuitive). Here both of those searches are offered about as clearly as one could hope for.

If we are mentally ticking things off on our Searcher's Toolkit list, the ability to use Boolean operators is not obvious, although we assume that it's there. The "Help" confirms this, along with supplying information about the other tools we're used to looking for, such as proximity operators and

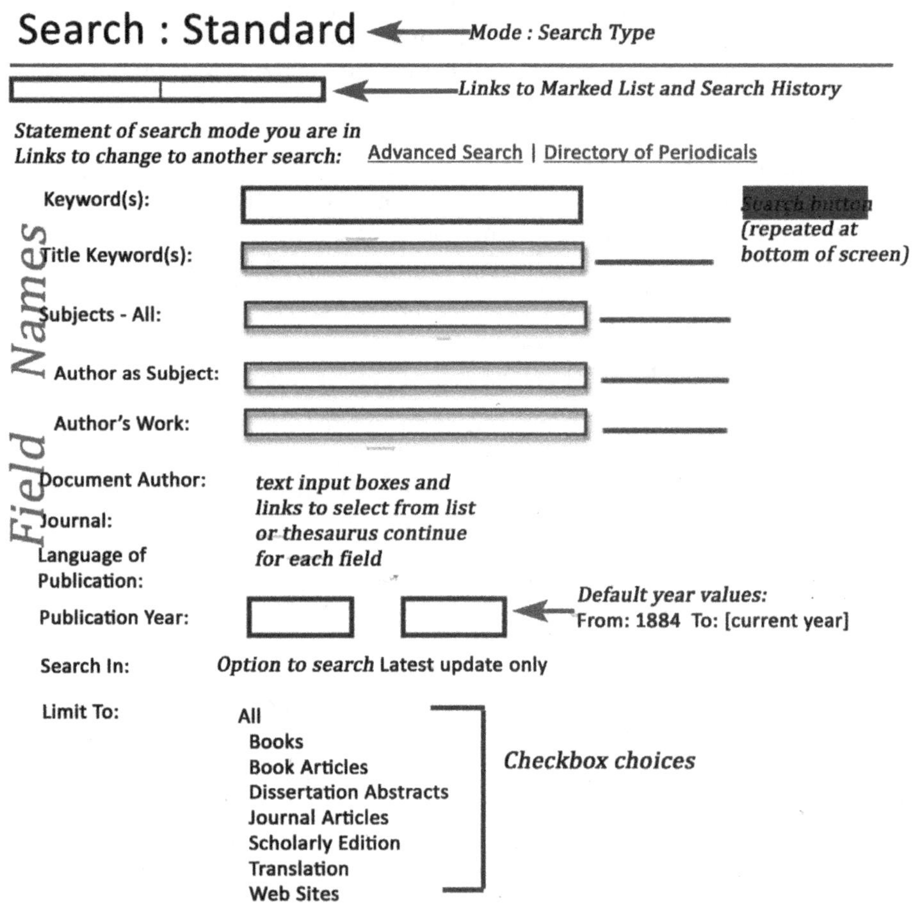

Search : Standard ◄————Mode : Search Type

◄————Links to Marked List and Search History

Statement of search mode you are in
Links to change to another search: Advanced Search | Directory of Periodicals

Field Names

Keyword(s):

Title Keyword(s):

Subjects - All:

Author as Subject:

Author's Work:

Names

Document Author:

Journal:

Language of
Publication:

Publication Year:

Search In:

Limit To:

Search button
(repeated at
bottom of screen)

text input boxes and
links to select from list
or thesaurus continue
for each field

Default year values:
From: 1884 To: [current year]

Option to search Latest update only

All
Books
Book Articles
Dissertation Abstracts
Journal Articles
Scholarly Edition
Translation
Web Sites

Checkbox choices

Figure 8.9. Representation of the Chadwyck-Healey *MLA IB* Standard search interface, with annotations.

wildcards. There is an implied AND between fields on a page. A set of document types appears explicitly labeled Limit to; other fields commonly used as limits are also available: Language of Publication and Publication Year. In the Figure 8.9 graphic, the lines following most of the fields represent links to "select from a list" (Title Keywords, Document Author, Journal, Language of Publication) or "select from thesaurus" (Subject—All, Author as Subject, Author's Work). In all, this version of MLA offers a total of 29 searchable fields, 24 of which have searchable index lists of values. The ability to explore all the possible values for specific fields is something we are seeing less often in databases (WorldCat via FirstSearch is the only comparable one in this book), so this is rather special.

Search Example 1: A Subject–Keyword Search

Our first search example is a topic that receives continuing attention from the literary community: examples of the use of cross-dressing in the works of Shakespeare. For our search strategy, we'll start with:

Search : Standard

Keyword(s):   cross-dressing

Author as Subject: Shakespeare

The results for this search start to demonstrate the breadth of coverage, in terms of document types and international reach, of this database. There are chapters from edited books, whole books, articles from theater, literary, and cultural journals, dissertations, papers from a conference, an article from a Chinese literary journal, records for articles and books in French, German, Romanian and Spanish, and electronic journal articles. Here are some examples:

Magnus, Laury: "Cross-Dressing, Comic Power Inversions, and 'Supposes': Performing the Beginning and the End of The Taming of the Shrew" *In* (pp. 200–204) Dupuis, Margaret (ed. and preface), Tiffany, Grace (ed., preface and introd.), *Approaches to Teaching Shakespeare's The Taming of the Shrew*, New York, NY: Modern Language Association of America, 2013. xii, 252 pp. (Approaches to Teaching World Literature 123). (2013)

Murray, Barbara A.: "'Strange Star': Same-Sex Love and William Burnaby's Love Betray'd or The Agreeable Disapointment (1703)" English Studies: A Journal of English Language and Literature, (93:2), 2012, 177–187. (English summary.) (2012)

Grant, Allison: "The Dangers of Playing House: Celia's Subversive Role in As You Like It" Selected Papers of the Ohio Valley Shakespeare Conference , (4:), 2011, (no pagination). (In special issue: "Shakespeare and Ethics." Electronic publication.). (2011)

Craig, Susan: "'Show Me . . . Like a Queen': A Study of the 'New' Globe Theatre's Cross-Dressed Productions of 'Antony and Cleopatra' (1999) and 'Twelfth Night, or What You Will' (2002)" Dissertation Abstracts International, Section A: The Humanities and Social Sciences, (71:5), 2010, 1499. (Drew U), (2010)

Thomas, Chad Allen: "On Queering Twelfth Night" Theatre Topics , (20:2), 2010, 101–111. (2010)

Cheang, Wai Fong: "A Crossdressed Judith Shakespeare?-Reconceptualizing the Representation of Women's Predicaments in Three Contemporary Shakespeare-related Movies" Wenshan Review of Literature and Culture, (2:2), 2009, 71–103. (Chinese summary; English summary.). (2009)

Asper, Helmut G.: "Die zögernde Prinzessin: Asta Nielsen spielt Hamlet" Film Dienst , (60:8), 2007, 16–17. (2007)

There are two additional points to note about the results screen in the Chadwyck-Healey MLA (Figure 8.10):

- Result records each have a check box to select, or Mark them. These entries are automatically added to the Marked List; if you view a full

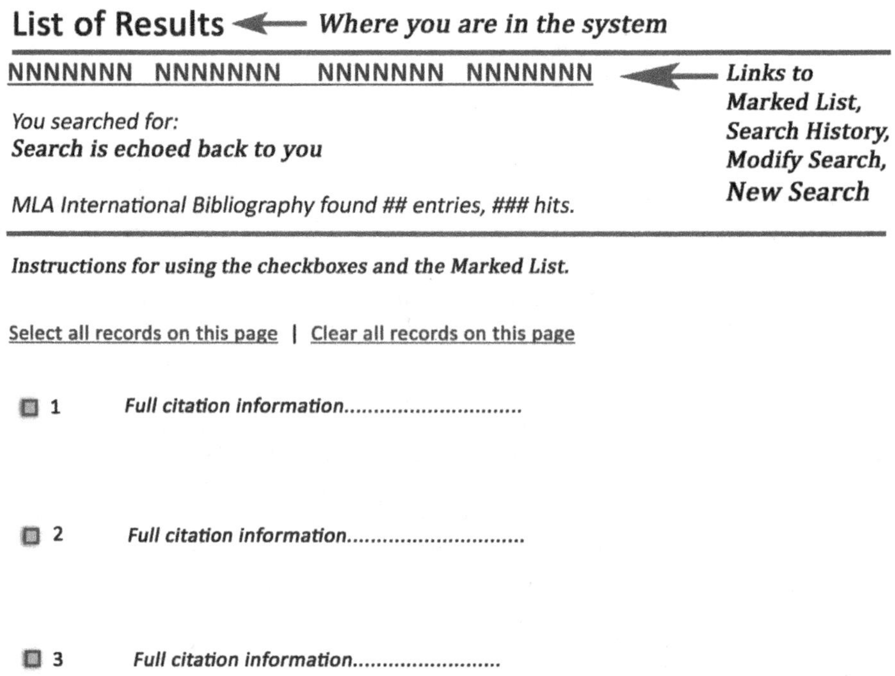

List of Results ◄─── *Where you are in the system*

NNNNNNN   NNNNNNN   NNNNNNN   NNNNNNN   ◄─── *Links to*
Marked List,
You searched for: *Search History,*
Search is echoed back to you   *Modify Search,*
New Search
MLA International Bibliography found ## entries, ### hits.

Instructions for using the checkboxes and the Marked List.

Select all records on this page | Clear all records on this page

▣ 1   *Full citation information.............................*

▣ 2   *Full citation information.............................*

▣ 3   *Full citation information.........................*

Figure 8.10. Representation of the Chadwyck-Healey *MLA IB* results display, indicating major features and functions.

record or page forward in the results, you won't lose your marked items.

- The system reports that the search retrieved "## entries" and "## hits." The entries count refers to the total number of citations, or records. The second, larger hits count measures the number of times that search terms appeared in records. A record in which a search term appears more than once causes the hit count to increase.

No matter which version of MLA IB you have access to, a Full Record display should begin to give you a sense of the detailed indexing performed on records in this database. Just like the search interface, the full record display in the Chadwyck-Healey version lines up the field names on the left, each with its value in a neat column to the right. In the record for an article titled "'Cattle of This Colour': Boying the Diva in As You Like It," there are nine subject fields, including four Literary Theme fields, a Period field, the Author as Subject field we used in our search, and so forth, as delineated in Table 8.2. (For an even more dramatic example, take a look at the record for "A Cross-dressed Judith Shakespeare?"—it has 33 Subject fields associated with it!)

Two Additional Search Samples

Returning to the Standard Search screen, let us set up one of those searches that students frequently need to do, but frequently do incorrectly,

Table 8.2. Example of list of Subjects in a full *MLA IB* record.

Subjects Field Name	Field Contents
National Literature:	English literature
Period:	1500–1599
Author as Subject:	Shakespeare, William (1564–1616)
Author's Work:	As You Like It (1598)
Subject Classification Term:	comedy
Literary Theme:	(treatment of) female protagonist
Literary Theme:	(relationship to) boy actors
Literary Theme:	cross-dressing
Literary Theme:	actresses

that is, a search for comment or analysis *of* an author or his work (a search for literary criticism). The "Author as Subject" field in the Standard Search screen is perfect for addressing this need:

Search : Standard

Author as Subject: Bellow, Saul

Such a search returns a huge number of results, however—more common would be a search for material about a particular work by an author. A strategy for finding materials that discuss a specific work by an author might be:

Search : Standard

Author as Subject: tolstoi

Author's Work: "war and peace"

This also provides the opportunity for a discussion of non-English names.

Non-English Names in the *Bibliography*

As has been pointed out several times, the scope of the *Bibliography* is international, and among those 327,000+ names in the Thesaurus are thousands of names from scores of nationalities, including names transliterated from non-Roman alphabets. For example, the MLA indexers prefer the spelling *Tolstoi*, not *Tolstoy*, for the author of *War and Peace*. The only problem is that if you look up Tolstoy in the Thesaurus, you will find it—but there is no "see" reference to guide you to the other spelling. To discover the Preferred Term, you need to select the entry Tolstoy, Leo, and then click the Related Terms button. Then you'll be told that the Preferred Term is: Tolstoi, Lev Nikolaevich. Working with Eastern European, Russian, and Chinese names (including place names) can be particularly tricky. For example, the controlled heading for the former leader of Communist China is *Mao Zedong*, not *Tse-tung, Mao*, or *Zedong, Mao*, forms and spellings that Westerners might be likely to try. If you can figure out a search that at least lets you see similar entries in the Thesaurus (for example, by searching on simply "mao" and then scanning), then you will see a listing for Mao Tse-tung that you can select, and *then* the Related Terms button will tell you that the "Preferred term(s)" is Mao Zedong. With so many names it is probably not realistic to ask the indexers to anticipate all the ways people might search for them, but getting the right version of a non-English name can be a bit tricky.

When working with names, be prepared to be flexible: use the Thesaurus if possible, but if the answer still isn't clear and you're getting frustrated, try searching the form of the name you're familiar with as Keyword(s), search parts of the name, or use truncation. You are likely to find records on the person you are after from a record where that form of the name appears in the title, and you can then see how that name is listed in the Subject fields of the record.

Search Example 2: Selecting from the Subjects—All Thesaurus

Our search objective now is to find some materials discussing dystopias in the literatures of various countries. We could go to the Advanced search and run our search specifically in the Genre field, but the danger is that we might miss some good material. Luckily, the Subjects—All field and its "select from thesaurus" link in the Standard search screen allow us to mine all of the specialized subject fields at once.

Going to the Thesaurus list for the Subjects—All field and looking for the term dystopia, we find quite a few headings to choose from. Like the WorldCat field indexes, this version of MLA displays the term you search on in context—you always see the four entries before your term and the continuation of the list after your term(s). As an example, here are our dystopia matches with the two (mysterious) entries preceding and following them:

Thesaurus : Subject List

- dystocia
- dystonia musculorum deformans
- dystopia
- dystopian drama
- dystopian fiction
- dystopian literature
- dystopian novel
- dystopian prose
- Dyula
- Dyula language

Each entry has a check box for selecting it; we choose "dystopia," "dystopian fiction," "dystopian literature," and "dystopian novel," then click the

Select button to transfer the information to the Search screen, appropriately ORed together, like this:

Search : Standard

Subjects—All: "dystopia" OR "dystopian fiction" OR "dystopian literature" OR "dystopian novel"

At this point the patron only has a vague idea of exploring how dystopias are depicted across cultures, so we will simply search these four headings and see what this very international database can give us. And what a response: almost 1000 results! The international scope of this database is indeed evident, with records for works in Spanish, Afrikaans, German, French, Turkish, and Russian. Scanning the results, however, the student notices that a number of the records seem to be chapters in a book about the *Hunger Games*. To quickly gather just those records, we use the "Modify Search" link to return to the Standard search screen, to amend it as follows:

Search : Standard

Keyword(s):   hunger games

Subjects—All: "dystopia" OR "dystopian fiction" OR "dystopian literature" OR "dystopian novel"

This neatly gathers all the records for chapters from the book *Space and Place in The Hunger Games: New Readings of the Novels*, as well as another edited book on the topic and some journal articles. Perhaps a research direction has been found!

Advanced Search

Like the Standard search, in the Advanced Search screen Chadwyck-Healey has made a deliberate decision to display all the searchable database fields in a list on the page rather than using drop-down menus (in exactly the same pattern as in the Standard search screen: [Field Name:] [text input box] "select from a list/select from thesaurus" link). The advantage is that the number and names of all the fields are obvious at a glance; the disadvantage is that it does make for a rather long screen. The full list of fields available in the Advanced search is provided in Table 8.3.

What a wealth of fields are available: every possible aspect of a publication has a searchable field, and now we see some of the other topical areas of this database being brought out, such as Folklore, Linguistics, and Performance. Note that you can search by "Language of Publication" (in the Publication Information fields), but in keeping with the Linguistics aspect of this database, there is also a field to search by "Subject Language," that is, the language being discussed in the article. For example, you could find articles written in French on the Kumak language. In addition to the same Limits that appear in the Standard search screen, the Advanced search has a limit for restricting results to journals that are Peer-Reviewed.

Table 8.3. Fields available in the Advanced search interface in the Chadwyck-Healey version of *MLA IB*.

All-purpose (first three fields)	Publication Information fields	Subjects fields
Keyword(s)	Publication Details	Subjects—All
Title Keyword(s)	Journal	Author as Subject
Document Author	Journal Volume	Author's Work
	Series Title	Folklore Topic
	ISBN	Genre
	ISSN	Linguistics Topic
	Language of Publication	Literary Influence
	Publication Year	Literary Source
		Literary Theme
		Literature Topic
		National Literature
		Performance Medium
		Period
		Place
		Subject Language
		Publisher Abstract

Cautionary Note

While I am obviously enthusiastic about having clearly labeled fields available for searching, that does not mean searching in specific fields is always the answer. Do not hesitate to fall back on a simple keyword search if a field search doesn't seem to be working. For example, a search on "women" as a Folklore Topic and "animals" as a Keyword made sense to me, but this retrieves no results. (Reversing the terms doesn't help.) Searching "women and animals" as Keywords, however, retrieves many results, which can then be browsed for the most on-target citations. (Information from those citations might then be used for building a slightly better search.) The MLA indexers are governed by many principles in choosing and assigning terms for entries, as indicated in the overview provided on the MLA website (MLA 2014b), but an overarching theme is that the indexing depends on *explicit* content. That is, a term will not be assigned to a record unless it is specifically mentioned in the content of the item. As the MLA indexers have seen the materials and you haven't, being too specific can lead to frustration. Always be ready to throw your net wider by simplifying your search.

The Marked List and Output

As mentioned previously, records in the Chadwyck-Healey MLA IB results list each have a check box for Marking them, and as you mark items they are immediately added to your Marked List. The entries in the Marked List accumulate in the sequence in which they were checked off in a Results screen, not in order by publication date. If you select the sixth result, then the first, and then the tenth, then look at your Marked List, you'll see them in the order: tenth, first, sixth (e.g., last in, first out). If you revisit some previous search results using the Search History, any additional records you mark will be added to the top of your Marked List; that is, they won't be automatically grouped with the earlier marked records from that search. There is nothing wrong with this, but it is worth mentioning because it might be somewhat confusing the first time you look at the Marked List. There are no options for sorting the items in the Marked List.

The Marked List is a fairly simple display: just a numbered list of records, each with a link to "remove from list." Above the list are links for the usual functions: Email records, Print view, and Download citations. The output interface for the email function includes a particularly nice feature: you can add an annotating note to *each* record in the list. The "Download citations" function is quite bibliographic-management-software savvy. There are options to export directly to RefWorks, or to ProCite, EndNote, or Reference Manager, to download a file compatible with importing into any of these four programs, or to download short or long versions of the citation records in plain text format.

Additional Feature: Directory of Periodicals

The third search option in the MLA IB is the Directory of Periodicals. (This is implemented in various ways by different database vendors: Sometimes the Directory of Periodicals content is integrated with the rest of the database, and sometimes it is necessary to search it as a separate database.) The Directory of Periodicals provides extensive, detailed information on over 5,800 journals and book series. The information provided is aimed both at users as *readers*—fields such as topical scope (subject), types of articles included, and subscription address—but even more at users as *writers*, as indicated by the fields just mentioned and an extensive series of fields devoted to instructions for authors: charge for submission, preferred editorial style, copyright holder, time from submission to decision, and time from decision to publication, to name just a few. If you were a graduate student specializing in Renaissance literature, the Directory of Periodicals would provide a very easy way to produce a list of journals or book series to which you might submit your work for publication (and not charge you for submitting). If you were an established scholar, you could quickly refresh your memory of the submission guidelines for the journal(s) in which you usually publish. Take note especially of the new Limit options in the representation of this screen in Figure 8.11; they all have to do with the user as a writer.

Quick Recap

The *MLA International Bibliography* (MLA IB) is produced by the Modern Language Association of America. The topical scope of the *Bibliography* is very broad, encompassing almost anything that could be described as

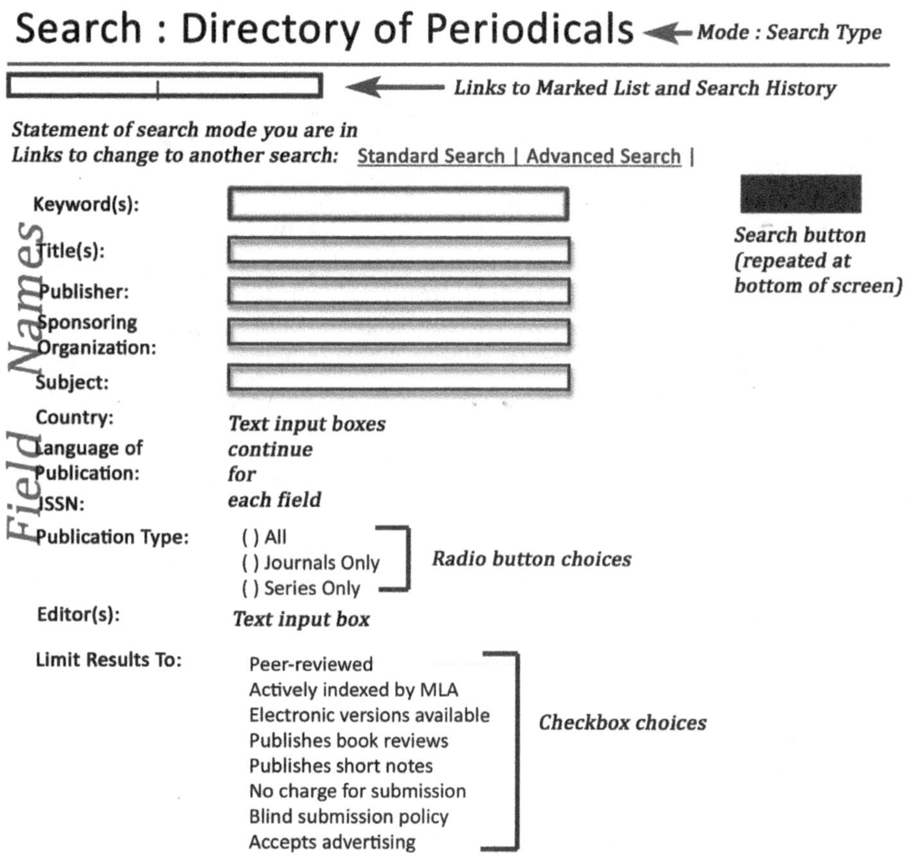

Search : Directory of Periodicals ◄— *Mode : Search Type*

◄————— *Links to Marked List and Search History*

Statement of search mode you are in
Links to change to another search: Standard Search | Advanced Search |

Field Names

Search button (repeated at bottom of screen)

Keyword(s):

Title(s):

Publisher:

Sponsoring Organization:

Subject:

Country:

Language of Publication:

ISSN:

Text input boxes continue for each field

Publication Type:

( ) All
( ) Journals Only   *Radio button choices*
( ) Series Only

Editor(s):   *Text input box*

Limit Results To:

Peer-reviewed
Actively indexed by MLA
Electronic versions available   *Checkbox choices*
Publishes book reviews
Publishes short notes
No charge for submission
Blind submission policy
Accepts advertising

Figure 8.11. Representation of the Chadwyck-Healey *MLA IB* Directory of Periodicals Search interface, indicating major features and functions.

human communication, for example, from literature and linguistics to folklore, dramatic arts, and teaching. Types of materials indexed include journal articles, books, book chapters, reference works, conference papers, dissertations, electronic publications, and works related to teaching, such as handbooks. Book reviews are *not* included. The MLA IB database is available from several different vendors; the version considered here is from Chadwyck-Healey, the specialist humanities imprint of ProQuest. This version supports special-purpose search fields, such as Author as Subject and Author's Work (as subject), in the Standard interface. The Advanced Search interface offers a long list of discipline-specific search fields, including Literary Influence, Literary Theme, Genre, and Performance Medium. An unusual feature in the email output option is that a "Notes" field is supplied for *each* record being sent, allowing the user to individually annotate the citations. An additional feature of the MLA IB is the Directory of Periodicals, which contains detailed publication, subscription, and submission information for over 6,000 journals and book series. Authors seeking to publish their work can use the Directory of Periodicals to identify appropriate publications and obtain submission instructions.

Additional Resources for Humanities

As in the previous chapters, the databases considered here are usually considered the key resources for the study of history and literature, respectively. The humanities, of course, encompass many more disciplines and there are literally hundreds of additional databases for humanities research. This section will attempt to provide a small taste of some other databases and vendors to be aware of in the area of "humanities." (For more, always remember the tip about the LibGuides Community site in Sidebar 5.1.)

In the group we might call "all purpose" humanities databases, JSTOR and *Project Muse* from Johns Hopkins University Press almost always lead the list, popular both for their scholarly content and for their full-text. Two other names to remember are *Humanities Full Text*, and *Humanities International Complete*, both from EBSCO, and of course the *Arts & Humanities Citation Index* within the Web of Science.

Continuing the two subject specialties in this chapter, *America: History & Life*, *Historical Abstracts*, JSTOR, and *Project MUSE* are usually the first choices for history research. A sampling of other databases for history includes: *America's Historical Imprints* Series I and II (Newsbank), *History Reference Center* (EBSCO), *Nineteenth Century Masterfile* (Paratext), and the primary source collections from Alexander Street Press, discussed as a group below.

For the very broad discipline of "literature," after the MLA IB could come any of a large number of databases, covering a gamut of publishers. Notable (and possibly familiar to you already) are the many, many resources in this area from the publisher Gale, which are equally at home in public, school, and academic libraries. Here is a partial list; comments have been added when the database title is not self-explanatory:

- *Black Literature Index* (ProQuest)
- *Early English Books Online* (EEBO) (ProQuest)—full text of books from the beginning of printing in England through 1700.
  - Good partner to the above: *Early English Books Online Text Creation Partnership* (from the Text Creation Partnership)—searchable and legible versions of the EEBO content
- *ESTC: English Short Title Catalogue* (British Library)—finding tool for books published from 1473–1800 in Britain and North America; has links to EEBO content when available
- HAPI (*Hispanic American Periodical Index*) (Latin American Center / UCLA)

Selection of Gale products:

  - *Biography and Genealogy Master Index*
  - *Contemporary Authors*

- *Dictionary of Literary Biography Complete Online*
- *Eighteenth Century Collections Online*
- *Nineteenth Century Collections Online*
- *Literature Criticism Online*
- *LitFinder*
- *Literary Index*

After all this exhausting literary research, however, you might simply want to find something to read for fun, something new but still in line with the kinds of things you like to read. For that, the *NoveList* database from EBSCO is ideal. This kind of resource is known as a Reader's Advisory tool, and is probably most frequently available through public libraries.

Other subject specific areas of the humanities include the following topic areas and significant databases:

Art: *Art Full Text* (EBSCO), *ARTbibliographies Modern* (ABM) (ProQuest), *Oxford Art Online* (Oxford University Press)

Film: *FIAF International Film Archive* (ProQuest), IMDb—Internet Movie Database (www.imdb.com), free Web resource; has achieved status as the authoritative source for film and television information[9]

Linguistics: *Linguistics and Language Behavior Abstracts* (ProQuest)

Music: *International Index to Music Periodicals* (ProQuest), *Music Index* (EBSCO), *Oxford Music Online* (Oxford University Press), *RILM Music Literature* (EBSCO)

Streaming audio: *Classical Music Library* (Alexander Street Press), *Magnatune* (published by Magnatune, open access), *Naxos Music Library* (Naxos)

Philosophy & Religion: *ATLA Religion Database with ATLA Serials* (EBSCO), *New Testament Abstracts* (EBSCO), *Old Testament Abstracts* (EBSCO), *Index to Jewish Periodicals* (EBSCO), *L'Annee Philologique* (EBSCO), *Philosopher's Index* (ProQuest), *Philosophy Online* (Philosophy Documentation Center), *Stanford Encyclopedia of Philosophy* (plato.stanford.edu), free Web resource hosted by Stanford University.

There are two additional database vendors that figure prominently in the area of humanities, whose products I decided to present here as groups by their *vendor* rather than mixing them in by topic above (with the one exception of Alexander Street Press' *Classical Music Library* listed under streaming audio).

Alexander Street Press has carved out a very interesting niche in the database world by focusing on *primary source materials,* and not limiting themselves to just text materials. These primary source materials are made available in full text or the appropriate media. This vendor has also chosen interesting, sometimes niche areas to build databases around, as demonstrated by the following sampling of titles.

Alexander Street Press databases:

- *African American Music Reference*
- *American History in Video*
- *Black Drama*
- *British and Irish Women's Letters and Diaries*
- *Early Encounters in North America: People, Cultures, and the Environment*
- *Gilded Age, The*
- *Scottish Women Poets of the Romantic Period*
- *Sixties: Primary Documents and Personal Narratives, 1960 to 1974*[10]

ABC-CLIO (publisher of this book) is also a vendor of databases, focusing on the school and entry-level academic markets. The products listed below are described in terms of reference resources or virtual textbooks rather than indexes to journal articles, thus they are more akin to the *AccessScience* database mentioned in the Additional Resources section in chapter 6 (but with very different content and intended audience, obviously). The databases listed below are aimed at the school library market; they are all also available in an "Academic" version aimed at the college market.

ABC-CLIO Databases:

- American Mosaic: The African American Experience
- American Mosaic: The Latino American Experience
- American Mosaic: The American Indian Experience
- World History: Ancient and Medieval Eras
- World History: The Modern Era
- World Religions: Belief, Culture, and Controversy

These resources for history and religion have received several strong endorsements from *School Library Journal,* as well as *Library Journal* and *Choice.*

Exercises and Points to Consider

1. Stanley Engerman, the professor in our first search example for *America: History & Life,* is also a prolific book *reviewer.* How would you pull up a list of his reviews of other people's books?

2. If you also have access to the *Web of Science* citation databases, try the cited reference search for Doris Kearns Goodwin's *No Ordinary Time* there. Compare the overall experience, specific capabilities, and results with search example 3 in *America: History and Life* (AHL). (Hints: search just on the author's name, and for year, put in 1994–1995.)

3. What are some archival sources being used by current historians that can provide a Mexican perspective on the U.S. war with Mexico (1846–1848)? Think about this carefully for a few moments: How are you going to get at that "Mexican perspective" part of the search? See the Endnotes for a Hint.[11]

4. A faculty member comes and asks for some titles of U.S. military history journals that would be likely candidates for a scholarly article on Gen. George S. Patton Jr. How many possible sources can you discover in AHL?

5. Many features of EBSCO's AHL did not fit into this discussion: find, explore, and discuss them. Which ones would you have included that I didn't?

6. Compare the version of MLA described here with the version at your school, if available (and different). What are advantages and disadvantages of each?

7. In the MLA Subject list (Thesaurus), how is the author of *Huckleberry Finn* listed? As Samuel Clemens, or under his pseudonym, Mark Twain? (Or both?) Compare this to your OPAC—which name is used there?

8. Consider the name of this Spanish author who was active in the late 16th and early 17th centuries: Lope Félix de Vega Carpio, often referred to simply as "Lope de Vega." Try searching "Lope de Vega" as Keyword(s)—how many results are there? Then choose a record, and see the form of his name used by the MLA indexers. Search on that, and compare the number of results with your previous search. (The Search History link is very handy if you forget to write down the number from the previous search.)

9. How many people have written their dissertation on Tolstoi's *War and Peace* (that MLA knows about)?

10. Look up Saul Bellow as an Article Author, then as the Subject of other people's articles, and observe the difference in the number of results. Explore the longer list, and come up with a way to focus your search.

11. The aforementioned searches focused on "classic" authors. What can you find about a modern author, Terry Pratchett, and his Discworld novels? Has anyone written a dissertation on Pratchett's work yet?

Beyond the Textbook Exercises

Exercises using databases from the Additional Resources section are available in the Student Resources tab at http://www.abc-clio.com/LibrariesUnlimited/product.aspx?pc=A4596P.

Notes

1. Note that it's not "Americ*an*"; this is a mistake people frequently make.

2. Note: BCE stands for "Before the Common Era"; CE stands for "Common Era." Political correctness comes to history.

3. I find the evolution of the terminology used in these interfaces interesting: A couple of years ago, these panels were all labeled "Narrow by." Now the wording is "Refine." How nice, we are getting more refined rather than narrower!

4. One does wonder where the "full words" come from, however, and one suspects possibly OCR (optical character recognition) scanning technology, given the number of "Worm War" and "Worm War H" (i.e., places where the words World War or World War II have been incorrectly interpreted by the OCR software) entries in the cited reference database. References are frequently wrong, and people mistype things, but not *that* much. Try searching just "worm war" (with quotes) in the Cited Source field to see what I mean.

5. Your reaction to the output of the "Find Similar Results" link may vary; to me, SmartText searching simply produces A LOT of results, not necessarily better than what is produced in the course of a regular search.

6. The MLA deep-date coverage isn't just lip service, either: if you search simply the date range 1884–1885, there are sixty entries (as of July 2014)! Note also that it is interesting that you can do that, i.e., simply search a year range without entering any kind of keywords or other values at all.

7. Having written that, of course I just encountered the first instance I've ever seen of an MLA IB record with an abstract. I can't find any explanation at the MLA website, in the literature, or on the Web; we'll have to just accept it as an anomaly for now.

8. Each vendor, of course, has its own user interface that is based on that vendor's field structure, so your experience searching the same database offered by different vendors can vary a great deal. If your institution subscribes to MLA from a different vendor, you will see distinct differences between that version and the one described here. For example, other versions may not offer as many document types or as many search fields, such as the specialized search for "Author as Subject." Another difference you might notice is that other vendors implement field searching as drop-down menu choices (e.g., EBSCO), rather than listing all the fields. Be ready for differences, and use them as a constructive exercise: Which implementation seems to work better, either for specific types of searches or overall?

9. It is regularly listed on library guides for finding film information.

10. What a great combination this database would be with *America: History & Life* and a topic from the Sixties era of the AHL CLIO Notes feature.

11. Hint: If you were writing about something from the Mexican perspective, in what language would you probably be writing? Search "Mexican War" as a Subject and limit it by language.

9
Numerical Databases

This chapter takes us into some very different territory. Rather than citations to textual materials, we're going to explore the idea of searching for numerical information: data, statistics—*numbers* about things. There are very few commercial databases that have tackled the issue of providing numerical information, but a great many websites have done so. We'll look at one of the major players in the commercial world, ProQuest's *Statistical Insight*, and two free government websites, American FactFinder (from the Census Bureau), and the Bureau of Labor Statistics. Before leaping into the databases, however, let's set the stage with some thoughts about finding numbers.

Finding Numbers

If you are not a specialist with years of experience—and even sometimes when you are—reference questions that involve finding statistics or data are probably the most challenging ones that you'll face. Let's be honest: for most of us, numbers are scary! There was a reason we weren't math majors. Don't be discouraged, however. Numbers questions don't always have to give you that deer in the headlights look: as with all of the other subject areas, my intent in this chapter is to try to give you some basic tools to help you to approach the question in an informed fashion, and to increase your chances of connecting the patron with the information requested. To begin with, I'm going to share with you my worldview about some basic number concepts: what determines the collection of numbers, how they can be categorized, who does the collection, and what sources to try for various categories.

> ## Sidebar 9.1: Numerical Terminology
>
> *Data* refers to individual numbers, for example, the original computer file of all the numerically coded responses to a survey, which usually looks like just a series of numbers. This is a *data* file, usually called a *data set*. Data are actual values. One value in a data set is a data point.
>
> When you process data, grouping like data points and expressing them as percentages, then you have *statistics,* which are groups of numbers, usually expressed in terms of percentages. The data (number) and the statistical percentage it represents both appear in the following sentence: "Almost 9 million (data) young Americans, or about 15 percent (a statistic) of all children, are overweight."
>
> In my experience, people who are not in numerically oriented fields (economics, business, sociology, etc.) tend to use the terms *data* and *statistics* almost interchangeably. They will ask for *data* about something, when they are really interested in statistics. (This is good, because statistics are usually easier to find.) If a person really does want a series of values to analyze, then he or she really does want a data set. A person in this position is usually quite aware of the difference between data and statistics, and you should be, too.

Concepts about Numbers

Collection of Numbers

First and foremost in working with a numerical question is to consider whether it will have been worth someone's time and effort to collect the information and make it available in the way the user desires. Numbers take a lot of time and effort to collect: real effort, often by real people. For example, the year 2000 Census cost a total of $4.5 billion, or $15.99 per person counted. By 2010, the estimated costs had ballooned to $13 billion, or $42.11 per person counted (Beine 2013). The first reports based on 2010 Census data only began to appear in May 2011, because collecting the numbers is only the beginning. Next, the data have to be analyzed and formatted into reports that either benefit the collecting organization (e.g., for planning or allocating) or are interesting enough to outside parties that they'll pay money for them.

In my previous position as a data librarian, I was frequently faced with people who felt they had an absolutely reasonable and rational numerical request, and that "certainly the information should be out there." And while what they're looking for might sound reasonable and rational to me too, it doesn't mean that the information actually is out there, or that it exists in exactly the way they envision.[1] If the government doesn't have it (our best free source), and a nonprofit organization such as the Inter-university Consortium for Political and Social Research (ICPSR) or possibly a trade organization[2] doesn't have it, then it means it would have to be information collected by a for-profit organization. Obviously, it was collected to help the company make that profit, so they have no incentive to disseminate it for free while it is still relevant. If the information isn't strategically vital or tactically important, and the company thinks it can sell the data (or reports based on the data) for more than the cost of collecting and analyzing the information, then those numbers might be available (for a fee). Again, as stated at the beginning of this section: If it's not worth somebody's time and effort, it probably won't be counted, and then exactly *because* it's worth time and effort, it might not be freely available.

Categories of Numbers

It can be helpful to think of collected numbers as falling into three broad categories: people, business, and financial. Numbers that get collected about People are things such as population counts, demographics (race, income, etc.), and vital statistics (births, deaths, etc.) Business numbers include broad information *about* business, such as numbers of companies, production, and workers in various industries, as well as numbers related to *doing* business, for example, market research or sales figures for a particular company. There are certainly business numbers that are financial (e.g., historical stock prices), but my third category, financial numbers, has to do with money or monetary equivalents (e.g., stocks) in a broader sense: information such as gross domestic product, banking data (total currency in circulation, total value of money in savings accounts, etc.), exchange rates, and aggregate numbers associated with the stock market, such as the Dow Jones Industrial Averages.

Fitting a numbers question into one of these categories helps to organize my plan of attack, because the categories tend to be associated with certain kinds of collection agents. This means that I'll get some ideas of where to look first, and that I'll have a sense of whether the information might be freely available or fee based.

Who Collects Numbers

In the United States, the U.S. government is probably the largest collector and publisher of numbers. This can probably be said of other developed countries as well. These organizations are termed the *public sector* and usually the information that they make available is free (your tax dollars at work).

At the opposite extreme, we have the *private sector*: trade or business organizations, professional associations, market research companies, and polling and surveying organizations. Usually information produced by a private-sector organization isn't free, although some trade and professional groups may provide some statistics on their websites. In general, however, numerical information collected by the private sector ranges from possibly affordable (say, from $20 to $500, which would probably be acceptable to a small-business owner or to a library buying a reference book), to prices meant for large corporations (e.g., $7,000 market research reports).[3]

Between the public and private sectors is the nonprofit area of academic researchers. Mentioned earlier, the ICPSR was organized specifically to gather and archive the data collected in the course of social science research conducted by scholars across the United States. The ICPSR is probably the largest social science data archive in the world. Your institution must be an ICPSR member for you to download their data. The membership fees reflect the magnitude of their organization and offerings (but for high-volume users, the cost per data set becomes quite inexpensive). If your institution is a member, it is likely that you will have a data librarian on staff, and ICPSR probably is his or her first or second most frequently used resource for serious number requests (i.e., for raw data that needs statistical processing, usually for advanced research). Although ICPSR is always working to make its resources more understandable to nonexpert users, it is still an advanced resource, and not as commonly found on institutional subscription lists as most of the databases in this book. Because I wish to keep the discussion at the beginning to intermediate level, using resources that are fairly common, I won't go into more details about ICPSR here. If you are interested in finding out more, their website is very helpful and informative: http://www.icpsr.umich.edu.

Try the Public Sector for . . .

When a reference question involves numbers having to do with people, my first move would be to try a government source (as long as the question is about people as *people*, and not as *consumers*). A government exists to govern people, and governing bodies are quite interested in information about their constituents. Governments are also very interested in the businesses in their countries: These companies are, after all, what keep the country solvent. For questions involving numbers of businesses, shipments of product X, employment, etc., try government sources. There are public-sector sources for some financial numbers questions as well. For questions involving monetary figures in a nationwide sense for the US, try the Federal Reserve Bank; for monetary figures at the worldwide level, try the World Bank. For US economic data, try the Bureau of Economic Analysis, and so forth.

Try the Private Sector for . . .

As mentioned previously, the government is my first choice for questions about people as people (heads that get counted). If someone wants to know about people as consumers, however, or what people are thinking, then it's more likely that the answer will come from a private-sector source: a market research report, a survey report from a company such as Harris Interactive, or perhaps a Gallup Poll. (It will probably also cost money.)

Questions about numbers for specific businesses almost always come from private-sector sources: trade organizations or publications that specialize in a particular line of business. Who cares most about home appliance manufacturing? The Association of Home Appliance Manufacturers. Hosiery? The National Association of Hosiery Manufacturers. Oil, airlines, and milk? They all have trade associations devoted to (among other things) collecting numbers pertinent to their mission, purpose, etc. Certain private-sector publishers specialize in trade reports: Crain Communications (e.g.,

Advertising Age, Plastics News), Ward's Communications (*Ward's Automotive Yearbook*), and the Beverage Information Group (beer, wine, and liquor handbooks). For any line of business, remember to consider associations as a source of information. This is perhaps especially true for service businesses, that is, for any line of work that does not involve producing a product, be sure to check for a related professional organization. This might be the only source of statistics about the profession.[4] (For example: want to know what butlers earn? Try the website of the International Guild of Professional Butlers at http://www.butlersguild.com/.)

There are two types of business numbers that are, surprisingly, freely available on the Web. One is stock quotes for particular companies: current quotes are available from any of several websites, and Yahoo! Finance offers a remarkably deep historical stock quote reporting system (the catch is that it works only for companies currently in business and trading on U.S. stock exchanges). Also accessible on the Web are the financial statements of public companies, which must be filed with the Securities and Exchange Commission (SEC) and are public documents. This information is available in a number of places, including the SEC's Edgar system (http://www.sec .gov/edgar.shtml), and the company's own website,[5] where the figures appear in the company's annual report.

Financial number questions that can involve a fee-based source tend to be ones that require a series of historical values (e.g., an exchange rate for a particular currency over a 30-year period), or financial information for another country, or a combination of the two (e.g., a table of 20 years of debt values for Nigeria). *Global Financial Data* is a commercial database product that deals in extended time series data and other specialized data series. The International Monetary Fund also charges for access to its data. In a rather jaw-dropping development in 2010, however, the World Bank opened its entire data archive for free access on the Web: see http://data.worldbank .org/. The United Nations is another likely source for financial and other numbers about countries; some of their data are freely available and some aren't. It's worth a try: http://www.un.org/en/databases/.

Quick Recap

This section has provided some background to the whole idea of finding numbers, and has given an overview of the major free and fee-based resources for numbers. A basic premise is that it takes time and effort to collect, format, and publish data or statistics. Without a financial or other strong motivation to prompt the process, data are unlikely to be collected. If information has been collected, it may not be available for free. In the United States, the government (the *public sector*) is probably the largest collector and provider of freely available data about people, industries, and economics (national-level financial information). Nongovernmental organizations, notably the World Bank, may also offer their data for free on the web. Numbers relating to businesses that can also be found at no charge on the Web are financial statements (balance sheet, income statement, etc.) for public companies and current stock quotes. Information that is rarely, if ever, free includes market research and data about specific businesses, which are most likely to be collected by survey companies, trade associations, or trade publishers (the *private sector*). One exception is trade associations, which occasionally make data related to their organization available on their websites.

A Comment about Searching for Numbers

One of the frustrating things about searching for numbers is that, all too often, whatever the person asks for, the numbers that you can find won't be exactly the ones that the patron wants:

You: "Here are some great figures about spotted hyenas!"

Patron: "Oh. Thanks, but I really wanted *striped* hyenas. . . ."

Remember that this does not represent a failure on your part: if you have done a rigorous search, it probably means that no one has cared enough yet about striped hyenas to collect and publish numerical data about them. Don't be discouraged. It is amazing, on the other hand, the numbers that you *can* find! Let's learn about the first of the three sources that we'll cover in detail, ProQuest's *Statistical Insight*.

Statistical Insight from ProQuest

Background and Coverage

Originally developed in 1998 by LexisNexis and Congressional Information Service, Inc., the database then known as *Statistical Universe* was the first to tackle the idea of indexing statistical reports rather than text documents. In essence, to put finding numbers on the same footing as finding articles.

It was a very smart partnership: Congressional Information Service (CIS) had a long history of publishing, in hard copy, three major abstracting and indexing tools: *American Statistics Index* (ASI), *Index to International Statistics* (IIS, which covers international intergovernmental organizations, e.g., the United Nations, World Bank, and the Organisation for Economic Co-operation and Development), and *Statistical Reference Index* (SRI, which indexes statistical information published by state governments, private sector publishers, and universities). By putting the content from the CIS A&I services, plus additional statistical information culled from government and other sources, into an online database under one search interface, enhancing it with indexing, and adding GIF images of the data tables, users could both search for and immediately access numerical information. And even though much of the data, especially that from the U.S. government, is freely available on the web, the task of locating it amid the plethora of government websites can be frustrating and difficult. In addition, the need to preserve and continue to provide access to earlier editions of files is not consistent across all government websites. Putting the materials into a database increases the chances of preserving a complete run of historical reports. All of these factors made *Statistical* a product definitely worth paying for.

In 2010, the whole data division of LexisNexis was purchased by Pro-Quest. Efforts to add more data, more quickly, were initiated: data are now added weekly instead of monthly, and the source list is continually expanding. I continue to see an increase in more recent content, more international content, and more frequent availability of full-text PDFs. The change in ownership has taken this unique and much-needed statistical product from strength to strength.

"Much-needed" is the key term because *Statistical Insight* is still, as of this writing, the most broadly based, general-purpose finding tool for statistical information on the market. We will discuss some complementary tools in the Additional Resources section, but there really are no direct competitors to *Statistical Insight* in the marketplace or on the free Web.

Date Coverage

Date coverage has somewhat different connotations in a numerical database than it does in a bibliographic or citation database. The range of *publication* dates—how far back the database goes—is not necessarily as important, because in the world of numbers it's very common to find recently published material that deals with the distant past, for example, "crop losses . . . 1948–1997" (published in 1999) or "acres harvested . . . 1930–1998" (published in 2006). There may be times when someone needs numbers published in a particular historical time period, but often it doesn't matter so much *when* the document was published as long as it has the right data. That said, to make the description of this database consistent with descriptions in the other chapters, we'll note that the basic *Statistical Insight* subscription provides material *published* from 1999 to the present. Adding on the ASI, SRI, and IIS modules provides indexing and abstracts back to 1973, 1980, and 1983, respectively (with recent options for full text as well). Any of these records can refer to information that is much older, however, so if you need to know the effect of weather and technology on corn yields in the Corn Belt, 1929–1962, or information about "spatial inequality" as an aspect of [economic] development "By Country, Selected Years and Periods 1767–1975," this is the place to go.

The options for the Publication Date limit recognize this difference. After doing a search, you have the option to filter your results by Date *Covered* (1700–2090—yes, you read that right![6]) or by Date *Published* (potentially from 1973 to the current year). This is a far cry from the typical date-limit field in a database, so pause and ponder it for a moment. Having said all this, I will admit I tend to avoid using date filters when searching for data; my preference is to try and identify (any and all) sources first, and simply see what date coverage is available in the results.

Notes and Search Examples

Perhaps surprisingly by now, we are going to spend our whole search experience in *Statistical Insight* in the Basic search mode. The Facet options

(ProQuest's term for filters) on the results page work so well that it is seldom necessary to go into the Advanced Search mode. Searching for numbers is just *different* from searching for words: getting too specific in the Advanced Search can actually end up being frustrating and detrimental to your searching, unless you are searching for a known item (e.g., a specific report title or similar). For once, a simple keyword or broad subject heading approach that retrieves *lots* of results that you then facet usually works more successfully.

Search Example 1: Finding Data by Occupation

As a first dip into *Statistical Insight*, we will demonstrate how to find data on a particular occupation. Feel free to try substituting whatever occupation you are interested in pursuing. Here, we will see what kinds of numbers we can find about librarians.

The Basic search screen for *Statistical Insight* adheres to the model for the Basic interface for all ProQuest databases: one search box, some colorful pictures (for this database, of things that get counted, such as fruit, trees, oil production, or highways and traffic), advice on how to search, and access to the Advanced search. I believe unique to *Statistical Insight* is the option to "Add a row" in the Basic search, access to the list of controlled subject headings ("Index Terms"—alerting us that Basic Tool No. 2, controlled vocabulary, is available here), a date limit option, and a list of topics under the label "Statistics in the News"—instant searches on hot topics. Note well that the default date limit is Previous 5 years; if you are doing an in-depth search you'll want to remember to change this to All Available Dates.

Overall, it is very clean, very simple—so much so that I think we do not need an image. You search, then you apply facets. Easy!

As you start to type in the Basic search box, after three letters the system starts suggesting things, a kind of auto-complete function such as we saw in PubMed (and that was first used by Google—what else?). But in this case, the suggestions are not just things other people have searched for: they are *programmed* suggestions that come solely from the Index Terms list (e.g., subject headings) and the issuing Source list (the names of the agencies that produced the reports). Somewhat like the Ovid interface to PsycINFO, the database designers are trying to steer users to the human-applied subject headings that have been applied to all the records. So while you could, as the interface suggests, "Improve [search] using Index Terms," it's not imperative to do a special look up in the Index Terms list; if we get close enough, the system will simply supply any available subject headings.[7] If you start typing: informat . . . you will get a rich list of headings, including information industries, information sciences, information security, and if you keep typing, information technology (for those of you who want to go into IT).

For this example, we will choose the suggestion "librarians," and hit enter to run the search.

Narrowing by Facets

On the results page, our options for sorting and faceting our results are available on the left, as shown in Figure 9.1. The sorting options are

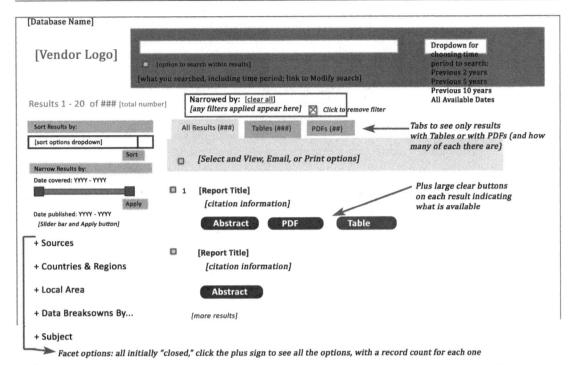

Figure 9.1. Representation of Statistical Insight results display, annotated and highlighting major features.

the usual Relevance (the default—take note!), or Date (most recent or oldest first). The "Narrow Results by" facets are organized into broad categories starting with Date Covered / Date Published slider bars, then Source, Countries & Regions, Local Area, Data Breakdowns By . . . , and Subject. As noted in Figure 9.1, by default these broad categories are first shown "closed;" clicking the plus sign for any of them reveals the possible options in that category for focusing your results, either as further sub-menus to be opened or as an immediate list. For a search like this, you might want to drill down under Source, then Associations, and choose only reports from certain associations (such as the American Library Association or the Special Libraries Association—after all, who cares more about librarian salaries than they do?). The "Data Breakdowns By . . ." offerings are always very useful; these facets are the ways people most often want to see the data, such as by age, commodity, educational attainment, income, industry, race, sex, etc. These options are sorted alphabetically. The entries under Subject, however, are sorted by frequency. Each entry in every category includes a number, indicating how many records you will have if you choose that facet: a wonderful feature. As you choose facets, the numbers will change—you'll always know the point at which your results are about to go to zero.

Say we try faceting by Source: Associations: All Associations, and Data Breakdowns: by race and ethnic group (leaving the "previous 5 years" limit in effect). This gives us just 4 results (we knew it would, from the record count, but we chose that facet anyway). Not enough? Simply remove any facet you've "Narrowed by" by clicking the orange box associated with it, or clearing them all (area just above the AI Results tab in Figure 9.1). Maybe it would be better to look for information from a federal agency. If you open that list under the Source facets, you'll see the Bureau of Labor Statistics listed, which we will visit later in this chapter. Maybe that source would have more information. If not, simply remove it and try something else. The bottom line is, it is extremely easy to apply one or more facets, see if you are getting what you want, then remove those and try other facets if you aren't. You can slice and dice your results with just clicks.

Search Example 2: Experimenting with Huge Results Sets

This example is actually an interactive exercise: It depends on your having access to *Statistical Insight* and being able to get online and experiment. Start by setting the date drop-down to Previous 10 years, and typing the following into the search box:

Earn

The suggestion: "earnings" will retrieve the largest set of results, thus giving you the greatest number of facets with which to experiment. (If the system for some mysterious reason decides not to provide that suggestion, simply type in "earnings"—with the quotes—yourself.)

Using the large result set for "earnings," start experimenting. Change the overall "Sort by:" order from Relevance to Date (most recent first). Try selecting various options under the "Data Breakdowns By . . ." and/or Subject facets. Then see if you can add facets from the Countries and Regions, or Local Area lists. (Definitely open the Countries and Regions facet, and then the sub-facet for Europe: roughly speaking, I think every country in Europe is represented now. Amazing: earnings information for *Albania*. Solid evidence of the increase in international sources.) See what is happening under the Tables or PDF tabs at any point in your explorations; these represent "full text" in this context. How about finding projections and forecasts for earnings? (Hint: Look under Subjects, and you may have to facet by region first.) If a facet (or combination of facets) produces no results, simply remove one or more and try something else. The following set of facets on the broad "earnings" search produces an interesting set of results:

Narrowed by: [Clear all]

Countries & Regions: US Total/Regional > Total US

Data Breakdowns by . . . : by educational attainment AND by occupation

(Underlying message: finish your degree, it's worth it.)

Search Example 3: Searching by Keyword, Enhanced with Toolkit Items

The emphasis so far has been on starting with a fairly broad search, typing a single word or phrase into the search box, observing what the system suggests, going with a suggested subject heading, and then using the Narrow Results options to focus your results. Please do not get the impression that this is the only good approach, however. You can also search simply by keywords (e.g. salaries librarians) or put the tools you've learned about to work in this basic search box: double quotes to indicate phrases, truncation with the asterisk, Boolean operators, and parentheses to nest statements. Here is a search constructed to find material about travel time or commuting (or commute or commuters) to work using public transport:

("travel time" OR commut*) AND work AND "public transport*"

[date setting]—Previous 5 years

Sort your results by Date (most recent first), then scan the titles. Again, you'll see many international entries, from the *Statistical Abstracts* or *Statistical Yearbooks* for other countries. Narrowing the results to "US Total/Regional > Total US" leaves us with an interesting set of results. Here are some examples:

Modes Less Traveled: Bicycling and Walking to Work in the U.S., 2008–12: American Community Survey Reports (18 p.) Published: 2014, Source: Bureau of Census, Record Number: 2014 ASI 2316-14.22. Data Summary: Commuting workers bicycling and walking to work, by commute mode, city, region, and selected demographic characteristics, aggregate 2008–12 with some trends from 1980. *[Results display has Abstract button; PDF of full text report is available on the Abstract page]*

Rural Transit Fact Book 2013 (41 p.) Published: 2014, Source: Small Urban and Rural Transit Center (University Research Centers> North Dakota State University), Record Number: 2014 SRI U3630-1. Data Summary: Rural population mass transit access and use, and travel characteristic, incl data on vehicle ownership and commuting habits, with comparisons to urban areas, 2009 or 2009–11 period, annual rpt *[Results display has Abstract button; full text PDFs of both the 2013 and 2012 Fact Books are available on the Abstract page]*

Transportation: ProQuest Statistical Abstract of the U.S. 2014: ProQuest Statistical Abstract of the U.S. 2014 Online Edition (42 p.) Published: 2014, Source: ProQuest (Commercial Publishers), Record Number: 2014 SRI C7095-1.23. Data Summary: ProQuest Statistical Abstract of the US, data on transportation by mode, 2014 annual data compilation *[Results display has Abstract button; all the tables are available on the Abstract page, in XLS, GIF, and PDF format]*

Principal Means of Transportation To Work [Selected Years, 1989–2011] (Page no.072 Table no.042) Published: 2014, Source: Bureau of Transportation Statistics (Department of Transportation) . . . *[Example of a record for an individual table; results display has Table button]*

Statistical Insight Results and Records

Results in *Statistical Insight* have at least one of the following buttons associated with them: Abstract, PDF, and Table.

The Abstract display represents the full record. It includes the complete publication information (presented in two ways, as "Title Info" and "BIB Data"), an abstract, and any or all of the following: the Index, Category, and/or Geographic Terms applied to the record, Related Tables, access to all the tables (in GIF format) and/or PDFs available for the record, and a copyright statement.

Hovering over a PDF button in the results list brings up a link to go directly to the PDF (which will usually then open in your browser). Hovering over a Table button brings up a preview of the table image, with options to download it as an Excel (XLS) file or to see the Source Document PDF (the entire report in which the individual table appeared), as well as icons for emailing or printing. Clicking through displays the table full size, with all the same output options. (Note: Emailing does not send the table image, only the links to the Excel and PDF files. More about this in the next section.)

Outputting Records

As you can see in Figure 9.1, the results lists in *Statistical Insight* have the familiar check boxes for selecting those entries that you wish to output. Simply check box the results you want, and then choose from the three options, View, Email, or Print, that are always present at the head of the results list. It seems all very easy and straightforward, but if you are expecting to receive attachments (or to print out) all the tables and PDFs from a group of records—that isn't how it works.

There isn't a way to mass output tables or PDFs from *Statistical Insight* (at least not at this time; who knows what may happen in the future?). You need to download each table or PDF one by one. If you are in a hurry or not on your own computer, the easiest thing might be to mark the records you're interested in, and then Email those results to yourself. You'll get a message containing a brief citation for each marked record, and a "Permalink" back to the record in the database, where you can then download or print the table or PDF. (Tip: when you access a record with a table in this manner, click the "Durable URL" link in the record to display the table.)

Getting to Full Text

While more and more records provide a PDF or an image of a specific table, there are still going to be records where the full text is not right there.[8]

Or you find the perfect report, but it's a little old, and you wish there was a newer one. Then what?

To be honest, the first thing I always do is to Google the title. I have had incredible luck getting to the full text online this way. This tactic has also been very effective in getting me to either more recent or older editions of the same reports from their source websites. The combination of the source name (the agency that cares about the topic) and keywords from the title of the report almost always get you very, very close if not exactly to what you're looking for (if it exists).

Next, with anything that appears to be a book-length document, try looking up the title in your institution's online catalog; your library may simply own it. Finally, look for evidence of identifying numbers: see if the record includes a SuDoc number (a government document identifier) or a mysterious annotation such as: "Record Number: 2005 ASI 7558-104." The former indicates that the item was published as a government document; if your institution has a gov docs collection, it's time to visit it. The latter number is an indicator that the whole publication is available on microfiche, part of a huge set of microfilmed documents behind the ASI (American Statistics Index, mentioned in the "Background and Coverage" section). The ASI's companion indexes, SRI and IIS, also have attendant fiche collections. Many university libraries own these fiche collections; go and consult your friendly microform collection librarian to find out more. When all else fails, there is always Interlibrary Loan.

Quick Recap

The beginning of this chapter introduced the whole topic of searching for "numbers" rather than articles, and introduced ProQuest's *Statistical Insight* as the only currently available multipurpose, entry-level subscription database for identifying numerical data.

The basic search in *Statistical Insight* is sufficient in almost all cases, although an Advanced search is available. Typing into the basic search box causes suggestions to appear, all of which are Index or Subject terms. You can choose a suggested term or compose your own search strategy, and then easily apply and remove facets from the extensive set provided on the left side of the results screen. Each facet option includes the number of results that will be available when that facet is applied. Each record in the results list will be clearly marked as to the availability of full text (the Table and PDF buttons), or you can look only at the records having a Table or PDF by choosing those tabs above the results list. If the full text of an item is not available in the database, doing a Google search for the report title (or the name of the issuing agency and part of the title) is a good approach; searching the local online catalog for the document title or consulting with a government documents librarian, if available, are other good strategies.

Even if the *Statistical Insight* database does not contain the full text of the data you are interested in, it is a far more efficient way of searching for and *identifying* what data might work and where it comes from, because it is custom built for that purpose. Having identified a report or an agency, one can then do a Google search for that known information. *Statistical Insight* provides a controlled entry into the crazy, messy world of numbers.

American FactFinder

Leaving the (relative) safety of the commercially crafted *Statistical Insight*, our first stop out on the wild frontier of numbers is the U.S. Bureau of Census (http://www.census.gov), home of *American FactFinder*.

Background and Coverage

In addition to everything else it provides, the Census Bureau website is home to a wonderful resource called *American FactFinder* (http://factfinder2 .census.gov). This is a good tool that keeps getting better. Reviews when it initially launched were highly positive (Jacsó 2000; Gordon-Murnane 2002), and subsequent reviews no less so. In 2006 Durant declared that: "All but the smallest academic and public libraries should link to it" and summed up his review of *American FactFinder* as "Highly recommended" (Durant 2006). Having used it since the early days, I can attest that this site has steadily gotten easier to use and understand, with one period of interregnum (captured in the third edition of this book) that is better to simply draw a veil over. As of this writing the Census Bureau has, thank goodness, restored the straightforward "Community Facts" one-box search, making the complex wealth of information they collect once again accessible to anyone who can type a zip code in a box.

The data accessible through *American FactFinder* include the current and previous decennial Census (i.e., from 2000 and 2010). The 2010 Census used only the short form, which is literally short. It's only 10 questions, covering only the most basic information: age, Hispanic or Latino origin, sex, race, living arrangements (e.g., type of housing, own or rent, household relationships and size). Luckily, *American FactFinder* also draws data from many other surveys that are more detailed and administered annually. (Although only to a sample of the population: it would be impossible to collect detailed survey results from 100% of the population every year, which is why the official Census is only administered every 10 years. The results from these annual surveys—a *statistical sampling*—are used to create estimates for the larger population.) The additional surveys include multiple years of the American Community Survey (ACS), the American Housing Survey, the Puerto Rico Community Survey, annual Population Estimate reports, the five-year Economic Census reports, annual economic surveys such as the Annual Survey of Manufactures and County Business Patterns, and even more. (It truly is a "wealth" of information.)

Notes and Search Examples

The American FactFinder homepage, as of this writing, is shown in Figure 9.2. It offers several ways to search (Community Facts, Guided Search,

Figure 9.2. The American FactFinder home page, as of June 2014.

and Advanced Search) but if you are only interested in information for one place, the Community Facts search is all you need.

Search Example 1: Getting "Community Facts"

You'd like to know how well you fit in (statistically, at least) in your community.

It is interesting to examine statistics that have been gathered about the community you live in, and see how you "fit"—in terms of age, marital status, income, etc., in the place you call home. The *American FactFinder* Community Facts system provides a good profile of every community in the United States, and requires nothing more than typing in a zip code or the name of a town, city, county or state. If you are searching by location name, type enough in to disambiguate which location you mean, and let the auto-suggest system do its work. If the name still matches more than one geography, choose the place you want from the list the system generates (Figure 9.3).

Navigating the Community Facts Display

An example of the initial Community Facts display is shown in Figure 9.4A. Information relating to the first button on the left is displayed in the main area of the screen, consisting of a prominent key number for that topic, the source of that number, and then a very manageable list of "Popular

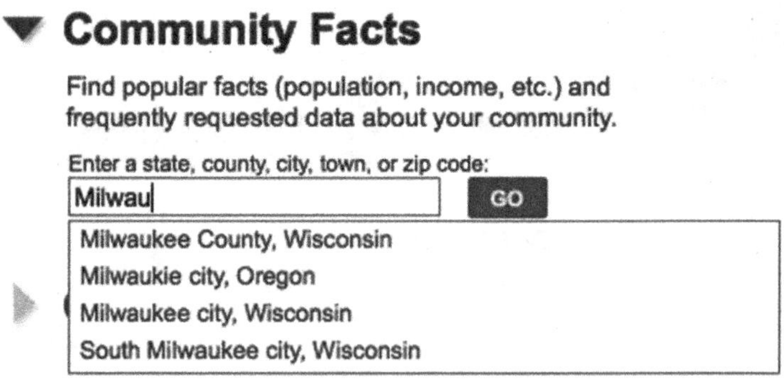

▼ Community Facts

Find popular facts (population, income, etc.) and frequently requested data about your community.

Enter a state, county, city, town, or zip code:

Milwau | **GO**

Milwaukee County, Wisconsin
Milwaukie city, Oregon
Milwaukee city, Wisconsin
South Milwaukee city, Wisconsin

Figure 9.3. American FactFinder suggestion system in action, as of June 2014.

tables for this geography," arranged by the survey from which the tables are derived. Clicking another button on the left changes the display to a number and popular tables for that topic (e.g., Total Housing Units for the Housing button). Yes, it is simplistic at this point, but the display always reminds you that if you want more, to use the Guided or Advanced search. Clicking into any of the suggested tables launches you into the rich detail of the survey; *then* things get interesting and you begin to appreciate having your hand held up to that point.

For example, if we choose the table on Demographic and Housing Estimates from the 2012 American Community Survey, we are suddenly looking at *lots* of numbers, but it's actually quite easy to spot that Milwaukee city, Wisconsin (as the Census Bureau refers to it) is a "young" city demographically: the largest percentage of the population falls in the 25 to 34 year age range (Figure 9.4*B*).

Using the topic buttons and tables retrieved by your zip code, what can you find out about your community? Spend some time looking through this information, and experimenting with the "Actions" available when you are looking at a specific table: Modify Table, Bookmark, Print, Download, Create a Map. Modify Table is truly amazing: you can show or hide rows and columns, move them around, change how a column is sorted, filter rows, and more, on-the-fly and right in the browser. You do have to wait for the screen to refresh after each action, so realistically it might be more efficient to Download the table and work with it in Excel. Still, you can't deny the "wow" factor of being able to make your own changes to the table right there on the screen. The Create a Map feature is also quite impressive, but be ready to be very, *very* patient. (Tip: watch the Create a Map video tutorial to learn how it works.)

Can you find the "Commute Time" for the place where you live? (Hint: this is an aspect of "Business and Industry.")

Guided Search Example

Community Facts are wonderful for easily finding lots of information about one location at a time. But what if you wanted one item of information for many places? As the display keeps reminding us, if we "want more,"

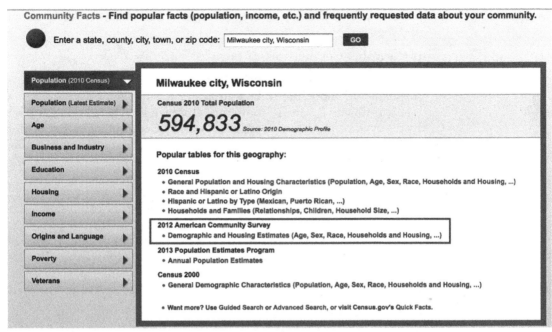

Figure 9.4*A*. American FactFinder initial "Facts" display, as of June 2014.

	Milwaukee city, Wisconsin			
Subject	Estimate	Margin of Error	Percent	Percent Margin of Error
SEX AND AGE				
Total population	594,328	+/-71	594,328	(X)
Male	284,831	+/-1,033	47.9%	+/-0.2
Female	309,497	+/-1,031	52.1%	+/-0.2
Under 5 years	48,128	+/-699	8.1%	+/-0.1
5 to 9 years	43,156	+/-1,000	7.3%	+/-0.2
10 to 14 years	43,349	+/-903	7.3%	+/-0.2
15 to 19 years	49,435	+/-704	8.3%	+/-0.1
20 to 24 years	56,343	+/-822	9.5%	+/-0.2
25 to 34 years	97,136	+/-1,052	16.3%	+/-0.2
35 to 44 years	74,135	+/-806	12.5%	+/-0.1
45 to 54 years	73,067	+/-821	12.3%	+/-0.1
55 to 59 years	31,767	+/-884	5.3%	+/-0.1
60 to 64 years	23,529	+/-746	4.0%	+/-0.1

Figure 9.4*B*. Detail of the "Demographic and Housing Estimates (Age, Sex, Race...)" table linked on the initial "Facts" display, as of June 2014.

we should try the Guided Search or the Advanced Search. Let's see if we can find the average commuting time for all the major cities in the US. Go get online, and see if you can walk through getting this data set with me. Since this is a free website, I know you can go see it for yourself, so I'm going to try only explaining the process in words. Use your eyes, and see if you can follow along, and even adapt if necessary if something has changed.

1. On the *American FactFinder* homepage, choose Guided Search. (Or if you are already in *FactFinder* looking at something else, simply

choose Guided Search in the bar right under the *FactFinder* name and logo.)

a. Click the "Get me started" button.

2. Now we have to decide: does "commuting" represent information about people, housing, or businesses or industries? (We don't know what "dataset" it comes from, and while we could cheat and search by a keyword in the table title, we won't.) Commuting is something that People do, so let's choose the first option, "I'm looking for information about **people**."

a. Click the Next button.

3. Now we are in step 2, Topics, and we have a list of expandable categories to choose from. Hmm. Commuting is something you do to get to work, so let's look at what's listed when we expand (click the + sign) for Employment. Bingo! "Commuting (Journey to Work)." Choose that topic, and notice how it flies over into the Your Selections box.

a. Click the Next button.

4. Step 3: Geographies. Here is where we get to choose multiple places for which we want this commuting time information. Use the "—select a geographic type—"drop-drown menu, and scroll it down until you find the top-level geography "Metropolitan Statistical Area/ Micropolitan Statistical Area" (e.g., not the similar heading indented under State).

a. Choose that value.

b. This brings up another list to choose from; choose either "All Metropolitan Statistical Areas within United States" (or the "All Micropolitan" option, if you like smaller places.)

c. Click the Add To Your Selections button (should be directly below the list), causing your choice to again fly over to the Your Selections box.

d. Click the Next button.

5. Step 5 gives us the chance to find data by Race/Ethnic Groups. That's not our focus in this question, so use either the Skip This Step button or simply click Next.

6. And now we're looking at our Search Results! There are many tables listed, but the most recent ones are at the top. Take a look at the table of "Selected Economic Characteristics" from the "[most recent year] ACS 1-Year Estimates" and see what it has to say about Commuting to Work in major cities across the US. (Notice the paging navigation in very small print just above the table; this is only 18 columns out of a total of over 1400 in the whole table. Use the tiny forward-arrow to see the next set of columns.) You might want to

compare these figures to the ones in the ACS 3-Year Estimates or ACS 5-Year Estimates.

And there you are: a detailed set of data for travel time to work in every major metropolitan area of the United States. You can find numbers!

Quick Recap

This section has looked at *American FactFinder*, the interactive system created by the Census Bureau for accessing data from the decennial Census and many other, more frequent surveys, including the annual American Community Surveys. We looked at two ways to search *American FactFinder*: Community Facts and Guided Search. Community Facts provides a lot of data about one geography at a time, manageably "chunked" by topic. With Guided Search, you can retrieve information for multiple geographies via a step-by-step process. The text input boxes in *American FactFinder* are designed to offer suggestions as you type; it can be worth typing more slowly (so the system can keep up) to take advantage of those suggestions. If no suggestions are offered, go ahead and try your search anyway. When you are looking at a particular table, there are many powerful options to choose from, including the interesting Create a Map function.

From "People" to "Workers"

The Census Bureau keeps track of the state of people in the United States: that is, how many people there are, how old they are, what sex they are, what race they belong to, where they live, and so forth. The Census Bureau notes whether people are employed or not, their income, and whether they are below the poverty level. For more detail about working America, however, we need to go to the Bureau of Labor Statistics.

Bureau of Labor Statistics

The Bureau of Labor Statistics, or BLS (http://www.bls.gov), tracks and provides exactly what the name says: everything about labor—working—in the United States. And it does mean *everything*—as of this writing, the BLS home page is featuring current news, a "By the Numbers" essay, regional information, "Latest Numbers," links to career information and BLS publications, and finally additional lists in small print at the bottom of the page. Even though it is a lot of information, it is cleanly structured and easy to understand. When we mouse over "Subjects" at the top of the page, however, I can understand if you start to feel overwhelmed (Figure 9.5). If you invest some time in studying it, however, you'll find that the designers have done their utmost to lay it out in a sensible and well-organized way, to try and connect you with the information you want as easily as possible. You will almost always find something new and useful, too. (And, besides, how can you help but feel friendly towards a government agency that uses

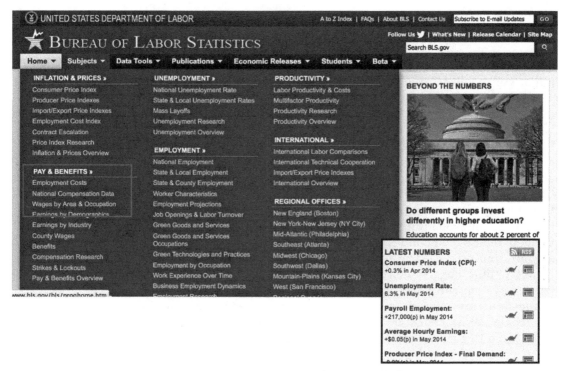

Figure 9.5. Subject Areas menu on the BLS home page, with Pay and Benefits section high-lighted, as of June 2014.

a little green dinosaur icon to indicate "historical" data? See the inset in Figure 9.5).

For our first example, we will focus on one section, about wages.

Pay & Benefits at the Bureau of Labor Statistics

Search Example 1: Part 1, Wages by Area & Occupation

Suppose the person closest to you has announced that as soon as you get done with your degree, he wants to go back to school and pursue *his* life-long dream of becoming a registered nurse. This causes you to wonder about job prospects, and especially salaries for nurses.

On the BLS home page, mouse over "Subjects" in the row of menus just below the agency name, as shown in Figure 9.5. Don't panic at the myriad choices; simply look under the heading "Pay & Benefits" for the "Wages by Area & Occupation" link (boxed area in the figure).

The next thing to decide is for what geographic area you want wage information: national, regional, state, or metropolitan area. When you're doing research for a particular person, it makes the most sense to look at data for a particular metropolitan area, since you'll be living and working in some specific place. (The other categories are more appropriate for more theoretical, comparative research purposes.) So let's look under the heading Wage Data by Metropolitan Area, and try the option: "For 375 metropolitan

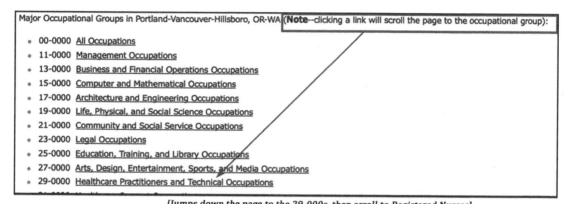

Figure 9.6. BLS page for Occupational Employment and Wage Estimates for Portland-Vancouver-Hillsboro, OR-WA metropolitan statistical area, selected portions, as of June 2014.

statistical areas (MSAs), 34 metropolitan divisions, and over 170 nonmetropolitan areas," because it seems to offer more than the "major metropolitan areas" option (which only offers "80 metropolitan areas").

Clicking this link takes us to a straightforward page where you simply have to scroll to the state you want and choose a city name (or do a "find in page" for a city name). For instance, the two pertinent parts of the "Occupational Employment and Wage Estimates" web page for the metroplex of Portland-Vancouver-Hillsboro, OR-WA, is shown in Figure 9.6.

If you have an idea of which broad category the occupation you are interested in belongs to, just click the link in the initial list and jump to that category (and then you may need to scroll to find the exact occupation you're looking for). But if you aren't sure what broad category the occupation you're looking for falls into, all you need to do is search the page for a word in the occupation title (e.g., "nurses" or "systems analyst") using the Web browser's Find function. Find is listed under the Edit menu, or can be invoked with "ctrl-f" on a PC or "command (⌘)–f" on a Mac.

Occupation Information at the Bureau of Labor Statistics

Search Example 1: Part 2, the *Occupational Outlook Handbook*

Continuing with the search example started earlier, your second concern was about the job outlook for nurses. The *Occupational Outlook Handbook* is the perfect answer. Wherever you are in the BLS home page, you can quickly get to the *Occupational Outlook Handbook* by mousing over

Publications in the menu bar. It is listed there and in several places on the BLS homepage.

The *Handbook* is a classic source of career guidance, first in hard copy and for many years now on the Web. It received a complete makeover in 2011–12, and now offers a number of very useful features not previously available (Figure 9.7).

There are various ways to use the *Handbook*, depending on your need. If you have a specific position in mind, as in this case, you can use the search box or browse the A–Z Index. If you are looking for a very specific job title, or the sorts of trendy titles that crop up in the tech industry ("chief creative officer"), you might not find an exact match in the *Handbook*, but doing a search might still bring up jobs that are related.

If you are looking for ideas for your future career, however, you have a number of options. You can browse Occupation Groups, or jump straight into the lists of Highest Paying, Fastest Growing, or Most New Jobs. Using the drop-down menus under Select Occupations By, you can create a personalized set of criteria and generate a list of jobs matching those criteria. This feature in particular could open your eyes to lines of work you'd never considered before.

But we know exactly which occupation we're interested in, so we head to the page for Registered Nurses. These 'occupation pages' bring together an extremely useful package of information presented as a series of tabs: Summary, What They Do, Work Environment, How to Become One, Pay, Job

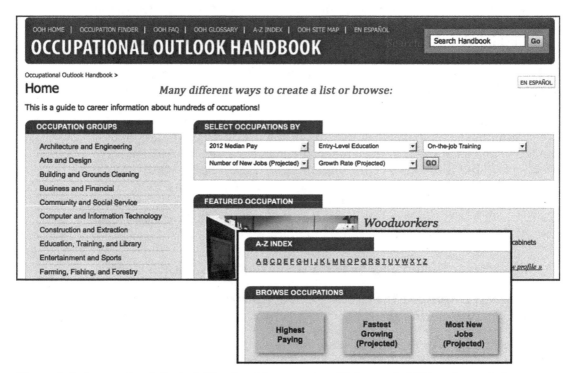

Figure 9.7. *Occupational Outlook Handbook* homepage, with inset of additional search features, as of June 2014.

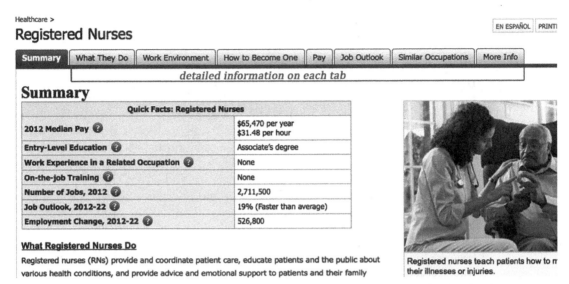

Figure 9.8. Example of an "occupation" page from the *Occupational Outlook Handbook*, annotated, as of June 2014.

Outlook, Similar Occupations, and More Info. The Summary page is always shown first, and provides a set of quick facts and summaries of the other tab's content (Figure 9.8). The other tabs then go into detail for their topic (and even include a "Suggested Citation" for the material).

The current *Occupational Outlook Handbook* content for registered nurses gives us the encouraging news that "Overall job opportunities for registered nurses are expected to be good" and that "Employment of registered nurses is expected to grow by 19 percent from 2012 to 2022, faster than the average for all occupations" (Bureau of Labor Statistics 2014). This could be a good career move!

The only bad news is that this information is provided at the nationwide level only. Finding information on job *outlook* (as opposed to current employment) by state or city is, regrettably, beyond the entry-level scope of this text, and you are encouraged to go talk to your friendly local business librarian.

Quick Recap

The *Bureau of Labor Statistics* tracks and provides information about employment and occupations in the United States, along with limited international information. Other topics covered by the BLS are pricing, inflation, consumer spending, and time use. We looked at only two of the hundreds of resources at the BLS: wage information by occupation, based on geographic location (e.g., salaries for librarians in Boston versus Omaha), and the *Occupational Outlook Handbook*. The *Handbook* pulls together a range of useful information for each job described to provide a clear picture of what work in that field is like, prospects for employment and pay, and organizations or websites to visit for more information. The BLS is a vast and incredibly rich resource for data of every kind about working in the United States.

Additional Resources for Statistics

One of the most comprehensive, all-time-best resources for quantitative information about almost anything in the US is a publication called the *Statistical Abstract of the United States*. Published annually by the Census Bureau from 1878 up until 2012, it was available in print and as PDFs freely available from the Census Bureau website. As of the 2012 edition, however, the Census Bureau could no longer afford to fund the office that collected and published the *Statistical Abstract*, and ceased publication. The data world swooned, but ProQuest charged in and saved the day by taking over the data collection and publication, and going one better: they turned the *Statistical Abstract* into a searchable database.[9] (This product integrates very nicely with the *Statistical Insight* database.) The *Statistical Abstract* has always been a cornerstone of numerical reference resources, and if you have only a limited budget (and mostly US-centric requests for numbers), this is the product to get. Having done it for the US, ProQuest then launched another new database called the *Statistical Abstract of the World*.

In early 2006, Cambridge University Press published the *Historical Statistics of the United States Millennial Edition* as a hardcopy book and an online database. As suggested by the title, the emphasis here is on *history*. This is an excellent resource for very-long-time series of strictly American data, in fairly broad topic areas (it is based on Census data). The emphasis here is on depth rather than breadth, for the past rather than the present. (Tables can go back as far as 1790, but generally stop in the 1990s, with a few going up to 2000.) An added extra of the *Historical Statistics* is that in addition to tables, it also provides detailed essays on major topics written by experts. The essays contain links to the tables that support the discussion, tying the two aspects of the database together.

Other fee-based services include the OECD's iLibrary, the International Monetary Fund's *International Financial Statistics*, *Statista* (from Statista, Inc.), and specialty applications for mapping, such as SimplyMap and PolicyMap.

Statista is a fairly new entrant on the statistical database stage, and is quite different from all the other sources. Not stuffy or formal at all, both the types of data they collect and the way they present it are very *au courant*. A spiffy colorful infographic on something to do with music? *Statista* had 20 on offer as of this writing. Or if you want a quick chart of Global iPhone sales, World of Warcraft subscribers, NFL teams by number of Super Bowls won, for the current year, this is the place. *Statista* is amazing for its coverage of trendy topics and its currency: almost nowhere else will you find data for the current year (but it may not be available for the *topic* you are searching for). For these topics, what you get is simply a bar chart with one or two sentences of explanation, source information, and suggestions for other charts you might be interested in, etc. *Statista* does also offer in-depth "dossiers" and market research, but I have to admit, I tend to associate it with these one-chart wonders (which are great if that's all you need).

Finally, we cannot leave a discussion of numerical databases without mentioning the World Bank again. As noted in the introductory material for this chapter, in 2010 the World Bank made the momentous decision to provide "free and open access to data about development in countries around the globe" (at http://data.worldbank.org). What is available now goes far beyond the former subscription product, *World Development Indicators*, which had been another mainstay in reference collections for many years. Now anyone with an Internet connection can access all the data collected by the World Bank, get tables, view data in the form of graphs or maps, run their own data analyses or visualizations (and share the results with others), and much, much more. The World Bank's Open Data Initiative is truly a gift to the world.

Numbers and the Reference Interview

Numeric Reference is somewhat of a specialty, involving a lexicon all its own. Information from surveys gets turned into data sets, which are then defined in terms of four distinct characteristics. I have listed here four specific things to try to find out during a reference interview with any patron requesting "data."

- The *population*, often referred to as the "universe" in data-speak: whom is the patron interested in? All of the people who live in rural areas of the United States? Nurses? Railway workers in the 19th century?

- *Date*: Most current available? One particular date (usually a year) in the past? Or a "time series," that is, a set of values over a particular period (e.g., the gross national product for the United States from 1948 to now)?

- *Frequency* (for a time series): Annually? Quarterly? Monthly?

- *Place, or geographic region*: The whole United States? Alabama? Spain?

It would be nice to provide you with a succinct, complementary list of actions to take based on the answers to these questions, but that probably requires a book unto itself. Suffice it to say that these definitely *are* the four questions to ask, and that eliciting information about these four things is useful in several ways, both practically and psychologically:

- The answers to these questions should help to determine if the patron really does want a data set, or just some statistics.

- If the request is vague, obviously the questions should help to clarify it, and asking them collects useful information (while also buying some time in which to rack your brain).

- Going through the process also provides a structured approach to fall back on (e.g., go back and ask the *right* questions), if you thought you understood the question and could get an answer pretty quickly, but your first resource isn't working out.

- Finally, answers to these questions are intended to help *you* to decide where to go looking for the information, but they will be equally helpful if you need to refer the patron to someone else in the library. Capturing the answers is a useful thing to do that makes the patron feel that a help process has been started, and forwarding the information will make the next librarian's task much easier, as well as saving time for both the librarian and the patron.

Exercises and Points to Consider

1. In the opening to this chapter, some broad categories of the following types of numbers were mentioned. If you are using this book in a class, have a class discussion and see how many specific types of the following sorts of numbers or statistics you can come up with:

   "People" type

   "Business" type

   "Financial" type

2. Similar to search example 1 in *Statistical Insight*, start typing "immigration" into the search box, and observe the suggestions that appear. Choose the suggestion "immigration and emigration," and then again spend time experimenting with the facets and with sorting by Date Published as opposed to Relevance.

3. Using *Statistical Insight*, can you find the total amount of wine imported to the US in [the most recent year available]? How about exported? For what other countries does *Statistical Insight* offer wine import data?

4. Still in *Statistical Insight*, what statistics can you find about traffic accidents due to texting? Start with a simple search (e.g. traffic accidents texting), then try to increase the number of results by learning from your results (Is there a better index term/phrase? What is the word used in many of the report titles for this type of activity? etc.). What are the coverage and published date ranges for each iteration of your search?

5. Can you find how many people *bicycle* to work in the US? What are the proportions of men versus women who bike to work? Create a Map to display the areas of the country with the highest percentages of people who commute by bicycle. Hint: In *American FactFinder*'s Guided Search, use the "I want to search for a **table number** or a **table title**" option, and search on the word bicycle. Then choose your geography (United States, or any local area of interest to you). In the "top 10 search results" returned, notice how the arrangement and degree of detail is slightly different depending on the table (one of the tables even includes how many people get to work by streetcar or trolley, or by ferry).

6. As mentioned in the Quick Recap for the BLS, this agency also conducts surveys and provides data on time use, that is, how Americans spend their days (and their spending habits). Find the link to this information under Subject Areas, and take a look at the HTML version of the latest American Time Use Survey. You are after something called "Table 1. Time spent in primary activities (1) and percent of the civilian population engaging in each activity, averages per day by sex, [latest year annual averages]." Take a look at the categories, gender differences, etc.—does this "look like you"?

Beyond the Textbook Exercises

Exercises using databases from the Additional Resources section are available on the Student Resources tab at http://www.abc-clio.com/Libraries Unlimited/product.aspx?pc=A4596P.

Suggested Readings

Kellam, Lynda M., and Katharin Peter. 2011. *Numeric Data Services and Sources for the General Reference Librarian*. Cambridge, UK: Woodhead Publishing Limited. The perfect gentle introduction to working with "data questions" for the nonspecialist. The authors are members of IASSIST, the professional organization for data librarians.

Ojala, Marydee. 2004. "Statistically Speaking." *Online* (Weston, Conn.) 28 (March/April): 42–44. A more in-depth look at "where numbers come from," similar to the opening discussion in this chapter. Full of good advice and strategies from a master in the field.

Xia, Jingfeng, and Minglu Wang. 2014. "Competencies and Responsibilities of Social Science Data Librarians: An Analysis of Job Descriptions." *College & Research Libraries* 75 (3): 362–388. Thinking of becoming a data librarian? This article provides an analysis of what employers are looking for.

Notes

1. This continues in my role as business librarian, but not as frequently. Business students seem to "get it" much more quickly that data collection costs money, and if the collecting agency can't recoup their costs, the numbers may not have been collected.

2. Note that nonprofits and trade organizations usually do not provide data for free; *nonprofit* does not mean "no fee" (and trade organizations need to recoup their costs, too).

3. What one might call the "ha ha, you must be kidding!" price category.

4. Obviously, Google does a good job of finding Web sites for organizations, but *Associations Unlimited*, the database equivalent of that reference staple, the *Encyclopedia of Associations*, is handy for identifying associations—especially the international ones, whose Web site might not be in English.

5. Look for links with the word "Investor" in them: Investor Relations, Investor Center, etc.

6. The year range you get for this limit will depend on what you search, of course. This was a simple search on the word "corn," for "All available dates." Most searches would not produce such an amazing "Date covered" range, but this is fun for its shock value.

7. Somewhat unfortunately, they do not TELL you that they are suggesting subject headings. The tip-off is that all the suggested terms are enclosed in double quotes, even the single word ones. If you do a look up in the Index Terms list, you'll see that headings you choose from there get pasted into the search box enclosed in quotes. It seems to be a very subtle code for "this is a controlled term."

8. Note, however: even a record that doesn't have a PDF button on it in the results page sometimes has a link to the PDF buried at the end of the Abstract display. It can pay to check.

9. At which there was much rejoicing in library and data land.

10
Focus on People

This entire book so far has been concerned with the mechanics of databases: what they are, how to use them, and how they differ by discipline. But it's important to pause and reflect on the ultimate reason *why* we're interested in learning this: to assist other people in their research process. Understanding the people who might benefit from using these databases and how they feel about doing research (there are a lot of emotions involved, it turns out) can inform how you interact with them. This chapter provides an examination of the general theoretical underpinnings of what researchers are going through: the whole process of *information seeking*. Indeed, information seeking is all around us, "always embedded in the larger tasks of work, learning, and play" (Nel 2001). Whether you're motivated by the question of locating the nearest coffee shop or a desire to find information on a rare form of cancer, although you might not have thought of it this way, those who study information seeking behavior see you as engaged in a complex set of interacting dimensions of work tasks, search tasks, time, and "individual, contextual, and environmental attributes"—all of which influence your information seeking and retrieval strategies (Xie 2009). If you are a librarian trying to facilitate information seeking, it's important to have the process in the back of your mind as you engage in a reference interview. Understanding the information seeking process also helps to inform your whole strategy of questioning in the reference interview (e.g., the use of "open" and "closed" questions) and helps to ensure greater satisfaction on both sides: librarian and patron.

This chapter is based on selected articles and other sources from the library literature that I found helpful for conveying the major points that I wish to make. These articles range from scholarly and erudite to down-home and practical (often the informal, one- or two-page pieces offer some of the best down-to-earth advice). This is by no means a comprehensive review of the literature; indeed, the examples listed in the section on Applied Studies are only a very select sample of articles that have been published since 2012 (when the previous edition of this book came out).

Interest in information seeking has a remarkably long history, as demonstrated by a study of the reference interview dating from the 19th century (Green 1876). Countless other studies have followed, making the information seeking literature vast and continually growing. Entire journals are devoted to the study of information needs and information seeking. *Information Research* (ISSN 1368-1613) is an "open access, international, peer-reviewed, scholarly journal" that made its debut on the Web in 1995 and has been actively publishing ever since (Information Research home page 2014). This e-journal probably now offers the largest freely available body of research papers in the world on the essential question of how people seek to fulfill their information needs and how librarians can better assist in the process.

Part 1: Information Seeking Behavior

The information seeking literature can generally be characterized as belonging to one of two groups: the *theoretical*, which discusses the topic in abstract terms and seeks to define it in terms of structured models, and the *applied*, which discusses it in terms of real-world observations and interactions. This section provides an introduction to some of the theory and the applied studies on people's information seeking behaviors.

Some Theoretical Background on Information Seeking

Robert S. Taylor's 1968 article is a classic in the area of theoretical information seeking studies. In it, he presents a model that identifies four levels of questions:

- Q1   the visceral need
- Q2   the conscious need
- Q3   the formalized need
- Q4   the compromised need

According to Taylor, information seeking can range from an unconscious, not-even-expressible information need, to a very fuzzy but vaguely discussible need, to a point at which the person can clearly voice the question, and finally to the compromised need—the question "*as presented to an information system*" (emphasis mine). An example of the question as presented to an information system is what a person types into the Google search box. (The source quoted lists "library or librarian" as the first kind of possible "information system," but as we know, and as is amply demonstrated in the literature, the Web is by far the first choice of information seekers today.)

In his 2001 article, Johannes Nel surveys the subsequent theoretical literature and the models of information seeking with an emphasis on the emotional states that accompany the various stages of the search process.

Table 10.1. Information Search Process Stages in Kuhlthau's Model (1991).

Stage	Task	Emotions
Initiation	Recognize a need for information (result of awareness of lack of knowledge).	Uncertainty, apprehension
Selection	Identify and select general topic or approach.	Optimism (upon achieving task)
Exploration	Need to locate information about topic, become informed, integrate new information with previously held constructs, reconcile sources providing inconsistent or incompatible information	Confusion, uncertainty, discouragement, frustration, sense of personal inadequacy
Formulation	Focus, personalize topic by identifying and selecting ideas from all the information retrieved.	Increased confidence, sense of clarity
Collection	Gather information related to the restated, focused topic; clearer sense of direction allows for more efficient, relevant interactions with information systems.	Confidence increases, interest in project increases, uncertainty subsides.
Presentation	Prepare presentation of findings.	Relief, satisfaction (or disappointment if search has not gone well)

He describes the classic model of the "information search process" by Carol Kuhlthau (1991) in detail; it has many stages and affiliated emotions, as indicated in Table 10.1. (This model was revisited in the very different world of 2008 by Kuhlthau and her colleagues, and found to be still valid [Kuhlthau, Heinström, and Todd].) Taken overall, this process amounts to quite an emotional roller coaster for the poor information seeker. Looking over the stages, we could envision it as in Figure 10.1.

A study by Ethelene Whitmire (2003) demonstrates that when it comes to undergraduates faced with writing research papers, Kuhlthau's model fits exactly. This model also fits with my own experience with academic information seekers, although the process doesn't necessarily progress steadily from one stage to another. Such seekers frequently go through several iterations of the 'select, explore, formulate, collect' stages. Ross J. Todd applied Kulhthau's model to adolescent information seeking (2003), adding in his version of the model the associated cognitive processes (thoughts: from vague to focused to increased interest), and physical actions (exploring to documenting).

Dr. Jannica Heinström, who has worked closely with Todd and Kuhlthau, has published several articles on her research in this area. Her work brings

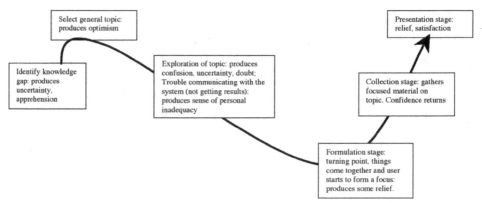

Figure 10.1. The research roller coaster.

the ideas in Kuhlthau's model (i.e., stages, tasks, and emotions in information seeking) to a next step (i.e., testing the influence of disciplinary area, study habits, and personality on information seeking in students) within the current, online-dominant information world. She has looked at patterns in information seeking both in master's level students and in middle and high school students. She has identified three characteristic information seeking patterns relating to the students' preferences for exploration or specificity, which she has named *fast surfing*, *broad scanning*, and *deep diving*. She found these various styles to be "grounded in personality traits" and could be "linked to the students' study approaches." Only in the social sciences did discipline appear to have an influence on information seeking style (Heinström 2006). Table 10.2 attempts to capture the results of her studies on master's level students in a shorthand format.

Note the "good critical evaluation skills" of the broad scanners. In looking over this table, don't you find it easy to recognize fellow students or information seekers of any kind that you have worked with?

The role of uncertainty, fear, or anxiety in the information seeking process continues to be a subject of study. Researchers have found these negative emotions continue to plague academic researchers of all ages, both in-person and online (Chowdhury, Gibb, and Landoni 2011; Radford et al. 2011b; Owens 2013). Savolainen (2014) provides a useful review of the theoretical literature concerning emotions in the information seeking and retrieval process, and further pursues the role of "emotions and feelings . . . as motivators for information seeking." Theory, in all these cases, seems to accord well with reality, and the "reality" of information seeking behavior is a favorite topic of library literature.

Applied Research on Information Seeking Behavior

Literally hundreds of studies have been done on information seeking behaviors in academic settings. Donald O. Case, in his 3rd edition of *Looking for Information: A Survey of Research on Information Seeking, Needs and Behavior* (Case 2012) continues to provide an excellent review of the study of information seeking behavior and the literature it has produced. The following

Table 10.2. Information Seeking by Fast Searchers, Broad Scanners, and Deep Divers.

	Fast Surfers	**Broad Scanners**	**Deep Divers**
Amount of effort	Minimal	Active, but highly spontaneous; serendipitous	Considerable, strong search engagement
Information acquisition pattern	Hasty, unstructured	Unstructured exploration	Focused and structured, systematic. preference for precision over recall
Preferred types of content	Easily accessible and digestible: overviews, restatements of views already held	Inspiring, challenging, presenting new ideas	High scientific quality, specific
Discipline (area of study)	No influence	Significant connection found between social sciences students and this approach	No influence
Study approach	Surface, low motivation	No influence	Focused, structured; desire for thorough understanding; deep or strategic approaches to studying; high motivation.
Personality traits	Low conscientiousness: "easily distracted, impatient, easygoing"; low openness to experience and high sensitivity result in "avoidance of challenging information content"	Extroversion but low agreeableness, openness to experience: "outgoing, curious, and competitive"; good critical evaluation skills.	No "significant influence of personality" but a positive connection between openness and conscientiousness to deep diving

Based on Heinström 2006.

(highly selective) list of articles that have appeared since the previous edition of this book are intended to give you a sense of the scope of this research:

- Mbabu, Bertram, and Varnum (2013) have studied undergraduates' use of scholarly databases, and Denison and Montgomery (2012) studied undergraduates' perceptions of the information seeking process and their emotional reactions; a recent study of graduate students was done by Sloan and McPhee (2013). In Israel, Greenberg and Bar-Ilan (2014) have looked at university students, while Bronstein (2014) did a study specifically of LIS students. Nkomo, Ocholla and Jacobs (2011) looked at web information seeking behavior by both students and staff at South African universities.

- Recent studies of the information seeking behavior of faculty include business faculty (Hoppenfeld and Smith 2014); education faculty (Rupp-Serrano and Robbins 2013); and academic scientists (Niu and Hemminger 2012).

- Medical information seeking by both physicians and patients is a perennially hot topic. Kannampallil et al. (2014), CILIP (2014), and Clarke et al. (2013) have studied healthcare professionals in the US; studies of professionals in other countries include the Philippines (Gavino et al. 2013), Japan (Sayama, Tsutsumi, & Oshida 2013), and Greece (Kostagiolas et al. 2012). Cyrus (2014) provides a broad-based review of the literature on patient information seeking; Kim and Syn (2014) do the same specifically for teens. Loos (2013) ponders the threat of cyberchondria for patients doing their own health information searching.

- Studies of very specific groups or topics include music students' use of YouTube (Lai 2013), information seeking behaviors of theatre professionals and journalists (Olsson 2013), and an in-depth study of the nature and ramifications of information seeking as a collaborative activity (Shah 2014).

Again, the above is only a tiny sample. Searches in the *Social Science Citation Index* (part of the *Web of Science*), *Library Literature,* LISTA,[1] or an advanced search in Google Scholar for the exact phrase: "information seeking behavior of" only in the title, will produce many, many more. Those from Google Scholar are particularly international.

School media specialists and public librarians have also actively contributed their observations and advice about the information seeking behaviors that they observe in the clientele of their libraries. Authors writing on the topic of information seeking by children, youth, or adolescents include Large, Nesset, and Beheshti (2008); Dresang and Koh (2009); and Bowler (2010). In later work, Nesset (2013) proposes two models for the research process in the K–12 environment, and after studying children aged 7, 9 and 11, Foss et al. (2013) examined how young people 14–17 years old search on the Internet. Sherry Crow has written a number of articles on intrinsic motivation in information seeking at the grade school level, most recently as a way to make it a "joyful" process (Crow 2013).

At the other end of the age spectrum, the public library community is concerned about the information seeking behaviors of baby boomers, in the US (Bennett-Kapusniak 2013; Williamson, Bannister, and Sullivan 2010) and in Canada (Cavanagh and Robbins 2012). There are also concerns about public libraries and librarians being called on to handle health information seeking from their clients (Smith, Hundal, and Keselman 2014).

Information Seeking in the Internet Era

The recent applied research on information seeking behavior in wired societies has consistent themes. People tend to turn first to the Internet or to friends or colleagues when they have an information need. As much as they love the Internet, they still do like interacting with humans. Given the choice between someone they know—a friend, a teacher, or a colleague—and a librarian (whom they do not know), they'll start with the former. With social networking sites, users now have the best of all worlds: doing their information seeking with friends and doing it conveniently, online. (Kim, Sin and Tsai [2014] provide an in-depth study of the use of social media for information seeking.) Another finding has to do with time: in studies old and new, users consistently complain about lack of time. Information seekers try to save time whenever possible, which leads to opting for convenience over quality to the point of convenience as the governing factor in their information seeking (Young and Von Seggern 2001; Connaway, Dickey, and Radford 2011).

In a pre-Google era study, participants described a "dream information machine" as something intuitive (a mind reader), a thing they can interact with in natural language. Their dream information machine is also a single source: comprehensive, complete, portable, and accessible 24 hours a day, 7 days a week (24/7) (Young and Von Seggern 2001). Quite likely, these study participants would regard Google as the answer to their dream. This is a good place to pause and consider:

Why People Love the Internet

The immediate, obvious answers are that it's easy (or appears to be) and it's ubiquitous. But we need to remember all those emotional underpinnings to the search process—those play a huge role in people's love affair with Web searching. According to the literature, at the beginning stages of the research process information seekers are anxious and nervous (unless they are teenagers or undergraduates, born into the Web world and quite confident of their abilities to find things). One of the big problems is getting started. An information seeker gets very discouraged and might even quit if he or she doesn't get results. They prefer one source, they want it fast, and they want it everywhere, all the time. On the Internet you work on your own, in your own way. Your thoughts don't have to be as clearly formulated as they would be to express your question to someone whom you don't know well.

Embarrassment is therefore avoided, and

- Starting is easier because you simply type something in and almost always get results.

- Anxiety is immediately reduced, because you got *something* (you probably have gotten much more than just something—perhaps thousands of hits—but it is better, quite literally, than nothing).

- You feel like you must know what you're doing. Confidence is increased because you got something, so you don't need help.

- It appears to be "one source" because you can get something on practically any topic from one search engine.

- It's fast, it's available 24/7, and it's almost ubiquitous, especially now that you can get to it on your mobile device.

What's not to like? There are, however, many negative emotions connected with searching on the Internet.

Downsides of Internet Searching

Some of the negative emotions and aspects of doing one's own searching on the Internet include the following:

- Doubt, uncertainty
- Confusion
- Frustration
- Time pressure
- Being overwhelmed with results
- Never knowing when you're finished or if you've found all there is to find

Uncertainty in information seeking in the digital environment is a frequent research topic, for example, Chowdhury, Gibb, and Landoni (2011). You have undoubtedly encountered many of these negative emotions yourself when searching the Internet. Having to sift through long lists of results, visiting various pages, evaluating, clicking deeper within a site to try to figure out why it was included in the results, then backtracking and trying not to get lost can definitely elicit all of these emotions. From the literature and my own experiences with users, the user mind-set appears to be something like this:

> Web searching can be very frustrating, but at least you suffer in private. You don't have to confess or try to explain your topic to a stranger: a librarian (especially if it isn't totally clear to *you* yet). Perhaps you've been working on this idea for a while and think you're quite on top of it, so how could someone (a librarian) totally unfamiliar with it be any help? You'd have to explain so much, and that would take too much time. Besides, you got results, so you obviously know how to search, and you're sure the information you want is out there. You want it, and it sounds reasonable to you that such information should exist, therefore it must be there, because you can find anything on the Internet, right? Somewhere. It must just be a matter of trying again, and again, frustrating as it is.

Not to close this section on a down note, we are reminded by a wonderful study by Flavián-Blanco, Gurrea-Sarasa, and Orús-Sanclemente (2011) that the emotions *during* an online search session run the gamut of surprise, hope, joy, distress, liking, and dislike, and *after* searching everything from joy, relief, or pride to regret, frustration, disgust, or anger.

Effect of the Internet Mind-set on Information Seeking

For some years now the literature about information seeking behaviors has scarcely questioned that users go straight to the Internet; that is a given. Now what is studied is how the Internet mind-set affects their information seeking, or search, habits. And what researchers have found and continue to find are the use of very simplistic searches involving only one or two keywords, and many iterations: search and scan (the results), search and scan again, and again (Novotny 2004; Moulaison 2008). Rather than trying to evaluate or analyze why a search didn't work, users simply change topics or the direction of their research, proceeding "erratically" through their search process (Taylor 2012) and rapidly abandoning searches that don't appear to work. Users rarely, if ever, take advantage of advanced search features, and Boolean scarcely enters the picture; they search subscription databases exactly as they do Google (which they return to again and again) (Bloom and Deyrup 2012). Users either don't know how or can't be bothered to refine large result sets; instead, they scan quickly for one or two likely looking titles (Kim and Sin 2011). Overall, digital search habits seem to be characterized by a trial-and-error approach, and a general lack of critical, analytical skills (Todd 2003, Taylor 2012)—or at least, a failure to employ same (Kim and Sin 2011). The title of Eric Novotny's 2004 article captures it exactly: "I Don't Think I Click." Although Heinström's (2006) study was not about the specific actions of the research participants, the type of searching described here sounds very much like what fast surfers and broad scanners would do, although she notes that the broad scanners are better at critiquing their results.

Is all this a death knell for the powerful, sophisticated interfaces developed for subscription databases? My hope is no. I hope that features such as Boolean operators and field searching will continue to be available, to be used by those who know how (by Heinström's third group, the deep divers, and by information professionals). At the same time, one can already see that the way keyword searches are handled behind the scenes in these databases is getting better and better, so that simple keyword searches in a sophisticated database produce useful results. We have also seen in previous chapters an emphasis on providing ways to refine results *after* searching, to (try to) help users who don't take advantage of the various options in the search interface. Is there any hope of teaching students and others to use more effective search methods, such as synonyms, Boolean logic, limits? In my opinion, trying to do this on the large scale, that is, teaching whole classes to be expert searchers, is probably not realistic. As teaching moments arise, one on one, introducing just one or two of these concepts with the appropriate hooks—"This will make your searching much more efficient, it'll be much easier to get the information you need, and you'll get a better grade on your paper"—can be a successful approach in my experience. Woo them gently; the carrot is much more effective than the stick. The occasion for most of these teaching moments is in the reference interview, our next topic.

Quick Recap

The information seeking process has been described in the theoretical literature with various models. Taylor's model uses levels of questions, whereas Kuhlthau's model describes it as a series of stages and tasks, each with a good deal of emotion attached. Heinström studies information seekers in the Internet era, and characterizes them as fast surfers, broad scanners, or deep divers. Applied studies of academic users support these models and show two major trends: a person seeking information tends to consult (1) the Internet, or (2) friends and colleagues before turning to the library. Searching the Internet has many very appealing aspects, as well as frustrations, for information seekers. The predominance of Internet usage has affected how people search for information; their habits generally are characterized by speed, reliance on keyword searches rather than anything more sophisticated, and trial and error. Heinström's deep diver searchers are the exception.

Part 2: The Reference Interview

Since the composition of the third edition of this book two excellent texts on this topic have appeared: Susan Knoer's (2011) *The Reference Interview Today*; and Dave Harmeyer's (2014) *The Reference Interview Today: Negotiating and Answering Questions Face to Face, on the Phone, and Virtually*. Both are full of practical, useful advice and guidance. Knoer proceeds chapter by chapter through pertinent topics (face to face reference, various kinds of virtual reference, dealing with cultural differences, special needs, etc.), while Harmeyer's instruction takes the form of "Scenarios" or case studies drawn from his real life experience.

While this section cannot possibly cover as much ground as a whole textbook on the topic, after all the technical discussion of the preceding chapters I feel it is very important to remember the human element. We are trying to learn to be better searchers to help other *people* (or, indeed, to help ourselves—and we are people too!). Therefore we will take some time to explore this topic.

One could even ask, in this Google era where do libraries and librarians fit in? Courtney Young's (2013) advice to librarians is to "make peace with the fact that patrons use Google first," because "user frustration with inadequate Google results often pushes students to seek help from librarians." Ahhh! That is a positive mind set: we pick up where Google leaves off. Yes, this means we get "more of the harder questions and fewer of the quick and easy ones" (Knoer 2011), at least in face-to-face reference (questions asked via chat or texting are still somewhat weighted towards the quick and factual). Most of the time this makes the job more interesting.[2]

Having users turn to us later in the research process and having to work with more difficult questions means, however, that it is actually even more important to have a good reference interview skill set. To sort out these more difficult questions and elicit useful information from people who are convinced that they are already good searchers who have done everything possible, you need all your best communication and people skills. Indeed, the oft-quoted dilemma, as phrased by Robert Taylor in 1968, still applies:

Without doubt, the negotiation of reference questions is one of the most complex acts of human communication. During this process, one person tries to describe for another person not something he knows, but rather something he does NOT know.

Essential Components of the Reference Interview

As noted in the description of Harmeyer's (2014) text on the reference interview, the essential parts or goals of that process are to

- Establish contact with the user

- Determine what the user's information need actually is

- Check to make sure that the answer actually meets that need completely.

The wording is modern, but the goals are the same as when Green first wrote about the "Personal Relations between Librarians and Readers" in 1876 (Knoer 2011). Let's look at what goes into meeting each of these goals.

Component 1: Establish Contact

Once upon a time, librarians sat passively at a reference desk and waited for patrons to (conquer their anxiety and) approach with a question. No longer. Now we reach out: we rove, we are embedded, we hold office hours and provide private one-on-one meetings in our offices, and we are everywhere virtually. "Virtual reference is responsive to the patrons' need for convenient access to reference service" (RUSA 2010), and lends itself to point-of-need service that is convenient, fast, and non-threatening (e.g., most virtual reference systems allow the participants anonymity). Indeed, "[t]oday's college students often seek help from a librarian via their cell phone or mobile device, which makes it possible to ask questions on the go while multitasking." And after a successful virtual encounter, students say they are more likely to seek out face-to-face reference encounters, where they know it's easier to explain a not-fully-formed question and to build a personal relationship (Ruppel and Vecchione 2012). (See also the article by Magi and Mardeusz on the topic of students' continued desire for face-to-face reference in the Suggested Readings at the end of this chapter.)

Having provided the means for establishing contact, we then need to be responsive and approachable (look up and smile in person, answer the chat/text/etc. quickly and with a positive greeting). Contact has been initiated; now to figure out "the information need."

Component 2: Determine the Actual Information Need, or, What Is the Real Question?

One of the most challenging things about the reference interview is simply that people do not ask for what they really want. This is a recurring theme in the literature: "inquirers seldom ask at first for what they want"

(Taylor 1968), and "librarians have long recognized the tendency of library users to pose their initial questions in incomplete, often unclear, and sometimes apparently covert terms" (Dewdney and Michell 1997). Mary Ellen Bates (1998) expressed the issue succinctly as "finding the question behind the question." Catherine Ross (2003) is strongly in favor of a reference interview in "almost every" transaction, because even a very brief exchange helps people to "clarify in their own minds what their question really is." The importance of "query clarification" in face-to-face reference is reiterated in the opening literature review in Radford et al. (2011a).

Why is this asking of a question so difficult? Why don't people simply ask what they really want to know? It turns out there's a lot more to *asking* a question (let alone answering one) than meets the eye. For example:

- The question might be used as a way to make contact, to see if you're available. Indeed, it has been suggested (Dewdney and Michell 1996)[3] that the initial question actually be treated as "four unspoken questions":

  o Am I in the right place?

  o Are you available to help me?

  o Are you listening and willing to help me?

  o Have you understood my topic (in general)?

- People all have worldviews and their own ideas (mental models) of how things work, even if they have no actual experience on which to base that idea. Because of this, they ask a question that they think you can answer. They couch their need in terms of something they think that you can provide. This is what Taylor meant by his fourth type of question, the "compromised need." The person deliberately recasts the question "in anticipation of what the files can deliver" (Taylor 1968), or in the form he or she thinks "is the sort of thing one should ask" (Fister 2002).

- As illustrated by the extended quotation from Taylor at the beginning of this section, people don't ask an exact question because they might not know exactly what they want or know any better way to phrase what they want. If you were a 6-year-old trying to ask your school librarian for something to read that would explain why your parents always seemed to be taking your older brother to the doctor, how well do you think you could express it? You may discover that many people become about 6 years old on approaching a reference librarian.

- Communication barriers—because of age, language, jargon, or mishearing or misinterpreting what was heard—can interfere in asking questions.

- Many questions can sound quite reasonable but just aren't. When you start to examine them more closely, they turn out to be impossibly broad.

- The exact information need might not be expressed because of embarrassment at having to ask, feeling "stupid for not already knowing the answer" (Ruppel and Vecchione 2012) or because of the nature of the question.

- Having to ask a question may bring up feelings of fear that are even stronger than embarrassment: fear from not knowing what to expect when they ask (What if the librarian says something impatient or belittling?) You can well imagine that patrons/information seekers in that situation would be very careful about the question they asked, and that it might be a long way from what they really want to know (Fister 2002).

"Not the Real Question": Some Examples

Here are some examples, drawn from real life and from the literature, of questions that were asked based on the motivations described earlier, or questions that are open to several interpretations.

- The totally misdirected question: "Could you read my paper and tell me if my arguments are right and if I've made any mistakes?" In reality, what the person wanted were some better, more scholarly sources.

- The question that they think you're more likely to be able to answer: "Where are the issues of *Mergers & Acquisitions*?" The real question: The student's professor had suggested a particular article in *M&A*, and the student was going to browse until he found it.

- Here is a wonderful example of six possible situations that could be lurking behind the very simple question, "Where are the cookbooks?" (Peterson 1997):

  1. Polly wants to browse a wide range of cookbooks to get different recipe ideas.

  2. Edna is looking for a specific recipe on authentic Italian Alfredo sauce.

  3. Mary is considering modifying her diet for health reasons and could really use some books on health and nutrition.

  4. Jenny is conducting a cooking seminar and needs information on how to structure her classes.

  5. Joe wants to be a chef, and what he really needs are books on job-hunting strategies.

  6. Marty is looking for *The Anarchist's Cookbook*, which is not a cookbook at all and is located in a completely different section.

- The question that sounds reasonable and isn't: "I need a list of the top 50 undergraduate programs in math, computer science, and engineering *worldwide*" [emphasis added]. There are directories of such programs (in the United States): *U.S. News and World Report* is famous for its "Best Colleges" rankings lists, similar tallies of the top 50 or top 100 this or that are sometimes found in other publications, and so this initially seems like a reasonable request. (But it's not; don't try it!)

- The failure of communication question (mishearing the original information). A classic example: an undergraduate asks for *Oranges and Peaches*, by Charles somebody, and gets more and more upset as the librarian can't find it. Finally, he happens to say, "but my professor said it was the Bible of evolution!" and the librarian realizes that what he meant was *Origin of Species* by Charles Darwin (Dewdney and Michell 1996).

Question Negotiation in the Reference Interview: Using Open and Closed Questions

It is possible to discover the real question, however. A combination of good communication skills, emotional intelligence, practice, and experience are the keys. The major component of good communication skills for the reference interview is known as *question negotiation*.

Question negotiation, which in reality is quite a complex process, sounds simple: You try to elicit information by asking questions. The questions have a particular style, known as open and closed. *Open questions* invite your interlocutor to tell you more, to expand on the topic in a free-form way (like the famous interview question: "Tell me about yourself"), whereas *closed questions* are used to request a specific piece of information and usually require only a yes or no, or a one- to two-word response.

Here are some examples of open questions that are good to use in the reference interview (they tend to begin with words such as how, where, what, why, and the useful phrase, "can you tell me . . ."):

- Can you tell me something more about what you're working on? (to try and determine if it's a class assignment, personal interest, etc.)

- What would you like to find out (about the topic)?

- How much material were you hoping to find?

- What have you tried already?

- What else have you found, or do you have any papers on this topic already that we could look at?

- Where did you find (example, if presented)?

Similar to these, but with some interesting variations, is an excellent set of questions suggested by Mary Ellen Bates (1998), a noted authority on searching:

- What do you mean by _____?

- What do you already know about _____?

- What do you expect me to find?

- Are there any sources you have already checked or that you would recommend?

- If you were writing an article about this subject, what would the headline be?

- If I can't find exactly _____, what would be second-best?

- How will you be using the information?

- So, in other words, what you'd like me to find is _____, right?

Following are some examples of closed questions:

- Are you looking for a specific item or a list of materials on a topic?

- Do you want a comprehensive search or a few good items?

- Did you try (the catalog, the Web, or a particular database)?

- When do you need this by?

- Do you need scholarly (research, journal) articles, or are popular (*Time, Newsweek*) articles okay?

- Are you looking for recent information, or are you doing historical research?

- Have you used (particular resource) before?

Both open and closed questions are important and useful in question negotiation; don't fall into the trap of equating open with good and closed with bad. Open questions are a good way to get things going, to start developing a big picture, and to get the user talking and thus providing subject words. Closed questions are useful for focusing the topic, making sure the interaction proceeds efficiently, and helping to rule out courses of action that might be unproductive. Strive to avoid a question negotiation session that uses only closed questions; rather, try to employ a mix of both. If you encounter a situation for which closed questions seem to be all that is required, however, don't feel guilty. It can happen, especially around basic questions, or in a text-messaging environment. What you want to avoid is falling into the habit of asking only closed questions from laziness or disinterest.

In coming up with questions, keep in mind what you are trying to do:

- Understand the problem and its literature—the topic.

- Find out what the person has already done (if anything).

- Develop search vocabulary and alternatives (synonyms).

- Determine limits (date, etc.) and levels (research or popular literature?).

- Discuss retrieval goals (How much? How many? How soon?).

- Develop an overall strategy to help you to select appropriate resources (database, Web, etc.).

- Establish a positive working relationship with the other person.

Overall, the question negotiation process in the reference interview should help you to understand the problem context, that is, *who* and *why*. Who is your questioner: a 5-year-old, your mom, an undergraduate, or a sales manager in your company? Your choice of words, your questions, your suggestions, and the amount of time spent—every part of your interaction—should be adjusted based on whom you are talking to. For example, most of the open questions suggested here aren't very appropriate for an elementary school student.[4] The second primary part of the context is *why* are they asking—what is motivating the search? Is it just exploratory, a personal interest? Is it specific, a class assignment or preparation for an upcoming interview? Again, this affects the whole nature and direction of the search.

Component 3: Check That the Answer Met the Need

One of the most important criteria of a successful reference interview is how it is concluded. In person or online, asking "Does this completely answer your question?" or simply "Does this answer your question?" not only tends to improve user satisfaction, it also tends to increase your accuracy rate (Radford et al. 2011a) (since, if your answer *didn't* meet the need, you will then get a second chance to get it right). Another set of ways to check might be, "Is this what you needed/were looking for/were hoping to find?" The final question (which, if it's been a long encounter, is sometimes hard to remember to ask) is, of course, "Is there anything else I can help you with?" After that, it's a matter of leaving the person with an open invitation to come back.

It is crucial to leave the user with the feeling that the door is open to further interactions, by saying "if you don't find it, come back" or "if this doesn't work, come back; we'll try again." If you have the opportunity of seeing the person a bit later, asking a follow-up question (e.g., "Did you find it?" "How did that work out?") is also very powerful in terms of the user's sense of satisfaction, even if things actually didn't work out. What you want to avoid is *negative closure*: simply sending someone off to another part of the building to browse, not asking if the need was met, not offering any sort of follow-up option, or any of several other negative verbal or body language tactics (Ross and Dewdney 1998). Virtual equivalents would include not asking if the question was answered, not asking if the person has another question, not inviting the person back, or at the very least closing with a friendly statement (e.g., "Have a good day!" or "Good luck! Bye for now.").

Finally, although you may now have the impression that every reference interview is going to be a huge affair, that you'll need to ask all kinds of questions, and that you should follow up on each one if possible—relax. They definitely won't all be like that. Some will be quite simple and brief, and even so, satisfying to both you and the patron. It's not only important to know about all these skills but also to employ them wisely. Use your emotional antennae and your ability to read the other person's body language (or other cues in a virtual environment), and don't go overboard if the patron is obviously in a hurry or not very interested. Give her what she seems to need and let it go. Something that is every bit as true today as when it was written in 1982 is Somerville's advice: "Part of the skill in conducting an effective interview is to know when to stop."

Interpersonal Communication Skills in the Reference Interview

Establishing contact, asking questions, and remembering to follow up are the mechanics. What makes a truly successful reference interaction happen are excellent interpersonal communication skills and qualities that are more intangible: friendliness, approachability, and the ability to quickly assess and respond to another person on his terms. Accurate answers are important, but users also value "a pleasant interpersonal encounter" (Radford and Connaway 2013). A major survey of practicing librarians (436 librarians from 212 institutions) regarding their perceptions of core competencies showed a particular emphasis on interpersonal skills. Verbal communication skills, listening, and approachability were chosen by more than 90 percent of the participants as three of the top five desirable skills, "closely followed by written communication skills and sense of humor, which received 87.8 percent and 85 percent of votes respectively" (Saunders 2012).

As Tyckoson (2003) said: "It is the interaction, the process of communication, which is often more important than the content or a specific answer," a premise that had been part of the original *Guidelines for Behavioral Performance of Reference and Information Service Providers,* which stated: "the positive or negative behavior of the librarian (as observed by the patron) becomes a significant factor in perceived success or failure" (RUSA 2013). The importance of establishing "rapport" with patrons is a recurrent theme, most recently studied by Owens (2013).

How can these nebulous qualities of approachability and rapport be achieved? The ALA *Guidelines* provide a complete guide; a quick subset is provided here. In a face-to-face encounter you might use:

- Giving positive nonverbal cues: projecting an approachable attitude and using welcoming body language, such as looking up (rather than staring fixedly at your computer screen), smiling, making eye contact, and presenting an "interested face."

- Active listening: verbally or nonverbally indicating interest, attentiveness (saying "uh huh," nodding), and empathy (facial expressions that mirror the other person's feelings, "ouch"), using approachable language.

- Conveying understanding of the information need either verbally by paraphrasing: "So you'd like (xyz); is that right?" or nonverbal cues (nodding).

The emotional underpinnings of the whole situation cannot be emphasized too much, and thus the need for "emotional intelligence" in conducting the exchange (Eidson 2000). People generally pick up on tones of voice and negative body attitudes quickly and unerringly (Ross 2003) and will be more satisfied with a helpful and friendly, even if incorrect or incomplete, answer than one that is correct but cold (Fagan and Desai 2003, Harmeyer 2014).

Online, you need to compensate for the lack of nonverbal cues and employ (textual) techniques for rapport building, strategies for relationship development, and evidence of deference and respect. This can be done by

- Responding promptly and with a friendly greeting when virtual contact is initiated.

- "[S]eeking and offering confirmation, using inclusive or informal language, self-disclosure or self-correction, offering encouragement and empathy, using positive interjections and humor" (Radford 2006).

- Even more specifically, Owens (2013) suggests "using contractions, abbreviations, emoticons, or exclamation points" to increase rapport.

A school librarian's list of important communication skills emphasizes the following points, which are definitely applicable to any situation (Riedling 2000):

- Positive, respectful responses

- Encouraging words

- Avoiding premature answers

The last point deserves extra attention, because it is a trap that is so easy to fall into. Even if students have been asking for the same thing for a week, it's important to treat each instance as if it were new. You never know—the 15th time it might actually be something a bit different.

In discussing communication skills and pitfalls, a public librarian is emphatic about not using library jargon, and points out terms that people frequently either mistake or use in a different sense from the "library" sense (Cramer 1998):

- Bibliography for biography

- Reference book for nonfiction work

- Equating "fiction" with "not true," and thus pejorative

- "Check out" for "look at"

This point also bears some further elaboration. We need to remember that we use a very specialized professional vocabulary that is unfamiliar to most people outside our profession. For many people, "entering a library is like going into a foreign country, where a foreign language is spoken" (Ross 2003). We should ask questions and provide an atmosphere that allows patrons to "describe their information need in their own terms" and in their own language (Ross 2003), and then give "a usable answer in plain language" avoiding the use of jargon altogether (Knoer 2011).

Technologies and environments change, people—and the skills for working with people effectively—remain essentially the same. As Knoer says about new technologies, "the good news is that they all use the same skill sets, just in a different setting" (Knoer 2011).

Beyond the Face-to-Face Reference Interview

There are many modes in which the reference interview can take place nowadays: in addition to one-on-one meetings and the telephone, reference happens by email, by chat, texting, and even by video technologies such as FaceTime or Skype, to the point that "virtual reference" has become "ubiquitous in academic libraries" (Breitbach and DeMars 2009). Each move away from the face-to-face situation presents some hurdles but also, surprisingly, some advantages. (Although the video technologies take us right back to the fears that plague face-to-face encounters, but with the convenience of not having to go to the library.)

Reference Interactions on the Telephone

On the telephone, you have no visual cues, but the auditory ones are still there. You can tell a lot about people's ages and situations by their voices, and because it's usually easier to talk than to type, you can ask and receive more information. On the negative side, you might find that conversing with a non-native–speaker over the phone seems much harder than in person; perhaps we unconsciously rely much more on visual cues, facial expressions, and the like when it is difficult to understand what we are hearing. It can also be more cumbersome to explain a process (e.g., navigating through various computer screens and interacting with an interface) over the telephone, but it's not terrible if the other person is sitting in front of their computer. Also, there seems to be something about our telephone expectations: people are usually quite accepting of an offer to be called back if you can't find what they need immediately. This gives you time to think and explore without the pressure of being watched or knowing that someone is on hold.

Virtual Reference Interviews: Email, Chat, and Beyond

With email, chat, and texting both the visual and auditory cues are gone, and all you have are words (or abbreviations) on a screen, which does present a challenge for nuanced communication. If you have no body language or gestures, and no voice intonation or accents, what do you do? In fact, it's not that bad. The typed environment is such a part of our lives now that it is more nuanced than one might expect: frustration and humor come through fairly obviously, and appropriate responses can be given. "[T]one and mood words, capital letters, and repeated punctuation reveal a lot about the writer's state of mind" (Fagan and Desai 2003). Owens (2013) suggests that the use of lower case represents deference, upper case more self-assurance, especially when deliberate choices seem to be being made about capitalizing the personal pronoun "I" or not. Other tactics that are probably second nature to you are the use of emoticons (smileys), descriptions of gestures, and language that is more like how you would speak than write (Ronan 2003). The trailing three dots of ellipsis can be very expressive; they can be used to indicate that an action is taking place ("let me give them a call . . ."), or to soften a statement (Owens 2013). Something as simple as typing "hmmm" adds "an explicitly human dimension" to the virtual interaction (Radford et al. 2011b). On the other hand choices about typos, punctuation, and spelling suddenly become "important elements of the communication act" in live chat (Radford et al. 2011b). If you are too perfect, you may be perceived as robotic and cold, if too informal, you may be perceived as young and inexperienced (Waugh 2013). A certain amount of mirroring your interlocutor seems to be the best compromise.

While sharing the limitations of text-only communication, each of these modalities—email, chat, text messaging—has certain advantages, either for the user, the reference librarian, or both.

Getting a reference request by email gives you plenty of time to think and compose a thoughtful, structured answer. You can attach files with screenshots to help explain something if needed. You can check your "script," and always remember to have positive closure by including phrases such as, "did this help?" and "let me know how this goes" or "ask again if this doesn't work out; we'll think of something else." In email, the requester may very well follow up with you, and depending on the email system, all of your exchanges might stay listed in the message, so you can quickly review what you've said and done so far. The typed environment can actually be a plus for people having to communicate in a foreign language, because accents are not in the way, and the people on both sides of the conversation have time to study the words to figure out what is being said. The downside of email is that it doesn't lend itself to an extended reference interview: having a question answered only with more questions is frustrating and not what the requestor is looking for. A better approach is to respond with an answer, some kind of actionable information, with a statement such as, "I think you are looking for [x], so let me explain how to do that. If this isn't right, though, please let me know where I went wrong and I'd be happy to try again!"

Email is asynchronous and may take place over days. In contrast, conversing by chat is immediate, which users appreciate. This often implies to the chat operator that there is a greater *immediacy* to the question than if the patron had emailed, but that is not necessarily so. Either by asking up front, "do you need this right away?" (Ronan 2003), or providing linguistic cues: "may wind up" (read: will take time) (Radford et al. 2011b), or by frequently communicating to the user that you are working on the question, the person at the other end may turn out to be fairly patient (Kern 2003; Fagan and Desai 2003). Indeed, they may be more than happy to let the encounter take its time while they multitask. Ruppel and Vecchione (2012) observed a significant change between 2002 and 2012 in the value students place on being able "to work on other tasks while chatting or texting with a librarian."

Ronan (2003) describes how to use the time-honored techniques of open and closed questions, encouragement, interest, and follow up in the chat environment, and how to modify them for the medium (e.g., try to keep both your questions and your responses brief and relatively informal). You'll probably end up using mostly closed questions, and that's all right; it's appropriate here. In a large study of chat reference transactions at a public library system, Kwon and Gregory found that the five behaviors most likely to result in user satisfaction were "receptive and cordial listening, searching information sources with or for the patrons, providing information sources, asking patrons whether the question was answered completely, and asking patrons to return when they need further assistance" (Kwon and Gregory 2007).

Breitbach and DeMars (2009) offer a number of suggestions for enhancing the chat encounter by taking it beyond just text by incorporating images, video, or web page annotation using free or low-cost software. More useful advice may be found in the description of the "best practices in chat reference" used by Florida's virtual reference librarians (Ward and Barbier 2010), and a detailed study of "query clarification" in chat reference based on a huge set of transcripts from the *QuestionPoint* cooperative virtual reference service administered by OCLC (Radford et al. 2011a).

Even quicker and shorter is the terse, character-limited world of text messaging. Lili Luo provides an excellent list of competencies needed and suggestions for training specific to text-based reference. Of the top 10 competencies, seven are common to all forms of reference, and only three are unique to the texting environment:

- The ability to compose answers to patrons' questions concisely, quickly, and accurately

- The ability to interpret patrons' information needs with limited context in text messages

- Familiarity with the software/hardware (Luo 2012)

To me, the second point is the most important and most difficult: "librarians have to be perceptive in uncovering users' real information needs in such a compacted communication format" (Luo 2012). And while text messaging does not "lend itself to comprehensive back-and-forth question negotiation," such questions are "usually simple and straightforward," and usually don't require a reference interview (Luo 2012).

If chat and instant messaging weren't enough, Saunders (2012) advises that "librarians must also be comfortable reaching out to users and communicating with them through social media sites such as Facebook and Twitter." Beyond that, with technologies such as FaceTime, Skype or Google video chat, we are right back to face-to-face reference service. On the plus side is the convenience; on the minus side can be technology (software and bandwidth) and expertise issues.

All the forms of textual virtual reference offer some significant intangibles. Gone is the embarrassment at having to approach a desk, where other people can see and possibly hear the interaction. A 2010 study of adults and members of the Net generation revealed that both groups "found chat to be the least intimidating form of reference" (and the most convenient) (Connaway and Radford 2010).[5] In fact, the removal of inhibitions may work a little *too* well, causing users to make far more, and more personal, requests than they would in person (Westbrook 2009, Luo 2012). Also gone is the reluctance to interrupt someone busily at work at something else. (If you're the chat operator, that's all you're doing, right? They can't see that you're multitasking as well.) Although there are no visual cues to use in positive ways, those same visual cues aren't there to influence either party in negative ways either: the librarian can't see that you have 29 body piercings, and you can't see that the librarian looks like the neighbor who always yelled at you for playing ball in the backyard—someone who can't possibly understand you.

Can a True Reference Interview Happen Online?

Librarians have questioned whether a decent reference interview can occur at all in an online situation, but looking at the world around us, this question has become moot. Our users are online, so that is where we need to be. And as the Oblingers (2005) point out, "Personal does not always mean 'in person' to the Net Gen. Online conversations may be as meaningful as one that is face-to-face." You are simply meeting the users where they are, instead of making them come into your physical space: it's convenient, it eliminates some of the worst impediments to asking questions (fear and embarrassment), it can definitely work, and the key remains communication. The technical skill sets for the different media vary, but very similar interpersonal skills can be used in them all. Verbal, nonverbal, and textual: all offer ways to communicate effectively and positively. And "[s]uccessful communication . . . regardless of the medium over which that communication takes place—implies success in the reference process" (Tyckoson 2003).

Why Is the Reference Interview So Important?

Obviously we can't all be subject specialists in everything, but we need to gain our patrons' confidence enough that they will work with us. Being attentive, asking questions, and taking an interest can help with this. You *are* a specialist in the search field. However, at the moment the person you are working with is the specialist in his field (i.e., what he wants), and you are a layperson. You can still "achieve an intelligent and collegial interest" in their work, and this is "the level the search specialist should try to achieve" (Harter 1986). This situation calls for good communication skills and rapport, because you're depending a great deal on the person you're working with to supply the terminology describing her search need. You then work with her to think of synonyms, and using that knowledge, try to match the terminology against an appropriate database's thesaurus, or simply try the terms given to you as keywords in a multidisciplinary database, a Discovery Service, or the Web, and proceed to learn from your results. The initial set of terms describing the topic usually needs to come from the patron, however.

The reference interview is how you are going to connect people to the information they need. Through an exchange of questions, you help them to clarify what their question really is, which ultimately saves their time, because you haven't, through misunderstanding or lack of probing, pointed them at something that is not useful (Kern 2003). Tyckoson (2003) sums it up by saying: "The reference interview is the most important skill that a reference librarian can learn. Tools and sources will always change, but the process will always begin with the reference interview."

To me, it's really all about two simple things:

You want to help, and

You want them to come back.

A positive reference interaction, wherever or however it takes place, helps that to happen.

Quick Recap

The reference interview is meant to establish contact, identify the real question, and check that the need has been met at the end. For several reasons, the initial questions that people ask in a reference situation frequently do not represent their real information need. A good reference interview includes question negotiation, involving a good mix of open and closed questions, and good interpersonal skills, such as a positive, encouraging attitude, welcoming body language, and avoiding the use of specialized vocabulary. It is important to end the reference interview by checking that the question has been answered and inviting follow up. It is also important to know when to stop. Reference interviews that do *not* take place face to face (by phone, email, chat, texting) have their advantages and disadvantages, but techniques can be employed to make these exchanges equally successful. Technologies such as FaceTime, Skype, and Google video chat bring us full circle back to the advantages (and some disadvantages) of one-on-one reference interviews. A good reference interview is important because it leaves the patron with positive feelings and more likely to return to the library, physically or virtually, with future questions.

Exercises and Points to Consider

1. School media specialists: What would be a good list of questions to use with your clientele?

2. Communication barriers were mentioned in a general way in this chapter, and a few examples were given (e.g., language, age differences). Can you elaborate on these? How many other communication barriers can you think of?

3. What would welcoming body language look like? How about unwelcoming?

4. How would you feel if you asked a question at a reference desk, and the librarian responded by turning immediately to his or her computer and typing?

5. Have you had many interactions with reference desks where you were the patron? Which ones do you remember? What do you remember about them?

6. Say that you were at the reference desk, and a woman approached and said she was looking for information about sign languages used with children who are *not* deaf. What are some questions you might try asking her? What are some other things you might do?[6]

Suggested Readings

The information seeking literature can quickly become overwhelming. The following short list of books, and a single important article, might be more manageable:

Aspray, William, and Barbara M. Hayes. 2011. *Everyday Information: The Evolution of Information Seeking in America*. Cambridge, MA: MIT Press.

Harmeyer, Dave. 2014. *The Reference Interview Today: Negotiating and Answering Questions Face to Face, on the Phone, and Virtually*. Lanham, MD: Rowman & Littlefield.

Knoer, Susan. 2011. *The Reference Interview Today*. Santa Barbara, CA: ABC-CLIO.

Magi, Trina J., and Patricia E. Mardeusz. 2013. "Why some students continue to value individual, face-to-face research consultations in a technology-rich world." *College & Research Libraries* 74 (6): 605–618. After all the discussion of how reluctant people are to approach librarians, and their fondness for the anonymity of virtual reference, a reminder that students (and undoubtedly others) still appreciate the benefits of face-to-face reference assistance and why they find it valuable.

Notes

1. In *Library Literature & Information Science* and LISTA, try a search on: (Information-seeking behavior OR Information-seeking strategies) as Subjects.

2. The rest of the time—well, every job has its frustrations. It's better if you don't bash your head on your desk when people can see you, though.

3. Ignore the date. Human nature doesn't change; these "unspoken questions" are just as true today as when Dewdney and Mitchell first proposed them.

4. For guidance on reference interviews with children, see Pattee (2008).

5. It's terribly hard to pick just one article to recommend on the topic of chat reference, but if I *really* had to, this might be the one. It's a great balance of formal study, extremely important topic (especially because of the two groups of people in the study), and accessible writing.

6. Skilled questioning, or even more likely, a session with appropriate databases employing good "learning from your results" tactics, are needed to recast this question as "methods of nonverbal communication used with autistic children." Unless you're an expert in this field (in which case presumably you don't need help finding such information), this is not the language you are likely to use in everyday speech. To get the best results most efficiently, it helps tremendously to have the question reformulated into this language.

11

Choosing the Right Resource for the Question

By this point in this book, or in your course if the book is being used as your textbook, you may be feeling somewhat overwhelmed: There are so many databases, and there's the whole Internet. How are you supposed to know what to use when? Specifically, you might wonder:

1. Should you always try to use a database first? (What if you have no subscription databases?)

2. Is it wrong to use the Web?

3. Are there guidelines for when you should use a database and when you should use the Web?

4. Where do you start?

First and foremost: Don't panic. Everybody feels this way at some point in his or her library school career, and frequently during the training on their first (and second, and third . . .) job as well. While there are no hard and fast rules for what to use when (like so many things, with time and experience you'll develop a style that is effective for you), there is an answer to the first two specific questions. Question 1: Should you always try a database first? Not at all. You should start with whatever seems most appropriate for the question and where you feel most comfortable starting, given the resources you have available. If you have no subscription databases, a growing number of high-quality resources are now available without a subscription on the Web: not only Google Scholar, ERIC, and PubMed, but also a number of others. This chapter will devote a section to these resources. In answer to Question 2: It is never wrong to use the Web, as long as you also use database resources if the question suggests that they might be helpful (and you have databases available to you).

The rest of this chapter will address Questions 3 and 4, as well as discussing the range of situations you may encounter on the job: from having a huge selection of commercial databases available to none. In all cases, but especially the latter, the section on free, high-quality databases on the Web will be of interest. We will start with Question 4 because that is actually the beginning of the process, and the question, "Where do I start?" has a simple and direct answer. It's the same answer that applies to anything in reference service: start with a good reference interview.

Start with the Reference Interview

The reference interview, whether it is in depth or only a two- or three-line dialogue, is the key to everything that happens next. That is how you find out what the patron wants, which should then suggest to you what resource(s) would meet the need. The reference interview should reveal factors such as the following:

- What is the subject area?

- What is the person looking for? For example, a specific factoid, a few good articles, an overview, or some statistics?

- Does the requester want current or historical information?

- How much material is needed: a great deal, or again, "a few good articles"?

- Does the person require research-level material (also known as scholarly or peer-reviewed) or popular material?

These points are discussed in the reference interview section of Chapter 10. Your reference interview should also provide some keywords or phrases with which to start your search. You now have a body of information to work with (context, guidelines, intent, and subject) and can make an initial decision as to whether it sounds like a database question or a Web question. Note that I said "initial decision"—you can always change your mind and take a new approach as you work on the request; you don't have to get it right the first time.[1]

Now let's tackle the harder issue—guidelines for using databases or using Web search engines. What should you be looking for in the information that you gather during the reference interview to help address that issue?

Questions for Databases

When trying to decide when to use databases and when to use a Web search engine, remember that people are using the Web to answer many questions on their own, and by the time they approach a librarian, it's likely that more sophisticated resources are called for. That said, in this section you'll find the hallmarks of questions that indicate *to me* that a database might be the answer, and questions for which a Web search might be a better approach. Never get the impression that any of this is carved in stone. As you gain experience, you will undoubtedly come to identify further or different indicators based on the clientele you are serving that will whisper to you: "database" or "Web." You will find yourself instinctively making good choices most of the time.

Why and When to Try a Database

Why choose a database over a Web search engine? (Note my terminology here: I am specifically referring to *search engines* such as Google or Bing, not Google Scholar. We will talk about Google Scholar in the context of free *databases* on the Web. Google Scholar will inevitably creep into the conversation in other places as well, no doubt.) The reasons are basic: authority and credibility. Databases can contain material with errors, but in general, there is a presumption that the material has been vetted somewhere in the process, and part of what you are paying the database vendor for is taking some responsibility for the quality of the material. Nancy Bloggs, writing web pages in her bedroom, doesn't necessarily assume any responsibility at all. You can be more confident providing patrons with information from a commercial database than the free Web in many cases. Even with information such as a formula from a *CRC Handbook* or a dictionary definition, which can be readily available on the Web, if this material is being provided to *someone else*, in most cases there is an inherent authority and credibility if it comes from a database. In situations in which the patron really wants to be sure of getting credible information, she won't be left wondering, "Who wrote this? Can I trust it to be right?" The Web is a useful tool for starting searches, but in cases where credibility and authority are crucial, usually you won't want to stop at what you find on the Web.

Inevitably in the following descriptions of when to try a database you will find that Web searching is mentioned as well. It really is impossible to draw hard and fast lines between the two types of resources, because so often they do complement each other well, but I have tried to keep the discussions focused as much as possible on databases.

Requests Involving Articles

If your reference interview has shown that *articles* are involved in any way, it is usually a strong indicator to try a database. Articles represent content that has been formally published, usually in hard copy, and then distributed and made available for a fee. The publishers of the magazines, journals, and newspapers the articles appeared in are (usually) not giving them away free on the Internet. Yes, it's true that on the Web you can find papers that authors have posted on their websites or archived in their organization's institutional repository. If you're after a known item, a Web search might work, but it's not as organized, efficient, and comprehensive as searching a good commercial database (or Discovery Service). Using your institutional databases also increases your chances of getting the full text, either directly or via a linking system. Google Scholar is rapidly closing the gap with commercial databases, but it doesn't have all the features and options they offer. (It can be a great place to start, however, especially in a subject area you are unfamiliar with, or when you want to figure out new terminology or places to look if you are having no luck in the databases you are trying.)

For example, in an academic situation involving a student writing a paper, in almost every case your best choice is an article or encyclopedia database. The ability to search by subjects, to use various limits, and to know that the material you'll retrieve has all made an appearance in the commercial press all firmly call for such a database. Again, the full text or links to full text in so many commercial databases is another obvious reason to go to a database.

Another type of "article request" is to find materials *citing* an article. However, it is now much less clear-cut whether this type of question is something to be answered with a database (*Web of Science*) or the Web in the form of Google Scholar. Google Scholar's "Cited by" numbers are usually higher than those in the *Web of Science* (because Scholar includes a broader spectrum of document types, and employs an automated collection process). But how and where is Google getting that information? How accurate is that count? What does it include? Researchers de Winter, Zadpoor and Dodou (2014) provide some answers to those questions and a thoughtful and thought-provoking analysis of Google Scholar versus the *Web of Science* in their study. Frankly, the authors make me nervous about the future of one of my favorite subscription databases, but still: if the *Web of Science* is available to you, my advice is to try that first, every time. It is a vetted, known resource of long-standing and created under very high standards of quality. A person wanting to know where something has been cited is usually after high-quality, published, find-able articles.

Of course, articles come from journals. Although patrons seldom ask, "Where is the *Journal of XYZ* indexed?" this often becomes an implied question for the librarian in the course of answering the question they did ask. Usually the most efficient course of action is to check the *UlrichsWeb* database to see where the journal is indexed. (Of course, you can also simply go to a likely database and use its "publication browse" feature, to see if the requested journal is listed.)

Requests for an "Overview Article"

Patrons often want an article that provides an *overview* of some topic. There are a couple of problems with such a request. One is, you hear the word *article*, and you do think database, which is right. The problem is, it is not that easy to find general, overview-type articles in the periodical literature, unless the author is writing a review of the literature or a tutorial on the topic,[2] or the topic falls within a discipline that publishes special-purpose survey journals, such as *Computer Surveys*. In general, articles tend to focus on a particular, finite topic rather than providing a broad introduction.

A better source for an introductory or overview treatment of a topic is often an encyclopedia entry (or a chapter in a prominent textbook for that field). Thousands of specific-topic encyclopedias are available, and more and more of them are being offered in online versions. (The *AccessScience* database introduced in the Additional Resources in chapter 6 is a good example.) Such a commercial encyclopedia database could indeed provide an authoritative, trustworthy overview.[3]

Book Questions

With the advent of mega online book vendors such as Amazon.com, Barnes & Noble, or Powells.com (which covers the gamut of new, used, and out of print), and the availability of WorldCat on the Web at WorldCat.org, the line between whether to use a subscription database or a Web resource for book questions has grown much more indistinct. Obviously, if the patron wants to know if your library owns a particular book, you'll go to your library's OPAC. After that, it may depend on what resources you have available. If you have access to WorldCat via FirstSearch (and enjoy all the options that interface offers) and *Books in Print*, you might try those databases first for book-related questions (e.g., verifying or completing book citations, finding books on a topic, or identifying a particular title that might be old or unusual). Because the subscription databases are not trying to *sell* the books, there is less "noise" on the screen to ignore, and thus they can be more efficient. You cannot beat the comprehensiveness of WorldCat, which helps to avoid the possibility of having to look at several online book and out-of-print vendor websites. And if it's quicker and easier to type "worldcat.org" into your browser than to click through a couple of library web pages to find the link to the subscription version, by all means use the Web version. On the other hand, if the patron is a student who wants a textbook (and is surprised that you don't have all the textbooks on Reserve), head off to Amazon.com immediately, to show him the deals on used copies.

Business Questions

Just by the nature of the beast, if it's a business question, it is usually safe to assume that the answer is worth money and thus is less likely to be freely available on the Internet. Business questions frequently involve articles, which we have already discussed as a database indicator. Another typical business query is the request for lists of companies in a certain line of business or in a specific geographical area. Although there are free telephone directories and other similar resources on the Web, the best directories for companies are commercial databases such as *Reference USA*, mentioned in the Additional Resources in chapter 5. Business documents such as market research reports or analyst's reports almost without exception come from subscription or other fee-based resources. A major exception to this general rule of using databases for business questions is in the case of certain business numbers, which we encountered in chapter 9. Stock quotes and the financial reports (e.g., annual reports) of current public companies can usually be found on the Web. Another exception has to do with research in the murky realm of "competitive intelligence," in which almost anything goes: almost any information could be valuable. Competitive intelligence research moves us to Questions for the Web territory, since information from blogs, wikis, newspaper websites (often providing content not available in their printed versions), anything and everything are fair game.

Law Questions

In this highly specialized area of reference, official legal databases are definitely your first choice. Although it is possible to find the text of some states' statutes (e.g., Texas Statutes) or laws (often referred to as "code," as in U.S. Code or N.Y. Code) online, it is probably easier to find the information needed using a commercial legal database. Especially in this topic area, the authority of a commercial, subject-specific database is very important. (And the assistance of a skilled law librarian is even more important.)

Medical Questions

Things become somewhat fuzzier when it comes to helping patrons with medical questions. Because, as with law, we are again working in a very serious and specialized topical area, you should start with databases if possible to take advantage of their authority and credibility. If you are working with medical professionals or medical students, obviously you'll turn to PubMed. Additional medical databases were discussed in the Additional Resources section of chapter 6. However, there is also an immense amount of medical information available on the Web that people are more than happy to tap into on their own, usually without recognizing the risks involved: the need to be very aware of the credibility of the source, the date of the information, etc. We'll revisit this issue in the Questions for the Web section.

Quick Recap

This section has attempted to address the issue of when you should try a database rather than a Web search engine. Questions for which you will want to try to use databases are those hallmarked by an underlying need for authority and credibility. Requests that mention a need for articles for research purposes, such as writing a paper, are usually best answered by appropriate databases. Requests expressed as a need for an overview article are often better served by material from an encyclopedia entry. Questions about books are sometimes answered equally well by subscription databases and free websites, such as Amazon.com or WorldCat.org. Business-related questions usually involve material that has been expensive to collect, and such questions usually need to be addressed with commercial databases. Preference should also be given to commercial databases for law and medical questions, due to the specialized and serious nature of the topic areas. The particular need in those situations for authority and credibility demands that only professionally produced and professionally acknowledged resources be used.

Choosing a Database

If you're faced with a question that seems like a database question, you could be in one of three situations: having many databases at your disposal (the assumption so far in this book), a few databases, or none at all. In this section we'll look at how to make a choice in each of those three scenarios.

Scenario 1: An Embarrassment of Riches

If you're at an institution that subscribes to literally hundreds of databases, the natural question is this: How do you decide which one to use? Or do you even need to decide; does your institution have a Discovery Service product that makes picking a specific database (at least to begin with), moot? If you don't have a Discovery Service or find it less efficient, then determining which database to start with involves many of the factors you use to *evaluate* a database (a topic addressed again in chapter 12):

- What subjects does the database cover? (If the topic is well defined, definitely in one subject area, a subject-specific database such as *Art Index* or *EconLit* could be the right resource. If the topic seems fuzzy, or interdisciplinary, a multisubject database such as ProQuest's *Research Library* or EBSCO's *Academic Search* or *MasterFILE* may be a better answer.)

- What types of material are included? Magazines? Scholarly journals? Books or book chapters? "Working papers"? Other materials? Or do you need a numeric or directory database?

- What *level* of material? (Is it popular level or research level?)

- What is the date coverage of the database? Does it cover the right time period? If you are trying to find or verify a really recent article, you'll want to check how frequently material is added to the database you're thinking of using, and how up to date it is.

- If the database does not provide full text, are the sources mostly available in your library (or in another database)?

- How searchable is the database? Does it offer controlled vocabulary to focus your search, or does it offer keyword searching of all fields if you need to find a needle in the haystack? Which fields are searchable? If you only have one piece of information, but that field isn't searchable in the database you've picked out, you have a problem. If you're looking for a particular *kind* of article, like a book review, you want a database that lets you limit or search by article type, and one that includes book reviews. Is it possible to limit by scholarly or peer-reviewed articles, if that's what you need?

You also don't have to pick just one database. You could identify two or three candidates and test your most specific search term in each one to see which shows the most hits. Especially if you're venturing into a new subject area, try your most specific term in the database that you've chosen, and see how many hits there are. If the database has a subject list or a thesaurus, look up your term to see if it is listed, and how many records are associated with it.

This list of factors to consider probably sounds like it would take far too much time, while the patron is sitting there expecting immediate action. As you gain experience, however, you will find that you can do this analysis of "database or the Web?" quite quickly. If you're at a major university or large public library that subscribes to a large number of databases, it's very likely that library staff have already created web pages that organize the databases into groups by subject, and often by whether or not they are full text. If you're working in a subject area that is unfamiliar to you, start by looking at databases by subject, or look at guides developed by librarians that might suggest the best databases for that subject area. Quickly scan the descriptions of the databases' *coverage*, *currency*, and *material* types. Go into the database(s) that seem most appropriate and test them for subject coverage, availability of appropriate fields, and limits, as mentioned in the earlier bulleted list. This all comes across as taking action on the question to the patron, and results will probably follow pretty quickly.

Of course, you have the free Web as well. Even when you have hundreds of subscription databases at your fingertips, it's a perfectly acceptable strategy to run a quick search in a Web search engine or in Google Scholar, just to see if the term is out there and in what context it is used, especially for an unfamiliar topic area (think of this as a reality check). As mentioned before, your subscription databases and the Web can complement each other well.

Scenario 2: A Few Good Databases

This scenario could apply to a school library with a handful of databases available, or to a corporate, law, or other special library. In each case, the limited number of databases was chosen for its appropriateness to your clientele and your mission, so in a way, you could consider this an advantage: some pre-selection has taken place, and these should already be the most likely databases for the questions that you expect to encounter. Given this, you can still look at your databases in light of the factors discussed earlier. Which one(s) might be most appropriate, given their *coverage*, *currency*, *searchability*, and ability to identify research? You can jump into one or more and test your search terms. Frankly, in many ways you have the advantage over those libraries that have hundreds of databases, because you can be thoroughly familiar with each of your resources, and have a much better idea which one is likely to be most useful for any given question, without any testing or analysis at all. And, of course, you have the free Web as well.

Scenario 3: No Subscription Databases at All

It would certainly be sad and frustrating, after learning about all these nifty fee-based resources, to find yourself in a situation in which you don't have any subscription databases. As long as you have an Internet connection, however, this is not nearly the dire situation it once was. First, you may find there are some (subscription) databases provided at no cost to you through your local public library system. Explore their website, find out what is available and what you need to do to gain access (e.g., a current library card with a barcode number). Next, as we have seen already in this book, many U.S. government agencies provide free versions of their database content on the Web: PubMed from the National Library of Medicine, ERIC from the Department of Education, and endless data from the Bureau of Census, the Bureau of Labor Statistics, and the World Bank. Other free government databases not mentioned previously include Agricola, from the National Agricultural Library (http://agricola.nal.usda.gov/), and ToxNet, another database from the National Library of Medicine, covering toxicology, hazardous chemicals, environmental health, and toxic releases (http://toxnet.nlm.nih .gov/). With WorldCat.org you have the riches of OCLC's WorldCat at your fingertips. Google Scholar has also been mentioned several times; let's take a closer look at this remarkable resource.

Google Scholar

Google Scholar (http://scholar.google.com) is a true database of scholarly content: peer-reviewed articles from commercially published scholarly journals, conference proceedings, theses, patents, legal opinions and journals, case law, book content from Google Books, scholarly content from the open Web (such as from institutional repositories), and who knows what else may have been added by the time you see this; coverage and content seem to be in a continuous state of expansion and improvement (Chen 2010; de Winter, Zadpoor and Dodou 2014). It is a wonderful resource, incredible and vast (as everything to do with Google is), and is utterly nonsectarian in its approach to subjects: it is truly multidisciplinary. (Google Scholar's effectiveness may vary according to the subject area of your search—definitely try it for an engineering literature search, for example [Cusker 2013]—but as with anything Google, you're almost guaranteed to find *something*.)

The Google Scholar search interface is also continuously evolving, and looking more like a subscription database all the time. As of this writing, there are six personalization features offered at the top of the Google Scholar initial screen: My library, My Citations, My updates, Alerts, Metrics, and Settings. Settings allows you to control which Collections (articles, patents, case law) are searched, how many results per page to display, and whether or not to display links for importing citations into [your specified] citation manager program. Settings is also where you can set Google Scholar to display "Library links," e.g., you can integrate Google Scholar with your institution's link resolver system to help you get to full text available from your library's subscriptions. (Note the word "help" rather than simply "get." The Library links feature is a huge step, but is not a fool-proof answer, as we will discuss below.) Back on the initial search screen, you can set which collections are searched on a search-by-search basis using the options just below the search box.

Is there an Advanced Search? There is, but the Google interface designers have steadily made access to it more and more subtle (and what it offers more limited; I worry it will disappear entirely in the near future). For now, the extremely low-key downward pointing triangle at the end of the search box is your access to the Advanced Scholar Search. Clicking this tiny icon brings up an Ajax window with basic Boolean options ("find **all** the words," e.g. AND, "**at least one** of the words," e.g. OR, "**without** the words," e.g. NOT), a proximity option ("with the **exact phrase**"), and three quasi-field search options: title, author, and publication name. That is, you can specify that your search terms appear "anywhere," or in the Title of the article, you can search for "articles **authored** by," or "articles **published** in." Last, you can apply a simple year date limit, e.g. "articles **dated** between." (Of course, Google does not label these options with the word "search"—these field labels all begin with the word "Return." Again, only librarians like to search, everyone else wants to *find*.) Still, this is enough to let us set up a reasonably focused search:

Find articles

with the **exact phrase**: Google Scholar

where my words occur: in the title of the article

Return articles **dated** between: 2013—2014

In the results display, every result has links to Cited by ##, Related articles, All ## versions, Cite, and Save, all the features of first class subscription databases plus the extra "versions" option, something specific to the Web where there might well be several versions of a document. (Save is an "output function:" you can now Save records to your My library account for ongoing access and research.) You can adjust year ranges again on the results display, create an Alert, or see Metrics about these results—shades of the *Web of Science* Journal Citation Reports. But most significant of all (to me), the all-mighty Google, which has *always* decided for us that their relevancy ranking was all we needed, has now added a Sort by date option to the Scholar results screen. It seems so small, and we don't think twice about this in a subscription database where they have always provided this option, but in a Google product? It is a sea change.

All of this, and it's completely free. So why do we pay for subscription databases? First and foremost, at least to me, is that despite all the studies, etc. comparing the content of Google Scholar to specific subscription databases, we have no way to know what the total scope of coverage of Google Scholar actually is. Google does not provide lists of which publications are covered, for how many years, etc., something that is standard in any commercial database. Just because it's vast doesn't mean it's comprehensive. If you are looking for an article and aren't finding it—does it mean your information is wrong, or that Google Scholar's coverage of that journal doesn't go back that far? (Or doesn't include that journal? Or just didn't include that article?) The system is a complete black box in terms of content: you can search it, but there is no way to know what (if any) parameters are bounding your search.

Another huge factor in using Google Scholar is the issue of getting to the full text. Yes, many hits representing published articles will also have a link to the author's personal PDF, or of course if it is an open access journal all is well. Being able to integrate with your library's link resolver system is great, but even then, if you are off-campus and not running VPN (i.e., you do not appear to be coming from the authorized IP range for your institution's subscriptions), you will not be given access to the article. (Instead, you'll be politely asked to pay a sometimes jaw-dropping amount for the privilege of downloading it.) If you know enough to run VPN while off-campus, access will be seamless. Otherwise, it can be strange and fraught. And what if you are no longer affiliated with an institution and all its wonderful online journal subscriptions? Then you are truly out of luck, and it might never occur to you that if you visited the library at a local college or university, you might be able to access this material at no cost to you.

Finally, Google is a commercial venture: they have been providing Google Scholar for free for many years, continually tweaking and improving it, but what if they get bored with it, or decide to start charging? It could vanish as suddenly as it appeared. Don't get me wrong: I love Google Scholar. I use it a lot, but I'm not ready to see it as an all-inclusive alternative if you also have subscription databases or a Discovery Service available. Indeed, Discovery Services may finally represent a valid library alternative to Google Scholar.

In addition to the vast "omni-disciplinarity" of Google Scholar, a number of subject-specific, free Web databases have been mentioned in the Additional Resources sections of chapters 5, 6, 8, and 9. A good source for information on the latest, recommended free resources on the Web is the "best free reference" feature that appears annually in *Library Journal*, listed in the Suggested Readings. And, as ever, you can tap into the collective knowledge of librarian experts around the world at the LibGuides Community site, as described in Sidebar 5.1.

Quick Recap

This section has discussed the range of situations you might find yourself in once you leave school. If you work at another university or large public library, you are likely to have a full range of subscription databases available. At a school, smaller public, or special library, you may have a small collection of databases, but ones that are especially targeted at your user group and with which you are very familiar. At the farthest end of the spectrum, you may be in a situation where there are no subscription databases. In that case, it is worth checking with your local public library to see if there are databases accessible to you as a library cardholder. We then took a close look at Google Scholar, which is steadily getting more subscription database features. Issues with Google Scholar as a subscription database substitute are lack of transparency of its content and coverage, and problems accessing full text for users who are off-campus or no longer affiliated with an institution having online journal subscriptions.

Having looked at questions best answered by databases and database availability situations, it is time to consider what questions are best answered by the Web.

Questions for the Web

One is tempted to say, "What *isn't* a question for the Web?" because it seems that no matter what keywords you search for, they'll have appeared in some web page, somewhere. There are certainly topics, however, that are much more likely, or only, answerable by a Web search.

Personal Uses of the Web

We use the Web endlessly for personal research: finding books at Amazon.com, getting weather reports, identifying a plant or bird, making travel plans, checking movie times, buying almost anything, filling in the missing parts of song lyrics, or finding an answer to a software question (e.g., what is the key combination for putting a hard return in a spreadsheet cell?). It's quick, it's easy, and it's not the sort of information you'll find in databases. (For a review from *Consumer Reports* about something that we're thinking of buying, however, we wind up back at a database, because that's an article.) Because it's only for our personal information, we take the responsibility for deciding how authoritative the information is and whether that's important.

Professional Uses of the Web

Popular Culture, Local Information, and People

At the reference desk, questions about popular culture ("Who is the highest-paid player in the NFL?"), daily life or local information ("Where are all the HSBC bank branches in [city X]?" "Can I get a list of all the choral societies in [city Y]?"), or, one of my favorites, identifying the source of a song, poem, or quotation from a small fragment, are definitely Web search material. A question such as "Who did the music in the 2007 *Beowulf* movie?" is perfect for the IMDb; mentioned earlier as a free source of film and television information. The Web is also amazing (a little frighteningly so) for finding people. It doesn't always work, but we all know some pretty incredible stories about locating people by searching for them on the Web.

Citation Disambiguation

The Web has become my first stop for citation disambiguation. For almost any situation where someone is trying to track down a citation or flesh out an incomplete citation, my recommendation is to try Google or Google Scholar first rather than a specific subject database. (Although a Discovery Service search would also be a good choice.)

Even with Google (or your favorite search engine), if at first you don't succeed, remember it's okay to leave out parts of the supposedly "known" citation and try just keywords from it until you figure out where the problem lies. In doing a Web search, you are looking for the citation to appear on someone else's web page (where one hopes that it's correct and complete), or at least to gain some sense of context. In Google Scholar, you hope to retrieve a record for the citation itself, or again, as a cited reference in another document. If both of these approaches fail (and believe it or not, that is possible), try Googling for the author's web page and see how he or she referred to the work in question. Try anything you can think of to provide a clue. Once the correct information has been found, you can then turn back to the library's subscription resources to retrieve the full text, or whatever is needed.

Rare or Obscure Topics

You can also start with a Web search when the patron indicates that what she is looking for is quite obscure, and you want the biggest haystack possible in which to look for that needle. Of course, the patron has probably already searched on the Web, but perhaps you can do it better. Do a quick Web search if the topic is obscure *to you*, just to try for a quick sense of context and possibly some additional useful keywords.

Medical Questions from Laypeople

If you are working on a medical question with a patron who is not a member of the health services professions, it is hard not to use the Web in your research. As mentioned in the previous section about Medical Questions, the patron very likely has been searching the Web on his own, and one can't deny there is a great deal of medical information available there. What is imperative is that you impress on the patron that much of it is incorrect, misleading, and outright dangerous, unless it comes from a reputable source. Depending on the resources available in your library and the skill level of the patron, your approach might be to encourage a change not in *source* but in *methodology*. Rather than simply doing Web searches, you can try to get the patron to *browse* reputable sites, such as MedlinePlus.gov, FamilyDoctor. org, or the sites of other reputable organizations. Use Web searches to find those associations and organizations, but then urge the patron to go into those sites and browse or search within the site. You should be able to trust the authority of websites from the government (.gov), such as the Centers for Disease Control and Prevention (www.cdc.gov) or sites run by reputable organizations (.org), like the American Cancer Society (http://www.cancer .org). Results from these sources could then be augmented with results from databases such as *Health Reference Center Academic* or the *Virtual Reference Library*, both from Gale.

Standard Facts and Statistics

For someone looking for a specific, standard fact (e.g., in what year did the Berlin Wall fall?), the authority of an encyclopedia database is attractive, but you may well simply try a Web search, because it's likely to be quicker and just as useful. (It's a standard date, after all; if the page comes from a credible source, it should be right. Wikipedia should be fine in this case.) Of course, if the patron then wants historical background for the falling of the Wall, you should get back to the encyclopedia or article databases very quickly. The area of quotations and definitions can be equally murky: in a situation in which it doesn't matter that much, you can probably just do a Web search. At the reference desk, if you have a resource such as *Oxford Online*, it would be more authoritative and professional to use that.

As we found in chapter 9, government agencies provide quite a wealth of statistical and numerical information on the Web. There aren't as many databases available in this area, so I often find myself using the Web as an equal partner when a question requires statistics or numbers to answer it. (But again, if I have access to an appropriate database, it almost always provides a much more *efficient* way of getting the information and is usually more authoritative as well.)

Quick Recap

The overarching themes in this Questions for the Web section have been issues of daily life, popular culture, people, and connecting with the "informal college," that is, tapping into the web of other people's knowledge (e.g., for software questions, obscure topics, or fragment questions—lyrics, quotations, etc.). The Web is useful for providing clues, context, or a reality check. As discussed in the Free Databases section, it is rapidly becoming a viable place to do scholarly research as well. It is amazing—what *did* we do before?

Exercises and Points to Consider

1. What do *you* use the Web for? Try keeping a journal for a week in which you record every time you use the Web to answer a question, either at work or in your personal life. Can you detect any common themes in your Web use?

2. "Search madness" activity: If you are using this book as part of a class, have the class members come up with a list of questions that they have encountered in a library, in their studies, or in their daily life. Then add in questions from earlier chapters in this book, or from search assignments. For questions that required databases before, try them as Web searches. For the questions submitted by the class, decide which seem suitable for the Web, and which are for databases. Spend a class session just madly searching and comparing results.

3. Here is a research request that would lend itself well to a group search session: An upper-level undergrad wrote me an email saying she was "trying to find the percent of people that buy local, or try to buy local, or any type of data on numbers of people who buy local."

You have now been exposed to a whole gamut of databases, including numerical ones and free, high-quality resources on the Web. Although it might look like she only wants numbers (so you could try *Statistical Insight* or the Department of Agriculture website), for this particular topic, you might be better off going for articles that *discuss* the topic, and hopefully drop a number or statistic here or there. So, which databases? What about Google Scholar, or just Google? Decide how you'll divide up the work and how you'll share insights about search terms and tactics as you go along—and go to town!

4. Here is another topic for a "group think" session: in upstate New York, municipal reservoirs (water basins open to the air) always seem to have one or more fountains in them. Some days they are turned on, some days not. It's hard to imagine city governments paying for something that's just aesthetic. Can you find out anything about the purpose of these "fountains"? Start by asking yourself "Who would care? Who would be in charge of such things? What is the most likely reason, and who might write about the efficacy of this technique?" (Note: city reservoirs in other parts of the country may be similar, I am only familiar with my area.)

Suggested Readings

Etkin, Cynthia, and Brian E. Coutts. Best Free Reference. *Library Journal.* Since 2009, a list of free online reference resources has appeared as part of the annual feature on the best reference titles published during the preceding year. Different database vendors index this feature differently; a universally safe approach should be to search *Library Journal* in the journal name (aka publication or source) field and "best" AND "reference" in the title, adding Coutts in the author field if needed.

Tenopir, Carol. 2002. "Sorting through Online Systems." *Library Journal,* May 1, 32, 34. This is the shortest, sanest set of tips and advice for keeping the plethora of databases straight in your head. Even though some of the names have changed since 2002, the advice still applies. A must read.

Notes

1. For the record, this is a sea change from the early days of searching on systems like Dialog, where you paid by the minute and often by each record displayed. Then you really did do your homework thoroughly before going online, and it was generally expected that you would get it right the first time. The advent of databases on CD-ROM and now on the Web has totally changed this aspect of searching (for the better).

2. This varies a great deal by discipline: tutorial articles (which can also appear under a title of "Review" or "Survey") are common in the engineering and computer science literature. There is a standard format for articles in medical journals that

includes a literature review, and the more scholarly library science articles have this as well. A literature review might not be the same as an overview, however, and certainly in subject areas such as business, a real overview is fairly rare.

3. Unfortunately, I often find it hard to convince my patrons—who are generally undergraduates or graduate students—that an encyclopedia entry is a valid resource or way to start. I'm trying to point them to a specialized encyclopedia, but they seem to relegate anything with *encyclopedia* in the title to "little kid" status.

12
Evaluating Databases

This chapter provides a detailed list of issues to consider when evaluating a database: information to gather, factors to assess, and suggestions for benchmarking. It concludes with advice about how to use this information effectively in putting together a database subscription request. The previous chapter, on choosing the best resource for the question, also draws on this material; don't be surprised if you find yourself going back and forth between these two chapters.

In real life, you are probably not going to be called upon to do an in-depth formal evaluation of a database that frequently. Institutions don't change their database subscriptions that often: getting anything new usually means giving up an existing service, and changing between relatively equivalent products tends to be held in check by the overall community's resistance to change. (Users generally prefer a status quo they are familiar with, rather than a change that requires any amount of learning or adjustment in their habits. A replacement has to demonstrate obvious and significant improvements in ease of use or content to be accepted.) It is also likely that you won't be making such a decision alone: you will be part of a team and thus the whole responsibility will not rest solely on your shoulders. At the same time, you want to remain up to date on new databases in your subject area; therefore, familiarizing yourself with new and changing products may become a fairly steady undercurrent to your job (depending on the volatility of products in your subject area). Another motivation for doing a thorough study of a database is to write a review of it. Although reviewing is an excellent way to start getting published, it isn't something you do every day. Finally, you obviously want to master a database completely before teaching others about it, even though (as you'll find in the last chapter) you want to be judicious in how much of what you learn you choose to pass on to your audience.

This explains the position of this chapter in the book: almost at the end of the sequence rather than at the beginning. It's important, and I hope useful, but it is not information that you'll need to work through in its entirety very frequently. The list of factors is not as exhaustive as in previous editions of this book, but definitely covers all the major points and a number of minor ones; enough to let you make an informed purchase decision, write a good review, or become as familiar as you need to be with any database. You certainly will find that you use selected elements from this list regularly in your daily reference activities, as mentioned in chapter 11. Factors of database evaluation such as topical coverage, date range, availability of full text, and usability of the interface, you'll find yourself assessing almost automatically, and even memorizing for the databases you use frequently. For those situations requiring an in-depth examination, such as conducting a database trial or writing a review for publication, the following two sections offer a list of categories and associated factors to consider in evaluating and testing databases.

Basic Facts and Figures

Initial Factual Information to Gather

Database Vendor(s)

As with anything else, the same databases are sometimes available from different vendors, and it can pay to shop around. Vendors get the data in a raw format and then format and load it according to how they structure their database, what fields they want to use, whether those fields are searchable, etc. The search capabilities (and obviously the user interface) vary depending on the vendor, and you can have a really different experience searching the same database offered by different vendors. If you are seriously looking at a new database and more than one vendor provides it, be sure to try them all. Subscribing to a database is a big investment, and you owe it to your organization, and especially to your users, to get the version that will best meet *their* needs.

Existing Reviews

Before jumping in and possibly re-inventing the wheel, stop and check: has anyone already written a review of this database? A thorough database review is a large task, requiring hours of research and testing. Although you may still want to check the latest facts and figures if the review is a few years old, and you will always want to do your own testing, someone else's review is a very useful place to start. If you are using a database such as *Library Literature & Information Science* or *LISTA* to locate reviews, searching 'database evaluation' in the Subject Terms field and the name of the database as a keyword should quickly identify any commercially published reviews. The source titles you'll see most often are *Choice: Current Reviews for Academic Libraries, The Charleston Advisor,* and *Library Journal,* as well as *Booklist, School Library Journal,* and *Library Media Connection.* All are excellent sources of reviews. If more than one vendor offers the database, look for comparative reviews or individual reviews for the different versions. Remember that electronic versions of reference books are also often thought of as databases, and the best resource for reviews of those titles is ARBA, American Reference Books Annual (itself available as an online database, *ARBAonline*).

Coverage

There are many aspects to coverage, including the following:

Subject Coverage. This is also referred to as "scope." What is the subject emphasis of the database—is it devoted to just one topical area, or is it multidisciplinary? Especially for a subject specific database, what is the *level* of the material covered; that is, who is the intended audience? K–12 students? College students? Graduate students? Faculty? Specialists? The lay public?

Material Coverage. What types of material and formats are included? If only periodicals, what types? (Types to look for include popular, scholarly, trade journals, newspapers, news wires.) Is there one type that is emphasized; that is, are there mostly popular or trade journals, with only a few scholarly titles? For articles containing tables or graphics, are those elements included? If such tables or graphics are included, how are they reproduced? (A formatted table reproduced in plain text can be almost impossible to interpret.) If other kinds of documents are covered, what are they? (Possibilities include books, book chapters, theses, conference proceedings, government documents, speeches, audio transcripts such as NPR interviews, and photos or visual materials such as would be found in an image archive.) Are any primary source materials included? What formats are offered for full text: HTML, PDF, or both?

Source Coverage. The *number* of sources is something that vendors love to tout, but, like "database size," this number is almost meaningless nowadays. (Depending on your needs and your audience, numbers that might have some meaning are the number of popular and scholarly sources, if both types are included.) What matters are the specific source titles included (are the important journals for the discipline in the list, or has it been padded with a lot of unknown, "fluff" titles?), and the *selection policy*. That is, are the publications indexed cover-to-cover, or only selectively? Is this policy universal for all titles in the database, or does it vary by title? Does the vendor have exclusive rights to any titles; for example, is there a journal whose content you will only find in So-and-So's databaseX? How much information is provided: citations only (like the *MLA International Bibliography*), citations with abstracts (like the *Web of Science*), or citations and full text (rapidly becoming the norm)? This is also referred to as the breadth and depth of coverage: more source titles would indicate greater *breadth*, and cover-to-cover indexing would provide greater *depth* of coverage.

Date Coverage. Does the database provide only current, or current and retrospective coverage (e.g., how far back in time does indexing for most of the titles go)? Does the database use a "moving wall" date coverage system, wherein titles are covered up to a set number of years in the past (e.g., JSTOR titles are usually covered from the first issue up to issues from three to five years ago. Each year one more new year is added, but current issues are not available.).

Geographic Coverage. Does the database index just U.S. publications, or is the source list international? If it is international, are the materials in their original language? How many and which languages are represented? Are article titles and abstracts (if available) offered in translation?

Availability of Sources

For any database that doesn't offer complete, universal full text, a major consideration would be how accessible the material that it indexes will be to your users. How many, or what percentage, of the sources are available in full text? If the database you are evaluating has only partial or no full text, do you have other databases (or print holdings) that can provide a significant proportion of those documents, and do you have a way to get users to that material? Interlibrary loan is always an option, but people usually prefer to be able to put their hands on what they want locally and immediately.

Currency and Embargoes

Most databases now add material continuously rather than on a schedule, but it could be worth asking the question: how often is material added? Of more significance is: are there embargoes on certain titles (e.g., the publisher has decided not to make the most current issues available)? How many titles are embargoed and for how long? (Are they embargoed for weeks, months, a year or more?) If there are titles that are important to your users that are embargoed for six months or more, this would be a strong red flag. If the database is offered by more than one vendor, check the updating and embargo schedules for each one. Both of these factors can vary considerably by vendor.

So far this discussion has focused mainly on periodical databases, but what about a directory database? A list of associations might remain fairly stable, but the corporate world is much more dynamic: companies change their names or get bought, sold, and merged into other companies. For both associations and corporations, names of officers, their titles, phone numbers, etc., are likely to change. For any directory or corporate type of database, definitely find out how often it is updated and how the database vendor obtains their information.

Size

Mainstream commercial databases can probably all be described as huge in terms of number of individual records; that is, the number of records is so large as to be meaningless, and the rate at which records are being added is likely equally meaningless.[1] The one thing about "size" to be alert to is whether the database is *so* large that the vendor has divided it up into multiple sections, and on what basis the division(s) have been made: by date (e.g., current, backfile), or by subject or material group? A database broken into sections can be annoying to use if you frequently have to rerun searches in each section.

Database Aids

Database aids include both online and physical resources that provide help in using the database, teaching others to use it, and promoting it. Investigate the database's online Help function: is it easy to find, easy to understand, and easy to use? Is the help context sensitive, that is, different depending on which screen you are on, or always the same? Note that context sensitive is not necessarily always better than static: the system's interpretation of your context may leave you scratching your head and wanting to start at the beginning instead. Also, if this is a vendor supplying many databases, is the Help specific to the database at hand, or is it generic, a one-size-fits-all for all the databases they offer? (The latter can be very annoying if you are trying to find out something about a database-specific field or feature.) Is there an online tutorial, and is it useful? Are there "quick start" or similar brief "how to" cards or leaflets that the vendor can provide? Will the vendor send you promotional materials to help market the new database? Most vendors are anxious to provide train-the-trainer services, usually by webinar; this is usually a quick and efficient way to get up to speed.

Cost and Vendor Support

Vendors regularly experiment with new pricing models, and this can be a more intricate question than you might think. In academic situations, the database cost is frequently based on FTE, or how many *full-time equivalent* students there are on campus. Such a charge model usually then means there is no limit to the number of people who can use the database at the same time. At the other end of the spectrum from this model, some databases charge by number of simultaneous users, or *seats*, that you opt for, meaning that only a limited number of people can use the database at the same time. A database with deep date coverage may be divided into sections, and it might be worth checking to see if you can purchase only the most recent section (if that would meet your needs). Price negotiation can be full of wheeling and dealing: discounts might be available based on the number of years that you sign on for or by the number of databases purchased from the same vendor. The price can depend also on how desperate the sales rep is to make the sale. Your institution may be able to drive a harder bargain in December (when the reps are anxious to make year-end quotas) than in July. Again, such a decision will seldom be up to you alone: you will likely be working with a department head that is familiar with pricing and dealing with vendors. No matter how you look at it, however, database subscriptions are expensive, often starting at four figures and going up from there (business and science databases can easily run into the 5-to-100+ thousand dollar range). Many libraries now participate in library consortia, which act together to negotiate pricing with vendors. Because there are so many possible factors, database prices are seldom (if ever) posted on vendor websites or listed anywhere. The myriad shifting factors and lack of transparency in pricing is the reason this book makes *no* attempt to provide pricing information on any of the databases discussed. The best way to determine the cost for a particular database is to start with the collection development or acquisitions librarian in your library. If you are not currently in a library, call the vendor directly and speak with a sales representative.

Vendor Support

It's also useful to explore the kind of support that the vendor offers, in particular for usage statistics. Are usage statistics available? How detailed are they? How do you access them, or can a report be automatically sent to you on a regular basis? Do the statistics adhere to the standards suggested by Project COUNTER (Counting Online Usage of NeTworked Resources), that is, are they "COUNTER compliant"? (See http://www.projectcounter .org.) Standardized statistics allow you to really know what you are looking at, what has been counted, and what it means. If you decide to invest the money, it's very important to have some idea of how much the database is getting used.

Other vendor support issues to explore are the nature and availability of technical and search support (by phone? email? Web form? Is it 24/7 and 365 days a year?), and, as mentioned previously, train-the-trainer services. During your database trial period, besides working with the database itself, be sure to test the technical and search support services. Is it easy to reach a knowledgeable person? Were your questions answered accurately and in a timely fashion?

Finally, be sure to try the database under all the current favorite browsers, and on Macs, PCs, and Linux machines. If the database is only fully functional under IE on a PC, and most of your users have Macs and prefer Chrome or Safari, you have a disconnect. (Believe it or not, there are still some databases with such limitations on the market.)

Testing and Benchmarking

As mentioned earlier, prior to initiating a subscription request, you will want to get a database trial (or multiple trials if the database is offered by more than one vendor). This is a key component in your evaluation. I have never encountered a vendor who wouldn't offer some kind of trial access to their products. Do not abuse their good nature in this regard: don't ask for a trial if you aren't serious about the database for some reason (either for purchase or for review-writing purposes), or if you don't have the time to evaluate it properly. While you have the trial, make good use of it. If necessary, deliberately schedule several time slots on your calendar over the course of the trial to devote to working with the database. As they say, pound on it! You really need to know what you're talking about if you are going to recommend it for purchase. The following section describes aspects of the database to look for, assess, and compare (benchmark) during your database trial.

Testing

Record and File Structure

This topic takes us all the way back to the material in chapter 2. Factors to assess include: What fields are available? Are the fields appropriate and useful given the subject matter of the database? When vendors simply apply their standard interface to a new database, the result is usually less than optimal. Of the fields you see in a full record display, how many are also searchable? (Some fields may be "display only"—PsycINFO's list of fields clearly delineates which fields are searchable and which are display only.) Another way to think of the field question is: How many ways can you look up the same record? That is, how many "access points" do the records have? More fields aren't always better but can be helpful. Do the searchable fields each have their own index list, and can you browse that list? Think of the WorldCat database and its many indexes, to the point of having single-word versus phrase indexes. More indexes are impressive but not always better. The questions to have at the front of your mind at all times during an evaluation are these: Does this make sense for this database? Is it helpful? Does it help get me to better results more efficiently?

Linking is an aspect of record and file structure that you can divine simply by observation. In a record display, are there fields that are linked (e.g., Author or Subject), which allow you to pull up all other records with that author or subject immediately? Are there other linked fields in the record, and to what do they link?

Indexing and Cataloging Practices: Searchability

Don't be put off by the heading of this section: it is not a suggestion for you to try to find out the interior policies and work practices that the vendor uses. Rather, there are many things that you can observe during testing, or find out from the documentation, that reveal something about how the vendor has set up the indexes, and how much human intervention (cataloging) has been applied to the records. These things can be dubbed *searchability*, and you will find many of them familiar from earlier chapters:

- Are there stop words?

- What limits are available? Are they useful?

- In regards to controlled vocabulary:

  - Does the database use a set of a controlled vocabulary (e.g., subject terms)?

  - Is the subject list a straight alphabetical list of terms, as in EBSCO's *MasterFILE Premier* or ProQuest's *Research Library*?

  - Or is it a thesaurus: a hierarchical system, with "broader," "narrower," and "related" headings that shows relationships between terms, as you find in *PsycINFO* or ERIC?

- With any kind of list of subject terms, can you browse the list?
- If subject terms are assigned to each record, how many are assigned? (2 to 3? 5? 10 or more?)
- With any browsable indexes, do they offer a "paste to search" function, so you don't have to retype the entry in the search interface? (This saves time and the risk of typing errors.)

- In regards to abstracts:
  - Do the records offer abstracts?
  - Are they simply replications of the first paragraph of the article, or are they actually evaluative or summarizing? (The former are more likely to have been machine generated, whereas the latter are most likely to have been written by a person.)
  - Are the abstracts generally long and detailed or short?

- In regards to title enhancements:
  - If titles in this subject discipline's literature are frequently cute or clever rather than straightforward, is a supplemental title added, to clarify what the article is really about (and to give you a better chance of retrieving it with a keyword search)?
  - If the database offers materials in different languages, are the article titles offered in translation?

- If full text is available, does the database support proximity operators, which are better tools for searching full text?

- Does the database offer a "find more like this" function? If yes, does it pull up appropriate, useful material?

- Overall, does the database employ features and conventions that are similar to those in other databases?

An additional point that bridges both searchability and the next category, user interface, is the idea of search history. This is a user interface functionality that does not have to do with indexing or cataloging practices, but that certainly contributes to a database's searchability. Does the database keep track of your search history? Can you reuse previous searches? Can you combine searches with other previous searches or with new terms?

User Interface: Usability

This is an area that is open to both objective and subjective evaluation, and can be particularly important in the case of the same database offered by multiple vendors. As you work with the database, besides assessing the content and search function, keep track of your experiences and reactions to the interface—the *way* you access that content and those search functions. In the broadest sense you should ask, "Does it work? How well?" When you are comparing vendors, searching the same information through a different interface can feel like a totally different experience. Following are some specific things to be look for:

- Are different skill levels accommodated, such as novice and expert?

- Is the interface easily understood?

- Does the interface make it clear how to use it, both by layout and by the terminology used? For example, are field names clear and understandable to the user?

- If icons are used, are they meaningful?

- Is the interface so bare and simple that it's "naked," or is it cluttered, busy, or mysterious?

- Are there *too many* options (or too many ways to do the same thing)?

- How is color contrast used? Is color used to demarcate functional areas of the screen, or is everything uniform in color?

- Is the interface visually appealing? For instance, is the color scheme easy on the eyes? Are the fonts too small, too big, too hard to read, etc.? Are the colors or fonts adjustable, either on an individual basis by users to suit their personal preferences, or globally for the whole institution's account, by a local system administrator (or both)?

- How important are the navigation links built into the interface? For example, if you use the Back button rather than a "Modify search" link, does it wipe out your search? (This is very annoying.)

- Can you initiate a search by just pressing Enter, or is it necessary to always click a "Search" or "Go" button?

- How easy is it to adjust or modify your search? Do you have to go back to a main search screen, or is the search interface (or other kinds of refine options) available on the results screen?

- Are functions such as save, email, and download easy to see and understand?

- If the database has a "time-out" function, that is, you get disconnected after a certain period of inactivity, does it provide a warning before disconnecting you? Can the time-out period be adjusted?

- If the subscription is based on a limited number of users, what sort of message (if any) is displayed if all the "seats" are in use when you try to sign on?

- Again, is the database browser or platform dependent, that is, will it work only with a specific Web browser, on a specific type of computer (usually Windows rather than Mac, Unix, or Linux)?

- If the database is browser dependent, what sort of warning does it provide if you attempt to use it with an unsupported browser?

- If you encounter nonfunctioning tools (i.e., buttons/features that don't work), is it because you are on an unsupported platform? This is another good excuse to call the vendor's tech support line and evaluate how they respond.

Treatment of Research

How research is treated is an important factor for any institution that works with students who are writing papers. Terms frequently used for research articles are *peer reviewed*, or *scholarly*. Databases such as ProQuest's *Research Library*, EBSCO's *Academic Search Complete* and Gale's *Academic OneFile* offer both popular and scholarly articles, and provide a limit function for "Scholarly" or "Peer Reviewed."[2] Provision of such a limit or similar functionality only makes sense when a database includes a wide range of materials, however. Databases that consist entirely of scholarly materials, such as the *Science Citation Index* or *EconLit*, do not need this type of filtering functionality.

Based on the discussion above, questions to ask in evaluating a multidisciplinary database are the following:

- Does the database provide research-level material?

- Is there a limit in the search interface for retrieving only scholarly materials?

- Is there a way to distinguish scholarly materials in search results, even if you haven't used a limit (e.g., by an icon in the record, or by a separate tab in the results display that filters for scholarly articles)?

- Is there anything in the product literature to indicate how many journals, or what percentage of the sources, are scholarly?

- One other point to check: scholarly articles almost always have a bibliography of sources at the end. If the database provides full text in HTML rather than PDF format, check to be sure that such bibliographies are included.

Sorting/Display/Output Capabilities

The amount of control you have over the presentation and output of your results can make a big difference in the usefulness of those results. It affects the extent to which you can easily evaluate them, and the ease of working with them. Here are things you may want to assess for each function.

Sorting:

- How many sort options are there?

- What is the default sort order for displaying results? Can you change the default?

- Is there a limit on the number of results that can be sorted? Some databases offer a sort option only on results sets of, for example, 500 or less.

Display:

- How many results are displayed per page? Can you change the number?

- Are the search parameters (e.g., words searched, limits used) reiterated on the results list screen?

- Are search terms highlighted in the results display? If they are, is it possible to turn such highlighting off? (Many repetitions of highlighted terms can sometimes turn out to be more annoying than helpful.)

- Are format options indicated for each record, for example, icons indicating HTML or PDF availability?

Output:

- What formats are offered for output, especially of full text? Plain text, HTML, or PDF?

- Can you email records? What email options are offered: for example, sending the information formatted as plain text, as HTML, or as a PDF attachment? How much can you customize the email: Can you enter your email as the return address, put in your own Subject line, or add a note? Can you choose to include the search history with the emailed results?

- When printing records, do you get to choose what is printed (which fields)? Note the following especially in databases that provide full text: Can you select a group of records, and then print the full records in one continuous stream? Or are you forced to print full-text records one by one?

- If you have reason to believe that many of the people who would use this database use software programs such as RefWorks or EndNote to keep track of their citations, does the database offer an export function for bibliographic management software programs?

Benchmarking

The first three types of benchmark activities listed here are, obviously, most important when you are trying to choose between two databases, especially if you already subscribe to one and are contemplating whether to change to the other. The next point addresses the fact that in academia, there is always a set of schools with which your school compares itself, and such comparisons are important to administrators.

Source List Comparisons

In choosing between rival databases, a good first step is to compare their lists of sources, that is, which journals (or other document types) does each one offer? How much overlap is there? How many unique titles are there? Among the unique titles, which list has more titles that are of interest to *your* institution? Among the titles that are the same in both databases, is the coverage the same? That is, how do the dates of coverage and the availability of full text (if any) compare? If you can obtain the source lists in Excel format and merge them into one spreadsheet, it can greatly facilitate this comparison process. This comparison is also almost entirely quantitative and objective, and therefore it carries more weight in a request for purchase. And you might not have to do this comparison by hand with your own spreadsheets: ask colleagues in the collection development, acquisitions, or cataloging departments to see if any comparison tools are available to you.

Search Result Comparisons

Just as it sounds, you should run the same searches in the databases that you are comparing, and see how the number and nature of the hits compares. The number refers to how many results, and the nature refers to the quality of the results: if one database yields 10 more hits on a search, but of those extra 10, 8 are from popular magazines or are only brief articles, are you really getting any significant advantage? Absolutely equal searches are somewhat difficult to achieve, because each database could use differing subject terms, the default fields that are searched might be different, etc., but this is still a very useful exercise to do. Experiment with keyword searches, phrase searches, and field searches. If there are subject terms that are the same in both databases, those are ideal for benchmark searches. Simply spending some time with the two subject lists side by side on the screen can be useful, too. Try to get a sense of the level of detail of subject terms used and the nature of the language. Even in the realm of controlled vocabulary, there are some that are more formal, and others that sound more like natural language. Users are more likely to benefit by accident when the subject terms are less formal (e.g., because the terms they type in happen to match the subject vocabulary).

Be sure to keep a record of everything you do while you're benchmark searching: exactly what the search was, the number of results, and comments on the results. Don't count on your memory; by the next day the similarities and differences will be a blur. Keeping a good log helps this activity stay in the quantitative, objective realm, rather than the gut instinct, subjective realm.

Finally, be sure to test searching at different times of day to compare response times. Based on the vendor's location, figure out what represents peak hours and test during that time. Significantly slower response times or access refusals are not a good sign.

Technical Support Comparisons

If you are comparing two databases, come up with some questions for the technical support staff at both vendors. Compare the time required to get answers, how accurate the answers are, and the general effectiveness of the staff.

Peer Institution Holdings

As mentioned previously, administrators at colleges and universities are very aware of, and sensitive to, comparisons with other schools that are recognized as peers. It has nothing to do with the intrinsic worth of the database at hand, but if you can show that a significant number of your school's peer institutions already subscribe to this database, it may be helpful in persuading your administration to fund the purchase.

Making a Request for Purchase

As mentioned at the beginning of this chapter, one of the reasons that you would choose to go through this much work is if you were considering a new database subscription. Now that you've done the work, what can you do to try to make the new subscription a reality? You've done your homework well, but keep in mind that administrators, like the rest of us, have limited time and attention spans. They don't want to read 10 pages of detail, they just want to see a succinct argument that shows why database XYZ is necessary, how it will benefit library users, and, quite likely, how you propose to fund the purchase. Most organizations have a process in place for making such requests, but the following list of points probably meshes with, or can be used to enhance, the existing process.

Elements to Include in the Request

What Does This Database Bring to the Institution?

Show what material this database offers that is not available from any other existing service (this could include topic areas, material types, specific publication titles, date ranges, etc.). Use numbers rather than text as much as you can. Relate the database directly to the goals of your organization, for example, to specific classes, areas of expansion (new programs), and so forth. If you need to highlight textual elements such as publication titles, provide at most four key titles, and list any additional titles you think are important in an appendix. Once you have demonstrated why this database is unique, it is also important to address the following consideration.

How Does This Database Complement the Existing Collection?

Although, of course, the database needs to bring something new to your organization (otherwise, why would you be interested in it?), it's also important to demonstrate how the material in this database could complement and extend the existing library collections. For example, if your institution has a strong language program, you could probably make quite a strong case for a database of international newspapers in the original languages as it would provide a wealth of language content without any of the knotty issues of getting such things in print. Conversely, if you are trying to make a case for a new religion database, but your school doesn't offer any kind of religion degree, you certainly can say it brings something new to your resources, but what exactly would be the point? There would be little complementary material in the collection, and, unless there were popular religion courses offered in another department, it would be difficult to identify a strong user base.

If you are proposing to change from an existing database to a rival product, obviously you'll do many comparisons, as mentioned in the first two types of benchmarking. You'll want to emphasize differences in the new version of the database that are important to your stated audience for the database. The following section discusses this key point, the potential database users.

Who Will Use the Database?

Who will be interested in the material in this database? How many potential users will it have? If at all possible, try to get some of those potential users involved during the database trial period. Have them test drive the database, or at least take a look at the source list. Comments from users (e.g., "it helped me with a paper," "I needed this for my thesis research," "it seemed easy to use"), or even better, purchase requests from users (i.e., "the library should definitely have this resource"), can be very persuasive. If you found a database review that included a strong comment relating to the audience for the database, which matches your potential audience, include it here.

How Will the Database Be Marketed?

If you get the database, how will you let people know that the new resource is available? As always, strive for brevity, but try to outline all the avenues you propose to use to market the database. For example, try a mass email to department faculty and students (possibly more than once) that includes links to appropriate web pages or use posters, flyers, brown-bag (or better, free pizza) information or training sessions, etc. Put links to the new resource on as many pages of your website as are appropriate. People have a lot vying for their attention, and as vociferously as your users may have said they wanted this new database, you will still need to put out quite a bit of effort to get them to integrate the new tool into their work habits.

In addition, it's a good idea to include how you plan to evaluate database usage after a year. How well did your marketing work? Usage statistics are one obvious measure, but some kind of quick, informal survey (e.g., by email or a web page) of your target communities shows a bit more initiative on your part. Besides, such a survey has the added benefit of providing additional marketing as well as assessing usage, usefulness, etc.

How Will the Purchase Be Funded?

Funding is usually the make-or-break factor: what is the cost, and where will the money come from? With the cost, indicate whether it includes any discounts, which pricing model was used (e.g., if you opted for only two simultaneous users rather than five), etc. If you have competing price quotes from multiple vendors, indicate that you've chosen the most economical one (or if you haven't, why). The money may come from canceling something else (another database, or several serial titles), or, if your accounting system permits, from a permanent transfer of funds from a monographic to a serial budget. If you believe your case is strong enough, there is always the option of simply requesting additional funds to be added to your budget line to pay for the new subscription.

What Else?

If the database has been favorably reviewed, include citation(s) to the review(s) in an appendix. Particularly useful or pertinent quotes might be included in appropriate sections of the main document. If in the course of your review and testing you have discovered features that you feel are particularly compelling, mention those now. Indicate that you can provide detailed title comparisons, or search logs, if requested.

Your overall goal is to present a succinct, clear, and quantitative case as well as a qualitative case. Your first attempt might not be successful, but you will have shown that you can perform a rational and cogent analysis. Your funding agents are more likely to trust you and try to do their best for you when you try again. So take a refusal like a good sport, and just keep gathering data for the next attempt.

Exercises and Points to Consider

1. This list of things to consider in evaluating a database is fairly comprehensive (perhaps daunting?), but no list can ever be absolutely complete. You've been working with databases a lot by now: What other points or issues have *you* encountered that you'd add to this list? What points do you think aren't as important or that you wouldn't need to bother with?

2. A major project: Choose a database that is new to you, either from the resources available at your institution, or by requesting a trial from a vendor. Do a thorough evaluation of it, from the point of view of either writing a review of the database for publication or writing up a purchase request for your management. (If you aren't currently employed in a library or other type of information center, make one up.) Then, either:

   Write the review
   or
   Write up the purchase request.

If you choose the review option, write the review as if you were going to submit it for publication. Include the name of the publication to which you would submit the review, and follow its guidelines in terms of formatting, length, etc. (See "Instructions for authors" on the publication's website.) After your professor has seen it, she might well encourage you to follow through with the submission; this is a realistic goal.

If you choose the purchase request option, include a separate description of your (real or fictional) library or information center, to set the scene. Be sure to describe your user community and your institution's overall budget situation. Make it as realistic as possible. If you are currently working in a library or information center, choose a database you'd actually like to obtain. You may be able to put your work here to good use on the job.

In either case, do not feel compelled to work through every single point mentioned in this chapter. Choose the ones that make sense and are feasible for your chosen project.

Suggested Readings

Carroll, Diane, and Joel Cummings. 2010. "Data Driven Collection Assessment Using a Serial Decision Database." *Serials Review* 36, no. 4: 227–239. This is a report on the serial database tool developed in-house and used for selection and cancellation projects, evaluation of electronic journal packages, and collection assessment by Washington State University librarians.

Powers, Audrey. 2006. "Evaluating Databases for Acquisitions and Collection Development." In: *Handbook of Electronic and Digital Acquisitions,* edited by Thomas W. Leonhardt, 41–60. Binghamton, NY: Haworth Press. Powers's chapter covers much of the same ground as this chapter, but with some interesting differences, including a case study. It can be very helpful to read similar material presented in a different voice. Other chapters in this *Handbook* are useful as well; for example, chapter 4 discusses the special issues around aggregator databases.

Notes

1. For more on the question of database size, see Péter Jacsó's useful article, "How Big Is a Database Versus How Is a Database Big" (2007).

2. Tip: If a database includes both popular and scholarly materials, but doesn't provide any functionality for distinguishing between them but does use subject headings, then some subject terms that might help sift out research articles are "methodology," "sampling," "populations," "results," "variables," or "hypotheses."

13
Teaching Other People about Databases

If the thought of getting up in front of other people and speaking makes your blood run cold, and you were hoping that by becoming a librarian you could avoid having to do that kind of activity, I'm sorry to have to burst your bubble.[1] But *my* hope is that after reading through this chapter and getting some experience, you will change your mind and come to understand that teaching and presenting are a vital part of librarianship. Let us consider the importance and ramifications of presenting for a moment, and then we'll get into some more specific nuts and bolts.

The library profession needs spokespeople and champions. The focus of this book has been, of course, databases, but what good are a group of wonderful databases if you can't convey to others that they exist and how to use them? How long do you think funding for these expensive resources will last if you can't defend them? (Especially when you are in competition with free resources like Google Scholar.) In the larger scheme of things, it's never too early to get used to the idea of justifying your existence: public, school, and state-employed librarians need to be able to talk to their communities and to local and state legislatures. Academic librarians make points for their libraries in the eyes of the budget controllers by successfully engaging in the academic game: by giving presentations at conferences and holding offices in state and national professional organizations. Our profession might not be in crisis, but we certainly are challenged by the Internet as almost no other profession is. The Internet is free, and libraries are expensive: we are cost centers, not profit centers. It's difficult to quantify the value we give back. If you've chosen to become a librarian, or are already in the profession, presumably you've made that choice because you enjoy and believe in the library as an institution and librarianship as a vocation. Isn't it worth it to learn to get up in front of people and talk for a short time to ensure that your chosen path has a future? *Any* kind of speaking you do—whether it's an information literacy session for a freshman writing class, an evening program for adults at a public library, a talk at a conference, three minutes of impassioned defense before a state legislature, or even a brief discussion in an elevator—makes a difference. It makes a difference both for libraries in general, and for your own career, to be able to effectively tell others what we do, why our (expensive) tools are useful, and what benefits they bestow.

Teaching means getting up in front of people and talking. Humans like to communicate (look at the popularity and omnipresence of cell phones), and teaching is just another form of communicating. It's a wonderful improvement that all of the American Library Association–accredited library schools in the United States now offer at least one class on instruction (Roy 2011), but maybe that course didn't fit into your schedule, or maybe library school is a distant memory for you. Still, even if public speaking ranks right up there with getting a root canal in your list of favorite things to do, be assured that it can be done. It gets easier, and you might even enjoy it someday, honest.[2] Maybe you enjoy teaching and presenting already; if so, good for you! But if not, if public speaking gives you butterflies, the next two sections on teaching principles and coping with anxiety should go a long way toward making the experience much more manageable, even if your heart is still beating a little faster than usual.

Teaching Principles

The next chapter discusses the opportunities that librarians have to teach people about databases. Of the five types of teaching or public speaking opportunities considered, I count myself as quite lucky to have experienced them all (with the exception of the public or school library versions of the second point). These experiences have informed my thoughts about what works and what doesn't, and what's important and what isn't, in the process of conveying skills or knowledge from one person to another, from one person to a group, or asynchronously via technology. The process of writing up my thoughts for this chapter included double-checking my instincts against some representative examples from the teaching literature (see the Suggested Readings at the end of the chapter), including essays by professors who have been recipients of the undergraduate teaching award at my university. It was gratifying to find my instincts borne out by this review. A particular acknowledgment goes to Celia Applegate, former professor of history at the University of Rochester, whose list of rules both inspired and frequently informed the following list of principles.

These are guidelines that can be applied to any type of teaching, not just of databases, although there are underlying assumptions (e.g., in the emphasis on use of technology) that what is being taught is technical or online in nature. You'll find that the list ranges from the more philosophical "teach to your audience" to the very directive and practical "wait for someone to answer when you ask a question." You will be able to use these principles as a kind of checklist and support system as you strive to acquire all the hallmarks of an effective teacher. Repeated studies have shown that "concern for students, knowledge of the subject matter, stimulation of

Sidebar 13.1: Teaching the "Millennial" Audience

Millennials, Net gens, or *Generation Next* are the various terms used to refer to people born between 1981 and 2002 (also frequently spelled *millenials*).

Characteristics of Millennials	Effective Teaching Strategies for Millennials
• Don't like being passive recipients of information • Like trial and error (they have no fear of failure) • Like to learn from each other • Don't like formal instruction • Like to be engaged and entertained	• More self-directed • Very little lecture • Relaxed and informal • Lots of student engagement and activity; for example, they like competition

From Carter and Simmons (2007).

interest, availability, encouragement of discussion, ability to explain clearly, enthusiasm, and preparation" are the qualities that students cite most often in describing effective teachers (Feldman 1976). Those are your goals, and these suggestions will help you achieve them.

Principle 1: Teach to Your Audience

Be very clear who your audience is, and keep them firmly in mind as you prepare the session. Make your teaching objectives, material, and handouts—everything about what you're doing—appropriate to the needs and interests of *that* audience. It's quite easy to decide what you want to tell people, but it takes a good deal more effort to determine how to deliver your message in a way they will really *hear* and perhaps remember. Ten-year-olds, undergraduates, lawyers, or the PTA are all very different groups of people, and your approach needs to be different in each case.

Principle 2: Avoid Lecturing

Avoid pure lecture at every opportunity. As Professor Applegate (1999) puts it: "Never miss an opportunity to keep your mouth shut." You probably thought that if you were asked to teach or present, you should fill every moment, but silence truly can be golden. Do not be afraid of silence (Applegate 1999). People need time to process what you're saying, which means that you need to stop speaking from time to time. Give people time to "think about what they have been told" at regular intervals (Felder and Silverman 1988). Something as simple as pausing to write a point on the board, and not talking while you do it, can provide a moment of needed silence. We're lucky in our subject matter, too, in that when you're teaching about databases, you have all kinds of ways you can stop lecturing and give your audience time to *use* what they've heard as well as think about it. For example:

- In a hands-on situation, have people start doing their own searching. Try to make the searching, not your lecture, fill the majority of the class time. Talk about one idea, then have people try it, then go on to another idea, and have them try it. Alternate between talking and activity.

- In a demonstration (not hands-on) situation, you might present people with a search statement, and then have them work alone or with the person next to them, to come up with as many synonyms as they can for each of the concepts in the search.

- Use the projector to display a search request, or hand out a paragraph describing a search request, either in the form of discursive text, or as a dialogue between a patron and a librarian. Have the class—individually, in groups, or as a whole—figure out one or more search strategies to try. Then have members of the audience come up and type in the chosen searches.

- If you are going over a computer function of some kind (e.g., looking materials up in the online catalog), ask the class if anyone has done it before. (*Wait* for an answer.) Then have one or two volunteers come up and demonstrate how they do it.

- Use questions such as "What are all the uses you can think of for (XYZ)?" to start discussions. To get even the quiet people involved, hand out brightly colored Post-it notes to everyone, and have them *write* their ideas, one per note. Stick them up on a wall or a white board, in categories, and start a discussion from there.

In general, look at the list of concepts you wish to get across, and come up with alternatives to straight lecturing. Students in the "Net gen" or "millennial" generation (born between 1981 and 2002) seem to be especially adverse to lecture, and even the students' faculty have noticed that they learn more effectively from discussing issues with each other (Viele 2006). Small groups, discussion, writing on the board, Post-its, other hands at the instructor keyboard, any kind of physical activity or acting out (you can do some fun things with people acting out Boolean logic)—all of these are lecture alternatives. People learn best when they are developing and putting concepts into practice themselves, so aim for that if possible. You don't have to come up with all these teaching ideas on your own. Brainstorm with a colleague; it will be fun for both of you.

Principle 3: *Wait* for Answers

When you ask questions of your audience (which is definitely a good thing to do), first, ask with a purpose, that is, ask a question for which you really want an answer, and second, *wait* for someone to answer. Give your audience a chance to marshal their thoughts and come up with a response. Resist with every fiber of your being the desire to answer your own question. The moment you do, the audience will decide your questioning is all a sham, and they won't bother to make any further effort. You will have no chance of getting them to answer any subsequent questions.

Waiting for someone to answer is definitely one of the hardest things to do in a teaching situation. That silence seems to stretch out forever, but try to remember two things. One, the time seems much longer to you than it does to your audience. Two, the silence will eventually start to bother the people in your audience as well, and they will realize that you really mean it; you *do* want to hear from them. Sooner or later someone will crack and say something. If you really can't stand it, pick someone in the group and push the matter by asking, "What do you think?" in a friendly way.

Of course, the kinds of questions that you ask make a difference, too. Questions that ask people to relate things to their own lives or experience are generally more comfortable, and can usually get *someone* to pipe up. Once they do, if you're looking to foster more group discussion, don't immediately respond yourself—look around for someone else who looks on the verge of speaking and give that person an encouraging look, or again, just ask, "What do you think?" Try not to be the arbiter, the touchstone, for every response from the group. It is not necessary to "respond to every response" (Applegate 1999).

Principle 4: Less Is More

Don't overwhelm your audience by trying to do too much. Guided by Principle 1, choose only a limited number of concepts or instructions that you feel will be the most useful information for *that audience*. Take two or perhaps three things you think would be most helpful for *that audience* to remember or learn, and build your presentation around those items. One of the biggest pitfalls for new professors—and this extends to anyone new to teaching—is that they tend to over-prepare lectures and try to present too much material too rapidly. Successful teachers, however, present material "paced in a relaxed style so as to provide opportunities for student comprehension and involvement" (Boice 1992).

This may well sound like a recommendation that you set your sights pretty low, and you may feel that it's a disservice to show only a few features of a wonderful database that is loaded with functionality. The problem is, you can't possibly cover as much material in interactive, nonlecture classes as you can if you are only lecturing; such classes aren't very efficient in that sense. If you are adhering to Principle 2, sincerely trying to avoid pure lecture (which is the most ineffectual form of instruction anyway), and instead trying to foster discussion and engagement and active learning, you can't go over every bell and whistle. It will be frustrating at times. You'll find yourself worrying, "They should know this! They should know that, too! And this other thing!" Consider this, however: If you show them two or three things that get their interest enough so that they go back on their own, don't you think they might discover some of the other "things they should know" on their own? It's likely that they can. Motivated, interested people are pretty smart that way.

Overall, the outcomes of a nonlecture style of teaching can be much more useful and rewarding to your students. If you cover only two or three things in an interesting way that shows, "here's how this will benefit you," the participants are much more likely to remember at least some of the content. And, if you manage *not* to alienate your audience, and *not* make the session one they can't wait to get out of, they are much more likely to seek you out again for help later, in what is probably a more useful one-on-one appointment in your office.

Principle 5: Transparency in Teaching

Don't be inscrutable (Applegate 1999). Lay out clearly the goals and objectives for the class, the assignment, or the exercise—whatever you are doing. Always keeping in mind Principle 1, relate the goals and objectives to your audience. Do your best to make them feel that it's worth their while to be there. Keep things simple, straightforward, and honest—you are not a god(dess) or keeper of keys to special mysteries, you just happen to have some useful knowledge you'd like to share that you believe will make your audiences' lives better in some way. Honesty is important because of the next principle.

Principle 6: You Have the Right to Be Wrong

It is acceptable to be wrong occasionally, or not to know the answer to every question. Acting inscrutable is often allied with trying to be infallible, and both are terrible ideas. Of course you will have done your best to master your material (Principle 8), but it is still inevitable that someone will ask you a question to which you don't know the answer, or that some alert person will point out something you've gotten wrong, pure and simple. Laugh at yourself, thank the person (sincerely) for noticing, make a note to fix it for next time, and get over it. No one is perfect, and most audiences will relate to you more easily if they think that you're human rather than a remote and infallible being. Consider this wonderful quotation:

> Arnold Schoenberg wrote in the introduction to his 1911 text on musical harmony that ". . . the teacher must have the courage to be wrong." The teacher's task, he continued, "is not to prove infallible, knowing everything and never going wrong, but rather inexhaustible, ever seeking and perhaps sometimes finding." The more we can involve the students with us in this task, "ever seeking and . . . sometimes finding," the better . . . (Applegate 1999)

Ever seeking and perhaps sometimes finding—what a perfect expression for librarianship. So don't get upset if you make a mistake; you are in excellent company.

Principle 7: Teaching with Technology

If working with technology of any kind, there are two things to keep in mind: (1) slow down, and (2) anticipate technology failure.

When you are working with technology, that is, either a projected computer screen or a hands-on computer classroom, you need to build more time into presentation plans. Especially in a hands-on situation, in which people are looking back and forth from your (projected) screen to their own (and maybe back to yours yet again), *slow down*. It's essential to take more time. You know where you're going, but your audience doesn't. It is all uncharted territory for them. You must give the people who are trying to follow you time to process. Even if they are not trying to replicate what you are doing on their own computers and are just watching the screen, take your speed down a few notches. Don't scroll rapidly up and down, and practice calmly mousing from point A to point B without any additional whizzing around on the screen. These may sound like small details, but again, your audience is madly trying to follow you (and might also be trying to take notes); this is new territory for them, and their minds will be doing a lot more processing than yours. Excessive scrolling and mousing in that situation is distracting, if not downright annoying, so work on keeping it to a minimum. Be deliberate in your movements.

The other thing about technology: Be ready for things to go wrong. Plan for how you will handle it if the projector bulb burns out, or you can't get on the Net, or the computer crashes. For example, if you're leading a hands-on session and the projector malfunctions, simply designate one or two of the people in the class as your hands, and have them follow your directions while the other students gather around those computers. Invite all the students to help as backseat drivers. They'll probably all have more fun and get more out of it than if things had gone according to plan! If you're presenting in a non–hands-on situation and your projector fails, start a discussion instead. Ask the group something about what you have just been trying to cover. As noted earlier, questions that relate the material to their own experience ("What do you folks usually do when you need to find XYZ?") are good for getting the ball rolling.

If you're presenting somewhere other than your home location and intend to show something live on the Internet, take a PowerPoint file (with screenshots of what you intend to show live) along as backup. It's a fair amount of extra work (depending on the length of your presentation), and you might not need it, but oh, if you do need it, you will be intensely thankful that you took the time. So take the time. It also gives you a way to rehearse (if you take a laptop with you) on the plane or in the hotel room the night before.

If you're in your home situation and something goes wrong: first, call tech support (if you have it); second, restart the computer; and third, start some kind of discussion.[3] With students, ask them about their assignment (or whatever has brought them to you today), what they've done so far with it, and their familiarity with the library and its systems. In a nonacademic situation, ask them what brought them to the session, what they hope to get out of it, etc.

Above all, in a technology failure situation, do not betray your anxiety. Don't wring your hands and whimper helplessly. Groaning is permitted, as long as you also laugh. Maintain your aplomb. This is much easier to do if you've rehearsed in your mind what you'll do if the technology lets you down. Because it will: not every time, but at least sometimes. Dave Barry says that your household plumbing makes plans in the middle of the night for how it will go wrong and disrupt your big party. These devices—computers, projectors, servers, etc.—undoubtedly do the same thing. And speaking of rehearsal . . .

Principle 8: Practice

There is an old gag that asks, "How do you get to Carnegie Hall?" Answer: "Practice, practice, practice." Practice is essential. If you are not used to presenting, or are uncomfortable with it, I cannot emphasize enough the importance of rehearsal. Practice is crucial for several reasons. First and foremost, the time you are allotted will always be limited, and a live run-through is the only way to find out how long the session you have planned actually lasts (and usually you will find that you have more material than you think). Practicing also helps you to become more comfortable, and can help identify bugs in your presentation, saving embarrassment later. Let's look at the "limited time" issue in more detail.

No matter what sort of group teaching or presentation situation it is (information literacy, staff development, etc.), you will always be working within a specified time limit. Until you have run through what you plan to say—actually spoken the words *out loud*—you won't know how long your presentation really takes. Unless you have a lot of experience, you cannot mentally run through a talk at a slow enough pace to mimic a verbalized version reliably. Especially when a presentation or sample class is part of a job interview, practice it to be *sure* it fits within the time allotted. If you practice and find that your presentation is too long, the only option is reducing the amount of information that you attempt to convey. When in doubt, cut it out. Talking faster is *not* an option, nor is running over. Both things will irritate your audience. If you simply keep talking and have to be cut off before you're finished, you will look unprepared. Practice by yourself (but aloud!), even if it means talking to the wall and feeling like an idiot. If possible, the best option is to round up some classmates, friends, or family, and give your talk to them. Especially if you are trying to simulate a class situation, with questions and back and forth, practicing with friends is extremely helpful in determining your timing and pacing. They can also help identify any non-sequiturs or outright errors in your talk. In a job interview situation, if you teach only one thing but do it well, appear relaxed, interact with your audience, and stay within your time limit, your prospective employers will feel as if you've taught them much more, and will, in general, have far more positive feelings about you than if you try to cram in every last nuance, are forced to rush, and lecture the entire time. Unless you are unusually gifted in this area, your audience will almost always be able to tell whether or not you have practiced.

At the same time, being well rehearsed doesn't mean rattling off your script like—well, like a memorized script. Rather, it means full mastery of your material, so that you are talking about your topic naturally and easily, you are able to field questions or take small side trips (or encounter technical difficulties) without getting flustered or derailed from your main intent, and your enthusiasm and enjoyment of your topic come through. If you are suffering, your audience will suffer as well. Take some lessons from Hollywood: rehearse, know your lines, and deliver them with sincerity and enthusiasm. Act like you're enjoying it, even if you aren't. Your audience will enjoy it a great deal more (and you might, too). But what if, even with a presentation built on these solid principles and plenty of rehearsal, your heart is still pounding and your throat starts to close as you walk through the presentation room door? Let's get that anxiety under control.

Reframing Presentation Anxiety

You may be somewhat surprised by the heading of this section, and by what follows, because I'm not going to talk about "conquering" or "overcoming" or "preventing" presentation anxiety (stage fright). If you get nervous about public speaking, I'm not going to say "relax." Because a certain level of anxiety isn't all bad. Anxiety causes the heart rate to go up, which means more blood coursing around, and adrenalin is released. Up to a point, this is good: blood pumping, especially to your brain, is a good thing! You've undoubtedly heard of the basic human instincts of "fight or flight," and this stage of increased blood flow, heightened awareness, and muscles ready for action represents fight mode. It's when things get out of control, and your body goes into *flight* mode that things go bad: the blood rushes to your core to take care of your vital organs . . . which don't, strangely enough, include your brain. Your brain shuts down (rather than physically running away, think of this as your brain mentally taking off and leaving your body behind), rational thought comes to a dead stop, and the rest of your body is usually pretty paralyzed as well. In fight mode, something will happen (it may not be good, but it will be action of some kind)—but in flight mode, action stops (unless it's running away, which isn't helpful). So, a certain level of anxiety (which is unique to each of us) is not a bad thing. The trick is finding what that "certain level" is for you: at what point does your stress level go from fight to flight? The previous section provided a set of pedagogical tools to help you prepare and give you confidence; here I will go over some simple but effective physical routines for coping with the emotional and physical manifestations of stress. Overall, I want you to try to think of embracing the anxiety rather than trying to eliminate it entirely. Try to approach the signs of stress differently, to view them as things that make you stronger and more resilient—you want the blood to go to your brain, not rush back into your core where it doesn't do your brain and mouth any good!

A post from Seth Godin's blog sums it up perfectly. Under the title: "How do I get rid of the fear?" he writes:

Alas, this is the wrong question.

The only way to get rid of the fear is to stop doing things that might not work, to stop putting yourself out there, to stop doing work that matters.

No, the right question is, "How do I dance with the fear?"

Fear is not the enemy. Paralysis is the enemy.[4]

Let's dance. But first, let's warm up.

Warming Up: Breath, Voice, Body

Warming up for a presentation gets your breath, voice, and body ready. First and foremost is breathing.[5]

Breathing

Have you ever watched a baby sleeping? Have you noticed how they breathe? A baby's breathing involves its whole torso: the stomach goes out, the whole tiny torso inflates, and most of all it's really, really relaxed. Somehow as we grow up we lose the skill of breathing well. Instead of good, deep, relaxed breathing, it ends up confined to our upper chest and shoulders, and when we're anxious, our breathing becomes short and shallow (and sometimes simply stops altogether, at least for a few moments). The first step in your dance with anxiety is to re-learn how to breathe.

Start by standing with your feet about one foot apart, with confident, upright posture, but feeling relaxed. Breathe out as completely as possible. Then breathe in, slowly, imagining that you are starting your accumulation of air deep down between your hip bones and expanding up and out in every direction up to the level of your lower ribs. Reverse the process, exhaling completely, imagining that every bit of that air, from the farthest nooks and crannies at the base of your torso, is all going out. Then breathe in again as before. Place one hand at the level of your diaphragm and the other hand on your lower back, and see if you can feel the expansion in both directions (but don't force it). A variation on this simple beginning:

- Start a moderately paced counting tempo by snapping your fingers or beating time with your hand.

- Take one of these deep, slow, calm breaths on a count: breathe in on a count of four, breathe out on a count of six.

- Repeat, gradually increasing the count, always making the exhalation slightly longer. (Breathing in on eight and out on 12 is a good short-term goal.)

- Tip: breathing out on a "sssss" or an "fffff" sound will help control the rate of the exhale, and allow you to sustain it for longer.

As little as three deep, calm breaths will slow your heart rate from "flight" to "fight," and can be done inconspicuously before you enter the presentation room. While you are presenting, remember and use your deeper, calmer breathing as you pause between sentences (which will also ensure that you *do* pause between sentences). This deep, calming breathing technique is excellent for your heart rate, and it also forms the basis of more efficient and effective speaking.

Care of the Voice

Babies provide a good model for beautiful breathing. Their excellent breathing technique also enables them to make inordinately loud sounds for their size when they are awake, but that's a rather painful image. Instead, let us consider opera or other professional, classical singers (since you might find opera to be a painful image as well). How do they do it? How do they make all that sound come out of their bodies, for long periods of time, and make it look effortless?[6] It is all based in good breathing. The key is to breathe and speak from your *diaphragm*, not your throat. Draw in your deep, diaphragmatic cushion of air, and imagine it as a steadily rising, very solid and supportive column of air that is supporting your every word. If you find your voice getting tired and hoarse after only 20–30 minutes of speaking in a presentation situation, you are doing all your talking from your throat and not using your air to support your voice. (If you spend any time at all around singers, you'll have heard them talking about "support" and how their breathing technique allows them to "project" their sound to the back of the room with a minimum of effort.) Your lovely big cushion of air is your infrastructure. Now let's get your voice ready to speak clearly and confidently.

Start with gentle warm ups: hum, keeping your lips together but your teeth apart inside your mouth, and keep the buzzing, humming sensation up in your face: feel the buzz in your lips and the vibrations in your cheekbones. From humming, move on to simple, mostly closed mouth sounds: mum-mum-mum or pom-pom-pom, and then to more open sounds: bah-bah-bah or ta-ta-ta. Now it's time to move on to some articulation exercises (some might call them tongue twisters). What you are doing here is waking up all the parts of your vocal mechanism, and preparing yourself to speak as clearly, crisply, and effectively as possible. The first exercise is useful because it reminds you of *what* your vocal mechanism consists of, what are the things you are warming up and preparing to use:

- "The lips, the teeth, the tip of the tongue"
- "Zinga zinga zinga zinga zing"
- "Fettucini Alfredo I love you so . . ."
- "You know you love unique New York"

In each case, simply repeat the phrase faster and faster while maintaining absolute clarity. (Singers do some of these on various note patterns, but that's not necessary for them to be effective.) Nutty as these exercises sound, they really do make a difference in preparing you to speak effectively and clearly. Diction is a beautiful thing.

Overall during your presentation you want to strive for an even, confident, and energized pitch and tone, which you can then alter for emphasis. But what does "even, confident, and energized" sound like? Brace yourself: there is no way to tell except to record yourself—and listen to it. Simply read from a book or anything else, or a couple of lines such as, "Hi, I am [Name]. I have [color] eyes and [color] hair, and I am [##] years old today." Say it in different ways: happy, sad, thoughtful, angry, and notice your voice changes (volume, speed, articulation, etc.). Stop groaning in agony and beating yourself up over the sound of your own voice, and be analytical: what do you want to change? Identify just one or two things to change that you think would improve your delivery, and work only on those. Rome wasn't built in a day.

To close this discussion of the voice, one word: hydrate, hydrate, hydrate! This means water, pure and simple, not coffee, tea, soda, or alcohol, which are dehydrating. Be kind to your vocal mechanism; give your body plenty of water so your voice can function at its best. With your breathing and vocal warm ups, your brain and your mouth should be ready to go. Now let's make sure your whole body is ready too.

Care of the Body

First and foremost, the night before the presentation, get a good night's sleep. This is another totally simple and obvious bit of good advice that is too often overlooked or ignored, but that will make a huge difference in your performance the next day.

On the day, as you do your calming breathing and vocal warm ups, check in with various parts of your body: where is there tension? Most people carry their stress in their neck and shoulders: do some stretches to work out some of that tension.

- Stretch your hands to the sky, and feel the pull all the way down your torso. As you slowly bring your arms down, imagine yourself three inches taller, with absolutely wonderful posture.

- Stretch your arms out to the side and behind you, feeling the pull across your chest.

- Add some gentle stretches to each side: with your right arm overhead, bend to the left, feeling the stretch all along your right side, then switch and bend and stretch to the right.

- Stand straight but relaxed, and let your head relax toward your right shoulder . . . then gently roll it forward . . . then gently continue around until your head is over your left shoulder. Repeat a couple of times.

- Stretch your face! First do a "lion roar" face, as fierce and tense as possible. Then relax utterly into a "dumb face": no expression (and no tension) at all. Repeat a couple of times.

- Think of something that makes you happy. Does it prompt a smile? Let yourself smile: the simple act of smiling releases endorphins, giving your brain chemistry a little positive boost.

- Don't force any of these movements: go only as far as is comfortable and tension-releasing. If you push, you'll be working at cross-purposes.

If your answer to "where is the tension?" is "all over my body!" then stretch everything else too! Legs, feet, hands—nothing is off-limits. Stretch it out, then relax. Sure, some of the tension will return, inevitably, but hopefully not *all* of it.

These simple warm ups can make a significant difference in your performance. The state of your body can change your attitude as much as your attitude can change your body. You are now ready to walk into the presentation room.

In the Presentation Room

Remember that "absolutely wonderful posture" you experienced while stretching? Plant that image (and the effect) firmly in your mind and walk through the door with that great posture in place. Never let it slip once you're in the room: you will look assured and confident, and likely feel more that way too. Good posture should feel *good*, not rigid.

Along with that confident posture, engage in confident activities: look people in the eye, acknowledge them, act at home in the situation. Think of yourself as "owning" the space: act like you've been in that room in front of this group 100 other times. Notice the reiteration of the word "act"—this kind of thing is not innate for most people. Acting, playing a role, is a perfectly legitimate way to achieve your goal of giving a successful presentation. (Visualize yourself doing these things *before* you walk into the room.)

Mankind is blessed with two clever and wonderful appendages that all too often become a presenter's bane. "What do I do with my hands?!" is a common problem for new presenters. The answer is: *use* them when you have a reason to do so: to make points, to reflect emotions, or to engage the audience. For example, you can indicate time, distance, or size: gesturing to indicate "a thick file" or "a steep increase" is more impactful than just saying it. But when your hands aren't doing any of those useful things, let them be calm and still. Pointless motions, or nervous tics (continually adjusting your hair, for example) detract from your message.

Along with hands, feet can be a problem. The following are some important "Body Don'ts:"

- *Don't* pace!
- *Don't* sway!
  - To fix these problems, plant your feet in a V.
  - Even when seated: plant your feet on the floor; be grounded.
- Most importantly, *don't* turn your back to point to something on the screen. Keep your face and your heart to your audience.

That last "don't" is one of the hardest to adhere to: it is so *tempting* to point to something on the screen that you want your audience to pay attention to! But don't do it. They can see the screen. You can see your computer monitor. Rather than pointing, use a verbal tactic such as "notice the second bullet point" or "stop and read point number three to yourself"—pause and let them do it, and then discuss the point. It may help to think of it this way: you want to face your audience to keep your energy focused outward, toward *them*: the whole reason for your being there is to help them learn something or to get ahead in some way, or to share something you know or have discovered with them. It's more about them, not so much about you.

This section has tried to impart a lot of advice in a very few pages, and may come across as somewhat overwhelming. So many things to remember! So many dos, so many don'ts—how can you possibly remember them all *and* the topic of your talk? The answer goes back to Principle 8: Practice. Practice your posture, effective hand motions, and speaking with support before you walk into the presentation room. Once you're in there, let muscle memory take over for all the details. Make your conscious goals just to remember to smile occasionally (write yourself a note about it if necessary) and breathe. You can't panic when you're breathing deeply and slowly. So practice, then breathe, smile, open your mouth, and share the wonderful information you have with your audience. You'll be great!

Exercises and Points to Consider

1. Think back over all your schooling. Which teachers do you remember most vividly (both good and bad)? See if you can come up with a list of reasons why those instructors either worked (or didn't) for you. Use this information to form your own list of teaching principles.

2. Principle 7, Teaching with technology, includes a strong injunction to *slow down* in any kind of follow-the-leader activity. Prove to yourself how long it takes for people to look at your screen, back to their own and to perform some action, and then back to yours to check that their screen now matches by actually timing the process. Come up with an idea for what you want your audience to do (e.g., replicate a search that uses two input fields, one of which is to be searched in a particular field), then commandeer your classroom for five minutes. Have everyone pair up: one person is the timekeeper (most phones or other devices have a timer app) and the other is "the student." Have everyone get to the same screen you are on, and tell the time-keepers to start. Enter the search you want the "students" to replicate, have them do it, and indicate to their timer-partner when they feel they have successfully replicated what is on your screen. You will probably be surprised at how many seconds it really takes.

3. One of the most painful but effective ways to overcome any kind of verbal tic is to practice giving a talk in front of a friend who is armed with a bell or some kind of annoying noise-making device. Every time you say "um" or "you know" or whatever your verbal tic is, your friend rings the bell. It's amazing how quickly you will slow down and consider more carefully what is coming out of your mouth, and *that is ok*! (It is also a good deal less painful than watching yourself on video.)

Suggested Readings

Applegate, Celia. "Teaching: Taming the Terror." Chapter 2 in *How I Teach: Essays on Teaching by Winners of the Robert and Pamela Goergen Award for Distinguished Achievement and Artistry in Undergraduate Teaching*. Rochester, NY: University of Rochester, 1999. http://hdl.handle.net/1802/2864. As noted earlier, this short essay confirmed and supported many of my teaching principles.

Lippincott, Joan K. 2005. "Net Generation Students and Libraries." In *Educating the Net Generation*, edited by Diana G. Oblinger and James L. Oblinger. Boulder, CO: EDUCAUSE. http://www.educause.edu/educatingthenetgen/. An excellent source for learning more about and achieving a better understanding of this particular audience.

Notes

1. My opening statement to this chapter is based on years of informal observation and interactions with librarians from many different libraries; an excellent study by Kaetrena Davis now provides empirical evidence for it as well. In her survey, she found that most of the time people don't go into librarianship specifically with teaching in mind: "more than two-thirds of the respondents (64%) chose librarianship with a desire to help people, followed by a love of reading and literacy (52%)" (Davis 2007).

2. The magic time for jettisoning pre-class nervousness and anxiety seems to be between 51 and 60 years of age according to Davis's study (2007).

3. Tech support people may hate me for presenting these actions in this order, but if you restart the computer and that *doesn't* solve the problem, you've lost a lot of precious time before initiating contact with tech support, who will inevitably take some time to respond.

4. http://sethgodin.typepad.com/seths_blog/2014/04/how-do-i-get-rid-of-the-fear.html.

5. As silly as it sounds, it's true. This section is based on a workshop I have given a number of times, and the breathing exercises are what participants most often report later as "really helping."

6. Note: when done with the right vocal technique, it *is* effortless, or at least minimally so—it doesn't just *look* effortless.

14
Database Teaching Opportunities

Synchronous and Asynchronous Modes of Teaching

Let's take a look at the kinds of opportunities for teaching or presenting information about databases that you are likely to encounter as a librarian. In rough order of frequency of occurrence (from most to least), these can be summarized as follows:

- One on one: working with a person at a service desk or by appointment.

- One-off, one-time sessions, often known as information literacy classes (or sometimes *bibliographic instruction*) in college and university settings. Presenting such a class is a common part of an academic job interview. In a school library, these are usually referred to simply as classes and tend to be quite brief: 15 to 20 minutes. The public library equivalent might be an evening or noontime continuing education session.

- Via video tutorials created for the purpose of asynchronous instruction.

- A database introduction or review, such as one would present at a staff meeting or staff development session.

- A sustained, semester-long class.

These are all quite different sorts of encounters, yet you'll find that many of the principles given in the previous chapter apply to them all. What follows are some thoughts about applying the principles in each case to make your database instruction more effective.

Teaching One-on-One

This is probably the type of teaching encounter[1] that librarians often find most comfortable. It's intimate; you only have to deal with one person and can focus entirely on him or her. It's also reactive, rather than proactive; the person has *chosen* to approach the service desk or make an appointment with you, and after you focus on the topic of the moment the encounter is over. True, you can't prepare (Principle 8) exactly, but that can be a plus: you won't be over-prepared. You have your life knowledge, your library science education, and your professional experience, and you simply apply these in various ways to meet each person's individual information needs.

Introducing a patron to a database at a service desk or during a re-search appointment provides an opportunity for a teaching moment, but if you take advantage of that, keep it to a moment. Don't overwhelm (Principle 4, less is more). Pick one or two things to try to teach the patron, such as "This is how you get to the list of databases on (subject X)" and "See this drop-down? If you change it to Subject, the articles you get should be right on target." *Suggest* the power of the database, but don't try to impart all your knowledge. (As Carol Kuhlthau [1988] says in more formal terms, the reference encounter represents the ideal in terms of teaching, because it offers "intervention that matches the user's actual level of information need.") Go through the process with the patron, asking questions about the topic, etc., and explaining in a general way what you're doing, but without necessarily going into all the details. In other words, try to be transparent (Principle 5) without being overwhelming or lecturing (Principle 2). For example: "Let's try this database—it's got psychology articles" rather than "Well, first you should go to the list of psychology databases, and then read the descriptions to decide which one to use. . . ." Attempt to engage the patron gently, and be quiet from time to time. A good time to be quiet is when you're looking at a list of results together, so that the patron can study the screen and process. It's much better to hold back a bit and have the patron ask, "How did you do that?" than to overwhelm him or her with information. Let's face it, not everyone is that interested, or *needs* to do this kind of research again (Principle 1, Teach to Your Audience). Dropping a limited number of teaching seeds is more likely to result in further questioning and ultimate skill flowering than 10 minutes of unmitigated, and probably unappreciated, lecture.

Teaching an Information Literacy Session

The classroom situation a librarian is most likely to encounter is really quite the hardest: the one-off, limited time (usually only around an hour) class, whose purpose might range from the typical information literacy, or "library," session for freshman English students, to how to search the Internet in an evening class for adults at the public library. Now you as an instructor are facing a roomful of people who may or may not wish to be there, and with whom you will probably only have one class session. You are supposed to have some idea of what makes them tick, make contact with them, communicate, and impart two or three chunks of useful knowledge about a fairly sophisticated topic (i.e., database or Web searching) in the limited time allotted. Certainly it is a challenge, but by keeping the principles in mind, you can meet that challenge.

Even in this situation, you can still teach to your audience: You will have advance notice that the session is coming, which gives you time to find out something about who your audience is going to be. In any kind of school situation, the instructor should be willing to tell you the reason that he or she has requested an instruction session in the library, and something about the class (personalities, skill levels, etc.). In a community education situation, talk to other librarians who have taught such classes before: Who tends to show up? What are they usually most interested in? How are their skills? If you feel you need more information, do some reading; plenty of research has been done on teaching adults (and every other age group). Here's your chance to go to ERIC and get "a few good articles."

We'll assume that, based on your research, some demonstration or hands-on training with a database will be part of your session, or possibly two databases, or a database and the library's online catalog—but that is probably pushing the limits of Principle 4 (less is more). It depends on the point that you are trying to make with each resource. For example, for a first freshman introduction to the library, you might decide that a multidisciplinary database that offers mostly full text is the resource most attuned with their needs and interests, and therefore you will show them the pertinent features of that database. For an upper-level course, you might opt to demonstrate a subject-specific, abstracts-only database (or one of the *Web of Science* Citation Indexes), along with the library catalog, with an explanation of how the two can be used in concert. Here is where you can use self-exploration to great advantage: you could divide the class into small groups and have each one explore and report back on a different resource, allowing the class as a whole to cover a lot more ground. (A scenario based on this idea is described later.) One thing you can almost be sure of, no matter who is in your class, is that while they may be vaguely aware of databases, they won't have used them nearly as much as they have Google (or whatever search engine is hot at the moment). Use this to your advantage. You know one thing that represents familiar ground to them, so work it in: compare and contrast the search engine with the properties of databases to introduce what databases are. (What is frustrating is that if you have to explain that there are such things as databases, it uses up one of the precious two to three learning objectives.)

Examples of Class Scenarios

One of the most difficult things to convey to students of any age is that search mechanisms other than Google (or similar) exist. You might decide that all you want to make sure the students come away with are the ideas (1) that special-purpose databases exist, and (2) that these databases provide an efficient means to identify articles on a topic. Then structure the session to emphasize the comparison, and the strengths of the subscription databases that make them worth the couple of extra steps to access them. The winning strategy here is to start with databases offering full text, and to create activities—search challenges, if you will—that allow the students to discover the efficiencies and useful features of databases that are not found in Google.

Once you've convinced your class of the usefulness of the library databases, usually the next most difficult learning objective is raising their interest level enough to overcome the challenge of databases that don't include full text. If your institution has implemented a link resolver system such as 360 Link, your goals might be: (1) to get the students to recognize the link icon in the database records, (2) to demonstrate its effectiveness in connecting them with full text, and (3) to understand their options if full text is not immediately available. If they decide to give up at this point, you want that to be an *informed* decision, not just a frustrated reaction. You might start such a session by asking the group if any of them has ever worked with a database that didn't provide the full text, and how did they get from a citation to the full text? See if anyone knows, and have that person explain how she did it. Then go into the database(s) for this class, ask them to identify the icon/link to the 'text finder' system, and (briefly) demonstrate the possible outcomes when using it. Turn the rest of the session over to the students, with each one working on assembling a list of materials on their specific topic (active, engaged learning). You can then work one-on-one with individuals as needed, quite likely explaining over and over what you've just shown them as a class, but that's ok. The knowledge will really only stick when it is personal, when the outcome is affecting *them*. It's worth demonstrating for the whole class, to give them the idea, but definitely keep it brief (Principle 2: never miss an opportunity to keep your mouth shut). (For more nifty ideas for active-learning exercises to use with undergraduates, simply look at the latest crop of articles in *Library Literature* under "Subject: Bibliographic instruction—College and university students." There are always new great ideas out there.)

The examples here are oriented to undergraduates, but you should be able to turn the basic ideas, and the principles outlined earlier, to your advantage for whatever group you are teaching. For example, a class of adults from the community will, of course, have quite different learning objectives. Rather than finding articles to support research papers, they may want to learn how to find reputable health information on the Web, or how to assess the validity or quality of any Web resource. You might decide that your goals are to introduce the idea of advanced search, and how to use it to limit a Web search to .gov or .edu sites. If you are introducing article databases, it's probably for different purposes, for example, current events, genealogy, business, or investment research. No matter what the subject matter, the principles still apply: Try to determine what information will be most pertinent to *that* audience; don't just lecture; definitely ask questions (an adult group might actually answer, and it can be easier to get an interesting discussion going); don't try to do too much; and finally, be extra careful to take it slow in a hands-on session. An adult group is also probably more likely to point out a mistake, or ask you a new question, and that's great: You'll learn something, and they'll secretly enjoy the idea that they stumped the teacher. It's a win-win situation.

In general, although a brief, one-off session[2] can be challenging, it is challenging in a good way. (For an even greater-but-good challenge, consider doing such a session in 15 minutes. Arant-Kaspar and Benefiel [2008] demonstrate a real mastery of "knowing their audience" and "less is more" in their description of their successful outreach program of brief instructional visits to classrooms.) True, you don't have the opportunity to establish much rapport with the group, to see their growth or progress, or to repair any blunders in this week's class next week. On the other hand, you are forced to be really rigorous in developing your one class (draw up your list of learning objectives, and then cross most of them out), so that what your attendees receive is a carefully honed, very targeted product. The quality is just as high, if not higher, than that of many of their regular classes, and the session is likely to be more interactive and memorable as well. If nothing else, the class will come away knowing that (1) you exist, (2) something other than Google exists, and (3) you showed them something that would make their research process easier. Just as we discussed in the Reference Interview chapter, if you can leave them with a positive impression, it's more likely that individual students will later seek you out at a service desk, in your office, at your satellite location in their department if you have embedded yourself, or by email, chat, etc.

A Mock Instruction Session as Part of a Job Interview

Presenting a class as part of a job interview has been mentioned a few times already, but let me add some specific notes about it here. First, the time will probably be shorter (20–30 minutes) than in any real class. This will tend to force you into more of a lecture style of presentation, which your audience is expecting, but try to surprise them by working in at least one of the interactive, nonlecture approaches suggested under Principle 2. Second, though this may sound obvious: Do your homework. The library where you will be interviewing most likely has a website. If the library is part of an institution of higher education or a corporation, the organization probably has a website. Study these, and use them to inform your presentation. Make the class you create look as if you already work there. Base your presentation on a database available at that library, and make your audience a group at that institution (a particular class, with a real class number and professor's name, or a real group within the company or organization). For a public library, study the schedule of classes already on offer, and try to come up with a session that would augment or complement an existing class. If you decide that you want to demonstrate a database that is available only at your target library, and not wherever you currently are, call up the vendor and ask for a trial so that you can learn it, and use the library's link when you are on site. (Create a PowerPoint as a backup just in case.) Create one or more appropriate handouts to go with your presentation, and again, don't be shy about copying the library or organization's logo off their website to brand your handouts. In as many ways as possible, act like you're already on board. With this kind of preparation, perhaps you soon will be!

Video Tutorials for Asynchronous Instruction

Providing instruction via video tutorials can eliminate some of the anxieties associated with public speaking, but this medium definitely has its own set of challenges. A well-crafted video tutorial should offer a direct, clear message, in the shortest time possible, using the fewest words possible.[3] You will spend longer creating a good three-minute learning video than any 60-minute class session, guaranteed (and that's not even counting the time to master the software you decide to use, if you are not already familiar with it). And as soon as you finish it, something about the database will change, and you'll have to either live with it being out-of-date or re-do it.

So why are librarians (and every one else) investing so much time and energy into creating multimedia tutorials? There are several reasons that seem to be standard answers. One is to save staff time: to relieve librarians from answering the same questions over and over, freeing them up for other activities; to save class time (rather than having the librarian do an instruction session in the class, point them at the tutorial); to do a better job of reaching students with different learning styles (visual, auditory, kinetic)—Gravett and Gill (2010), Vaughan (2009), and Dawson, Jacobs, and Yang (2010) all mention all of these points. There is also the perennial argument that it allows students to "learn at their own pace outside of the classroom" (Dawson, Jacobs, and Yang 2010). It is quite true that it simply isn't possible to be there in person for every person who needs help, and answering the same question over and over is not a good use of professional time. But my feeling is that much of the original impetus was the "it will make us look hip and cool" factor, which was reinforced by enthusiastic faculty reactions to librarian-created videos (Gravett and Gill 2010, Vaughan 2009). This was followed rapidly by a sense that everyone is doing it so we need to too: by 2012 "tutorials made with screencasting tools" were "very common" (Mestre 2012). Not to mention an apparent mass consensus that "students like videos," which may have been an assumption that arose from the popularity of sites like YouTube. I believed all these things as much as everyone else, and have spent hours of time creating and tweaking screencast video tutorials in the belief that they were the right approach. In doing the background research for this section, however, I discovered Lori Mestre's 2012 article, "Student preference for tutorial design: a usability study." This was the only article I was able to find that truly attempted to test the *effectiveness* of video tutorials as a teaching tool. The four hypotheses she started with were all either disproven, or in one case unable to be tested due to lack of data. Her findings fly in the face of accepted wisdom: "this study indicated that students, across all learning styles, performed much better in recreating tasks when they used a static web page with screenshots than they did after viewing a screencasting tutorial, that they preferred the static web page tutorials with screenshots, and that they preferred the static images over text." The essential problem the students had with the videos (which were only three minutes long) was that it was too hard to go back to a particular point or concept; using the video was just **slower.** They found the static web pages with images faster to use. And for students trying to accomplish a task, speed and efficiency are key (watching funny cat videos on YouTube are a different matter).

Does this mean you should give up on creating video tutorials? Not at all, just approach them differently: not as magic be-all and end-all answers, but as a technique to be used when an animated demonstration is truly the best way to address a particular instructional need. Even Mestre (2012) concludes:

> Static web page tutorials are generally easier and faster to create and to update than the screencast tutorials. However, to create a balance, as well as to continue to provide multiple options for students, it is recommended that librarians incorporate a variety of multimedia into their tutorials. Students want to be able to pick and choose what is relevant for them and that may change depending upon their needs. By mixing it up and including multiple learning objects (either with links or embedded) on a page (images, charts, video clips, quick games, exercises, scenarios etc) it may be possible to reach a wider range of students. With multiple options included, the novice and expert can decide how much information they want or which sections they need to review. The kinesthetic learner can try something out, while the aural learner can choose to listen to the process."

Tips for Making Better Video Tutorials

A good video tutorial is a lot like an iceberg: the tip that you can see above the water (the finished product) is only a tiny portion of the whole that lurks below the surface. The bulk of the work of creating a good video is like the body of the iceberg: huge, and hidden.

First and foremost, follow Polonius' dictum: "brevity is the soul of wit." (Shakespeare, *Hamlet* Act 2, scene 2), or as Principle 4 says: Less is more. Keeping it short—around three minutes—is mentioned repeatedly in the literature (Charnigo 2009, Leeder 2009, Oud 2009, Vaughn 2009, Strom 2011, Mestre 2012). Set yourself a goal of three minutes or less; if you are creating a tutorial for an involved topic or complicated database, break it up into small chunks: modularize your message. (Since it is impossible to "future-proof" the tutorial [Gravett and Gill 2010], keeping it short also makes having to keep re-doing or updating it less painful.)

Second, to create such a short, focused message means that before you even turn to your computer, you need to *plan* (Charnigo 2009, Leeder 2009, Meehan and Hylan 2009). Analyze the need (Principle 1, Teach to your audience), determine exactly what goals you are trying to achieve. Write a script, and even follow Hollywood's example: storyboard your movie before you start shooting it. This can be done as simply as a series of quick drawings, or more formally by pasting screenshots into PowerPoint (I have used both methods to good effect).

Include in your planning exactly what effects, if any, you will use. The software packages for creating such tutorials include a plethora of sophisticated options and effects, but as David Strom says, "Resist the temptation to remake *Star Wars* here and just deliver the goods" (Strom 2011). In more formal terms, the problem with multimedia is that it puts much higher demands on short term memory (Oud 2009); you want to keep your video fairly simple to reduce the cognitive load on the user (Leeder 2009). Another factor to consider is accessibility: Oud's 2011 article "Improving Screencast Accessibility for People with Disabilities: Guidelines and Techniques" provides excellent guidance on this topic.

If the video is directly tied to something in the students' curriculum, include the instructors of the class(es) in your planning stages and throughout the process (Dawson, Jacobs and Yang 2010, Vaughan 2009). This is a wonderful opportunity to engage with the faculty, to ensure the tutorial is meeting the right needs, and to make sure the product of all your hours of work has their enthusiastic endorsement: "This [tutorial] is brilliant, especially the video!" (Gravett and Gill 2010).

To narrate or not to narrate? Having to record your own voice may bring up a whole new wealth of performance anxiety bugaboos, because you will have to then listen to yourself (over and over) as you edit, which can be painful for a lot of people. Meehan and Hyland (2009) struggled with their voiceovers, and ultimately recommend, "[v]oiceover won't always be necessary." This is true, but let your decision be driven by the nature and content of your video: some ideas or processes may be better conveyed with just a few text balloons inserted in the action; for others it may be better to talk your users through the process. The general trend seems to be in favor of audio narration, which as Laurie Charnigo (2009) points out allows students to "hear my voice as I narrate the tutorial," which provides "one way for librarians to lessen the 'facelessness' of online library services." If you decide to narrate your video, my recommendation is to use one of the commercial screencasting programs (discussed below) that includes the ability to record audio. Patching together audio from one program (such as Audacity) with video in another program is likely to be much harder and more frustrating.

After all these injunctions and the hours of work that will likely be involved in creating your video tutorials, my final note in this series of tips is: do *not* strive for absolute perfection. (In a way, Principle 6: You have the right to be wrong.) Relax (a little). Unless you are a trained, professional instructional designer, perfection is simply not a realistic goal, and you will spend too much time and drive yourself crazy. As Charnigo (2009) wisely says, "My in-classroom library instruction sessions aren't picture perfect, so I think it is okay to allow for a little element of humanness in the final product." I couldn't agree more: it is definitely "okay" to let some of your personality come through; if you can't meet with all your users in person you still want them to get to know you. As Jamie Price (2010) points out: "A tutorial with a personal touch can make all the difference." And besides . . . something will undoubtedly change in the very near future, requiring that you redo the tutorial anyway.

You may be surprised that the topic of "software" occurs last in this section, rather than first. There are two reasons for this. One, software, like interfaces, can be a moving target. Names given here may have disappeared by the time you see this book. The second reason is, for me, the more compelling: the most important part of creating any video tutorial is the justification and the planning process. Figure out *why* a video is the right answer, *plan* it, and then decide what kind of software will best execute that project (or what software you have available or can afford).

But on to software: the most well-known, professional choices at the time of this writing are Camtasia from Techsmith (versions for Windows and Mac) and Adobe Captivate (Windows and Mac). Prices for both are in the three-figure range (Captivate is generally more expensive than Camtasia), but both offer educational pricing that is more affordable. Two less expensive options that still offer plenty of features are Screenflow (Mac) and Snagit (Mac and Windows); useful reviews and download links for both of these programs are available on c|net (cnet.com). Two free options with far more limited features are Jing (Windows and Mac) and Screencast-o-Matic (no client, runs in the browser). Limitations are not all bad, however: fewer features will keep you from going overboard. If "free" is what you can afford, these are good options, and provide an opportunity to see how creative you can be in doing more with less.

Let us now return to our "in person" instructional opportunities.

A Staff Presentation

Teaching your colleagues about a database is quite different from all of the other situations described here. For one thing, knowing your audience shouldn't be an issue; even if you are a new hire right out of library school, you should have a pretty good sense of what librarians are interested in and want to know. Because they are your peers and colleagues (which can make the whole thing both more and less comfortable), it should be much easier to plan and deliver your message. Note, however, that if your group includes members from throughout the library and not just reference librarians, it changes the playing field a good deal. Staff from departments outside of reference, including computer support, may have little or no idea that databases exist or how they are used, and teaching in this situation is much more akin to teaching a group of adults from the community. But teaching a group of reference librarians about a database turns many of the formerly stated principles upside down.

- Principle 2—Avoid Lecturing. You might be able to get away with more lecture here than in any other situation. It will still be appreciated if you try to break things up, however, and give your audience time to absorb what you're saying from time to time. I think you'll find, however, that a lecture naturally devolves into a more participatory session, for the reason noted in the next point.

- Principle 3—Wait for Answers. You probably won't have to wait for answers or need to work at fostering discussion; your colleagues likely will be very forthcoming with comments and questions. This is a group that is truly interested in what you are talking about and eager to explore it with you. (They are glad that you've done the work to master this database, so that they can ask *you* questions.)

- Principle 4—Less is More. You can set higher goals for the amount of information you plan to impart. Again, this audience is *interested* and does want the details. They are already knowledgeable, and will be more interested in salient differences from what they know, rather than the basics. You can start at a much higher level of discussion. However, take some guidance from Principle 4 and don't overwhelm them. A rule of thumb might be to master as much of the database as you can, plan to present 50 to 60 percent of that (all of which is beyond the basics), and let questions bring out whatever else people want to know.

The other principles do not change much. Principle 5, Transparency in Teaching, still applies. These librarians are likely to have chosen to attend your session, and so they are willing participants, but it's still a good idea to outline clearly the goals and objectives of your talk; that is, give them good reasons to stay and listen. You will very likely get a good workout of Principle 6, You Have the Right to be Wrong. You are talking to a very knowledgeable audience, who will undoubtedly catch something or know something that you don't. Don't worry about it! It's a benefit, not a contest. The two technology points of Principle 7 (go slower, and be ready for it to fail), both apply as in any other situation. Just because they are librarians doesn't mean they can look from their screen to your projected screen (or from your projected screen to their notes) any faster than anyone else. In fact, it may take them longer, because they are studying all the details more closely. So give everyone plenty of time. If the technology fails, you probably will have a whole roomful of people ready to jump in and help, so it's not all up to you. Still, you will want to show that you can stay calm, and have a plan in mind for what to do if the technology lets you down. Of course, Principle 8 applies to every situation: *practice* your database demonstration, in as realistic a situation as possible (e.g., out loud, in front of people if possible), before heading off to your staff development meeting.

If an information literacy session presents the most challenging *format* for teaching, a session for your colleagues undoubtedly presents the most challenging *audience* for your teaching. But again, let it be a good challenge. Learn the database, practice, but don't kill yourself preparing. You'll never remember it all anyway, and you'll just make yourself nervous. If one of your "students" knows something that you don't, let him or her teach you. If someone asks a question that you don't know the answer to, and neither does anyone else in the room, make it an opportunity to explore and find out together. It's really much more interesting that way.

The Full Semester Class

Here at last we have a chance to aspire to what is truly important in teaching, that is, "connection, communication, and the stimulation of critical thinking" (Brown 1999). Instead of one session, you'll see this class over and over, get to know your students, and get beyond the limits of just a few how-tos of only one database. You'll be able to explore many databases and broader philosophical and technical considerations of databases and information seeking. Sadly, these opportunities are quite rare for librarians, so I will not spend much time on this topic. I would like to say enough to indicate that this is a *feasible* project, however. Should you ever get offered the chance to develop and provide such a class, think seriously about taking it on.

A full semester class, obviously, requires considerable planning, and there are entire books devoted to teaching and curriculum planning (the Suggested Readings include two titles, and a search of WorldCat or Amazon. com reveals many, many more). However, it is not an insurmountable effort. Consider these five steps that are recommended in planning a course (Davidson and Ambrose 1994):

- Assess the backgrounds and interests of your students.

- Choose the course objectives (note that these are often set by the department, and you simply need to determine how to achieve them).

- Develop the learning experiences within the course.

- Plan how to seek feedback and evaluate student learning.

- Prepare a syllabus for the course.

You are already familiar with the concept in the first point: Know your audience. With a full semester to work with, you can now choose overall course objectives, as well as objectives for each session. In both cases, however, you still need to be careful not to overwhelm your students. In each individual class meeting, you shouldn't try to deliver too much, and the sum total of all the sessions ultimately determines the amount of material that you can get through in a semester. You may find it useful to approach a semester-long course as an organizational activity: to work from large, overarching ideas, to the components of those ideas, and finally to the steps needed to teach those components. As you work out the steps, you can plan the best learning experiences to support them. As you determine the components, you can then plan ways to assess mastery of them. When all of that is done, you will have enough material to write up a syllabus.

A discouraging aspect of a whole semester's course for many people is that it seems like you have to come up with *so much material*. But, at least in the area of databases and research techniques, the large ideas—the overall objectives—can be broken down into many component parts. If you start analyzing, breaking down the knowledge or skills that you take for granted into a series of intellectually manageable chunks, you'll be surprised at the amount of material this represents. (Students like clearly defined chunks of information.) As you present the course, those component ideas build on each other, heading toward the overall course objectives. Along the way you are presenting learning experiences to convey those ideas, assessing to see if the ideas have been conveyed, and giving feedback. It's an organic, iterative, growing process. Go for it.

Exercises and Points to Consider

1. Decide what type of library you would be most likely to apply for a job in, then develop a 20-minute mock teaching session that could be used in your interview. This could be an academic, school, public, corporate, law, or medical library. In real life, outreach is an

increasingly important aspect in the services of all of these types of libraries (their very survival could depend on proving their value to the overall organization), so even if such a session is not listed as part of your interview schedule, be proactive and offer a session as an added extra to your interview.

2. Think of an assignment you've had where everyone in the class was looking for the same (kind) of thing, OR a database you're familiar with that has a particular quirk that you know from experience needs to be explained. Storyboard a 3-minute video to address the issue.

3. You have reached the end of this book: was there something in particular you learned along the way (either from the book, or in class, or in struggling with an assignment) that you'd like to share with other students? Design a conference poster to convey your story. This will involve learning what conference posters are, good design principles for such posters, etc. Then seriously consider submitting your poster to a major library conference.

Suggested Readings

Booth, Char. 2011. *Reflective Teaching, Effective Learning: Instructional Literacy for Library Educators*. Chicago: ALA Editions. One of my favorite books on this topic, as it is down-to-earth and full of "news you can use."

McKeachie, Wilbert J. 1994. *Teaching Tips: Strategies, Research, and Theory for College and University Teachers*. 9th ed. Lexington, MA: D.C. Heath and Company. A totally practical, down-to-earth guidebook covering every aspect of teaching. Although oriented toward the creation and delivery of a semester-long class, chapters 4 and 5, on Organizing Effective Discussions, and Lecturing; chapter 13, on Peer Learning, Collaborative Learning, Cooperative Learning; and chapter 19, Teaching in the Age of Electronic Information, are all universally applicable. Ignore the date; this book is timeless.

Mestre, Lori S. 2012. "Student preference for tutorial design: a usability study." *Reference Services Review* 40(2): 258–276. Extensively quoted in the video tutorials section, you owe it to yourself to go read the original in its entirety. Eye opening and very well done.

Veldof, Jerilyn. 2006. *Creating the One-Shot Library Workshop: A Step-by-Step Guide*. Chicago: American Library Association. If you didn't have the good fortune to have taken a course in instructional design, here is the ideal alternative. Veldof's guide is meant to address the need for a library session that is "one shot," but frequently requested, and that can be taught by different people. This book will help you design a session that can be consistently taught by different people and consistently received by any group of students, but the instructional design principles are useful for improving any kind of class development.

Notes

1. Frankly, it had never occurred to me to question that what happens at the reference desk is teaching, but if you have any doubts, there is a quantity of literature available to support the idea. See Eckel (2007), Elmborg (2002), and Gremmels and Lehmann (2007), all of which have strong "review of the literature" sections.

2. Actually, you might find that you get invited back to give a library session every time the professor teaches the class, so definitely keep your notes and whatever materials (e.g., PowerPoint) you used.

3. David Strom, a professional from outside the library world, provides the useful guidance that "A three-minute video will be about 500 words of script, give or take."

References

Preface

Tennant, Roy. 2004. *Metasearching: The Promise and the Peril*. Ithaca, NY, New York Library Tour 2004. http://roytennant.com/presentations/older/2004newyork/metasearch.pdf .

Chapter 1

Adams, K., A. Anstaett, E. Hays, & E. Pfeiffer. 2013. Web Scale Discovery Tools [Poster]. Available at: http://hdl.handle.net/10355/35124 (MOspace).

Calvert, Kristin. 2014. "Maximizing Academic Library Collections: Measuring Changes in use Patterns Owing to EBSCO Discovery Service." To appear in *College & Research Libraries*. Available at: http://crl.acrl.org/content/early/2014/01/17/crl13-557.full.pdf.

Computer History Museum. 2004. *Timeline of Computer History—Networking*. http://www.computerhistory.org/timeline/?category=net.

Daniels, Jeffrey, Laura Robinson, and Susan Wishnetsky. 2013. "Results of Web-Scale Discovery: Data, Discussions, and Decisions." *The Serials Librarian* 64 (1–4): 81–87.

Dialog (a Thomson Reuters business). 2005. *Company Background—Dialog History Movie Transcript*. http://www.dialog.com/about/history/transcript.shtml.

Encyclopædia Britannica Online. 2014. s.v. "digital computer." http://www.britannica.com/EBchecked/topic/163278/digital-computer.

Encyclopedia of Computer Science, 4th ed. 2003. s.v. "database management system (DBMS)." Anthony Ralston, Edwin D. Reilly, and David Hemmendinger, eds. Chichester, UK: John Wiley and Sons, Ltd., p. 517–520. (Accessed via the *ACM Digital Library*.)

Fagan, Jody Condit. 2011. "Editorial: Federated Search Is Dead—and Good Riddance!" *Journal of Web Librarianship* 5 (2): 77–79.

Fry, Amy. 2013. "Discovery Systems: The Promise and the Reality. A Report of the RUSA MARS Local Systems & Services Program, American Library Association Annual Conference, Anaheim, June 2012." *University Libraries Faculty Publications*. Paper 11. http://scholarworks.bgsu.edu/ul_pub/11.

Kemp, Jan. 2012. "Does Web-Scale Discovery Make a Difference? Changes in Collection Use after Implementing Summon." in *Planning and Implementing Resource Discovery Tools in Academic Libraries*, ed. Mary Pagliero Popp and Diane Dallis (Hershey PA: Information Science Reference): 456–68.

Lexikon's History of Computing. 2002. *Master Chronology of Events.* http://www.computermuseum.li/Testpage/01HISTORYCD-Chrono1.htm.

Oxford English Dictionary. 2014. s.v. "database." OED Online. Oxford University Press. http://www.oed.com/view/Entry/47411?redirectedFrom=database.

Vaughan, J. 2011. Investigations into Library Web Scale Discovery Services. *Information Technology and Libraries.* Available at: http://digitalscholarship.unlv.edu/lib_articles/44.

Way, D. 2010. "The Impact of Web-Scale Discovery on the Use of a Library Collection." *Serials Review* 36 (4): 214–220.

Chapter 3

Walker, Geraldene, and Joseph Janes. 1999. *Online Retrieval: A Dialogue of Theory and Practice.* 2nd ed. Englewood, CO: Libraries Unlimited, p. 63.

Chapter 5

Ross, Celia. 2012. *Making Sense of Business Reference. Chicago: American Library Association.* Tenopir, Carol. 2003. "Databases for Information Professionals." *Library Journal* 128 (October 1): 32.

Tenopir, Carol. 2004. "Eric's Extreme Makeover." *Library Journal* 129 (September 1): 36.

U.S. Department of Education. 2014. *50 Years of ERIC.* http://eric.ed.gov/pdf/ERIC_Retrospective.pdf?v=2.

Chapter 6

Bardyn, Tania. 2009. "An Interview with CINAHL: What's New in the Nursing and Allied Health Literature." *Journal of Hospital Librarianship* 9 (1): 81–88.

EBSCO. 2014. GreenFILE Environmental Awareness Database. http://www.ebscohost.com/academic/greenfile.

HLWIKI Canada. "Scopus vs. Web of Science." Last modified April 28, 2014. http://hlwiki.slais.ubc.ca/index.php/Scopus_vs._Web_of_Science.

Jacsó, Péter. 2004. "ISI Web of Science, Scopus, and SPORTDiscus." *Online* 28 (6): 51–54.

LaGuardia, Cheryl. 2005. "ISI Web of Science/Scopus." *Library Journal* 130 (1): 40–42.

Libmann, François. 2007. "Web of Science, Scopus, and Classical Online: Philosophies of Searching." *Online* 31 (3): 36–50.

Manafy, Michelle. 2004. "Scopus: Elsevier Expands the Scope of Research." *EContent* 27 (11): 9–12.

Marcin, S.E. 2006. "CINAHL." *Choice* 43 (7): 1198

Salisbury, Lutishoor. 2009. "Web of Science and Scopus: A Comparative Review of Content and Searching Capabilities." *The Charleston Advisor* 11 (1): 5–18.

Schnall, Janet G., and Terry Jankowski. "Scopus vs. Web of Science" in "Scopus." Last modified January 2, 2014. LibGuides at University of Washington Health Sciences Library. http://libguides.hsl.washington.edu/scopus.

Tenopir, Carol. 2001. "The Power of Citation Searching." *Library Journal* 126 (November 1): 39–40.

Thomson Reuters. 2014. "History of Citation Indexing." http://wokinfo.com/essays/history-of-citation-indexing.

Thomson Reuters. 2014. "Web of Science [next gen brochure]" http://thomsonreuters.com/products/ip-science/04_062/wos-next-gen-brochure.pdf.

Turner, Jan Loechell. 2008. "AccessScience revisited: 2.0, the Next Generation." *The Charleston Advisor* 10 (1): 5–8.

U.S. National Library of Medicine. 2014. "MEDLINE, PubMed, and PMC (PubMed Central): How are they different?" Fact Sheet. http://www.nlm.nih.gov/pubs/factsheets/dif_med_pub.html.

Vucovich, Lee. "Scopus." Last modified January 9, 2014. Lister Hill Library Guides. http://libguides.lhl.uab.edu/scopus.

Chapter 7

Flagg, G. 2006. "New WorldCat Search Site Offers Public Access." *American Libraries* 37 (September): 12–13.

Hane, Paula J. 2006. "OCLC to Open WorldCat Searching to the World." *NewsBreaks* Information Today, Inc. http://newsbreaks.infotoday.com/nbreader.asp?ArticleID=16951.

Helfer, Doris Small. 2002. "OCLC's March into the 21st Century." *Searcher: The Magazine for Database Professionals* 10 (February): 66–69.

Hogan, Tom. 1991. "OCLC Looks to End-User Market with FirstSearch." *Information Today* 8 (November): 1, 4.

Jordan, Jay. 2003. "Cooperating during Difficult Times." *The Journal of Academic Librarianship* 29, no. 6: 343–345.

OCLC. 2014a. *WorldCat: A Global Library Resource.* http://www.oclc.org/en-US/worldcat/catalog.html.

OCLC. 2014b. *What is WorldCat?* https://www.worldcat.org/whatis/default.jsp.

Chapter 8

Golderman, Gail. 2008. "History E-Reference Ratings," November 15. *Library Journal.com.* http://www.libraryjournal.com/article/CA6612291.html.

MLA. 2014a. *Scope of the Bibliography.* Modern Language Association. http://www.mla.org/bib_scope.

MLA. 2014b. *Descriptors and Indexing.* Modern Language Association. http://www.mla.org/bib_descriptors.

ProQuest LLC. 2014a. *Modern Language Association International Bibliography.* http://www.proquest.com/products-services/mla_interntl_bib.html.

ProQuest LLC. 2014b. *Literature Online.* http://www.proquest.com/products-services/literature_online.html.

Chapter 9

Beine, Joe. 2013. "The Cost of the U.S. Census." http://www.genealogybranches.com/censuscosts.html. Quoting Gauthier, Jason G. 2002. *Measuring America: The Decennial Censuses from 1790–2000.* U.S. Bureau of the Census/Dept of Commerce. Washington, DC: U.S. Government Printing Office. Appendix A, p. A-1. Cost per person calculated and added by Mr. Beine; 2010 data is from the GAO and U.S. Census Bureau Web sites.

Bureau of Labor Statistics. "Registered Nurses." *Occupational Outlook Handbook, 2014,* 15th ed. U.S. Department of Labor. http://www.bls.gov/ooh/health care/registered-nurses.htmDurant, D. 2006. "American FactFinder." *Choice* 43 (August): 177.

Gordon-Murnane, Laura. 2002. "Digital Government: Digital Tools for the Electronic Dissemination of Government Information: FirstGov and American FactFinder." *Searcher* 10, no. 2: 44–53.

Jacsó, Péter. 2000. "Peter's Picks & Pans." *Econtent* 23 (August/September): 84–86.

Chapter 10

Bates, Mary Ellen. 1998. "Finding the Question behind the Question." *Information Outlook* 2 (July): 19–21.

Bennett-Kapusniak, Renee. 2013. "Older Adults and the Public Library: The Impact of the Boomer Generation." *Public Library Quarterly* 32 (3): 204–222.

Bloom, Beth S. and Marta Deyrup. 2012. "The Truth Is Out: How Students REALLY Search." *Proceedings of the Charleston Library Conference.* http://dx.doi.org/10.5703/1288284315103.

Bowler, Leanne. 2010. "Talk as a Metacognitive Strategy during the Information Search Process of Adolescents." *Information Research: An International Electronic Journal* 15 (4), article number 449. http://files.eric.ed.gov/fulltext/EJ912756.pdf.

Breitbach, William, and J. Michael DeMars. 2009. "Enhancing Virtual Reference: Techniques and Technologies to Engage Users and Enrich Interaction." *Internet Reference Services Quarterly* 14, no. 3–4: 82–91.

Bronstein, Jenny. 2014. "The Role of Perceived Self-Efficacy in the Information Seeking Behavior of Library and Information Science Students." *The Journal of Academic Librarianship* 40 (2): 101–106.

Case, Donald O. 2012. *Looking for Information: A Survey of Research on Information Seeking, Needs and Behavior,* 3rd ed. Bingley, UK: Emerald Group Publishing Limited.

Cavanagh, Mary F., and Wendy Robbins. 2012. "Baby Boomers, their Elders and the Public Library." *Library Review* 61 (8/9): 622–640.

Chowdhury, Sudatta, Forbes Gibb, and Monica Landoni. 2011. "Uncertainty in Information Seeking and Retrieval: A Study in an Academic Environment." *Information Processing & Management* 47, no. 2: 157–175.

CILIP. 2014. "Health Managers and Information Use." *CILIP Update* 8–8.

Clarke, Martina A., Jeffrey L. Belden, Richelle J. Koopman, Linsey M. Steege, Joi L. Moore, Shannon M. Canfield and Min S. Kim. 2013. "Information Needs and Information-Seeking Behaviour Analysis of Primary Care Physicians and Nurses: A Literature Review." *Health Information & Libraries Journal* 30 (3): 178–190.

Connaway, Lynn Silipigni, Timothy J. Dickey, and Marie L. Radford. 2011. "'If It Is Too Inconvenient I'm Not Going after It': Convenience as a Critical Factor in Information-Seeking Behaviors." *Library & Information Science Research* 33, no. 3: 179–190.

Connaway, Lynn Silipigni, and Marie L. Radford. 2010. "Virtual Reference Service Quality: Critical Components for Adults and the Net-Generation." *Libri* 60, no. 2: 165–180.

Cramer, Dina C. 1998. "How to Speak Patron." *Public Libraries* 37 (November/ December): 349.

Crow, Sherry R. 2013. "Researching Stuff is the Best!" *Teacher Librarian* 41(1): 34–41.

Cyrus, John W. 2014. "A Review of Recent Research on Internet Access, Use, and Online Health Information Seeking." *Journal of Hospital Librarianship* 14 (2): 149–157.

Denison, Denise R., and Diane Montgomery. 2012. "Annoyance or Delight? College Students' Perspectives on Looking for Information." *The Journal of Academic Librarianship* 38 (6): 380–390.

Dewdney, Patricia, and Gillian Michell. 1996. "Oranges and Peaches: Understanding Communication Accidents in the Reference Interview." *RQ* 35 (Summer): 520–535.

Dewdney, Patricia, and Gillian Michell. 1997. "Asking Why Questions in the Reference Interview: A Theoretical Justification." *Library Quarterly* 67, no. 1: 50–71. Quoted in Marshall Eidson, 2000.

Dresang, Eliza T., and Kyungwon Koh. 2009. "Radical Change Theory, Youth Information Behavior, and School Libraries." *Library Trends* 58, no. 1: 26–50.

Eidson, Marshall. 2000. "Using Emotional Intelligence in the Reference Interview." *Colorado Libraries* 26 (Summer): 8–10.

Fagan, Jody Condit, and Christina M. Desai. 2003. "Communication Strategies for Instant Messaging and Chat Reference Services." *The Reference Librarian* 79/80: 121–155.

Fister, Barbara. 2002. "Fear of Reference." *Chronicle of Higher Education* 48 (June 14): B20.

Flavián-Blanco, Carlos, Raquel Gurrea-Sarasa, and Carlos Orús-Sanclemente. 2011. "Analyzing the Emotional Outcomes of the Online Search Behavior with Search Engines." *Computers in Human Behavior* 27 (1): 540–551.

Foss, Elizabeth, Allison Druin, Jason Yip, Whitney Ford, Evan Golub, and Hilary Hutchinson. 2013. "Adolescent Search Roles." *Journal of the American Society for Information Science & Technology* 64 (1): 173–189.

Gavino, Alex I., Beverly Lorraine C. Ho, Pura Angela A. Wee, Alvin B. Marcelo, and Paul Fontelo. 2013. "Information-Seeking Trends of Medical Professionals and Students from Middle-Income Countries: A Focus on the Philippines." *Health Information & Libraries Journal* 30 (4): 303–317.

Green, Samuel Swett. 1876. "Personal Relations between Librarians and Readers." *Library Journal* (October): 74–81. Quoted in David Tyckoson, 2003, and Susan Knoer, 2011.

Greenberg, R. and J. Bar-Ilan. 2014. "Information Needs of Students in Israel—A Case Study of a Multicultural Society." *The Journal of Academic Librarianship* 40 (2): 185–191.

Harmeyer, Dave. 2014. *The Reference Interview Today: Negotiating and Answering Questions Face to Face, on the Phone, and Virtually*. Lanham, MD: Rowman & Littlefield.

Harter, Stephen P. 1986. *Online Information Retrieval: Concepts, Principles, and Techniques*. Orlando, FL: Academic Press, p. 149.

Heinström, Jannica. 2006. "Broad Exploration or Precise Specificity: Two Basic Information-Seeking Patterns among Students." *Journal of the American Society for Information Science and Technology* 57, no. 11: 1440–1450.

Hoppenfeld, Jared and Michael M. Smith. 2014. "Information-Seeking Behaviors of Business Faculty." *Journal of Business & Finance Librarianship* 19 (1): 1–14.

Information Research home page. 2014. *Information Research: An International Electronic Journal*. http://informationr.net/ir/.

Kannampallil, Thomas G., Amy Franklin, Trevor Cohen, and Timothy G. Buchman. 2014. "Sub-optimal Patterns of Information Use: A Rational Analysis of Information Seeking Behavior in Critical Care." In *Cognitive Informatics in Health and Biomedicine*, pp. 389–408. London: Springer.

Kern, Kathleen. 2003. "Communication, Patron Satisfaction, and the Reference Interview." *Reference & User Services Quarterly* 43 (Fall): 47–49.

Kim, Kyung-Sun, and Sei-Ching Joanna Sin. 2011. "Selecting Quality Sources: Bridging the Gap Between the Perception and Use of Information Sources. *Journal of Information Science* 37, no. 2: 178–188.

Kim, Kyung-Sun, Sin, Sei-Ching Joanna Sin, and Tien-I Tsai. 2014. "Individual Differences in Social Media Use for Information Seeking." *The Journal of Academic Librarianship* 40 (2): 171–178.

Kim, Sung Un, and Sue Yeon Syn. (2014). "Research Trends in Teens' Health Information Behaviour: A Review of the Literature." *Health Information & Libraries Journal* 31 (1): 4–19.

Knoer, Susan. 2011. *The Reference Interview Today*. Santa Barbara, CA: Libraries Unlimited.

Kostagiolas, Petros A., Katerina Ziavrou, Giorgos Alexias, and Dimitrios Niakas. 2012. "Studying the Information-Seeking Behavior of Hospital Professionals: The Case of METAXA Cancer Hospital in Greece." *Journal of Hospital Librarianship* 12 (1): 33–45.

Kuhlthau, Carol C. 1991. "Inside the Search Process: Information-Seeking from the User's Perspective." *Journal of the American Society for Information Science* 42, no. 5: 361–371. Quoted in Johannes G. Nel, 2001.

Kuhlthau, Carol C., Jannica Heinström, and Ross J. Todd. 2008. "The 'Information Search Process' Revisited: Is the Model Still Useful?" *Information Research* 13, no. 4. http://informationr.net/ir/13-4/paper355.html.

Kwon, Nahyun, and Vicki L. Gregory. 2007. "The Effects of Librarians' Behavioral Performance on User Satisfaction in Chat Reference Services." *Reference & User Services Quarterly* 47 no. 2: 137–48.

Lai, Katie. 2013. "How Are Our Undergraduates Using YouTube? A Survey on Music Students' Use of YouTube and the Library's Multimedia Collection." *Music Reference Services Quarterly* 16 (4): 199–217.

Large, Andrew, Valerie Nesset, and Jamshid Beheshti. 2008. "Children as Information Seekers: What Researchers Tell Us." *New Review of Children's Literature & Librarianship* 14, no. 2: 121–140.

Loos, Amber. 2013. "Cyberchondria: Too Much Information for the Health Anxious Patient?" *Journal of Consumer Health on the Internet* 17 (4), 439–445.

Luo, Lili. 2012. "Professional Preparation for 'Text a Librarian'." *Reference & User Services Quarterly* 52 (1): 44–52.

Mbabu, Loyd Gitari, Albert Bertram, and Ken Varnum. 2013. "Patterns of Undergraduates' Use of Scholarly Databases in a Large Research University." *The Journal of Academic Librarianship* 39 (2): 189–193.

Moulaison, Heather L. 2008. "OPAC Queries at a Medium-Sized Academic Library: A Transaction Log Analysis." *Library Resources & Technical Services* 52, no. 4: 230–237.

Nel, Johannes G. 2001. "The Information-Seeking Process: Is There a Sixth Sense?" *Mousaion* 19, no. 2: 23–32.

Nesset, Valerie. 2013. "Two Representations of the Research Process: The Preparing, Searching, and Using (PSU) and the Beginning, Acting and Telling (BAT) Models." *Library & Information Science Research* 36 (2): 97–106.

Nkomo, Ntando, Dennis Ocholia, and Daisy Jacobs. 2011. "Web Information Seeking Behaviour of Students and Staff in Rural and Urban Based Universities in South Africa: A Comparison Analysis." *Libri: International Journal of Libraries & Information Services* 61 (4): 281–297.

Novotny, Eric. 2004. "I Don't Think I Click: A Protocol Analysis Study of Use of a Library Online Catalog in the Internet Age." *College & Research Libraries* 65 (November): 525–537.

Niu, Xi and Bradley M. Hemminger. 2012. "A Study of Factors that Affect the Information-Seeking Behavior of Academic Scientists." *Journal of the American Society for Information Science & Technology* 63 (2): 336–353.

Oblinger, Diana G., and James L. Oblinger. 2005. "Is it Age or IT: First Steps toward Understanding the Net Generation." In: *Educating the Net Generation*, edited by Diana G. Oblinger and James L. Oblinger, 2.1–2.20. Boulder, CO: Educause. http://www.educause.edu/ir/library/pdf/pub7101b.pdf.

Olsson, Michael. 2013. "Gently to Hear, Kindly to Judge: The Affective Information Practices of Theatre Professionals and Journalists." *Information Research: An International Electronic Journal* 18 (3), article number C22.

Owens, Tammi M. 2013. "Communication, Face Saving, and Anxiety at an Academic Library's Virtual Reference Service." *Internet Reference Services Quarterly* 18(2): 139–168.

Pattee, Amy S. 2008. "What Do You Know? Applying the K-W-L Method to the Reference Transaction with Children." *Children & Libraries* 6, no. 1: 30–31, 34–39.

Peterson, Lisa C. 1997. "Effective Question Negotiation in the Reference Interview." *Current Studies in Librarianship* 21 (Spring/Fall): 22–34.

Radford, Marie L. 1999. "The Reference Encounter: Interpersonal Communication in the Academic Library." Chicago: Association of College and Research Libraries. Quoted in Catherine Sheldrick Ross, 2003.

Radford, Marie L. 2006. "Encountering Virtual Users: A Qualitative Investigation of Interpersonal Communication in Chat Reference." *Journal of the American Society for Information Science and Technology* 57: 1046–1059.

Radford, Marie L., Lynn Silipigni Connaway, Patrick A. Confer, Susanna Sabolci-Boros, and Hannah Kwon. 2011a. "'Are We Getting Warmer?' Query Clarification in Live Chat Virtual Reference." *Reference & User Services Quarterly* 50, no. 3: 259–279.

Radford, Marie L., Gary P. Radford, Lynn Silipigni Connaway, and Jocelyn A. DeAngelis. 2011b. "On Virtual Face-Work: An Ethnography of Communication Approach to a Live Chat Reference Interaction1." *The Library Quarterly* 81 (4): 431–453.

Radford, Marie L., and Lynn Silipigni Connaway. 2013. " 'Not Dead Yet!' A Longitudinal Study of Query Type and Ready Reference Accuracy in Live Chat and IM Reference." *Library & Information Science Research* 35 (1): 2–13.

Riedling, Ann Marlow. 2000. "Great Ideas for Improving Reference Interviews." *Book Report* 19 (November/December): 28–29.

Ronan, Jana. 2003. "The Reference Interview Online." *Reference & User Services Quarterly* 43 (Fall): 43–47.

Ross, Catherine Sheldrick, and Patricia Dewdney. 1998. "Negative Closure: Strategies and Counter-Strategies in the Reference Transaction." *Reference & User Services Quarterly* 38, no. 2: 151–163.

Ross, Catherine Sheldrick. 2003. "The Reference Interview: Why It Needs To Be Used in Every (Well, Almost Every) Reference Transaction." *Reference & User Services Quarterly* 43 (Fall): 38–42.

Rupp-Serrano, Karen and Sarah Robbins. 2013. "Information-Seeking Habits of Education Faculty." *College & Research Libraries* 74 (2): 131–141.

Ruppel, Margie, and Amy Vecchione. 2012. " 'It's Research Made Easier!' SMS and Chat Reference Perceptions." *Reference Services Review* 40 (3): 423–448.

RUSA (Reference and User Services Association). 2013. *Guidelines for Behavioral Performance of Reference and Information Service Providers*. Reference and User Services Association, American Library Association. http://www.ala.org/rusa/resources/guidelines/guidelinesbehavioral.

RUSA (Reference and User Services Association). 2010. *Guidelines for Implementing and Maintaining Virtual Reference Services*. Reference and User Services Association, American Library Association. http://www.ala.org/rusa/files/resources/guidelines/virtual-reference-se.pdf.

Saunders, Laura. 2012. "Identifying Core Reference Competencies from an Employers' Perspective: Implications for Instruction." *College & Research Libraries* 73 (4): 390–404.

Savolainen, Reijo. 2014. "Emotions as Motivators for Information Seeking: A Conceptual Analysis." *Library & Information Science Research* 36 (1): 59–65.

Sayama, Satoko, Ryohei Tsutsumi, and Ikuko Oshida. 2013. "Information Needs and Information-Seeking Behavior of Physicians in Private Practice." (English). *Journal of the Japan Medical Library Association / Igaku Toshokan* 60 (4): 468–475.

Shah, Chirag. 2014. "Collaborative Information Seeking." *Journal of the Association for Information Science & Technology* 65 (2): 215–236.

Sloan, Marg and Kim McPhee. 2013. "Information Seeking in Context: Results of Graduate Student Interviews." *Partnership: The Canadian Journal of Library & Information Practice & Research* 8 (1): 1–18.

Smith, Catherine Arnott, Savreen Hundal, and Alla Keselman. 2014. "Knowledge Gaps among Public Librarians Seeking Vaccination Information: A Qualitative Study." *Journal of Consumer Health on the Internet* 18 (1): 44–66.

Somerville, Arleen N. 1982. "The Pre-Search Reference Interview—A Step by Step Guide." *Database* 5 (February): 32–38.

Taylor, Arthur. 2012. "A Study of the Information Search Behaviour of the Millennial Generation." *Information Research* 17(1) paper 508. http://InformationR.net/ir/17-1/paper508.html.

Taylor, Robert S. 1968. "Question-Negotiation and Information Seeking in Libraries." *College & Research Libraries* 29, no. 3: 178–194.

Todd, Ross J. 2003. "Adolescents of the Information Age: Patterns of Information-Seeking and Use, and Implications for Information Professionals." *School Libraries Worldwide* 9, no. 2: 27–46.

Tyckoson, David. 2003. "Reference at Its Core: The Reference Interview." *Reference & User Services Quarterly* 43 (Fall): 49–51.

Ward, Joyce, and Patricia Barbier. 2010. "Best Practices in Chat Reference Used by Florida's Ask a Librarian Virtual Reference Librarians." *The Reference Librarian* 51, no. 1: 53–68.

Waugh, Jennifer. 2013. "Formality in Chat Reference: Perceptions of 17-to 25-Year-Old University Students." *Evidence Based Library and Information Practice* 8 (1): 19–34.

Westbrook, Lynn. 2009. "Unanswerable Questions at the IPL: User Expectations of E-mail Reference." *Journal of Documentation* 65, no. 3: 367–395.

Whitmire, Ethelene. 2003. "Epistemological Beliefs and the Information-Seeking Behavior of Undergraduates." *Library & Information Science Research* 25: 127–142.

Williamson, Kirsty, Marion Bannister, and Jen Sullivan. 2010. "The Crossover Generation: Baby Boomers and the Role of the Public Library. *Journal of Librarianship and Information Science* (Folkestone, England) 42, no. 3: 179–90.

Xie, Iris. 2009. "Dimensions of Tasks: Influences on Information-Seeking and Retrieving Process. *Journal of Documentation* 65, no. 3: 339–366.

Young, Courtney L. 2013. "Librarians Can Finish What Starts with Google." *The Reference Librarian* 54 (4): 353–355.

Young, Nancy J., and Marilyn Von Seggern. 2001. "General Information-Seeking in Changing Times: A Focus Group Study." *Reference & User Services Quarterly* 41 (Winter): 159–169.

Chapter 11

Chen, Xiaotian. 2010. "Google Scholar's Dramatic Coverage Improvement Five Years after Debut." *Serials Review* 36 (4):221–226.

Cusker, Jeremy. 2013. "Elsevier Compendex and Google Scholar: A Quantitative Comparison of Two Resources for Engineering Research and an Update to Prior Comparisons." *The Journal of Academic Librarianship* 39 (3): 241–243.

de Winter, Joost C.F., Amir A. Zadpoor, and Dimitra Dodou. 2014. "The Expansion of Google Scholar versus Web of Science: A Longitudinal Study." *Scientometrics* 98 (2): 1547–1565.

Chapter 12

Jacsó, Péter. 2007. "How Big Is a Database Versus How Is a Database Big." *Online Information Review* 31 (August): 533–536.

Chapter 13

Applegate, Celia. 1999. "Teaching: Taming the Terror." In: *How I Teach: Essays on Teaching by Winners of the Robert and Pamela Goergen Award for Distinguished*

Achievement and Artistry in Undergraduate Teaching, 23–36. Rochester, NY: University of Rochester. http://hdl.handle.net/1802/2864.

Boice, R. 1992. *The New Faculty Member: Supporting and Fostering Professional Development.* San Francisco, CA: Jossey-Bass. Quoted in Richard M. Reis, *Tomorrow's Professor: Preparing for Academic Careers in Science and Engineering.* New York: IEEE Press, 1997, p. 276.

Carter, Toni, and Beverly Simmons. 2007. "Reaching Your Millenials: A Fresh Look at Freshman Orientation." *Tennessee Libraries* 57 (1): 1–4. http://www.tnla.org/displaycommon.cfm?an=1&subarticlenbr=124&printpage=true.

Davis, Kaetrena D. 2007. "The Academic Librarian as Instructor: A Study of Teacher Anxiety." *College & Undergraduate Libraries* 14, no. 2: 77–101. http://digitalarchive.gsu.edu/univ_lib_facpub/29.

Felder, R. M., and L. K. Silverman. 1988. "Learning and Teaching Styles in Engineering Education." *Journal of Engineering Education* 77, no. 2. Quoted in Richard M. Reis, *Tomorrow's Professor: Preparing for Academic Careers in Science and Engineering.* New York: IEEE Press, 1997, p. 265.

Feldman, K. 1976. "The Superior College Teacher from the Students' View." *Research in Higher Education* 5, no. 3: 243–288. Quoted in Richard M. Reis, *Tomorrow's Professor: Preparing for Academic Careers in Science and Engineering.* New York: IEEE Press, 1997, p. 261.

Roy, Loriene. 2011. "Library Instruction: The Teaching Prong in the Reference/Readers' Advisory/Instruction Triad." *The Reference Librarian* 52 (3): 274–276.

Viele, Patricia T. 2006. "Physics 213: An Example of Faculty/Librarian Collaboration." *Issues in Science and Technology Librarianship* 47 (Summer). http://www.istl.org/06-summer/article2.html.

Chapter 14

Arant-Kaspar, Wendi, and Candace Benefiel. 2008. "Drive-by BI: Tailored In-class Mini-instruction Sessions for Graduate and Upper-level Undergraduate Courses." *Reference Services Review* 36 (1): 39–47.

Brown, Theodore M. 1999. "Connection, Communication, and Critical Thinking." In: *How I Teach: Essays on Teaching by Winners of the Robert and Pamela Goergen Award for Distinguished Achievement and Artistry in Undergraduate Teaching*, 9–20. Rochester, NY: University of Rochester. http://hdl.handle.net/1802/2862.

Charnigo, Laurie. 2009. "Lights! Camera! Action! Producing Library Instruction Video Tutorials Using Camtasia Studio." *Journal of Library & Information Services in Distance Learning* 3 (1): 23–30.

Davidson, C. I., and S. A. Ambrose. 1994. *The New Professor's Handbook: A Guide to Teaching and Research in Engineering and Science.* Bolton, MA: Anker Publishing. Quoted in Richard M. Reis, *Tomorrow's Professor: Preparing for Academic Careers in Science and Engineering.* New York: IEEE Press, 1997, p. 277.

Dawson, Patricia H., Danielle L. Jacobs, and Sharon Q. Yang. 2010. "An Online Tutorial for SciFinder for Organic Chemistry Classes." *Science & Technology Libraries* 29 (4): 298–306.

Eckel, Edward J. 2007. "Fostering Self-Regulated Learning at the Reference Desk." *Reference & User Services Quarterly* 47 (Fall): 16–20.

Elmborg, James K. 2002. "Teaching at the Desk: Toward a Reference Pedagogy." *portal: Libraries and the Academy* 2 (July): 455–464.

Gravett, Karen, and Claire Gill. 2010. "Using Online Video to Promote Database Searching Skills: The Creation of a Virtual Tutorial for Health and Social Care Students." *Journal of Information Literacy* 4 (1): 66–71.

Gremmels, Gillian S., and Karen Shostrom Lehmann. 2007. "Assessment of Student Learning from Reference Service." *College & Research Libraries* 68 (November): 488–501.

Kuhlthau, Carol C. 1988. "Developing a Model of the Library Search Process: Cognitive and Affective Aspect. *RQ* 28 (Winter): 232–242. Quoted in Edward J. Eckel, "Fostering Self-Regulated Learning at the Reference Desk." *Reference & User Services Quarterly* 47 (Fall 2007): 16–20.

Leeder, Kim. 2009. "Learning to Teach through Video." *In the Library with the Lead Pipe* (October): 1–6. http://www.inthelibrarywiththeleadpipe.org/2009/learning-to-teach-through-video/.

Meehan, David, and Jack Hyland. 2009. "Video Killed the 'PDF' Star: Taking Information Resource Guides Online." *SCONUL Focus* Winter (47): 23–26.

Mestre, Lori S. 2012. "Student Preference for Tutorial Design: A Usability Study." *Reference Services Review* 40 (2): 258–276.

Oud, Joanne. 2009. "Guidelines for Effective Online Instruction Using Multimedia Screencasts." *Reference Services Review* 37 (2): 164–177.

Oud, Joanne. 2011. "Improving Screencast Accessibility for People with Disabilities: Guidelines and Techniques." *Internet Reference Services Quarterly* 16 (3): 129–144.

Price, Jamie B. 2010. "Screencasting on a Shoestring: Using Jing." *Reference Librarian* 51 (3): 237–244.

Strom, David. September 22, 2011. "Screencasting Tips and Best Practices." ReadWrite [tech news site]. http://readwrite.com/2011/09/22/screencasting-tips-and-best-pr#awesm=~oFF90lJQIbNT2N.

Vaughan, K.T.L. 2009. "Development of Targeted Online Modules for Recurring Reference Questions." *Medical Reference Services Quarterly* 28 (3): 211–220.

Index

About the Author

Suzanne S. Bell is the business librarian at the University of Rochester and an adjunct instructor for the School of Information Science at the University of Wisconsin–Milwaukee. Her previous positions have included computer science librarian at the Rochester Institute of Technology and at Carnegie Mellon University, Internet education specialist at the University of Rochester Medical Center, and economics librarian at the University of Rochester. Bell has a master's degree in library science.

DATE DUE

APR 2 2 2017	NOV 0 4 2017
APR 2 4 2017	DEC 0 1 2017
APR 2 8 2017	JAN 1 6 2018
MAY 0 5 2017	JAN 1 3 2018
SEP 2 0 2017	